How Expectancies Shape Experience

How Expectancies Shape Experience

Edited by Irving Kirsch

AMERICAN PSYCHOLOGICAL ASSOCIATION • WASHINGTON, DC

Published by
American Psychological Association
750 First Street, NE
Washington, DC 20002

Copies may be ordered from
APA Order Department
P.O. Box 92984
Washington, DC 20090-2984

In the U.K., Europe, Africa, and the Middle East, copies may be ordered from
American Psychological Association
3 Henrietta Street
Covent Garden, London
WC2E 8LU England

Typeset in Goudy by EPS Group Inc., Easton, MD

Printer: Sheridan Press, Ann Arbor, MI
Dust jacket designer: Berg Design, Albany, NY
Technical/Production Editor: Amy J. Clarke

Library of Congress Cataloging-in-Publication Data
How expectancies shape experience / edited by Irving Kirsch.—1st ed.
     p.   cm.
   Includes bibliographical references and indexes.
   ISBN 1-55798-586-3 (hardcover : acid-free paper)
   1. Expectation (Psychology).   2. Self-fulfilling prophecy.   3. Medicine, Psychosomatic.   I. Kirsch, Irving, 1943–
   BF323.E8H69   1999
   150—dc21   99-21132
                                                                      CIP

British Library Cataloguing-in-Publication Data
A CIP record is available from the British Library.

Printed in the United States of America
First Edition

To Giuliana,
with great expectations.

CONTENTS

CONTRIBUTORS

James J. Barrell, PhD, Department of Psychology, University of West Georgia, Carrollton

Thomas H. Brandon, PhD, Director, Tobacco Research & Intervention Program, H. Lee Moffitt Cancer Center & Research Institute, and Department of Psychology, University of South Florida, Tampa

Salvatore J. Catanzaro, PhD, Department of Psychology, Illinois State University, Normal

Amy L. Copeland, PhD, Department of Psychology, Louisiana State University, Baton Rouge

James R. Council, PhD, Department of Psychology, North Dakota State University, Fargo

Jack Darkes, PhD, Department of Psychology, University of South Florida, Tampa

Frances K. Del Boca, PhD, Department of Psychology, University of South Florida, Tampa

Andrew Eig, PhD, Department of Psychiatry, New York University Medical School, New York

Mark T. Fillmore, PhD, Department of Psychology, University of Waterloo, Ontario, Canada

Mark S. Goldman, PhD, Department of Psychology, and Alcohol & Substance Use Research Institute, University of South Florida, Tampa

Robert A. Hahn, PhD, Division of Prevention Research and Analytic Methods, Epidemiology Program Office, Centers for Disease Control and Prevention, Atlanta, GA

Edward R. Hirt, PhD, Department of Psychology, Indiana University, Bloomington

Michael E. Hyland, PhD, Department of Psychology, University of Plymouth, United Kingdom

Laura M. Juliano, MA, Tobacco Research & Intervention Program, H. Lee Moffitt Cancer Center & Research Institute, and Department of Psychology, University of South Florida, Tampa

Irving Kirsch, PhD, Department of Psychology, University of Connecticut, Storrs

Elisa Krackow, MSW, Psychology Department, State University of New York at Binghamton

Steven Jay Lynn, PhD, Psychology Department, State University of New York at Binghamton

James E. Maddux, PhD, Department of Psychology, George Mason University, Fairfax, VA

Catarina Maidhof, Dipl Psych, Department of Environmental Medicine, University Hospital Freiberg, Germany

Sean M. McCrea, BS, Department of Psychology, Indiana University, Bloomington

Jack Mearns, PhD, Department of Psychology, California State University, Fullerton

Eileen M. Palace, PhD, Department of Psychiatry and Neurology, Tulane University School of Medical, New Orleans, LA

David G. Payne, PhD, Psychology Department, State University of New York at Binghamton

Donald D. Price, PhD, Department of Oral and Maxillofacial Surgery and Neuroscience, Health Science Center, University of Florida, Gainesville

Guy Sapirstein, PhD, Westwood Lodge Hospital, Needham, MA

Nancy E. Schoenberger, PhD, Center for Research in Complementary and Alternative Medicine, Kessler Medical Rehabilitation Research Education Corporation, West Orange, NJ

Samantha C. Sodergren, BS, Department of Psychology, University of Plymouth, United Kingdom

M. Vogel-Sprott, PhD, Department of Psychology, University of Waterloo, Ontario, Canada

Harald Walach, PhD, Department of Environmental Medicine, University Hospital Freiberg, Germany

Joel Weinberger, PhD, Derner Institute, Adelphi University, Garden City, NY

PREFACE

IRVING KIRSCH

My interest in response expectancy began when I was an undergraduate student majoring in psychology at California State University, Los Angeles. It came about through a convergence of two influences, one involving my assessment of research and the other involving personal, non-academic experiences.

Early in my education, I found myself attracted to behavior therapy, especially to Wolpe's (1958) systematic desensitization. The outcome data convinced me of the efficacy of desensitization, but I had many doubts about the conditioning theories by which various psychologists were explaining it. The ideology of early behavior therapy was based on a strict, mechanistic interpretation of classical and operant conditioning. Having been influenced by the cognitive behaviorism of Tolman (1932), I saw this view of behavior as wrong. If the lowly rat learned by developing insight, expectancies, and cognitive maps of the world, then certainly cognitive processes must also be involved in the more complex learned behavior of human beings. If rats think, then why not people?

During my senior year as an undergraduate, I undertook a comprehensive review of the research data on systematic desensitization. The data, as I saw it, supported my contention that the changes it produced were cognitively mediated. Specifically, it seemed to me that they were brought about by changes in people's beliefs about themselves and about how they would react to the stimuli they had previously feared. Although I had not yet named it, what I had stumbled on was the construct of *response expectancy*.

When I was working on the literature review, I had a personal experience that further convinced me of the operation of response expectancies and of the generality of their effects. By intentionally changing my own response expectancies, I was able to change my long-standing aversion to hot, spicy foods into a craving for them. Later, I learned that the same technique could be used to change a person almost instantaneously from being uncontrollably ticklish to being unticklable.[1]

It can be argued that my perception of the research literature was at least partly due to the theoretical presuppositions with which I had approached it. As an expectancy theorist, I would be hypocritical to deny this. Early in my professional career, however, I subjected my response expectancy hypothesis about desensitization to rigorous experimental tests that could easily have led to its disconfirmation had it been incorrect. In the first of these studies, David Henry and I tested a variant of systematic desensitization in which we paired images of a feared situation (i.e., public speaking) with painful electric shocks (Kirsch & Henry, 1977). This duplicated the conditions under which a strict behaviorist theory predicts an increase in fear. Instead, our procedure was as effective as systematic desensitization in decreasing fear among a group of phobic participants. The key to the success of this strange therapy was the provision of a convincing rationale, as indicated by a significant correlation between its credibility and treatment outcome.

Many years and many studies later, I remain convinced of the basic correctness of my intuition about the self-confirming nature of response expectancies. Not only have my own data continued to substantiate it, but so have those of others, often to a degree that I have found satisfying but surprising. I had not expected the effects of expectancy to be as strong as the data—much of which is reviewed in this book—seem to indicate. Most recently, I was pleased to learn that the noted neurologist and neuropsychologist Marcel Kinsbourne (1998) had developed a model of basic brain function from which response expectancy effects can be predicted. This further strengthens my expectancy that the central thesis of this book is well founded. I predict that this expectancy will continue to be confirmed.

REFERENCES

Kinsbourne, M. (1998). Unity and diversity in the human brain: Evidence from injury. *Daedalus*, *127*, 233–256.

Kirsch, I. (1990). *Changing expectations: A key to effective psychotherapy*. Pacific Grove, CA: Brooks/Cole.

Kirsch, I., & Henry, D. (1977). Extinction vs. credibility in the desensitization of speech anxiety. *Journal of Consulting and Clinical Psychology*, *45*, 1052–1059.

Tolman, E. C. (1932). *Purposive behavior in animals and men*. New York: Appleton-Century-Crofts.

Wolpe, J. (1958). *Psychotherapy by reciprocal inhibition*. Palo Alto, CA: Stanford University Press.

---

[1] An extensive description of these phenomena can be found in the preface to my first book, *Changing Expectations: A Key to Effective Psychotherapy* (Kirsch, 1990).

How Expectancies Shape Experience

RESPONSE EXPECTANCY:
AN INTRODUCTION

IRVING KIRSCH

Response expectancies are anticipations of automatic reactions to particular situational cues. In 1985, I drew attention to the importance of these expectancies in understanding placebo effects, psychotherapy, and hypnosis, and I extended social learning theory by incorporating this new construct into its framework (Kirsch, 1985). Since that time, researchers in diverse laboratories have provided important advances, extending the understanding of the importance of response expectancies across disparate domains. Their research indicates that response expectancies are determinants of mood states, memory reports, fear and anxiety, sexual arousal, pain perception, asthmatic responses, drug use and abuse, depression, illness and health, and responses to psychotherapy and medical interventions. The strength of some of these effects indicates that response expectancy may be more than just another psychological variables to consider. For example, in an editorial on the response expectancy effects associated with antidepressant medication (see chap. 12 in this book), the editor of the British magazine *New Scientist* commented that "psychiatrists will need to rethink their views about how antidepressants work. They may also need to rethink their views about the causes of mental illnesses in the first place" ("Patient

3

Heal Thyself," 1998, p. 3). The exceptionally wide range of responses that are affected by expectancy suggests that it is more than the causes of mental illness that may need to be reconsidered. To paraphrase the editor, psychologists may need to rethink their views about the determinants of experience and behavior in general. The purpose of this book is to provide a comprehensive and up-to-date review of the burgeoning empirical literature that suggests this possibility.

Expectancies are seen as determinants of behavior in many psychological theories (e.g., Ajzen & Fishbein, 1980; Bandura, 1977; Mischel, 1973; Rotter, 1954; Tolman, 1932) and as mediators of classical and operant conditioning in contemporary learning theory (Rescorla, 1988, 1991). Most of the expected outcomes described in these theories are stimulus expectancies. They are expectancies of the occurrence of external events, such as money, school grades, recognition by others, and the like. Response expectancy theory begins by distinguishing between these stimulus expectancies and response expectancies.

RESPONSE EXPECTANCIES: WHAT THEY ARE AND WHAT THEY DO

Response expectancies are anticipations of one's own automatic reactions to various situations and behaviors. For example, a person may expect to feel more alert after drinking a cup of coffee, to feel less pain after taking pain medication, to feel intoxicated after drinking alcoholic beverages, and so on. Expected outcomes of this sort are among the things people consider in choosing courses of action (e.g., deciding whether to drink a cup of coffee or take pain medication). In this sense, response expectancies function in the same way as stimulus expectancies. However, response expectancies have an important characteristic that they do not share with stimulus expectancies: Unlike stimulus expectancies, response expectancies are directly self-confirming.

Students might hold expectancies of receiving particular grades on an examination. These stimulus expectancies might affect how much they study and, in this way, indirectly affect their grades, but the expectancy itself would not have any direct effect on the students' grades. Contrast this with the expectancy that drinking a cup of coffee will make one more alert. People holding these expectations report feelings of enhanced alertness after drinking decaffeinated coffee, but only if they are not aware that the coffee was decaffeinated (Kirsch & Weixel, 1988). These effects are automatic (Kirsch & Lynn, 1999), and people need not attend to the expectancy for its effect to be seen. Nevertheless, people are able to report their beliefs and expectancies when asked to do so, and this enables researchers to assess response expectancies as predictors of experience and behavior.

Although expectancies can produce nonvolitional responses, they are not the only causes of these experiences and behaviors. People are also affected by external stimuli, ingested substances, and proprioceptive feedback. As a result, when an expectancy is the only cause of a response, the response tends to be smaller than when the expectancy is augmented by other factors. In addition, expectancies vary along two dimensions: the strength of the expectancy (i.e., how confident one is that the response will occur) and the magnitude of the expected response. When a person has a strong expectancy for a relatively small change in response, the expectancy is likely to be confirmed. In contrast, a relatively weak expectancy for a large change in response is more likely to be disconfirmed. Because most of people's expectancies are held with less than complete confidence, unless boosted by some other factor, the resulting response tends to be somewhat weaker than anticipated. This tendency toward overprediction has been well established in the areas of fear and pain (Rachman, 1994; Rachman & Arntz, 1991) and seems to characterize the literature on hypnotic response expectancy as well.

WHY RESPONSE EXPECTANCIES ARE SELF-CONFIRMING

Although a stimulus expectancy does not affect the expected stimulus itself, it does affect the person's perception of it (Bruner, 1957, 1986). This phenomenon provides a key to understanding the self-confirming effects of response expectancies. The stimuli with which people are confronted have varying degrees of ambiguity. In preparing people to see the world in particular ways, stimulus expectancies help them to disambiguate it. For example, the perception of ambiguous stimuli like the young woman–old woman drawing can be influenced by a prior presentation of unambiguous versions of similar stimuli. When preceded by a series of unambiguous drawings of one figure or the other (e.g., drawings that are seen unambiguously as a young woman), the ambiguous drawing is more likely to be perceived as that figure.

In addition to establishing temporary perceptual sets, experience can lead to the development and cultural transmission of stable perceptual biases, as demonstrated in a classic study by Bruner and Postman (1949). In that study, students were tachistoscopically shown a series of playing cards, some of which were anomalous (e.g., a red 6 of spades). Both normal and anomalous cards were identified after brief exposures, but the anomalous cards were identified incorrectly. A black 4 of hearts, for example, might be misidentified as a normal 4 of hearts or as a 4 of spades. In these instances, what was seen was due to a combination of what was out there and what was expected to be out there.

The anomalous card experiment reveals the adaptive function of perceptual expectations: They enable more rapid recognition and classification of stimuli than would otherwise be possible. The price of speed is accuracy, but the trade-off is often worthwhile. Rapid recognition can have considerable survival value, even if it is sometimes inaccurate. Less harm may be done by mistaking a stick for a rattlesnake than by taking the time to examine a snake with enough care to reliably determine that it is indeed dangerous.

Brains evolved because they provide animals with an adaptive advantage; they are "anticipation machines" (Dennett, 1991, p. 178) that allow organisms to interpret and respond to their environments effectively and efficiently. According to Kinsbourne (1998, in press), the content of consciousness arises as a pattern of neuronal activity formed by the clash of two colliding waves, an incoming wave from receptors and an outgoing anticipatory wave. Thus, experience "is an inextricable amalgam of represented anticipation and represented perturbation" (Kinsbourne, 1998, p. 241).

When stimuli are ambiguous enough, sets or expectancies can lead to their being misperceived, even when they are examined slowly and carefully. For example, when 17th- and 18th-century biologists who believed in preformation examined sperm under the microscope, they reported seeing fully formed miniature beings. They saw miniature horses in the sperm of a horse, tiny chickens in the sperm of a rooster, and minuscule human babies in human sperm. The ambiguity of the stimulus allowed them to see whatever they expected to see.

Internal states are especially ambiguous; for that reason, people's perceptions of them are particularly prone to long-lasting expectancy effects. This became painfully apparent when the first paradigm of experimental psychology collapsed, as many introspective reports were found to be determined largely by the theoretically derived expectations of the introspective observer (Dodge, 1912; Kirsch, 1977). The influence of expectancy on subjective states was rediscovered in the 1950s and 1960s, with the revelation that placebos not only please patients but also produce alterations in symptoms and perhaps even underlying disorders (Harrington, 1997).

When expectancies alter people's perception of external stimuli, they do not simultaneously affect the stimulus itself. When people introspect, however, the distinction between percept and that which is perceived breaks down. The perception is not just *of* the experience, it *is* the experience. Therefore, changing people's perception of pain, anxiety, depression, and other psychobiological states is equivalent to changing these experiential states. In this sense, the self-confirming effect of response expectancy on experiential responses is a logically necessary consequence of the confirmatory effects of expectancy on perception. In addition, if one assumes that there is a physiological substrate for any experiential state, then a change in perception is always a change in physiology as well. For that reason, expectancy-induced changes in experience are always accompanied by at least some physiological changes.

To summarize, people are biologically structured to respond rapidly to the environment; in so doing, they use perceptual templates or expectancies to resolve stimulus ambiguities. Thus, stimulus expectancies alter perceptual responses, especially to ambiguous stimuli. Because internal responses function as highly ambiguous stimuli, expectancies about them (i.e., response expectancies) are self-confirming to a fairly substantial degree. For example, they can be sufficiently self-confirming as to override and reverse the effects of potent chemical agents (e.g., Ikemi & Nakagawa, 1962; Wolf, 1950).

AN OVERVIEW OF THIS BOOK

An impressive array of response expectancy effects have been documented in research laboratories throughout the world. The purpose of this book is to review this research and to evaluate its importance for understanding and affecting human function and dysfunction. The book is divided into four sections. The first covers the basic theoretical foundations of response expectancy. Part II demonstrates the wide range of areas in which response expectancy effects have been documented, including positive and negative moods, anxiety disorders, dysphoria, coping with stressors, memory, anxiety, sexual dysfunction, and asthma. In the third section of the book, response expectancies are considered in relation to the important topics of substance use and abuse. Finally, the last section explores the role of response expectancy in medical and psychological treatment.

Part I: Theoretical Foundations

Part I provides a theoretical context for understanding the data reviewed in the rest of the book. In the first chapter, James Maddux places the response expectancy construct in the broader social–cognitive perspective from which it was derived. Maddux explicates the basic principles that unite various social–cognitive theories and clarifies the confusion created by the different but overlapping ways that expectancy terms have been used. This is followed by a chapter in which Mark Goldman discusses the neural architecture that underlies expectancy operation. Goldman begins by reviewing current models in cognitive neuroscience and then applies these to an understanding of the ways in which expectancy affects experience and behavior.

Part II: Function and Dysfunction

The second section of the book examines the role of response expectancies in basic human function and dysfunction. It begins with a review by Salvatore Catanzaro and Jack Mearns of expectancy influences on both positive and negative mood states, especially as they relate to people's ability to cope with stress. Included in this chapter is an extensive review of data-derived studies using the Generalized Expectancies for Negative Mood Regulation Scale, which measures people's beliefs about whether their coping efforts will be successful in alleviating their negative moods. These data indicate that expectancy predicts dysphoric mood independently of actual coping responses, family support, negative life events, anxiety sensitivity, and self-confidence. In addition, prospective studies using the scale reveal that expectancy predicts changes in depression after exposure to stressors.

In chapter 4, Edward Hirt et al. explore the role of response expectancy in memory processes in general and in the creation of false memories in particular. The data they review indicates that expectancies based on past knowledge and experience influence how people remember the past. In addition, expectancies generated by external sources (e.g., by suggestions, misinformation, or misleading questions) can also alter what is recalled. Hirt et al. examine the relevance of these data to the important and contentious issue of the recovery of repressed memories and the creation of false memories of traumatic events (e.g., sexual abuse).

In chapter 5, Nancy Schoenberger updates the voluminous literature linking response expectancy to both normal and pathological fear and avoidance. These data indicate that phobic anxiety is highly correlated with anxiety expectancy and that improvement after treatment is highly correlated with pretreatment expectancies. The dependency of treatment outcome on clients' expectations has also been found in experimental studies. In a study of the effects of in vivo exposure on agoraphobia (Southworth & Kirsch, 1988), for example, only half the participants were told that the purpose of the exposure sessions was to lower their anxiety. The others were told that its purpose was merely to assess their anxiety. Clients provided with therapeutic expectancies showed substantially greater improvement and improved more rapidly than those who were led to believe that exposure was for the purpose of assessment.

In chapter 6, Donald Price and James Barrell examine the role of expectancy in the experience of pain. The effects of placebos on pain is one of the best known response expectancy phenomena, and data indicate that in some instances it may be mediated by the release of endogenous opioids in the brain. However, Price and Barrell also review data indicating that placebo effects can be obtained in circumstances that rule out the production of opioids as a causal mechanism. In addition, they review data linking placebo analgesia to classical conditioning and show that these conditioning effects are mediated by response expectancies.

In chapter 7, Eileen Palace presents compelling evidence that response expectancies are pivotal to sexual dysfunction and that changing them is central to treating this problem. In one of these studies, Palace used false biofeedback of vaginal blood volume (VBV) during exposure to erotic stimuli to test her hypothesis that sexual response expectancies alter sexual response. She reported that false VBV feedback indicating arousal increased actual VBV in 100% of sexually dysfunctional women. Furthermore, the increase in actual response occurred within 30 s of the expectation of an increase, thus providing strong evidence for the causal role of expectancy.

Finally, in chapter 8, Samantha Sodergren and Michael Hyland demonstrate that response expectancies can instigate and inhibit asthmatic reactions. The data they review indicate that expectancies can produce effects that are about two thirds the magnitude of those of active pharmacological agents. In addition, when pharmacological agents are administered with expectancy misinformation indicating effects opposite to those of their actual effects, the pharmacological effect is reduced by half.

Part III: Substance Expectancies and Substance Abuse

The third section of this book concerns substance use and abuse. In chapter 9, M. Vogel-Sprott and Mark Fillmore examine the impact of both response expectancies and stimulus expectancies on the use and reactions to socially used drugs (e.g., caffeine and alcohol). For example, they review data that indicate that response expectancies predict the direction and magnitude of changes in motor performance after the ingestion of placebo caffeine. In addition, these placebo-induced changes in performance can be altered by providing people with information about the effects of caffeine.

In chapter 10, Mark Goldman et al. provide a comprehensive overview of the immense literature on alcohol expectancy and alcohol abuse. Goldman et al. developed a widely used measure of alcohol-related response expectancy and documented the importance of these expectancies in the prediction, prevention, and treatment of alcohol abuse. These data indicate that (a) alcohol expectancies of adolescents, measured before the onset of drinking, predict subsequent social and problem drinking; (b) alcohol expectancies predict the outcome of treatment programs for problem drinkers; and (c) treatment procedures aimed at altering alcohol expectancies lower subsequent alcohol consumption.

In the last chapter of this section (chap. 11), Thomas Brandon et al.

extend the work on alcohol expectancy to the problem of nicotine addiction and attempts to stop smoking. The data they review indicate that nicotine expectancies predict levels of nicotine use, withdrawal severity, and success of efforts to quit smoking. Among the data indicating that the relation is causal is an experimental study in which smokers were given nicotine gum and information about the withdrawal symptoms to expect during smoking abstinence (Tate et al., 1994). Expectancy information significantly affected reported withdrawal symptoms, decreasing them among participants instructed to expect no symptoms and increasing them among those told to expect them.

Part IV: Specifics of Nonspecific Effects

The role of response expectancies in treatment is the focus of the last section of the book. In chapter 12, Irving Kirsch and Guy Sapirstein report a meta-analysis of the acute effects of antidepressant medication. Their meta-analysis indicates that at least 75% of the drug response is duplicated by inert placebos. However, there is reason to believe that much of the remaining 25% of the drug response may also be due to expectancy. First, the correlation between response to medication and response to placebos was exceptionally high ($r = .90$). Second, the proportion of the effect size duplicated by placebo was virtually identical (range = 74%–76%) across medication type (e.g., tricyclics, selective serotonin reuptake inhibitors, monoamine oxidase inhibitors). The biggest surprise, however, came when they examined the effect size for a subset of studies in which the active drugs (amylobarbitone, lithium, liothyronine, and adinazolam) were not antidepressants. The effect of these drugs on depression was as great as that of the most effective antidepressants, and again an inactive placebo duplicated 76% of this effect.

Kirsch and Sapirstein's meta-analysis was limited to studies of the acute affects of antidepressant drugs and placebos (the mean duration of the studies was 5 weeks). In chapter 13, Harald Walach and Catarina Maidhof extend these findings to long-term effects (6 months–3 years). Instead of using standardized mean improvement scores, however, Walach and Maidhof based their calculations on the number of patients showing long-term, clinically significant improvement in the drug condition and the number showing long-term, clinically significant improvement in the placebo condition. Across the studies they examined, 65% of the patients in the drug groups improved, compared with 46% of patients in the placebo groups. These data indicate that 71% of the long-term effects of antidepressants are duplicated by inert placebo.

Placebos can produce negative as well as positive effects, and this *nocebo effect* is the focus of chapter 14. In this chapter, Robert Hahn reviews data revealing that expectancies can produce unwanted noxious effects such as headaches, epileptic seizures, itchy nose, watering or burning eyes, plugged ears, tight or scratchy throat, nausea, dizziness, sleepiness, and depression. As Hahn concludes, response expectancies can make people sick as well as healthy.

In chapter 15, Joel Weinberger and Andrew Eig examine the important role of response expectancies in psychotherapy. The data they review indicate that improvement in psychotherapy can be predicted by pretreatment expectancies. Similarly, expectations and attributions predict relapse. Weinberger and Eig explore ways of enhancing therapeutic expectancies to maximize treatment outcome.

Hypnosis has been found to be an effective method of enhancing the effects of psychotherapy (Chambless et al., 1998; Kirsch, Montgomery, & Sapirstein, 1995). In the last chapter of the book, James Council examines the central role of response expectancy in eliciting hypnotic responses. Hypnotic inductions are shown to be similar to placebos, in that the contents of the induction are irrelevant as long as the person accepts the procedure as a legitimate induction. Furthermore, the experience and behavior of hypnotized people have been found to vary dramatically as a function of their expectancies about hypnosis. Finally, expectancy has been found to be a major determinant of how responsive a person will be to hypnosis. In one study, for example, an expectancy manipulation rendered 73% of the participants highly responsive to hypnotic suggestion, with all of the remaining participants being moderately responsive (Wickless & Kirsch, 1989). In the control group, few participants were highly responsive, most were moderately responsive, and a substantial number were unresponsive.

Taken together, the chapters in this book confirm that response expectancy is an important psychological factor with wide-ranging effects. It is a variable that should not be ignored in theories of normal and dysfunctional behavior, it is a fruitful area of future research, and it is an important consideration in the design and implementation of treatment for both psychological and physical disorders.

REFERENCES

Ajzen, I., & Fishbein, M. (1980). *Understanding attitudes and predicting social behavior*. Englewood Cliffs, NJ: Prentice Hall.

Bandura, A. (1977). *Social learning theory*. Englewood Cliffs, NJ: Prentice Hall.

Bruner, J. (1957). On perceptual readiness. *Psychological Bulletin, 64*, 123–152.

Bruner, J. (1986). *Actual minds, possible worlds*. Cambridge, MA: Harvard University Press.

Bruner, J. S., & Postman, L. (1949). On the perception of incongruity: A paradigm. *Journal of Personality, 28*, 206–223.

Chambless, D. L., Baker, M. J., Baucom, D. H., Beutler, L. E., Calhoun, K. S., Crits-Christoph, P., Daiuto, A., DeRubeis, R., Detweiler, J., Haaga, D. A. F., Johnson, S. B., McCurry, S., Meuser, K. T., Pope, K. S., Sanderson, W. C., Shoham, V., Stickle, T., Williams, D. A., & Woody, S. R. (1998). Update on empirically validated therapies, II. *The Clinical Psychologist, 51,* 3–16.

Dennett, D. C. (1991). *Consciousness explained.* Boston: Little, Brown.

Dodge, R. (1912). The theory and limitations of introspection. *American Journal of Psychology, 23,* 214–229.

Harrington, A. (1997). *The placebo effect: An interdisciplinary exploration.* Cambridge, MA: Harvard University Press.

Ikemi, Y., & Nakagawa, S. (1962). A psychosomatic study of contagious dermatitis. *Kyoshu Journal of Medical Science, 13,* 335–350.

Kinsbourne, M. (1998). Unity and diversity in the human brain: Evidence from injury. *Daedalus, 127,* 233–256.

Kinsbourne, M. (in press). Gehirn und bewusstsein [Brain and consciousness]. In J. Goetschl (Ed.), *Auf der suche nach dem selbst* [On the search for the self]. Graz, Austria: Urania Protokolle.

Kirsch, I. (1977). Psychology's first paradigm. *Journal of the History of the Behavioral Sciences, 13,* 317–325.

Kirsch, I. (1985). Response expectancy as a determinant of experience and behavior. *American Psychologist, 40,* 1189–1202.

Kirsch, I., & Lynn, S. J. (1999). Automaticity in clinical psychology. *American Psychologist, 54,* 504–515.

Kirsch, I., Montgomery, G., & Sapirstein, G. (1995). Hypnosis as an adjunct to cognitive–behavioral psychotherapy: A meta-analysis. *Journal of Consulting and Clinical Psychology, 63,* 214–220.

Kirsch, I., & Weixel, L. J. (1988). Double-blind versus deceptive administration of a placebo. *Behavioral Neuroscience, 102,* 319–323.

Mischel, W. (1973). Toward a cognitive social reconceptualization of personality. *Psychological Review, 80,* 252–283.

Patient heal thyself? Psychiatrists will have to rethink the way they test drugs like Prozac. (1998). *New Scientist, 159,* 3.

Rachman, S. J. (1994). The overprediction of fear: A review. *Behaviour Research and Therapy, 32,* 683–690.

Rachman, S. J., & Arntz, A. (1991). The overprediction and underprediction of pain. *Clinical Psychology Review, 11,* 339–355.

Rescorla, R. A. (1988). Pavlovian conditioning: It's not what you think it is. *American Psychologist, 43,* 151–160.

Rescorla, R. A. (1991). Associative relations in instrumental learning: The Eighteenth Bartlett Memorial Lecture. *Quarterly Journal of Experimental Psychology: Comparative and Physiological Psychology, 43B,* 1–23.

Rotter, J. B. (1954). *Social learning and clinical psychology*. Englewood Cliffs, NJ: Prentice Hall.

Southworth, S., & Kirsch, I. (1988). The role of expectancy in exposure-generated fear reduction in agoraphobia. *Behaviour Research and Therapy, 26*, 113–120.

Tate, J. C., Stanton, A. L., Green, S. B., Schmitz, J. M., Le, T., & Marshall, B. (1994). Experimental analysis of the role of expectancy in nicotine withdrawal. *Psychology of Addictive Behaviors, 8*, 169–178.

Tolman, E. C. (1932). *Purposive behavior in animals and men*. New York: Appleton-Century-Crofts.

Wickless, C., & Kirsch, I. (1989). Effects of verbal and experiential expectancy manipulations on hypnotic susceptibility. *Journal of Personality and Social Psychology, 57*, 762–768.

Wolf, S. (1950). Effects of suggestion and conditioning on the action of chemical agents in human subjects: The pharmacology of placebos. *Journal of Clinical Investigation, 29*, 100–109.

I

THEORETICAL FOUNDATIONS

1

EXPECTANCIES AND THE SOCIAL–COGNITIVE PERSPECTIVE: BASIC PRINCIPLES, PROCESSES, AND VARIABLES

JAMES E. MADDUX

Throughout psychology's history, much effort has been devoted to understanding human self-regulation, which is the capacity of people to think about the future, set goals, develop plans to attain these goals, and regulate their own behavior based on these goals and plans. At the heart of the ability to plan and self-regulate is the ability to anticipate or develop expectancies, to use past experience and knowledge to form beliefs about and predict future events and states (Olson, Roese, & Zanna, 1996, p. 211).

The expectancy construct and various expectancy theories and expectancy–value theories are among the most thoroughly investigated constructs and models in psychology (e.g., Feather, 1982). These theories are concerned with the expectation that specific behaviors will be effective in producing specific outcomes and with the value placed on these outcomes. Theories in the expectancy–value framework include Lewin's (1938) the-

I am grateful to Robert Lent and Stanley Gully for careful critical readings of an earlier version of this chapter.

ory of psychological fields, Tolman's (1955) principles of performance, Edwards's (1954) theory of decision making, Rotter's (1954, 1966) social learning theory, protection motivation theory (Maddux & Rogers, 1983; Rogers, 1975), the theory of reasoned action and planned behavior (Ajzen, 1988; Fishbein & Ajzen, 1975), self-efficacy theory (Bandura, 1977), and control theory (e.g., Carver & Scheier, 1982; Hyland, 1988).

The most recent innovation in theory and research on expectancies is Kirsch's (1985a, 1990) response expectancy theory. A *response expectancy* is an expectancy for a nonvolitional response, such as a subjective experience and its physiological concomitants (e.g., emotions, pleasure, pain). Thus, response expectancies are concerned with people's beliefs about their own reactions to events, reactions viewed by people as being automatic and not under direct volitional control. People actively seek some nonvolitional responses (e.g., sexual arousal) and actively avoid others (e.g., pain). Therefore, expectancies for nonvolitional responses serve the same function as expectancies for environmental events. One important difference between response expectancy theory and other expectancy theories is its emphasis on nonvolitional responses rather than volitional (intentional) behavior. A second important difference is that response expectancies are self-confirming; people tend to experience the nonvolitional responses that they expect (Kirsch, 1985a, 1990).

The utility of a new psychological construct is greatly enhanced when it is placed in the context of a general model or theory. Therefore, my goal of this chapter is to describe the larger theoretical framework in which response expectancy theory is embedded. Response expectancy theory is an extension of social learning theory, as originally developed by Rotter (1954; see also Woodward, 1982). As social learning theory evolved, it became more explicitly cognitive, as in Bandura's (1986) social–cognitive theory and Mischel's (1973) cognitive social learning theory. A number of other models might also be called *social–cognitive*: personal construct theory (Kelly, 1955), the theories of reasoned action and planned behavior (Ajzen, 1988; Fishbein & Ajzen, 1975), goal-setting theory (Locke & Latham, 1990), control theory (Carver & Scheier, 1982; Hyland, 1988), various theories of personality concerned with goals and their attainment (e.g., Cantor, 1990; Dweck & Leggett, 1988), causal attribution theories (e.g., Anderson, Krull, & Weiner, 1996), and various cognitive theories of psychological disorders and psychotherapy (e.g., Beck, 1976; Hollon & Beck, 1994).

Despite some differences, these theories have much in common. First, they share a set of principles or assumptions about the basic psychological processes or activities in which people engage. They also share a set of basic conceptual elements, units, or variables from which the principles and processes are built. Because of these similarities, it is appropriate to refer to the social–cognitive theories or the social–cognitive perspective when discussing this family of theories. A thorough understanding of response expectancy theory depends on understanding these common principles and understanding the similarities and differences among the basic elements.

In this chapter, I first describe several basic principles and processes held in common by the theories in this perspective. I then describe the basic elements, units, or variables from which these theories are built, including the often confusing similarities and differences among them that hinder theory development and research.

BASIC PRINCIPLES AND PROCESSES

The social–cognitive theories share several basic principles and hypothesized processes about human behavior and personality. The exact number of basic principles one derives depends partly on how one divides them into subprinciples. The basic four appear to be reciprocal causation, centrality of cognitive construals, self-regulation, and social embeddedness of self and personality.

Reciprocal Causation

Environmental events, cognition, emotion, and behavior are mutually interacting influences. People respond cognitively, affectively, and behaviorally to environmental events, but through cognition they also exercise control over their own behavior, which then influences not only the environment but also cognitive, affective, and biological states. The process of reciprocal causation has also been called "emergent interactive agency" (Bandura, 1986, 1989a). Although these influences are reciprocal, they are not necessarily simultaneous or of equal strength. A complete understanding of human behavior in any situation requires an understanding of all of these sources of influence: cognition, affect, behavior, and environmental events.

Centrality of Cognitive Construals

People have powerful cognitive and symbolizing capabilities. They cognitively construe (i.e., construct or build) their world, and it is these cognitive construals that have the greatest influence on behavior and emotions. People strive to understand and give meaning to their world. They encode (i.e., organize, categorize, and label) aspects of their world, including aspects of themselves and other people. Such encoding, once formed, resists change and greatly influences the construal of subsequent events. People attempt to explain events that have happened and to predict future events so that they can predict and control in the service of adaptation.

These explanations and predictions greatly influence what people feel and do. People often display apparent regularity in cognitive construals, which results in apparent regularity in behavior and emotion in particular types of situations. This apparent regularity is referred to as *personality*.

Because people observe others and form and retain verbal and nonverbal symbols of the actions of others and the consequences of those actions, they learn vicariously. In this way, people develop behavioral and cognitive competencies, beliefs about their ability to exercise those competencies under specific conditions, and beliefs about the possible consequences of exercising those competencies in certain situations.

The capacity for cognition also includes the capacity for consciousness, self-awareness, and self-reflection. People observe their own behaviors, thoughts, and feelings. They evaluate their ongoing behavior on the basis of how well it is working to accomplish their situational aims and objectives. People also note the influence of their behavior on the environment and the influence of the environment on their behaviors, thoughts, and emotions.

People are also capable of forethought and prediction, including the ability to imagine themselves thinking, feeling, and behaving in imagined future situations. They are capable of developing mental images of possible future events and states to be either attained or avoided (goals) and strategies for achieving or avoiding those future events and states (plans). Expectancies about the effects of certain behaviors under certain conditions and expectancies about the ability to perform those behaviors competently are the most important components of such strategies.

Self-Regulation

People are active shapers of their environments and of their own behaviors, thoughts, and emotions rather than passive responders to environmental events or internal psychological forces such as unconscious conflicts and endogenous traits. Their cognitive abilities provide them with the tools for self-regulation. The capacity to envision goals allows people to create incentives that motivate and guide their behavior. Through goals, people develop standards for their ongoing behavior, evaluate their behavior against these standards, and then make strategic choices about their behavior on the basis of these standards. People enter or avoid situations depending on the perceived relevance to their goals; these choices then shape their behavior by developing or limiting their competencies and skills and influencing their beliefs about their competencies. This is not to say that all goal-directed activity is intentional; much occurs automatically, without awareness of the behavior and its effects (Kirsch & Lynn, 1999).

Self-regulation consists of at least seven essential interactive elements: (a) goal setting (i.e., choosing what to try to accomplish), (b) planning (i.e., developing a strategy for attaining the goal), (c) implementation (i.e., implementing the plan through specific behaviors), (d) monitoring feedback (i.e., observing the impact of one's behavior on progress toward or away from a goal), (e) self-evaluation (i.e., formulating beliefs about personal abilities and probability of goal attainment), (f) affective reactions to feedback self-evaluation, and (g) corrective action (i.e., engaging in behavior designed to move one toward the goal more efficiently). This process is not linear but recursive. For example, change in the self-evaluation of competencies can lead to changes in goals, and affective reactions can interfere with planning, implementation, and monitoring feedback.

Social Embeddedness of the Self and Personality

People define themselves largely by what they think about, how they feel about, and how they behave toward other people. The individual's behavior is influenced and shaped by other people and by what the individual expects other people to think, feel, and do in response to his or her behavior. The most important learning is social learning, that is, what people learn from other people about how to think, feel, and behave. The most important cognitions are social cognitions, which are explanations and predictions about the behaviors, thoughts, and feelings of other people. Self and personality are perceptions (accurate or not) of one's own and others' patterns of social cognition, emotion, and action as they occur in patterns of situations. Thus, self and personality are inextricably embedded in social contexts, and an understanding of an individual cannot be achieved without understanding his or her social cognition and behavior in specific social situations, including the individual's social goals; situationally specific expectations; beliefs about social and situational norms; and how he or she selects, construes, and organizes information about the self and others. Because they are socially embedded, personality and self are not simply what people bring to their interactions with others; they are created in these interactions, and they change through these interactions. Thus, they are not entities; they are processes.

SOCIAL–COGNITIVE VARIABLES

The principles and processes shared by the social–cognitive theories depend on a relatively small number of elements, units, or variables. These elements are the most basic units from which these theories are built and from which additional variables are built. They are variables in that they are dimensions that can be measured and on which people can differ. Unfortunately, the taxonomies and labels for these variables, as well as their definition and measurement, are not consistent across the various social–

cognitive models, nor are they always consistent across studies examining a specific model. Variables are sometimes given different names in different models; sometimes variables are subsumed under other units, and sometimes researchers do not operationally define (i.e., measure) variables consistent with their conceptual definitions. These inconsistencies result in confusion about the definition and measurement of these variables and the relationships among them. Science is impossible without clear and consistent definitions of variables and without their valid and reliable measurement, and this confusion is an obstacle to research and theory development in the social–cognitive perspective.

For example, the considerable variation in the ways researchers have measured what Bandura (1997) called "self-efficacy" makes it difficult to compare the findings of one study on self-efficacy with another study that measured something else but called it "self-efficacy." A close examination of the measures researchers use to operationally define other basic social–cognitive variables such as expectancies, perceived control, and intentions also reveals similar inconsistencies across studies (cf. Kirsch, 1995; Maddux & DuCharme, 1997). The following list of variables is offered as a solution to some of this confusion.

Behavior–Outcome Expectancy

A *behavior–outcome expectancy* is a belief about the contingency between a specific behavior and a specific outcome (result, consequence) or set of outcomes. It is the belief that a specific behavior may lead to a specific outcome in a specific situation. All social–cognitive theories include a behavior–outcome expectancy, which is Mischel's (1973) name for this construct. Other names include "expectancy for behavior-reinforcement sequence" (Rotter, 1954, 1966, 1982), "outcome expectancy" (Bandura, 1977), "means–end belief" (Kirsch, 1995), "action–outcome expectancy" (Heckhausen, 1977), "response–stimulus expectancy" (Bolles, 1972), "response–reinforcer association" (Rescorla, 1987), and simply "expectancy" (Vroom, 1964).

The term *behavior–outcome expectancy* is preferable to the other alternatives for several reasons. First, the term *behavior* is more suitable for the social–cognitive perspective than is *response* because response, having its roots in traditional behavioral learning theory, suggests that the behavior is merely a reaction to an environmental event, a notion inconsistent with the principles of reciprocal causation, cognitive construal, and self-regulation. Second, the term *outcome* is preferable to the term *reinforcement* because outcome encompasses consequences one might want to avoid (aversive events) in addition to those one might want to attain (i.e., reinforcements). Third, behavior–outcome expectancy is also more specific and less confusing than outcome expectancy, which has been defined by researchers in various ways—a problem that is discussed later in this chapter.

Some theories subsume behavior–outcome expectancies under a composite construct. The theory of reasoned action (Fishbein & Ajzen, 1975) and the theory of planned behavior (Ajzen, 1988) include behavior–outcome expectancy in the assessment of two major predictors of behavioral intentions: attitudes about the behavior and social norms about the behavior. Both are assessed by asking people what outcomes they expect to result from the behavior in question and how much importance (value) they place on those outcomes. Kirsch (1995) proposed that behavior–outcomes expectancies are a component (along with self-efficacy expectancy) of what he called a "personal outcome expectancy," which is the individual's belief that his or her behavior will produce a particular desired outcome. Other composite constructs are Mischel's "plans and strategies," which are the means by which people intend to attain their goals, and "encodings," which are people's construals and categorizations of information about self, others, and the world (Mischel, 1973; Mischel & Shoda, 1995). Both constructs consist of various behavior–outcome expectancies, along with several other basic variables to be described later.

Two kinds of behavior–outcome expectancies can be distinguished on the basis of two different types of outcomes: environmental events and nonvolitional responses such as emotional reactions, sexual arousal, and pain. This is essentially a distinction between events that are external and internal to the person. A *behavior–stimulus expectancy* is the expectancy that a behavior will lead to an environmental event. Kirsch (1985a) called this a "response–stimulus expectancy." A *behavior–response expectancy* is the expectancy that a behavior will lead to a nonvolitional response. Kirsch (1985a) called this a "response–response expectancy."

Stimulus–Outcome Expectancy

Behavior–outcome expectancies are concerned with behaviors leading to outcomes. *Stimulus–outcome expectancies*, however, are concerned with beliefs that certain events provide a signal or cue for the possible occurrence of other events. This distinction was made by Mischel (1973), who distinguished between behavior–outcome expectancies and stimulus–outcome expectancies. Bolles (1972) made an identical distinction between response–stimulus expectancies and stimulus–stimulus expectancies. Rotter (1954, 1966, 1982) made a similar distinction by differentiating between expectancies for behavior–reinforcement sequences and expectancies for reinforcement–reinforcement sequences (i.e., beliefs that one reinforcement may lead to another reinforcement). Expectancies for reinforcement–reinforcement sequences, as described by Rotter (1954, 1966, 1982), are a kind of stimulus–outcome expectancy because they are concerned with beliefs about how much one particular kind of stimulus or event (i.e., reinforcement) predicts another of that same kind. Heckhausen's (1977) situation–outcome expectancy and Vroom's (1964) instrumentality are also stimulus–outcome expectancies.

Stimulus–outcome expectancies are important for two reasons. First, a stimulus may signal that a particular event either will or will not occur, depending on whether the individual engages in a specific behavior. In this way, a stimulus–outcome expectancy triggers a specific behavior–outcome expectancy, which may then influence behavior. Second, specific expected reinforcers and punishers gain part of their value from the extent to which people believe they will lead to other reinforcers and punishers.

Like behavior–outcome expectancies, stimulus–outcome expectancies can be divided into two types on the basis of the distinction between environmental events and nonvolitional responses. A *stimulus–stimulus expectancy* (Kirsch, 1985a) is the expectancy that a stimulus signals the probable occurrence of an external environmental event (e.g., that a siren predicts the appearance of an ambulance or fire truck). A *stimulus–response expectancy* (Kirsch, 1985a) is the expectancy that a stimulus signals the probable occurrence of a nonvolitional response (e.g., the expectancy that watching a sad movie will make one cry).

Self-Efficacy Expectancy

A *self-efficacy expectancy* is a belief in one's ability to perform a specific behavior or set of behaviors under specific conditions. Self-efficacy expectancy is not limited to beliefs about one's ability to engage in a simple motor act (although it may include such beliefs), but it does include beliefs in one's ability to "mobilize the motivation, cognitive resources, and courses of action to exercise control" (Bandura, 1990, p. 316) over a specific task demand in a specific situation. For this reason, it is not sufficient to simply say that self-efficacy is predictive of one variable or another; one must specify the domain (behavior and situation) of the self-efficacy measure. Because it is domain specific, self-efficacy expectancy is not a trait, and the term *expectancy* serves as a reminder of this. Self-efficacy expectancies, however, like other expectancies, may generalize from one situation or task to another. Self-efficacy expectancies pertain to behaviors and performances, not to outcomes or goals.

Most social–cognitive models do not make clear the distinction between the expectations that specific behaviors will lead to desired outcomes (behavior–outcome expectancy) and that one will be able to successfully perform the behaviors in question (self-efficacy expectancy), although the distinction had been alluded to before Bandura's work (see Kirsch, 1985a). Neither Rotter (1954, 1966, 1982) nor Mischel (1973) differentiated between self-efficacy expectancy and behavior–outcome expectancy in their original formulations, although both now acknowledge the importance of the distinction (Mischel & Shoda, 1995; Rotter, 1990). Self-efficacy expectancies are an important aspect of Mischel's (1973; Mischel & Shoda, 1995) plans, strategies, and encodings.

The definition of self-efficacy expectancy and its relation to other variables is the source of considerable controversy. Two conceptual issues are (a) the distinction between different types of self-efficacy expectancy and (b) the distinctions among self-efficacy expectancy, behavior–outcome expectancy, perceived behavioral control (as defined in the theory of planned behavior), and intentions (as defined by the theories of reasoned action and planned behavior).

Are there different types of self-efficacy? The variety of ways in which self-efficacy expectancy is measured in research certainly suggests so. The term *self-efficacy* is used in at least two different ways in research: as the perceived ability to perform a particular behavior, which Kirsch (1995) called "task self-efficacy," and as the perceived ability to prevent, control, or cope with potential difficulties that might be encountered when trying to perform the behavior, which Kirsch (1985a) called "coping self-efficacy" (see also Williams, 1995). Kirsch's task self-efficacy is similar to Bandura's (1977) original definition of self-efficacy expectancy as "the conviction that one can successfully execute the behavior required to produce the outcomes" (p. 193).

Researchers have used a myriad of items and scales to measure what they purport to be self-efficacy, often claiming that they are measuring different types of self-efficacy. Of course, just because researchers use the same term for two different measures does not mean that those different measures represent two different "types" of a common construct represented by the common term. These proposed different types of self-efficacy should be viewed not as different types of self-efficacy expectancies but as self-efficacy expectancies for different types of behaviors and performances, ranging from relatively simple motor acts to complex and challenging behavioral sequences and orchestrations. For example, "hammering nails" and "sawing wood" may be simple (but not always easy) motor acts, but "building a cabinet" is a complex undertaking. One can have a self-efficacy expectancy for each of these motor acts, and one can have a self-efficacy expectancy for building a cabinet. Each requires some "generative capability," although the generative capability required for hammering a nail is relatively small, whereas the generative capability required for building a cabinet is relatively large. Likewise, one can have a self-efficacy expectancy for "putting on a condom" and a self-efficacy expectancy for "engaging in safe sexual intercourse." The expectations concerning the ability to execute these different behaviors and sequences are not different types of self-efficacy expectancies; rather, they are self-efficacy expectancies for different types of performances.

Is the belief that one can attain one's goal also a type of self-efficacy expectancy? Should researchers apply the term *self-efficacy expectancy* to expectancies for attaining outcomes and goals as well as expectations for engaging in behaviors and performances used to attain outcomes and goals, such as getting an A in a course (e.g., Bandura, 1995; Mone, 1994)? The answer depends on how terms such as *performance, goal,* and *outcome* are defined. For example, getting an A in a course is neither a behavior nor a performance; it is an outcome that results from engaging in many behaviors and performances. Because a goal is a desired outcome, getting an A can certainly be a goal. Furthermore, getting an A is marker of performance attainment (Bandura, 1995) because the A is the marker that indicates that one's performance was ultimately successful. However, the A is a measure of the success of the performance, not the performance itself. Therefore, to talk about "self-efficacy for getting an A" expands the meaning of self-efficacy from beliefs about performing behaviors (however simple or complex) to beliefs about attaining outcomes and goals. Researchers should not call an expectancy for attaining an outcome (goal, performance marker) a self-efficacy expectancy if they also call an expectancy for performing a behavior a self-efficacy expectancy. What researchers call this expectancy for achieving outcomes is less important than acknowledging that it is not the same as an expectancy for performing a behavior or set of behaviors. Kirsch's (1995) personal outcome expectancy and Mc-Clelland's (1985) probability of success are reasonable candidates for this construct.

The relationship between self-efficacy expectancy and outcome expectancy is also a source of confusion and controversy (e.g., Borkovec, 1978; Corcoran, 1991; Kirsch, 1986; Maddux, 1995). This confusion stems partly from the fact that as Kirsch (1995) pointed out, the term *outcome expectancy* has been used to refer to both behavior–outcome expectancies (i.e., beliefs about the contingency between a particular behavior and an outcome) and personal outcome expectancies (i.e., the person's belief that he or she will or will not personally be able to attain a certain outcome). A personal outcome expectancy includes the belief that a behavior will produce a certain outcome and the belief that the person will be able to perform the behavior (a self-efficacy expectancy).

The relationship between self-efficacy expectancy and outcome expectancy depends on whether one is concerned with a behavior–outcome expectancy or a personal outcome expectancy (Kirsch, 1995). Self-efficacy expectancy and behavior–outcome expectancy are logically unrelated, but self-efficacy expectancy and personal outcome expectancy are logically related because personal outcome expectancy is composed of self-efficacy expectancy and behavior–outcome expectancy. Research indicates that in situations in which outcomes are perceived to be determined almost exclusively by one's behavior, self-efficacy expectancies greatly influence personal outcome expectancies, and personal outcome expectancies do not add significant predictive utility beyond that offered by self-efficacy expectancy. However, in situations in which outcomes are perceived as being determined by external factors (e.g., luck), personal outcome expectancies should be less closely tied to self-efficacy expectancies and should add to the prediction of behavior. Research also suggests that when defined and measured carefully and in a manner consistent with the conceptual distinction, behavior–outcome expectancy can be important in the prediction of intentions and behavior (e.g., Litt, 1988; Maddux, Norton, & Stoltenberg, 1986; Sanna, 1992; Stanley & Maddux, 1986).

Self-efficacy expectancy is similar to perceived behavioral control, as defined in the theory of planned behavior (Ajzen, 1988). Both involve beliefs that one has the resources and opportunities to execute a behavior or attain a goal. However, the lack of clarity in the definition and measurement of both self-efficacy expectancy and perceived behavior control raises some questions. In research, perceived behavioral control has been measured as perceived control over the behavior and as perceived control over goal attainment (e.g., Ajzen & Madden, 1986; DeVellis, Blalock, & Sandler, 1990; Madden, Ellen, & Ajzen, 1992; Schifter & Ajzen, 1985). These are different constructs.

This problem parallels the problem of self-efficacy expectancies for behaviors and self-efficacy for goals. As noted previously, for example, "getting an A" in a course or "losing weight" are not behaviors but are outcomes or goals that can be attained by implementing a behavioral plan (e.g., attending class, studying, and taking tests). Researchers cannot have it both ways. Perceived control over a behavior is a self-efficacy expectancy; perceived control over goal attainment is not. Perceived control over a goal attainment depends on both self-efficacy expectancy and behavior–outcome expectancy, which makes it identical to Kirsch's (1995) personal outcome expectancy and similar to what McClelland (1985) called the "probability of success." Much of the research on the theory of planned behavior assesses perceived control as perceived control over goal attainment. Calling this a measure of perceived behavioral control is a misnomer. Finally, if perceived behavioral control is the same as self-efficacy expectancy, researchers have no need for both terms.

The final source of confusion is the relationship between self-efficacy expectancy and intentions. Sometimes when people say "I can't," they are referring to beliefs about a lack of skills and abilities; other times they are referring to beliefs about their lack of ability to manage discomfort and distress and expressing their resulting unwillingness to do something that may be motorically simple. This distinction is particularly important in situations in which performing a behavior may lead to involuntary aversive reactions such as fear, pain, or discomfort (Baker & Kirsch, 1991; Corcoran & Rutledge, 1989; Kirsch, 1982, 1985b), situations in which the individual has strong response expectancies for aversive outcomes. When people anticipate aversive outcomes (e.g., fear or pain) and are not willing to engage in behavior that may produce those outcomes, their linguistic habit is to say that they cannot perform the behavior (low self-efficacy) rather than they will not perform it. Measures of willingness may simply be measures of intention as used in the theory of reasoned action. Therefore, in situations in which fear or pain is anticipated, measures of perceived ability to perform the behavior (self-efficacy) may be measures of intention to perform the behavior. This intention is determined primarily by the strength of the person's response expectancies. The mislabeling of intention and perceived ability may occur in other important domains in which people are asked to engage in behaviors that may lead to immediate discomfort, such as dieting, exercising, or violating personal norms (Baker & Kirsch, 1991).

The distinction between self-efficacy expectancy for simple motor tasks and self-efficacy expectancy for complex performances is important for understanding some of the confusion that has arisen about the relationship between self-efficacy expectancy and intentions. In situations involving anticipated pain, discomfort, or emotional distress (e.g., picking up a snake, asking an attractive person for a date, running a marathon), measures of self-efficacy expectancy for the simple motor behaviors involved in these complex tasks (grasping, talking, running) are strongly influenced by response expectancies and are thus largely equivalent to measures of willingness and intention (Kirsch, 1995). Self-efficacy expectancy for the complex performances (including self-efficacy for coping with disturbing thoughts, anxiety, and pain) are not the equivalent of willingness and intention.

Outcome Value

An *outcome value* is the value or importance attached to specific outcomes in specific situations. Outcomes can be either (external) stimulus events or (internal) nonvolitional responses. Other labels for the same construct include reinforcement value (Rotter, 1954, 1966, 1982), stimulus value (Mischel, 1973), incentive value (McClelland, 1985), and simply value (Vroom, 1964). The term *valence* is used for anticipated, as opposed to actual, satisfaction resulting from an outcome (Vroom, 1964), but making this distinction seems to be conceptual nit picking. An outcome can be valued because people want to attain it (e.g., money, better health) or because they wish to avoid it (e.g., cancer, obesity); thus, outcome value is a broader term than reinforcement value and incentive value. In addition, because outcomes can be stimulus events or nonvolitional responses, outcome value is a broader concept than stimulus value.

Outcome value appears in all the social–cognitive theories, although it is sometimes called something else or subsumed under another variable. For example, in various social–cognitive models of health behavior, such as protection motivation theory (e.g., Maddux & Rogers, 1983; Rogers, 1975) and the health belief model (e.g., Janz & Becker, 1984), the perceived severity of the health threat is an outcome value (Maddux, 1993). In the theory of reasoned action and planned behavior, outcome value is evident in the assessment of attitudes and social norms because, as noted previously, both are measured as the product of behavior–outcome expectancies and the value of those expected outcomes.

Goal

A *goal* is a valued outcome that one is consciously trying to attain or avoid, "a desirable future state of affairs one intends to attain through action" (Kruglanski, 1996, p. 600), and an end state or final product one wants to attain (Austin & Vancouver, 1996; Hyland, 1988; Locke & Latham, 1990). Goals differ from outcome value because a goal is a result one wants to achieve, whereas outcome value is the importance placed on that result. People can have various goals of varying degrees of importance, and several people can have the same goal but value it differently. Outcome value is that dimension of importance or value.

A goal is not a plan; plans are strategies people devise to attain goals (Austin & Vancouver, 1996). Nor is a goal an intention; an intention (discussed in the next section) is one's commitment to implementing the plan or the behavior that one believes will produce the goal.

A goal is not a motive or a need. Motive or need is usually defined as an affectively charged, biologically based "push" to work toward and derive satisfaction from a certain broad class of goals, such as "achieving" or "affiliating" (e.g., McClelland, 1985). Thus, a motive or need is a disposition, tendency, or inclination to value, strive toward, and derive feelings of satisfaction from attaining certain kinds of goals. A goal, however, is a more specific and situational outcome that one desires—either the attainment of a positive event or experience or the avoidance of an aversive event or experience. Bandura (1989b) made a similar distinction between biologically based motivation and cognitively based motivation; a goal is an example of cognitively based motivation.

Intention

An *intention* is what one says one will do. One can intend to implement a plan, or one can intend to engage in a specific behavior in a specific situation as part of a plan. Because implementing a plan consists of engaging in specific behaviors, the intention to implement a plan always involves, eventually, the intention to engage in or implement some specific behavior or another. Thus, as noted previously, an intention is not a plan because the plan is what one intends to do.

Although intention seems to be a simple notion, its definition and measurement pose some problems. In their theory of reasoned action, Fishbein and Ajzen (1975) defined an intention as "the person's subjective probability that he will perform the behavior in question" (p. 12) and said that it should be measured by "a procedure which places the subject along a subjective-probability dimension involving a relation between himself and some action" (pp. 12–13). Although seemingly straightforward, this definition of intention has been the subject of considerable debate. For example, this definition can be viewed as emphasizing people's estimates or predictions that they will or will not perform the behavior in question rather than an indication that they plan to perform the behavior. Of course, what people plan to do can be much different from what they predict they will do, possibly because when formulating a prediction people consider a wider range of possible influences than when formulating an intention (Sheppard, Hartwick, & Warshaw, 1988).

Some researchers have measured intentions consistent with Fishbein and Ajzen's (1975) original definition of one's estimate or prediction of what one will do. Others have defined and measured intentions as what one intends or plans to do. Research suggests that estimates (i.e., predictions) of future performance are better predictors of behavior than are intentions to perform the behavior (Sheppard et al., 1988).

An intention is not a goal, although one certainly can intend to attain a goal. An intention is similar to a goal in that both are cognitive representations of future desired states, but they are different because a goal is what one intends to attain. In common parlance, people use the word *intend* to refer to both their commitment to attaining a goal (e.g., "I intend to lose 10 pounds by summer" or "I intend to get an A on the next math examination") and their commitment to implement a specific plan or behavior to attain that goal (e.g., "I intend to walk 3 miles four times a week" or "I intend to study hard for the next math examination"). Gollwitzer (1993) made essentially the same distinction between goal intentions and implementation intentions (although the latter are more situation specific than most measures of behavioral intentions).

Unfortunately, researchers have sometimes used one definition and sometimes the other without acknowledging the difference. Some researchers have measured goal intentions (e.g., "I intend to lose 10 lb") and called them "intentions." Others have measured behavioral intentions (e.g., "I intend to cut down on sweets") and called them "intentions" (Maddux & DuCharme, 1997). The difference between goal intentions and behavioral intentions may be difficult to discern in some cases (e.g., studying 3 hr a night can be construed as both a goal and part of a plan for getting an A on a test), but it is related to the distinction between goals and plans in that plans consist of actions that one believes will help attain the goal.

If the distinction between goals and plans is important in the social–cognitive perspective, then so is the distinction between goal intentions and implementation intentions. However, because goal intention is almost identical to the notion of goal commitment (i.e., determination to reach the goal; Locke, 1996), it simply adds a new term without adding a new construct. Researchers may not need both terms. To avoid confusion, the term *intention* is probably best reserved for referring to one's commitment to implement a plan or engage in a behavior one believes will lead to a goal—a behavioral or implementation intention—rather than one's commitment to the goal.

Attributions

Causal attributions, or simply *attributions*, are explanations concerned with the motives, behaviors, thoughts, and feelings of self and others (Anderson et al., 1996). The social–cognitive emphasis on self-regulation or self-control is echoed in attribution theory and research in that attributions "allow us to create stable and generally useful views of the world around us in the sense that they enhance our ability to predict and control events" (Anderson et al., 1996, p. 273).

Attributions and expectancies are both concerned with perceived control. The crucial difference between them is that an attribution is an explanation for what has already occurred (perhaps at this very moment), whereas an expectancy is a prediction about what might occur (perhaps at the very next moment). Attributions and expectancies influence each other. One way behavior–outcome expectancies influence attributions is that events that are inconsistent with expectancies trigger attempts to explain them (Olson et al., 1996), and these expectancy-disconfirming events are often attributed to external and unstable causes (Olson et al., 1996). Research on this relationship, however, focuses on stimulus (event) expectancies, not on response expectancies; an unanswered question is the extent to which expectancy-disconfirming nonvolitional responses are also attributed to unstable causes, external causes, or both. This effect seems to hold, however, for self-efficacy expectancies. For example, people with low self-efficacy expectancies for an activity are more likely than people with high self-efficacy expectancies to attribute success in that activity (an expectancy-disconfirming event) to external rather than internal causes such as personal capability (Bandura, 1986, 1989a, 1992; Schunk, 1995).

Attributions also influence expectancies (Bandura, 1989b; Weiner, 1986). Explanations of past events, especially events interpreted as success or failure, influence expectations of future success or failure—both outcome expectancies and self-efficacy expectancies. For example, attributing success in an activity to internal causes leads to greater expectations for future success (Weiner, 1986). An expectation for success, however, typically consists of self-efficacy expectancies and outcome expectancies—a distinction not made in studies addressing the influence of attributions on success expectancies. Attributions seem to influence behavior and mood largely through their effect on self-efficacy expectancies (Bandura, 1989a; Maddux & Meier, 1995).

Competencies

Competencies are what people know about the world and what they know how to do in the world. They are what people are capable of doing to solve specific problems, attain specific goals, and overcome specific obstacles and challenges under specific conditions (but not necessarily what they usually do; Mischel, 1973; Mischel & Shoda, 1995). These competencies can be cognitive (intellectual), behavioral, or self-regulatory (i.e., the ability to modify behavior, cognition, and emotion to deal with changing conditions). They include "the quality and range of the cognitive constructions and behavioral enactments of which the individual is capable" (Mischel, 1973, p. 266) and the ability to "construct (generate) diverse behaviors under appropriate conditions" (Mischel, 1973, p. 265). Competencies include skills and abilities but do not include beliefs or expectations about skills or abilities (self-efficacy expectancies), although such beliefs are crucial to the effective use of one's competencies. Nor do they include beliefs about the possible outcomes or consequences of the exercise of one's competencies (behavior–outcome expectancies). However, the ability to develop strong and resilient beliefs about one's competencies and accurate beliefs about the consequences of one's behavior is a cognitive competency.

Affect

Whether affect should be considered a basic social–cognitive unit is debatable. On the one hand, contemporary theories of emotion agree that emotions result from the cognitive evaluation or appraisal of life events and that which is evaluated is the degree to which the event is wanted or unwanted, that is, to what extent it is construed as moving a person toward or away from a goal (Frijda, 1988; Lazarus, 1991a, 1991b; Mandler, 1984; Ortony, Clore, & Collins, 1988). Thus, it is possible to view affect as the result of the other social–cognitive units (e.g., behavior–outcome expectancies and outcome values) but not as a social–cognitive unit itself. On the other hand, research from the past two decades indicates that affective responses are relatively automatic and interact in important and complex ways with attributions, self-evaluation, and self-regulation (Bandura, 1989a,

1989b, 1997; Barone, Maddux, & Snyder, 1997; Mischel, Cantor, & Feldman, 1996). Thus, affect deserves a prominent place in the social–cognitive perspective.

CONCLUSIONS

The concept of response expectancy makes an important contribution to the social–cognitive perspective by focusing people's expectations concerning nonvolitional responses such as emotions and pain. A more complete understanding of response expectancies depends on a clearer understanding of the broader social–cognitive perspective and the relationships among response expectancy and other social–cognitive constructs.

The major theories of the social–cognitive perspective share a number of important principles and a relatively small number of basic elements, units, or variables. Among the major principles are those of reciprocal causality, centrality of cognitive construals, self-regulation, and social embeddedness of self and personality. These theories also share a relatively small number of basic conceptual elements or building blocks: behavior–outcome expectancies, stimulus–outcome expectancies, self-efficacy expectancies, outcome value, goals, intentions, attributions, competencies, and affect. Several other constructs found in one or more social–cognitive models—attitudes, social norm beliefs, personal outcome expectancies, plans and strategies, and encodings—can be built from these basic units.

The similarities among the basic principles, processes, and variables of the various social–cognitive theories strongly suggest that they are not different models but simply variations on a few basic themes. Because there are few differences on which to base competing hypotheses, research that pits one model against another in an attempt to support one and refute the other is difficult to design and may not be the most productive use of researchers' efforts, as research on the social–cognitive models of health behavior suggests (Maddux, 1993; Maddux, Brawley, & Boykin, 1995; Weinstein, 1993). Because these models are more similar to than different from each other, theorists and researchers might better direct their energies toward integration rather than competition. The goal of research should then be to determine not whether one model is better than another, or even whether one variable is more important than another, but to determine the relative utility of the different variables and changes in relative utility with different behaviors and situations over time.

Bandura (1995) lamented that "we are now in the era of cafeteria-style theorizing in which constructs are plucked from divergent theories and strung together in various combinations as alternative conceptual schemes" (p. 354), as when similar factors bear different names and higher order variables constructed from lower order variables are presented as a new type of determinant. As a solution, Bandura suggested a focus on broad integrative constructs. The conceptual analysis and the list of basic variables described in this chapter are offered as a place to start. However, the delineation of commonalities among models and an attempt at integration need to go beyond what has been attempted here. The other social–cognitive models noted previously, each of which incorporates several of these basic principles, processes, and variables, eventually need to be included in the mix.

A major source of confusion is that the social–cognitive perspective has a large number of different words but a relatively small number of different ideas. Theorists and researchers need to resist the urge to add words that do not add ideas because doing so will probably add confusion. Perhaps the best way to avoid doing this is to become familiar with the words and ideas already out there. No new words were suggested in this chapter, although some preferences for certain words over others were expressed, along with some rationale for those preferences. However, more important than agreeing with these suggestions for what words to use for what ideas is agreeing that theorists and researchers need to agree. Theoretical integration will not be facilitated by the further proliferation of social–cognitive terms.

Finally, researchers need to move beyond models and constructs and concern themselves with measurement. The most important definitions of variables are operational definitions—how they are measured. If researchers agree on the verbal definition of concepts and variables but cannot agree on their measurement, they will make little progress toward understanding them. In fact, they will probably mislead and confuse themselves by believing they have consensus and understanding when they do not.

Is the effort worth it? Some would suggest that it is not. B. F. Skinner once referred to the study of cognition as the "creation science of psychology" (Skinner, cited in Baum & Heath, 1992). According to Lee (1989), theories of behavior based on social–cognitive constructs share a number of problems: (a) They confuse description of behavior change with explanation of behavior change, (b) they rely on poorly defined and unobservable interactions among poorly defined variables, and (c) they are unable to make precise predictions about behavior. Lee concluded that social–cognitive models are not testable and therefore not useful. The pros and cons of using cognitive constructs in explanations of human behavior have been discussed repeatedly since the days of Watson and Pavlov and cannot be given full treatment here. Social–cognitive constructs indeed present definitional and measurement problems, but refinement and consistency in definition and measurement are likely to develop as theorists and researchers become aware of these difficulties and address them. This chapter offers a place to begin.

Decades of research on such social–cognitive constructs as attributions, expectancies, goals, and intentions amply demonstrate the measurability of covert variables and their utility in at least predicting behavior (e.g., Bandura, 1986; Barone et al., 1997; Fiske & Taylor, 1991). The extent to which theories based on these constructs truly explain behavior remains a question on which psychology's philosophers of science have yet to agree.

REFERENCES

Ajzen, I. (1988). *Attitudes, personality, and behavior.* Homewood, IL: Dorsey Press.

Ajzen, I., & Madden, T. J. (1986). Prediction of goal-directed behavior: Attitudes, intentions, and perceived behavioral control. *Journal of Experimental Social Psychology, 22,* 453–474.

Anderson, C. A., Krull, D. S., & Weiner, B. (1996). Explanations: Processes and consequences. In E. T. Higgins & A. W. Kruglanski (Eds.), *Social psychology: Handbook of basic principles* (pp. 271–296). New York: Guilford.

Austin, J. T., & Vancouver, J. B. (1996). The goal construct in psychology: Structure, content, and process. *Psychological Bulletin, 20,* 338–375.

Baker, S. L., & Kirsch, I. (1991). Cognitive mediators of pain perception and tolerance. *Journal of Personality and Social Psychology, 61,* 504–510.

Bandura, A. (1977). Self efficacy: Toward a unifying theory of behavior change. *Psychological Review, 84,* 191–215.

Bandura, A. (1986). *Social foundations of thought and action.* New York: Prentice Hall.

Bandura, A. (1989a). Human agency in social cognitive theory. *American Psychologist, 44,* 1175–1184.

Bandura, A. (1989b). Self-regulation of motivation and action through internal standards and goal systems. In L. A. Pervin (Ed.), *Goal concepts in personality and social psychology* (pp. 19–86). Hillsdale, NJ: Erlbaum.

Bandura, A. (1990). Some reflections on reflections. *Psychological Inquiry, 1,* 101–105.

Bandura, A. (1992). On rectifying the comparative anatomy of perceived control: Comments on "Cognates of personal control." *Applied and Preventive Psychology, 1,* 121–126.

Bandura, A. (1995). On rectifying conceptual ecumenism. In J. E. Maddux (Ed.), *Self-efficacy, adaptation, and adjustment: Theory, research, and application* (pp. 347–375). New York: Plenum.

Bandura, A. (1997). *Self-efficacy: The exercise of control.* New York: Cambridge University Press.

Barone, D., Maddux, J. E., & Snyder, C. R. (1997). *Social cognitive psychology: History and current domains.* New York: Plenum.

Baum, W. M., & Heath, J. L. (1992). Behavioral explanations and intentional explanations in psychology. *American Psychologist, 47,* 1312–1317.

Beck, A. T. (1976). *Cognitive therapy and the emotional disorders.* Madison, CT: International Universities Press.

Bolles, R. C. (1972). Reinforcement, expectancy, and learning. *Psychological Review, 79,* 394–409.

Borkovec, T. D. (1978). Self-efficacy: Cause or reflection of behavioural change? In S. Rachman (Ed.), *Advances in behaviour therapy and research* (Vol. 1, pp. 163–170). Elmsford, NY: Pergamon Press.

Cantor, N. (1990). From thought to behavior: "Having" and "doing" in the study of personality and cognition. *American Psychologist, 45,* 735–750.

Carver, C. S., & Scheier, M. F. (1982). Control theory: A useful conceptual framework for personality–social, clinical, and health psychology. *Psychological Bulletin, 92,* 111–135.

Corcoran, K. J. (1991). Efficacy, "skills," reinforcement, and choice behavior. *American Psychologist, 46,* 155–157.

Corcoran, K. J., & Rutledge, M. W. (1989). Efficacy expectation changes as a function of hypothetical incentives in smokers. *Psychology of Addictive Behaviors, 3,* 22–28.

DeVellis, B. M., Blalock, S. J., & Sandler, R. S. (1990). Predicting participation in cancer screening: The role of perceived behavioral control. *Journal of Applied Social Psychology, 20,* 639–660.

Dweck, C. S., & Leggett, E. L. (1988). A social–cognitive approach to motivation and personality. *Psychological Review, 95,* 256–273.

Edwards, W. (1954). The theory of decision making. *Psychological Bulletin, 51,* 380–417.

Feather, N. T. (1982). *Expectations and actions: Expectancy-value models in psychology.* Hillsdale, NJ: Erlbaum.

Fishbein, M., & Ajzen, I. (1975). *Belief, attitude, intention, and behavior: An introduction to theory and research.* Reading, MA: Addison-Wesley.

Fiske, S. T., & Taylor, S. E. (1991). *Social cognition.* New York: McGraw-Hill.

Frijda, N. H. (1988). The laws of emotion. *American Psychologist, 43,* 349–358.

Gollwitzer, P. M. (1993). Goal achievement: The role of intentions. *European Review of Social Psychology, 4,* 141–185.

Heckhausen, H. (1977). Achievement motivation and its constructs: A cognitive model. *Motivation and Emotion, 1,* 283–329.

Hollon, S. D., & Beck, A. T. (1994). Cognitive and cognitive–behavioral therapies. In A. E. Bergin & S. L. Garfield (Eds.), *Handbook of psychotherapy and behavior change* (4th ed., pp. 428–466). New York: Wiley.

Hyland, M. E. (1988). Motivational control theory: An integrative framework. *Journal of Personality and Social Psychology, 55,* 642–651.

Janz, N. K., & Becker, M. H. (1984). The health belief model: A decade later. *Health Education Quarterly, 11,* 1–47.

Kelly, G. A. (1955). *The psychology of personal constructs: A theory of personality* (2 vols.). New York: Norton.

Kirsch, I. (1982). Efficacy expectations or response predictions: The meaning of efficacy ratings as a function of task characteristics. *Journal of Personality and Social Psychology, 42*, 132–136.

Kirsch, I. (1985a). Response expectancy as a determinant of experience and behavior. *American Psychologist, 40*, 1189–1202.

Kirsch, I. (1985b). Self-efficacy and expectancy: Old wine with new labels. *Journal of Personality and Social Psychology, 49*, 824–830.

Kirsch, I. (1986). Early research on self-efficacy: What we already know without knowing we knew. *Journal of Social and Clinical Psychology, 4*, 339–358.

Kirsch, I. (1990). *Changing expectations: A key to effective psychotherapy*. Pacific Grove, CA: Brooks/Cole.

Kirsch, I. (1995). Self-efficacy and outcome expectancies: A concluding commentary. In J. E. Maddux (Ed.), *Self-efficacy, adaptation, and adjustment: Theory, research, and application* (pp. 331–345). New York: Plenum.

Kirsch, I., & Lynn, S. J. (1999). Automaticity in clinical psychology. *American Psychologist, 54*, 504–515.

Kruglanski, A. W. (1996). Goals as knowledge structures. In P. M. Gollwitzer & J. A. Bargh (Eds.), *The psychology of action: Linking cognition and motivation to behavior* (pp. 599–618). New York: Guilford Press.

Lazarus, R. S. (1991a). Cognition and motivation in emotion. *American Psychologist, 46*, 352–367.

Lazarus, R. S. (1991b). Progress on a cognitive–motivational–relational theory of emotion. *American Psychologist, 46*, 819–834.

Lee, C. (1989). Theoretical weaknesses lead to practical problems: The example of self-efficacy theory. *Journal of Behavior Therapy and Experimental Psychiatry, 20*, 115–123.

Lewin, K. (1938). *The conceptual representation and the measurement of psychological forces*. Durham, NC: Duke University Press.

Litt, M. D. (1988). Self-efficacy and perceived control: Cognitive mediators of pain tolerance. *Journal of Personality and Social Psychology, 54*, 149–160.

Locke, E. A. (1996). Motivation through conscious goal setting. *Applied and Preventive Psychology, 5*, 117–124.

Locke, E. A., & Latham, G. P. (1990). *A theory of goal setting and task performance*. Englewood Cliffs, NJ: Prentice Hall.

Madden, T. J., Ellen, P. S., & Ajzen, I. (1992). A comparison of the theory of planned behavior and the theory of reasoned action. *Personality and Social Psychology Bulletin, 1*, 3–9.

Maddux, J. E. (1993). Social cognitive models of health and exercise behavior: An introduction and review of conceptual issues. *Journal of Applied Sport Psychology, 5*, 116–140.

Maddux, J. E. (1995). Self-efficacy theory: An introduction. In J. E. Maddux (Ed.),

Self-efficacy, adaptation, and adjustment: Theory, research, and application (pp. 3–33). New York: Plenum.

Maddux, J. E., Brawley, L., & Boykin, A. (1995). Self-efficacy and healthy decision-making: Protection, promotion, and detection. In J. E. Maddux (Ed.), *Self-efficacy, adaptation, and adjustment: Theory, research, and application* (pp. 173–202). New York: Plenum.

Maddux, J. E., & DuCharme, K. A. (1997). Behavioral intentions in the theories of health behavior. In D. Gochman (Ed.), *Handbook of health behavior research* (pp. 133–152). New York: Plenum.

Maddux, J. E., & Meier, L. J. (1995). Self-efficacy and depression. In J. E. Maddux (Ed.), *Self-efficacy, adaptation, and adjustment: Theory, research, and application* (pp. 143–169). New York: Plenum.

Maddux, J. E., Norton, L. W., & Stoltenberg, C. D. (1986). Self-efficacy expectancy, outcome expectancy, and outcome value: Relative effects on behavioral intentions. *Journal of Personality and Social Psychology, 51,* 783–789.

Maddux, J. E., & Rogers, R. W. (1983). Protection motivation and self-efficacy: A revised theory of fear appeals and attitude change. *Journal of Experimental Social Psychology, 19,* 469–479.

Mandler, G. (1984). *Mind and body.* New York: Norton.

McClelland, D. C. (1985). How motives, skills, and values determine what people do. *American Psychologist, 40,* 812–825.

Mischel, W. (1973). Toward a cognitive social learning reconceptualization of personality. *Psychological Review, 80,* 252–284.

Mischel, W., Cantor, N., & Feldman, S. (1996). Principles of self-regulation: The nature of willpower and self-control. In E. T. Higgins & A. W. Kruglanski (Eds.), *Social psychology: Handbook of basic principles* (pp. 329–360). New York: Guilford.

Mischel, W., & Shoda, Y. (1995). A cognitive–affective system theory of personality: Reconceptualizing situations, dispositions, dynamics, and invariance in personality structure. *Psychological Review, 102,* 246–268.

Mone, M. A. (1994). Comparative validity of two measures of self-efficacy in predicting academic goals and performance. *Educational and Psychological Measurement, 54,* 516–529.

Olson, J. M., Roese, N. J., & Zanna, M. P. (1996). Expectancies. In E. T. Higgins & A. W. Kruglanski (Eds.), *Social psychology: Handbook of basic principles* (pp. 211–238). New York: Guilford.

Ortony, A., Clore, G. L., & Collins, A. (1988). *The cognitive structure of emotions.* New York: Cambridge University Press.

Rescorla, R. A. (1987). A Pavlovian analysis of goal-directed behavior. *American Psychologist, 42,* 119–129.

Rogers, R. W. (1975). A protection motivation theory of fear appeals and attitude change. *Journal of Psychology, 91,* 93–114.

Rotter, J. B. (1954). *Social learning and clinical psychology.* Englewood Cliffs, NJ: Prentice Hall.

Rotter, J. B. (1966). Generalized expectancies for internal versus external control of reinforcement. *Psychological Monographs, 80*(1, Whole No. 609).

Rotter, J. B. (1982). *The development and application of social learning theory: Selected papers*. New York: Praeger.

Rotter, J. B. (1990). Internal versus external control of reinforcement: A case history of a variable. *American Psychologist, 45*, 489–493.

Sanna, L. J. (1992). Self-efficacy theory: Implications for social facilitation and social loafing. *Journal of Personality and Social Psychology, 62*, 774–786.

Schifter, D. B., & Ajzen, I. (1985). Intention, perceived control, and weight loss: An application of the theory of planned behavior. *Journal of Personality and Social Psychology, 49*, 843–851.

Schunk, D. H. (1995). Self-efficacy and education and instruction. In J. E. Maddux (Ed.), *Self-efficacy, adaptation, and adjustment: Theory, research, and application* (pp. 281–304). New York: Plenum.

Sheppard, B. H., Hartwick, J., & Warshaw, P. R. (1988). The theory of reasoned action: A meta-analysis of past research with recommendations for modifications and future research. *Journal of Consumer Research, 15*, 1206–1210.

Stanley, M. A., & Maddux, J. E. (1986). Cognitive processes in health enhancement: Investigation of a combined protection motivation and self-efficacy model. *Basic and Applied Social Psychology, 7*, 101–113.

Tolman, E. C. (1955). Principles of performance. *Psychological Review, 62*, 315–326.

Vroom, V. H. (1964). *Work and motivation*. New York: Wiley.

Weiner, B. (1986). *An attributional theory of motivation and emotion*. New York: Springer-Verlag.

Weinstein, N. D. (1993). Testing four competing theories of health-protective behavior. *Health Psychology, 12*, 324–333.

Williams, S. L. (1995). Self-efficacy, anxiety, and phobic disorders. In J. E. Maddux (Ed.), *Self-efficacy, adaptation, and adjustment: Theory, research, and application* (pp. 69–107). New York: Plenum.

Woodward, W. R. (1982). The "discovery" of social behaviorism and social learning theory, 1870–1980. *American Psychologist, 37*, 396–410.

2

EXPECTANCY OPERATION: COGNITIVE–NEURAL MODELS AND ARCHITECTURES

MARK S. GOLDMAN

In a popular "Far Side" cartoon by Gary Larson (1995), a man is standing alongside a flying saucer. Disembarking from this saucer are a number of aliens, each shaped like a bowling pin with legs and what looks like a gloved hand at the top. The caption reads, "Inadvertently, Roy dooms the entire earth to annihilation when, in an attempt to be friendly, he seizes their leader by the head and shakes vigorously."

This cartoon exquisitely demonstrates expectancy operation. It shows that people routinely behave in accord with their preexisting expectations about how the world is organized. It suggests that behavior influenced by these expectancies is most often not thought out in some deliberative fashion but is automatic in nature; in fact, it is the ability to function without attention-demanding deliberation in relation to the myriad of circumstances people encounter that is the essence of such expectancy-guided

Portions of this work were supported by National Institute on Alcohol Abuse and Alcoholism Grant R37 AA08333. I thank Jack Darkes and Fran Del Boca for comments on earlier drafts of this chapter.

behavior. It also shows that behavior that occurs in this fashion easily can be mistaken, perhaps with serious consequences.

Organisms must have some system for reducing the degrees of freedom intrinsic to the information in the environment. Simple organisms reduce uncertainty by receiving relatively little information. Not far up the evolutionary ladder, however, are sensory systems capable of receiving information that would be overwhelming in the absence of some preexisting template for organizing such information and guiding ensuing behavior. The need for such a template is so compelling that some aspects of this template are even hardwired at birth. Consider, for example, the visual system with its capacity to respond to increasingly complex (but predetermined) stimulus configurations (i.e., lines in various orientations, patterns, movement) as information is passed up the hierarchies of cells in first the retina, then the lateral geniculate bodies, followed by layers of the visual cortex, and on to more frontal cortical structures (Maunsell, 1995). High level adaptive behavior requires plasticity, however, so higher organisms also use templates acquired from experience (Grossberg, 1995) and are capable of alteration by relevant new information. Even aspects of the visual system, once thought to be hardwired, have been found to be adaptable (see Singer, 1995). This fundamental capacity for storing information to organize later perceiving and responding is what Tolman (1932) called "expectancy."

When introduced, the concept of *expectancy* was criticized by behavioral theorists of the time (e.g., Guthrie, 1935, p. 172), who did not have modern computer and information-processing models on which to base theoretical accounts. It was not clear to them how a nonsubstantive process (i.e., information processing) could produce movement. It is now evident that information-processing devices (computers) can control actions through a wide variety of servo mechanisms.[1] In fact, evidence is now available that in living organisms, some information storage (memory) systems are so closely integrated with muscle systems that they reside in the periphery of an organism, not within the central nervous system (Grillner, 1996). The behaviorist view also proved limited in accounting for the capacity of organisms to learn at one time point without displaying this learning until later. Instead, cognitive views of expectancy prevailed (Bolles, 1972; Goldman, Brown, Christiansen, & Smith, 1991; Kirsch, 1985; MacCorquodale & Meehl, 1954; Mischel, 1984; Rotter, 1954).

Expectancy research has not yet availed itself fully of the exploding knowledge base in computer science, cognitive neuroscience, and artificial intelligence that began after World War II. In this chapter, I suggest models from these realms that might be usefully applied to expectancy research.

---

[1]An automatic device that uses small amounts of power to control a system of much greater power.

Furthermore, in the past decade, efforts have begun to blend cognitive models with models of affect and emotion (Bower, 1981, 1992; Lang, 1979) in the recognition that these domains are significantly related in the nervous system and routinely function together to influence behavior (Gray, 1990). As modern theories of personality have been articulated and related to these theories of emotion, it has also become possible to tie together cognition, affect, and personality within a general model of expectancy operation.

The premise of my chapter is that expectancy is not a narrow theoretical process but an umbrella term for processes that influence all behavior. The term *expectancy* refers to dynamic information templates stored in the nervous system that are processed to produce behavioral output. These templates are called "expectancies" because they prepare the organism for future circumstances similar to circumstances already encountered. They are dynamic in that they are not static "photographs" but instead unfold as they are activated. In general, they are of two sorts: those that are compared with incoming sensory input to organize and interpret this input and those that structure output.

The pervasiveness of these processes is underscored by recent expectancy-based neurocomputational models of brain functioning. Consider, for example, the following observations: "Neural networks that match sensory input with learned expectations help explain how humans see, hear, learn and recognize information" (Grossberg, 1995, p. 438), and "learning is driven by . . . expectations about future salient events . . . [and output of] . . . dopaminergic neurons . . . signals changes in the predictions of future salient or rewarding events" (Schultz, Dayan, & Montague, 1997, p. 1593). Models of this type do not require complex deliberation but might be based on nothing more than the detection of information patterns that match previously stored patterns. When input is sufficiently similar to the stored representation, information templates representing associated response patterns are in turn activated. These response expectancies then activate associated affective and motor pathways and may result in behavioral output. The word *may* is used because other information templates are almost certainly activated at the same time; these multiplex activation patterns compete for influence over final behavioral output.

Expectancy systems do not operate passively, however. They also selectively influence the perception of incoming stimuli. Consider an example by Grossberg (1995), who credited Richard Warren:

> Suppose that you hear a noise followed immediately by the words "eel is on the . . . ." If that string of words is followed by the word "orange," you hear "peel is on the orange." If the word "wagon" completes the sentence, you hear "wheel is on the wagon." If the final word is "shoe," you hear "heel is on the shoe." (p. 439)

According to Grossberg, expectations activated by the final word in the sequence influence the perception of the first word in the sequence that is held in working memory.

Many of these systems are now described in the literature without reference to the term *expectancy* (see, e.g., Miller, Galanter, & Pribram's, 1960, test–operate–test–exit model of basic self-regulation or Austin & Vancouver's, 1996, model of goals). The term *expectancy* is used here in deference to its historical roots, descriptive appropriateness, and usefulness in linking a diverse body of research. Also, the term *expectancy* itself has had a variety of meanings at different times and in different areas in psychology (e.g., probability of reinforcement, response–outcome correlations, stimulus–stimulus correlations; see chap. 1 in this book). The present usage is consistent with Tolman (1932) and more recent broad views of expectancy (e.g., Bandura, 1986; Bolles, 1972; Goldman et al., 1991; Kirsch, 1985; MacCorquodale & Meehl, 1954; Overmeier, 1990; Rotter, 1954).

The purpose of this chapter is to relate recent models and findings in computer science and cognitive neuroscience to the expectancy concept first advanced by Tolman (1932). I argue that placing these models and findings under the expectancy umbrella connects them to functional behavior in the real world. In the following two sections, I review the models and findings that may be applied to the understanding of expectancy operation. Other sections follow that extend these concepts to the domains of affect and personality.

COMPUTATIONAL MODELS

In 1950, Turing presented the "universal machine," designed not for a single purpose but to perform an unlimited range of tasks. This model served as the basis for the modern computer. Turing's concepts also had enormous implications for models of nervous system functioning, however. The notion of a machine with adaptable functions, which in some configurations even could be said to "learn," provided obvious referents for the nervous system. To clarify this apparent association, Newell (1970) articulated a range of views about the relation between computing and cognition, from computing as an interesting metaphor to cognition as a literal species of computing. Since that time, findings from neuroscience research support the latter view (see, e.g., Maunsell, 1995, and Singer, 1995, on the visual system).

The "biological computer" that may reside in the nervous system is much more complex than any electronic computer yet developed, however, not just because it is in some sense more advanced but because it developed in layers over many stages of evolution. That is, simpler and more limited systems for accomplishing similar functions developed earlier in evolution and are still present in organisms lower on the phylogenetic scale. As more sophisticated systems evolved, these systems elaborated and overlaid the simpler systems, but they did not necessarily replace them. As one example, neuroscientists have recently shown that the dopaminergic system in the nucleus accumbens and dorsal striatum works in part by tagging certain stimulus environments as having incentive salience; that is, dopamine is released when stimuli are encountered that have been associated with reinforcement in the past (Schultz et al., 1997). This system may be directly activated by drugs that have abuse potential. Such a system for the "attribution of incentive salience" (Robinson & Berridge, 1993, p. 249) essentially serves as an expectancy mechanism without complex intervening cognitions. These layered systems may work together in higher organisms or may compete for control of behavioral output. For example, certain drugs may be "wanted" more, even though they are subjectively "liked" less (Robinson & Berridge, 1993). This is not how a computer engineer would design an efficient system.

When one is discussing behavior, it is common to differentiate structure from function. In cognitive science, the structure of a system that can be programmed is referred to as its "architecture" (Newell, Rosenbloom, & Laird, 1989). Two basic architectures have been developed for computers. Overwhelmingly present in everyday computers is the architecture for serial processing. The second architecture supports parallel processing.

In a serial processing system, an addressable memory is separate from a central processing unit that runs the program. The program (designed by a programmer on the basis of analysis of the function to be performed) calls up information from memory and transforms it in accord with the function to be performed. All program steps are performed one at a time. These computers are fast because their electronics are fast. Problems are solved, however, by brute force over many steps and always require an external agent to design the algorithm appropriate to the desired function.

Parallel processing appears to be more consistent with nervous system functioning. Because neurons operate in milliseconds, human processes (the simplest of which take approximately 100 ms) can involve only 100 or so steps. Feldman (1985) has called this the "100-step program" constraint. Serial programs typically require far more steps to perform a function of consequence. Hence, human neural functioning must involve considerable parallel processing. Such processing involves activation of molecular information ("bits") from a large number of storage points, which is then linked in successive steps to form complex patterns. Because information must be accessible from many locations at the same time, the underlying architecture for a parallel system takes the form of a network in which elements are highly interconnected. In a parallel system, the configuration of assembled information guides output.

Consistent with this conceptualization is the accumulating evidence that complex memories (stored information that serves as the expectancy template) are not maintained intact continuously but are assembled from parts when needed. For example, Ungerleider (1995) wrote that

> information about all the different visual attributes of an object is not stored in a unified fashion in any single area of the cortex . . . . [It] seems to be stored in a distributed cortical system in which information about specific features is stored close to regions of the cortex that mediate the perceptions of those features. (p. 771)

The hippocampus creates linkages between different cortical areas to form higher order concepts, but, once formed, the prefrontal cortex activates the multiple areas that constitute the concept.

When assembled, these complex associations correspond to the constructs of schema (concepts at different levels of abstraction) and script (complex action patterns, how to do something such as preparing a meal; see Schank & Abelson, 1977) used in cognitive and developmental psychology. Despite different terminology, these associational networks conceptually and functionally overlap the expectancy concept. Both organize and interpret incoming information and guide responses.

To simulate the nervous system, cognitive scientists have articulated two general computational models of network operation. The parallel distributed processing, or "connectionist," model relates electronic elements in a manner thought to be similar to the relation of biological elements in the nervous system. In this "neurally inspired" (Rumelhart, 1989) system, information resides in the rules (weights) that associate (connect) one electronic element to another. With a complex set of processing units (usually three hierarchically arranged levels of units), a connectionist network can perform complex functions and can "learn," in the absence of programming, through feedback loops that convey the discrepancy between actual and desired output. This capacity makes connectionist models appealing. Other theorists have noted that these networks' appeal is limited, however, because it is impossible to understand how they perform a task; solutions reside in temporary activation patterns (numerical weights) between units. No direct representation of any object or event is stored. In addition, these networks typically need an extraordinarily large number of trials to produce a predesignated output.

A second network model stores representations of the external world as codes or symbols. In these symbolic network models, molecular concepts are represented as "nodes" that are closely or distantly linked on the basis of intrinsic meaning and learning history. Higher order concepts are assembled when activation spreads from node to related node. Pylyshyn (1989,

p. 62) argued that human systems must include symbol manipulation because humans process relationships, not just concrete stimuli. For example, once a child learns to place a red ball in a blue box, he or she also knows how to place a blue ball in a red box. This characteristic is a natural consequence of symbol architectures, but it must be enforced in nonsymbol (e.g., connectionist) architectures, which are more stimulus bound.

Pylyshyn (1989) further suggested, however (as did Simon & Kaplan, 1989), that processing occurs at multiple levels that may include connectionist and symbol networks as well as higher order semantic (knowledge) networks. The connectionist networks would correspond to the physical or biological level of processing. These levels would then serve as the substrate for symbol and semantic processing in a hierarchical fashion.

MATHEMATICAL APPROACHES FROM COGNITIVE PSYCHOLOGY

Cognitive psychologists have offered other mathematical approaches for modeling symbolic networks. Estes (1991) suggested that memory "traces can be viewed as vectors or lists, as nodes in a network, or as points in a multidimensional space" (p. 12). These formal schemes are not mutually exclusive; each point in multidimensional space could represent a node in a network. Each node may also represent the activation of a subnetwork that reflects a collection of elementary characteristics of the concept. Because of this flexibility, Chang (1986; also see McNamara, 1992) recommended network theory as a general theory of cognitive representation from which specific theories can be developed. Higher order network models can serve as a computational basis for symbolic and semantic memory.

Formalizing symbolic or semantic memory models as networks implies a basis for memory process as well as memory structure. One of the earliest computational models of how memories assemble from individual parts (Quillian, 1962) evolved into the spreading activation scheme of Collins and Loftus (1975). In this scheme, nodes are located more or less distantly apart in the network depending on how closely they are associated in memory. When triggered by a stimulus, activation spreads across this network and then dissipates. The coactivated nodes represent an associational set or higher order concept (schema, script) and are thought of as being part of declarative (episodic and semantic) memory. If thought of as sequences of activated information that organize movement, procedural memory (repetitive motor sequences) could also be based on network architecture, perhaps in a different brain location (e.g., cerebellum, motor strip; see Raymond, Lisberger, & Mauk, 1996; Squire, 1987, 1992). Given the current knowledge of neurocognitive systems, however, spreading activation is best conceived of as a useful heuristic rather than as a precise theory.

These mathematical approaches may be best understood by examining graphical representations. Figure 2.1 shows a simple hypothetical network in which spreading activation operates to form a concept, and Figure 2.2 shows how a network might be inferred from data on similarity judgments plotted using multidimensional scaling. Multidimensional scaling locates data points in multidimensional space using a distance metric. Note that these data, from research on alcohol expectancies, is well described by a two-dimensional (2-D) solution, with a bipolar dimension ranging from bad to good as the horizontal dimension and a vertical dimension ranging from sedation to arousal. These dimensions serve primarily to locate the data points in a visual space; more critical is the assumption that the spatial relations (distances) among the individual data points model a network. In such a network model, activation that begins at one data point (node) spreads outward to nodes in the closest proximity. The nodes that jointly activate make up the concept or schema. Because activation is assumed to dissipate with distance, only nodes proximal to the original activation point become part of the concept.

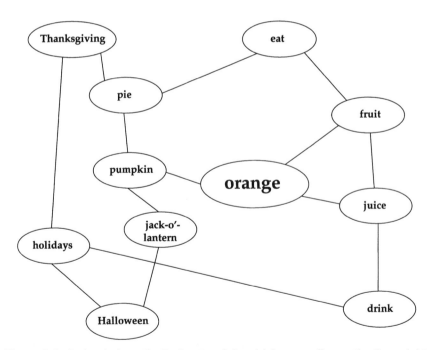

Figure 2.1. A simple hypothetical network in which spreading activation might form a concept. If activation spreads to the left from a starting point at the word *orange*, the concept is much different than if activation spreads to the right.

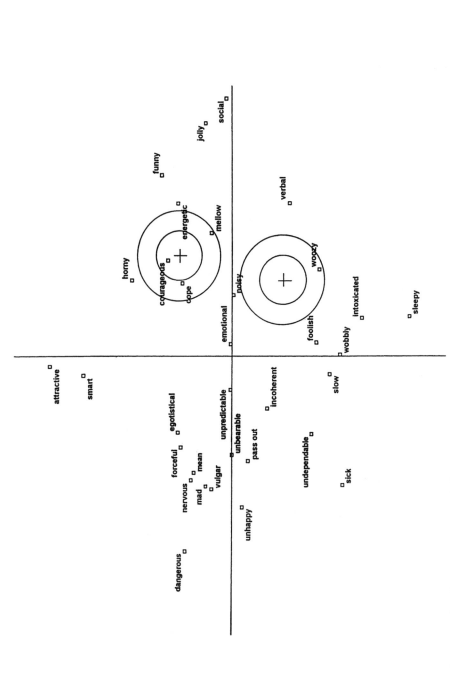

Figure 2.2. An example of expectancy words located in two-dimensional space after being subjected to multidimensional scaling. In this example, hypothetical starting points for the activation of the expectancy network have been located in keeping with findings that used such auxiliary scaling methods (see Rather & Goldman, 1994). The plus sign in the upper right quadrant is the hypothetical starting point for light drinkers; the plus sign in the lower right quadrant is the hypothetical starting point for heavy drinkers. Once activation begins, it may be presumed to spread like ripples on a smooth lake (as characterized by the concentric circles).

EXPECTANCY CONSTRUCT: SURPLUS MEANING

Because expectancy has been defined in so many ways within different psychological traditions, it has accumulated meanings that are, in the current context, superfluous. A common understanding within some traditions is that expectancy-guided behavior is "top-down." The precise meaning of this term often goes unexamined, but it seems to imply that expectancies operate from only the "highest" levels of cognition. Top-down influences contrast with "bottom-up" processes (another term rarely examined), which are "stimulus driven." It should be evident by now that in the hierarchical neural environment, "top" and "bottom" are highly relative. In any instance, the higher level of processing may be low in the overall architecture.

An often associated view is that expectancies must operate by becoming "conscious" and must use attentional resources. None of the models discussed require conscious processes or focused attention for effective operation. They postulate only that previously stored information is used to organize incoming information. Consciousness and focused attention may be most related to the processing of serial information in the real-time environment of the temporal world.

Given the amount of simultaneous information people must process (consider even the simplest stimulus array in the real world), most likely in the context of parallel neural processing systems perceptual and behavioral control are mostly "automatic" in nature (operate without awareness). It should come as no surprise, then, that much behavior happens with minimal or no awareness and certainly without a sense of volition (Kirsch & Lynn, 1999). Berns, Cohen, and Mintun (1997) identified specific brain regions that even are responsive to environmental novelty in the absence of awareness, presumably by comparing incoming information with stored patterns (i.e., expectancies). People regularly carry out behavioral sequences not planned in advance and of which they were only marginally aware or were even unaware they "intended" to perform. (Consider the common experience of arriving home from work and not being able to recall just how one got there.)

In this sense, Sigmund Freud and others since his time may have misled psychologists; rather than treating behavior in the absence of awareness as requiring explanation (or even as pathological), such behavior is likely to be modal (see Banaji & Hardin, 1996; Bargh & Barndollar, 1996; and Jacoby, Lindsay, & Toth, 1992; Kirsch & Lynn, 1999). Some recent models treat awareness (attention) as a limited resource, with specific behaviors involving more (or less) of this resource (Shiffrin & Schneider, 1977). Logan (1995) was more consistent with expectancy models when he ascribed the speed advantage of automatic processing to "the theoretical and empirical principles that govern memory" and suggested that "performance is automatic when it can be supported by traces retrieved from memory instead of costly algorithmic computation" (p. 751; see also Logan, 1996). These traces are essentially expectancies.

Sometimes consciousness may be no more than observing oneself behave automatically. The subjective experience of consciousness is instead the conundrum. Hence, apparently "magical" phenomena such as hypnosis or the placebo effect may be mysterious only when the assumption of conscious control is overextended. From the perspective of modern neurocomputational models, it is no surprise that the control of behavioral output and the subjective sense of conscious intention could become decoupled. This book offers many such instances.

Also note that in some areas of psychology (e.g., attitude theory), the term *belief* is associated with the expectancy concept. This term seems to imply conscious, verbalizable information, which certainly may derive from the information-processing systems discussed earlier but does not include all of them. The verbal expression of beliefs is likely influenced by a number of expectancy sets working in both constructive and competitive ways (e.g., constraints imposed by expectancies of appropriateness to particular settings and by interpersonal norms).

The argument for the pervasiveness of automatic processing in no way implies that deliberative (conscious) processing is not important. Attention-demanding, "controlled" processing may be, from an evolutionary perspective, the most recent means for enhancing behavioral plasticity and adaptability. Deliberative processing may increase survival potential by intruding into automatic processes that may at times be maladaptive. (Alternatively, some theorists have suggested that deliberative thought may be merely a by-product of the development of complex neural systems capable of more than the functions that gave them an advantage in natural selection.) The relative influence of controlled and automatic processing is not yet well articulated, however, and the importance of automatic processing is underscored by the automatic nature of even the selection of particular information for processing by deliberative systems (i.e., the choice of much of the material that people "think" about without making an effort to recall it). Nevertheless, rule-based information-processing algorithms (e.g., logic, mathematics) and the planning of activities over medium-to-long term intervals have given humans wide adaptability to environmental conditions. However, the use of rules to guide future behavior (i.e., to anticipate upcoming circumstances) may be regarded as another level of expectancy processing.

INTEGRATING AFFECT AND PERSONALITY

Cognitive science has traditionally been less attentive to individual differences and to motivational systems than to "cold" cognition. In recent years, however, cognitive researchers have been led by their data to consider affective regulation (Bower, 1981, 1992), and emotion researchers have begun to use cognitive models similar to those described earlier (Gray, 1990; Lang, 1979, 1995). Because expectancies are directed in part toward the anticipation of reward and punishment and because these conditions are intimately tied to affective responses, a neurocomputational model of expectancies would not be complete without integrating affective responding. Furthermore, because recent theories of personality are built on the ongoing relationship of affective responding to behavioral consistency, these discussions inevitably lead to an expectancy view of personality. In the next two sections, I address these issues.

Affect

A pure information-processing (computational) model fails when applied to organismic functioning in one major respect: There is ultimately no mechanism to tell it what to strive for (provide motivation, goals) in the absence of an outside agent. In living organisms, primary needs (e.g., hunger, thirst), closely allied with affect and emotion, appear to play this role. Because being alive requires behavior (even doing nothing is a behavioral option), it is perhaps most helpful to think of these systems as steering behavior (rather than inducing it) or making some behavioral options more salient in the face of a wide range of possibilities. This perspective on emotion can be readily coupled with an information-processing view of neural functioning (i.e., affect may be seen as an internal governor of which computations are initiated, are interrupted, or take precedence among the competing possibilities available). Indeed, Gray (1990) pointed out that neural systems underlying affect are so closely integrated in the living brain with those that support cognition as to be virtually indistinguishable.

In recent years, theorists in the affect domain have converged on two prevailing models of the fundamental mathematical dimensions of affect. One model includes two bipolar dimensions located in 2-D space (e.g., Russell, 1979, 1980): affective valence, ranging from pleasant to aversive, and arousal, ranging from extremely unaroused (or even asleep) to highly aroused. The second model emphasizes two other (unipolar) dimensions of positive and negative affectivity (Watson & Tellegen, 1985). Whereas Russell's model regards valence and arousal as independent (orthogonal), Watson and Tellegen's model combines valence and arousal on each of the two unipolar dimensions. These dimensions can be distinguished by their different orientations in the same 2-D space (at a 45° rotation from Russell's dimensions; i.e., if Russell's dimensions were drawn from 12 o'clock to 6 o'clock and from 9 o'clock to 3 o'clock, the new dimensions would have their upper anchors at 7 min 30 s and 52 min 30 s). Others theorists, taking a similar position, have referred to the latter two dimensions as "behavioral activation" and "inhibition" (Fowles, 1980; Gray, 1982) or as "reward seeking" and "harm avoidance" (Cloninger, 1987). Arguments continue about the relative merits of these different models, how they might be integrated (see Larsen & Diener, 1992), and the time course of activation (tonic or phasic) of these systems. All models presume individual differences in the tendency to experience and express these emotions. In fact, one simple way of understanding the concept of temperament would be to consider it an individualized predisposition to respond with one or another affective pattern.

The continuing debate over the "true" dimensions of affect and temperament occurs because these dimensions are thought to reveal a limited set of basic physiological processes (two or three at most) that are the substrates for affective responses. For example, in the type of model espoused by Russell (1980; also advanced by Lang, 1995), the valence dimension represents the operation of two opponent systems located in related but separate brain areas. The nucleus accumbens, caudate nucleus, and putamen are often cited as the substrates for approach behaviors and the amygdala as the substrate for aversive reactions; alternatively, Davidson (1993) located the substrate for approach-related affective responses in the left anterior cortex and withdrawal-related affective responses in the right anterior cortex. It is then assumed that the more complex array of emotions people experience results from combinations of different levels of the two or three more basic emotions. Left at this point, however, one might infer that these complex affective combinations are created afresh on each emotional occasion solely from the activation of these limited numbers of physiological systems. Put another way, in this view, many of the emotions people experience have no unique existence; they are perceptual combinations in the same fashion that most colors are combinations of reception in only three basic receptor types.

Because the nervous system seems to store representations of its own activation patterns, however, one may suppose that beginning at birth (and perhaps even earlier), a representation of each particular affective response, and the stimulus conditions within which it occurred, is stored in memory, just as other expectancy information is stored (see Izard, 1993; Lang, 1979; LeDoux, 1995; and Shaver, Schwartz, Kirson, & O'Connor, 1987). These affective memory networks, presumably stored in part in cortical structures, are linked to the subcortical systems that activate the more primitive affective responses (appetitive and defensive reactions; see Lang, 1995). Thereafter, affective responding results both from activation of the pathways that mediate primitive affective response and from activation of those same pathways through activation of the previously stored memory patterns of that affective response. That is, once the template of stimulus conditions relevant to an affective response is sufficiently matched by a newly encountered stimulus, then the stored representations of the previous affective response in that circumstance are activated and in turn activate primary (physiological) affective systems. Once again, these conditions describe the operation of an expectancy system. In this way, expectancies may be viewed as influencing affective responding.

Any given affective response may be either more or less a "raw" physiological event. Physiological activation triggered innately by a real external stimulus might be indistinguishable from physiological activation triggered by the stored representation of that affective response in memory, regardless of whether the external stimulus would have reached threshold for triggering such a response innately. This is essentially a cognitive explanation for classical conditioning; it is not dissimilar to Rescorla and Wagner's (1972; see also Siegel & Allan, 1996) model, in which the organism is understood to learn correlations, rather than acquiring wired connections, between unconditional and conditional stimuli and responses. Models of this kind relating affect to cognition have recently become central in comprehensive accounts of affective functioning (see Bower, 1981, 1992; Lang, 1979, 1995; and LeDoux, 1995).

Such models not only can be used to explain affective psychopathology (in which affective responses are apparently triggered by otherwise inconsequential events) but can also help resolve a major debate within the field of affect studies itself. Ratings of affect and emotions, when located in multivariate space, have frequently been found to fall approximately in a circular pattern in a 2-D plane (circumplex; see Russell, 1979, 1980). Procedures such as factor analysis either reveal "basic" dimensions or not depending on the rules for inclusion of affect indicators (words). As noted earlier, some theorists argue for particular dimensional solutions (e.g., Watson & Tellegen, 1985), whereas others suggest that the circumplex is most representative and that dimensions located in this space are arbitrary (i.e., that affect has no intrinsic simple structure). In the model presented earlier, even shortly after birth it becomes impossible to identify "basic" emotions using only ratings of overt emotional output because such output reflects stored affective information, not just the primary physiological reactions. In this view, rating systems for affect based on subjective responses are therefore incapable of revealing "true" (physiologically based) dimensions of affect (Larsen & Diener, 1992).

Note that in Figure 2.3, the space occupied by the domain of affective words is not dissimilar to the multidimensional scaling model of alcohol expectancies presented earlier. In a similar vein, therefore, researchers can use these models of affective space to model a working parallel processing network of affective activation. Affective nodes located more closely are assumed to be more likely to coactivate. If a hypothetical threshold of activation is achieved in this information storage system, activation then proceeds to the physiological systems for affect expression, resulting in the experience of emotion. Furthermore, because it is likely that particular

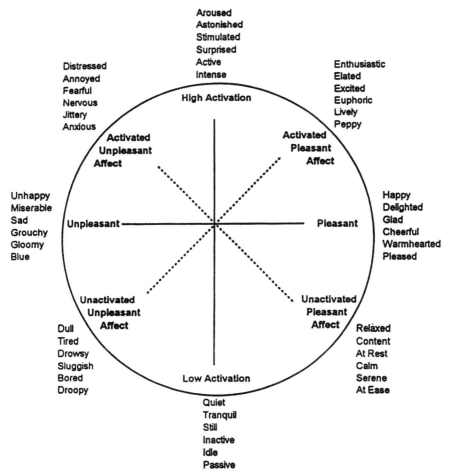

Aroused
Astonished
Stimulated
Surprised
Active
Intense

Distressed
Annoyed
Fearful
Nervous
Jittery
Anxious

High Activation

Enthusiastic
Elated
Excited
Euphoric
Lively
Peppy

Activated
Unpleasant
Affect

Activated
Pleasant
Affect

Unhappy
Miserable
Sad
Grouchy
Gloomy
Blue

Unpleasant ——————————————— Pleasant

Happy
Delighted
Glad
Cheerful
Warmhearted
Pleased

Unactivated
Unpleasant
Affect

Unactivated
Pleasant
Affect

Dull
Tired
Drowsy
Sluggish
Bored
Droopy

Relaxed
Content
At Rest
Calm
Serene
At Ease

Low Activation

Quiet
Tranquil
Still
Inactive
Idle
Passive

Figure 2.3. The domain of affective words (self-reported affect circumplex) as described by Larsen and Diener (1992). Note that if the words listed on the periphery of the circle were placed into the space within the circle, there would be considerable overlap with the locations of the words shown in Figure 2.2. From "Promises and Problems With the Circumplex Model of Emotion" (p. 31), by R. J. Larsen and E. Diener, 1992, in M. S. Clark (Ed.), *Emotion*, Newbury Park, CA: Sage. Copyright by Sage Publications, Inc. Reprinted with permission.

groups of affective nodes activate conjointly, a hierarchy of affective responses is suggested (see Bower, 1992; and Shaver et al., 1987). Once again, this is essentially an expectancy model of affective response.

Personality

To weave what psychologists call "personality" into the same expectancy (anticipatory information-processing) scheme, one need only to view personality as a set of relatively consistent behavioral patterns that develop over time as manifestations of the above information–affective networks (see Meyer & Shack, 1989; Pervin, 1994; and Revelle, 1995). Such a model readily reflects the consistency as well as the changeability of behavior over time, as the networks are modified to accommodate changing life circumstances and physical maturation. According to this view, the relative stability in personality is seen to result from the core information nets that begin developing at birth (or even before). It is difficult for long-standing information patterns, which are continually strengthened by inherited physiological predispositions, to be easily changed.

In support of the notion that personality can usefully be viewed as the behavioral manifestation of information–affective (expectancy) networks, research shows that commonly identified traits and types (including the Big Five; see Costa & McCrae, 1995) are consistently related to lo-

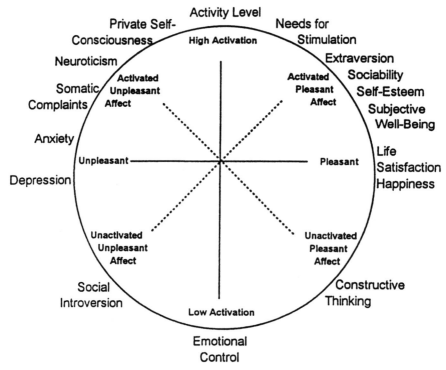

Figure 2.4. The relationship of personality constructs (traits) to locations on the affective circumplex shown in Figure 2.3. Repeated activation of affective information nodes could result in behavior patterns described by these trait labels. From "Promises and Problems With the Circumplex Model of Emotion" (p. 39), by R. J. Larsen and E. Diener, 1992, in M. S. Clark (Ed.), *Emotion*, Newbury Park, CA: Sage. Copyright by Sage Publications, Inc. Reprinted with permission.

cations on the affective circumplex that reflect the most salient affective dimensions (Larsen & Diener, 1992; Meyer & Shack, 1989). Figure 2.4 shows the locations on the affective circumplex that correspond to recently articulated personality constructs. Again, the circumplex model may be construed as a graphic representation of a network model in which spreading activation can serve as a heuristic for network operation. Furthermore, as with affective space, dimensions drawn through 2-D space can be construed as higher order personality characteristics under which lower order characteristics (or facets) are subsumed in a hierarchical arrangement (Costa & McCrae, 1995). These hierarchical networks (expectancy templates) constitute the substrate for an expectancy-based view of personality functioning. In this conceptualization, part of the consistency in behavior that psychologists call personality derives from the processing of complex expectancy templates that have been developed over the years.

INTEGRATION

The pieces are now in place to explain how even complex behaviors can be influenced by actual experience, observed (vicarious) experience, or even in the absence of experience but guided by an acquired concept about appropriate behavior (e.g., "hypnotic" behavior based on the individual's knowledge of what hypnosis is supposed to do). The activation of an expectancy template can directly initiate a behavioral sequence (script) previously associated with that "recognized" stimulus. Such a template in the same way can also directly activate an affective experience. In a more indirect fashion, the activation of an expectancy can indirectly produce a behavior that is associated with or results from the activation of an affective state. For example, a person may become more socially outgoing because he or she is affectively aroused. Expectancy operation can even produce the relatively stable behavior patterns psychologists refer to as "personality," consistent with the same processes repeated over many occasions. In fact, it is this type of processing that is the essence of modern conceptualizations of personality (see Revelle, 1995). Thus, expectancy processing can be used to explain simple, time-limited behavioral and affective sequences as well as much more complex affective and chronic (stable) behavior patterns.

Research Approaches

Because expectancies are treated here as a central psychological construct, it would not be too far-fetched to say that the broad domain of methodologies used anywhere in psychological (i.e., cognitive, affective, or neural) science may be applied to expectancy research. Researchers who specifically wish to study expectancies from the vantage point of parallel processing, network-type models are encouraged, however, to construct such models specific to the domain in question in advance of empirical tests. For example, the expectancies of consequences of alcohol or drug use, behaviors while hypnotized, affective responses to particular circumstances, or any specific behavioral repertoire could be modeled. In keeping with well-known findings in the realm of attitude research, the more specific to a particular context and circumstance are the expectancies, the more likely they are to be scientifically useful.

As discussed elsewhere in this book, such models may be constructed theoretically or with the assistance of exploratory empirical techniques (e.g., for the collection of word-association norms, see Nelson, Schreiber, & McEvoy, 1992; for multidimensional scaling and clustering, see Cooke, Durso, & Schvaneveldt, 1986; Goldman & Rather, 1993; Rather & Goldman, 1994; and Smith & Medin, 1981). Factor analysis may be less helpful in this regard because units of information that serve well as nodes in a network structure may be "predicted" by a limited set of factors that are inherently opaque about process or mechanism (see Goldman, Greenbaum, & Darkes, in press) and because bipolar concepts may not be well represented in factor analytic models (see van Schuur & Kiers, 1994). The utility of these models for explaining empirical findings and for predicting other relationships then becomes the criterion for the continued use of the model (as in all other research). Of course, models generated in these ways at best can be only imperfect representations of what are presumed to be largely automatic or implicit processes. It is the iterative development of these models over successive rounds of exploratory and confirmatory studies that helps sharpen their utility.

Practical Applications

The formulation of psychological processes as expectancy models suggests that behavior change can be effected through disconfirmation of existing expectancies (see Goldman, 1994; and Stangor & McMillan, 1992). Most current cognitive therapy techniques can be construed as variations on expectancy disconfirmation procedures. For example, Beck (1991) suggested that clients should "experiment" to test (and disconfirm) their beliefs. What modeling of expectancies as networks can bring to this process is a "roadmap" of the expectancies that are central in the network and perhaps most related to behavioral outcomes. Hence, the disconfirmation of these expectancies might have the most robust effect on behavior.

Efforts to disconfirm expectancies in a real-world context are likely to be more effective than are abstract discussions of expectancy operations. Much of the material commonly presented in treatment may be viewed as discussions of expectancy operation. In these instances, psychologists depend heavily on the successful intrusion outside of the therapy office of conscious processes into the stream of automatic processing. Because automatic processes seem to take little or no effort and do not need conscious cues to operate, it is difficult for controlled systems to effectively counter unwanted automatic behaviors over an extended time period. Because expectancies are acquired from experience, they are most likely to be activated and disconfirmed in a context that approximates or matches the original experience (but has a different outcome; see Goldman, 1994). The prevailing practice in therapy is to repeatedly remind the client of expectancy-disconfirming material (using controlled processes) in the hope that he or she will experience an actual disconfirming event as a result.

CONCLUSION

Recent advances in cognitive and neural science, and the computational models that often underlie them, have strengthened the scientific basis for psychological investigations. It therefore would behoove researchers in any domain of psychology to gain some familiarity with these advances. Although many of these advances have been accomplished without reference to the expectancy concept, in this chapter I argued for the reciprocal utility of these views. The expectancy concept readily benefits from these advances because they offer a foundation for models of expectancy operation. However, because expectancy theorists have always attended closely to the functional basis of behavior, researchers in other areas of scientific inquiry also might do well to attend to the broad domain of expectancy as a means of conceptually relating their systems to real-world adaptive functioning. Both lines of development have the potential to further enhance practical and therapeutic applications of psychological concepts. To underscore the advantage of reciprocity, I note that Tolman (1932) titled his major book on the expectancy concept *Purposive Behavior in Animals and Man*, with *purposive* being the key word.

REFERENCES

Austin, J. T., & Vancouver, J. B. (1996). Goal constructs in psychology: Structure, process, and content. *Psychological Bulletin, 120,* 338–375.

Banaji, M. R., & Hardin, C. D. (1996). Automatic stereotyping. *Psychological Science, 7,* 136–141.

Bandura, A. (1986). *Social foundations of thought and action.* Englewood Cliffs, NJ: Prentice Hall.

Bargh, J. A., & Barndollar, K. (1996). Automaticity in action: The unconscious as repository of chronic goals and motives. In P. M. Gollwitzer & J. A. Bargh (Eds.), *The psychology of action* (pp. 457–481). New York: Guilford Press.

Beck, A. T. (1991). Cognitive therapy: A 30-year retrospective. *American Psychologist, 46,* 368–375.

Berns, G. S., Cohen, J. D., & Mintun, M. A. (1997). Brain regions responsive to novelty in the absence of awareness. *Science, 276,* 1272–1275.

Bolles, R. C. (1972). Reinforcement, expectancy, and learning. *Psychological Review, 79,* 394–409.

Bower, G. H. (1981). Mood and memory. *American Psychologist, 39,* 129–148.

Bower, G. H. (1992). How might emotions affect learning? In S. Christiansen (Ed.), *The handbook of emotion and memory: Research and theory* (pp. 3–31). Hillsdale, NJ: Erlbaum.

Chang, T. M. (1986). Semantic memory: Facts and models. *Psychological Bulletin, 99,* 199–220.

Cloninger, C. R. (1987). A systematic method for clinical description and classification of personality variants. *Archives of General Psychiatry, 44,* 573–588.

Collins, A. M., & Loftus, E. F. (1975). A spreading activation theory of semantic processing. *Psychological Review, 82,* 407–428.

Cooke, N. M., Durso, F. T., & Schvaneveldt, R. W. (1986). Recall and measures of memory organization. *Journal of Experimental Psychology: Learning, Memory, and Cognition, 12,* 538–549.

Costa, P. T., & McCrae, R. R. (1995). Domains and facets: Hierarchical personality assessment using the revised NEO Personality Inventory. *Journal of Personality Assessment, 64,* 21–50.

Davidson, R. J. (1993). Parsing affective space: Perspectives from neuropsychology and psychophysiology. *Neuropsychology, 7,* 464–475.

Estes, W. K. (1991). Cognitive architectures from the standpoint of an experimental psychologist. *Annual Review of Psychology, 42,* 1–28.

Feldman, J. A. (1985). Connectionist models and their applications: Introduction. *Cognitive Science, 9,* 1–2.

Fowles, D. C. (1980). The three arousal model: Implications of Gray's two-factor learning theory for heart rate, electrodermal activity, and psychopathy. *Psychophysiology, 17,* 87–104.

Goldman, M. S. (1994). The alcohol expectancy concept: Applications to assessment, prevention, and treatment of alcohol abuse. *Applied and Preventive Psychology, 3,* 131–144.

Goldman, M. S., Brown, S. A., Christiansen, B. A., & Smith, G. T. (1991). Alcoholism and memory: Broadening the scope of alcohol expectancy research. *Psychological Bulletin, 110,* 137–146.

Goldman, M. S., Greenbaum, P. E., & Darkes, J. (in press). A confirmatory test of hierarchical expectancy structure and predictive power: Discriminant validation of the Alcohol Expectancy Questionnaire. *Psychological Assessment, 9,* 145–147.

Goldman, M. S., & Rather, B. C. (1993). Substance use disorders: Cognitive models and architecture. In K. S. Dobson & P. C. Kendall (Eds.), *Psychopathology and cognition* (pp. 245–292). San Diego, CA: Academic Press.

Gray, J. A. (1982). *The neuropsychology of anxiety: An inquiry into the functions of the septo-hippocampal system.* New York: Oxford University Press.

Gray, J. A. (1990). Brain systems that mediate both emotion and cognition. In J. A. Gray (Ed.), *Psychobiological aspects of relationships between emotion and cognition* (pp. 269–288). Hillsdale, NJ: Erlbaum.

Grillner, S. (1996). Neural networks for vertebrate locomotion. *Scientific American, 274,* 64–69.

Grossberg, S. (1995). The attentive brain. *American Scientist, 83,* 438–449.

Guthrie, E. R. (1935). *The psychology of learning.* New York: Harper & Row.

Izard, C. E. (1993). Four systems for emotion activation: Cognitive and noncognitive processes. *Psychological Review, 100,* 68–90.

Jacoby, L. L., Lindsay, D. S., & Toth, J. P. (1992). Unconscious influences revealed: Attention, awareness, and control. *American Psychologist, 47,* 802–809.

Kirsch, I. (1985). Response expectancy as a determinant of experience and behavior. *American Psychologist, 40,* 1189–1202.

Kirsch, I., & Lynn, S. J. (1999). Automaticity in clinical psychology. *American Psychologist, 54,* 504–515.

Lang, P. J. (1979). A bio-informational theory of emotional imagery. *Psychophysiology, 16,* 495–512.

Lang, P. J. (1995). The emotion probe: Studies of motivation and attention. *American Psychologist, 50,* 372–385.

Larsen, R. J., & Diener, E. (1992). Promises and problems with the circumplex model of emotion. In M. S. Clark (Ed.), *Emotion* (pp. 25–59). Newbury Park, CA: Sage.

Larson, G. (1995). *The far side 1995 off the wall calendar.* Kansas City, MO: Andrews & McMeel.

LeDoux, J. E. (1995). Emotion: Clues from the brain. *Annual Review of Psychology, 46,* 209–235.

Logan, G. D. (1995). The Weibull distribution, the power law, and the instance theory of automaticity. *Psychological Review, 102,* 751–756.

Logan, G. D. (1996). The CODE theory of visual attention: An integration of space-based and object-based attention. *Psychological Review, 103,* 603–649.

MacCorquodale, K. M., & Meehl, P. E. (1954). Preliminary suggestions as to a formalization of expectancy theory. *Psychological Review, 60,* 125–129.

Maunsell, J. H. R. (1995). The brain's visual world: Representation of visual targets in cerebral cortex. *Science, 270,* 764–769.

McNamara, T. P. (1992). Priming and the constraints it places on theories of memory and retrieval. *Psychological Review, 99,* 650–662.

Meyer, G. J., & Shack, J. R. (1989). Structural convergence of mood and personality: Evidence for old and new directions. *Journal of Personality and Social Psychology, 57*, 691–706.

Miller, G. A., Galanter, E., & Pribram, K. H. (1960). *Plans and the structure of behavior.* New York: Holt.

Mischel, W. (1984). Convergences and challenges in the search for consistency. *American Psychologist, 39*, 351–364.

Nelson, D. L., Schreiber, T. A., & McEvoy, C. L. (1992). Processing implicit and explicit representations. *Psychological Review, 99*, 322–348.

Newell, A. (1970). Remarks on the relationship between artificial intelligence and cognitive psychology. In R. Banerji & M. D. Mesarovic (Eds.), *Theoretical approaches to non-numerical problem solving* (pp. 363–400). New York: Springer-Verlag.

Newell, A., Rosenbloom, P. S., & Laird, J. E. (1989). Symbolic architectures for cognition. In M. I. Posner (Ed.), *Foundations of cognitive science* (pp. 93–131). Cambridge, MA: MIT Press.

Overmeier, J. B. (1990, September). *Expectations: From the laboratory to the clinic.* Paper presented at the Pavlov Society of America, Philadelphia, PA.

Pervin, L. A. (1994). A critical analysis of current trait theory. *Psychological Inquiry, 5*, 103–113.

Pylyshyn, Z. W. (1989). Computing in cognitive science. In M. I. Posner (Ed.), *Foundations of cognitive science* (pp. 49–91). Cambridge, MA: MIT Press.

Quillian, M. R. (1962). A revised design for an understanding machine. *Mechanical Translation, 7*, 17–29.

Rather, B. C., & Goldman, M. S. (1994). Drinking-related differences in the memory organization of alcohol expectancies. *Experimental and Clinical Psychopharmacology, 2*, 167–183.

Raymond, J. L., Lisberger, S. G., & Mauk, M. D. (1996). The cerebellum: A neuronal learning machine? *Science, 272*, 1126–1131.

Rescorla, R. A., & Wagner, A. R. (1972). A theory of Pavlovian conditioning: Variations in the effectiveness of reinforcement and nonreinforcement. In A. H. Black & W. F. Prokasy (Eds.), *Classical conditioning: II. Current research and theory* (pp. 64–99). New York: Appleton-Century-Crofts.

Revelle, W. (1995). Personality processes. *Annual Review of Psychology, 46*, 295–328.

Robinson, T. E., & Berridge, K. C. (1993). The neural basis of drug craving: An incentive sensitization theory of addiction. *Brain Research Reviews, 18*, 247–291.

Rotter, J. B. (1954). *Social learning and clinical psychology.* Englewood Cliffs, NJ: Prentice Hall.

Rumelhart, D. E. (1989). The architecture of mind: A connectionist approach. In M. I. Posner (Ed.), *Foundations of cognitive science* (pp. 133–159). Cambridge, MA: MIT Press.

Russell, J. A. (1979). Affective space is bipolar. *Journal of Personality and Social Psychology, 37*, 345–356.

Russell, J. A. (1980). A circumplex model of affect. *Journal of Personality and Social Psychology, 39*, 1161–1178.

Schank, R. C., & Abelson, R. P. (1977). *Scripts, plans, goals, and understanding.* Hillsdale, NJ: Erlbaum.

Schultz, W., Dayan, P., & Montague, P. R. (1997). A neural substrate of prediction and reward. *Science, 275*, 1593–1599.

Shaver, P., Schwartz, J., Kirson, D., & O'Connor, C. (1987). Emotion knowledge: Further exploration of a prototype approach. *Journal of Personality and Social Psychology, 52*, 1061–1086.

Shiffrin, R. M., & Schneider, W. (1977). Controlled and automatic human information processing: II. Perceptual learning, automatic attending, and a general theory. *Psychological Review, 84*, 127–190.

Siegel, S., & Allan, L. G. (1996). The widespread influence of the Rescorla–Wagner model. *Psychonomic Bulletin and Review, 3*, 314–321.

Simon, H. A., & Kaplan, C. A. (1989). Foundations of cognitive science. In M. I. Posner (Ed.), *Foundations of cognitive science* (pp. 1–47). Cambridge, MA: MIT Press.

Singer, W. (1995). Development and plasticity of cortical processing architectures. *Science, 270*, 758–764.

Smith, E. E., & Medin, D. L. (1981). *Categories and concepts.* Cambridge, MA: Harvard University Press.

Squire, L. R. (1987). *Memory and brain.* Oxford, England: Oxford University Press.

Squire, L. R. (1992). Memory and the hippocampus: A synthesis from findings with rats, monkeys, and humans. *Psychological Review, 99*, 195–231.

Stangor, C., & McMillan, D. (1992). Memory for expectancy-congruent and expectancy-incongruent information: A review of the social and social developmental literatures. *Psychological Bulletin, 111*, 42–61.

Tolman, E. C. (1932). *Purposive behavior in animals and man.* New York: Appleton-Century-Crofts.

Turing, M. A. (1950). Computing machinery and intelligence. *Mind, 59*, 433–460.

Ungerleider, L. G. (1995). Functional brain imaging studies of cortical mechanisms for memory. *Science, 270*, 769–775.

van Schuur, W. H., & Kiers, H. A. L. (1994). Why factor analysis often is the incorrect model for analyzing bipolar concepts, and what model to use instead. *Applied Psychological Measurement, 18*, 97–110.

Watson, D., & Tellegen, A. (1985). Toward a consensual structure of mood. *Psychological Bulletin, 98*, 219–235.

II

FUNCTION AND DYSFUNCTION

3

MOOD-RELATED EXPECTANCY, EMOTIONAL EXPERIENCE, AND COPING BEHAVIOR

SALVATORE J. CATANZARO AND JACK MEARNS

Experiencing pervasive, enduring negative moods undermines one's physical and mental well-being. Therefore, factors that terminate negative moods, or enhance and maintain positive moods, should promote greater adjustment and health (Bryant, 1989; Gross & Muñoz, 1995). One of these salutary factors, which we have studied over the past 15 years, is mood-related expectancy. In this chapter, we review two lines of research investigating response expectancies related to mood. This research shows that (a) specific expectancies for positive and negative mood states are strong predictors of those moods (e.g., Klaaren, Hodges, & Wilson, 1994) and (b)

Preparation of this chapter was supported in part by Grant 1R15 MH55870-01 from the National Institute of Mental Health and by a university research grant from Illinois State University. We gratefully acknowledge the contributions of our thesis students, research assistants, and independent study students, without whom many of the studies reviewed in this chapter might not have been completed. Although we cannot list them all by name here, several are cited in this chapter and many more are acknowledged in the original publications to which they contributed. Several of the studies described herein were supported by grants from Illinois State University. We thank M. Christina Birbaum and Sherlynn Robinson for their assistance in the preparation of this chapter.

individual differences in beliefs about one's ability to alleviate unpleasant affect predict the coping responses people use to face life problems and the effectiveness of that coping. We call these beliefs generalized expectancies for negative mood regulation (Catanzaro & Mearns, 1990).

EXPECTED EMOTIONAL STATES

Researchers in seven studies investigated the relationship between expected positive or negative mood and measures of later mood or mood-related cognitions. Expected mood has consistently predicted experienced mood, and experimental studies document a causal relation with experienced mood.

Positive Task Expectations

Catanzaro (1989) investigated the effects of expecting to enjoy an experimental task on subsequent performance expectancies, minimal goal statements (i.e., the lowest level of performance participants would find satisfactory), and self-reported enjoyment of the task. Before the experimental procedures were described to them, participants were asked to rate how much they expected to experience positive outcomes (e.g., enjoy themselves) and negative outcomes (e.g., feel nervous) during the experiment. They then performed a level of aspiration task (Rotter, 1942). Participants who expected to enjoy the experiment (a) rated the task and their performance more positively, (b) stated performance expectancies that were closer to performance levels, and (c) stated lower minimal goals relative to performance and expectancy levels. Because setting minimal goals relatively low entails lowering one's standards for an acceptably positive outcome, it maximizes one's opportunities for positive reinforcement and hence enjoyment (see also Catanzaro, 1991; Phares, 1972; and Rotter, 1954). This study shows that individuals who expected to enjoy themselves behaved in ways that made their enjoyment more likely.

Expected Humor

Wilson, Lisle, Kraft, and Wetzel (1989) conducted two studies in which they manipulated (a) participants' affective expectations about how funny cartoons would be and (b) whether those expectancies were confirmed or disconfirmed. (All the cartoons had previously been rated as not very funny.) Participants who had been led to believe the cartoons were funny rated them as funnier and liked them better than did individuals in a control group. Most important, participants who expected funny cartoons also showed more signs of facial mirth (e.g., smiling and laughing). Thus, the expectation of being amused caused actual amusement, even though the cartoons were not amusing.

Expectancy Versus Experience

Klaaren et al. (1994) conducted two studies examining the influence of affective expectations on people's subjective evaluations of experiences and on their decisions about whether to have those experiences again. In the first study, college students were asked about their affective expectations for an upcoming winter vacation. When they returned to campus at the beginning of the following semester, their actual experiences and overall evaluation of their vacations were assessed. Affective expectations—assessed several weeks earlier—were a robust predictor of overall judged quality of vacation irrespective of what happened on that vacation.

In Study 2, both affective expectations and objective experience were experimentally manipulated. Participants were randomly assigned to either a neutral expectation condition or a positive expectation condition in which they were told that the experiment was easy, fun, and liked by previous participants. They then watched a 20-min Charlie Chaplin movie under either pleasant or unpleasant conditions (e.g., soft vs. harsh lighting). The results were startling: Expectations were more important than actual viewing conditions in determining enjoyment of the experience and willingness to participate again. Follow-up analyses suggest that the participants' expectations led them to discount or reinterpret experiences that were inconsistent with their expectations. These results suggest that the power of affective expectations is considerable: They appear not only to influence experience but also the later interpretations of experience. This again underscores the self-confirming nature of affective expectancies: By influencing cognition, they determine how a situation is interpreted.

Mood and Menstruation

Researchers in two studies examined the role of mood-related expectancies in women's daily mood fluctuations during the menstrual cycle. Fradkin and Firestone (1986) led women to believe that premenstrual symptoms were either universal biological consequences of the menstrual cycle (strong negative mood expectancy) or psychological artifacts caused by negative societal myths (weak negative mood expectancy). Those who believed that premenstrual distress was an artifact reported much less negative mood than did either the strong negative expectancy group or a control group. These self-report findings were corroborated by husbands' reports of the participants' moods.

Olasov and Jackson (1987) randomly assigned women to one of four experimental groups. Two groups received expectancy manipulations: They viewed videotapes featuring an attractive, professional-looking "scientist" who delivered lectures designed either to increase or decrease beliefs that women experience negative moods during menstruation. Results indicate that individuals who believed the premenstrual phase was characterized by negative moods reported more negative moods throughout their menstrual cycle than did the other groups. Furthermore, expected mood was significantly correlated with menstrual and premenstrual moods during the ensuing 40-day period.

Mood and Nicotine Withdrawal

Tate et al. (1994) examined the effects of expectancy on symptoms during nicotine withdrawal. They led some participants to expect psychological and somatic withdrawal symptoms. Others were led to expect no complaints. Those who expected no complaints reported much less mood disturbance during withdrawal than did those in a no-expectancy control group, but other group differences were weak. Tate et al. suggested that the strength of preexisting response expectancies for mood symptoms during withdrawal might have limited the impact of their expectancy manipulation.

Alcohol-Related Mood Change

Greenwood's (1990) study also supports the conclusion that how people expect to feel predicts how they eventually feel independent of what happens to them in the meantime. He examined the role of expected positive and negative affect in alcohol-related mood change. Participants completed self-reports of positive and negative affect (Watson, Clark, & Tellegen, 1988) before receiving bogus success or failure feedback that induced a positive or negative mood. They then performed a tasting task in which they rated several beverages, including flat tonic water labeled either as a mixed drink (placebo alcohol) or plain tonic water. Before each task, mood expectancy was assessed; before and after each task, actual moods were assessed.

Results provided strong support for the role of expected mood in predicting actual mood assessed after the taste rating task, even when concurrently assessed mood was statistically controlled. In addition, an intriguing pattern of interactions emerged. First, the relation between expected affect and subsequent affect was strongest among those participants who knew they were drinking plain tonic water. This finding clearly supports the response expectancy hypothesis because no mood influence can be attributed to tonic water.

Among individuals who believed that they had imbibed alcohol, though, the relation between expected affect and subsequent affect depended on how much of the placebo beverage they consumed. For those who drank relatively small amounts of placebo alcohol, the relation between expected and subsequent affect was similar to that of the tonic water group. However, among those who drank relatively large amounts of placebo alcohol, the relation between expected affect and affect change was largely absent. These individuals may have been exhibiting unanticipated reactions to the experimental procedures. Nonetheless, Greenwood's (1990) results suggest that affective expectations are strong predictors of future affect, except in unusual situations (e.g., when a deceptive experimental manipulation has unanticipated consequences).

Summary

We reviewed seven studies examining expectancies for positive or negative affective states. These studies all yielded results consistent with the response expectancy hypothesis (Kirsch, 1985). Expected affective states are strongly related to subsequent emotional experience, judgments about one's performance, changes in performance goals, and judgments of the quality of one's experience. Researchers of all the studies reviewed, except Greenwood (1990), manipulated expectancy experimentally; these studies demonstrate the causal impact of expected mood. Only Tate et al. (1994), who attempted to manipulate nicotine withdrawal symptoms in relatively small groups, provided mixed results. Greenwood's (1990) correlational results indicate that mood expectancy effects are independent of one's current mood. Finally, relations among expected mood, behavior, and subsequent mood can be characterized as *mood congruent* (Bower, 1981); people tend to behave in ways that ensure that their affective expectancies will be confirmed.

EXPECTANCIES FOR NEGATIVE MOOD REGULATION

Over the past 15 years, we have been investigating the role of generalized expectancies for negative mood regulation in determining (a) how people cope with stressful life events and (b) coping outcomes related to health and mood. Our research suggests that assessing these expectancies can provide valuable prediction of important variables in the coping process.

In a seminal study, Franko, Powers, Zuroff, and Moskowitz (1985) examined generalized expectancies for affective self-regulation, defined as "an expectancy that some overt behavior or cognition will alleviate a negative state or induce a positive one" (p. 210). They interviewed children aged 6–11 years about their experiences with sadness, anger, and happiness. Children as young as 6 had well-developed beliefs about how to make themselves feel better when they were sad or angry. Consistent with Rotter's (1954, 1982) social learning theory, these beliefs exhibit both situational specificity (e.g., strategies described for use with mothers differed from those for use with peers) and generality across situations. Franko et al. (1985) suggested that such beliefs, conceptualized as generalized expectancies for the success of mood regulation strategies, should predict coping efforts and their outcomes.

Generalized Expectancies for the Negative Mood Regulation Scale

On the basis of the work of Franko et al. (1985), we defined *generalized expectancies for negative mood regulation* as beliefs in one's ability to terminate or alleviate a negative mood state (Catanzaro & Mearns, 1990). We developed the Generalized Expectancies for Negative Mood Regulation (NMR) Scale to measure these beliefs. The prototypical high scorer on the NMR scale believes that "If I try to feel better, I will feel better." Numerous studies indicate that the NMR scale is highly internally consistent and temporally stable across a wide range of the life span (Brashares & Catanzaro, 1994; Catanzaro, Horaney, & Creasey, 1995; Catanzaro & Laurent, 1996). Catanzaro, Laurent, Mearns, and Krogen (1995) reported comparable results with a version adapted for children, the NMR-Y scale.

A major task in scale development was establishing the discriminant validity of our NMR scale from social desirability, depression, and other personality constructs. Catanzaro and Mearns (1990) reported modest correlations of the NMR scale with social desirability and Rotter's (1966) Locus of Control Scale. Catanzaro (1994) provided strong evidence of discriminant validity from depression using confirmatory factor analysis. Holeyman (1995) found that the NMR scale correlated at a low level with the Big Five personality dispositions of Anxiety (also called Neuroticism) and Openness to Experience (McCrae & Costa, 1987). Catanzaro (1993) showed that NMR expectancies are modestly correlated with anxiety sensitivity (Reiss, Peterson, Gursky, & McNally, 1986; see also chap. 5 in this book). In summary, the NMR scale is a highly reliable measure across the life span, with discriminant validity from social desirability, locus of control, depression, personality traits, and anxiety sensitivity.

Over the years, we have consistently observed that NMR expectancies correlate with emotional distress. To understand how NMR expectancies become associated with problems such as depression, we next review studies examining the role of these expectancies in the process of coping with stressful events.

Cross-Sectional Studies of NMR Expectancies and Coping With Stress

Catanzaro and Mearns (1990) and Franko et al. (1985) posited that NMR expectancies should be related to efforts to cope with stressful events based on the social learning theory tenet that when individuals believe a behavior will lead to a desired outcome, such as feeling better, they are likely to engage in that behavior (Rotter, 1954, 1982). Kirsch, Mearns, and Catanzaro (1990) first studied the associations among NMR expectancies, coping responses to stressful events, and symptoms. They found NMR expectancies to be associated with more frequent use of active coping responses and less frequent use of avoidant responses. Furthermore, NMR expectancies were associated with fewer reported symptoms of depression and minor physical ailments, and this relation was independent of coping responses: Irrespective of how people reported coping with stress, NMR expectancies were negatively associated with symptoms. Finally, active coping responses—which were uncorrelated with depressive symptoms—were positively associated with depressive symptoms when NMR expectancies were statistically controlled.

This last finding was intriguing; it was unexpected, but researchers in subsequent studies (described later) replicated the result. Kirsch et al. (1990) suggested that problem-solving attempts may be ineffectual unless the individual believes they will succeed. A lack of confidence in one's coping strategies might result in individuals trying a greater variety or frequency of coping responses but with only half-hearted effort and little success. Another possibility is that even if people successfully solve life problems, their dysphoric moods might persist unless they also have confidence that their coping efforts have helped them feel better (Catanzaro & Greenwood, 1994). Whatever the reason, it is clear that not believing that one's coping responses will be successful increases the likelihood that they will indeed be unsuccessful.

Two studies with older adults show that NMR expectancies were negatively associated with avoidant coping responses and with depressive symptoms even when stress levels and coping responses were controlled. In Brashares and Catanzaro's (1994) study, a sample of women who were caregivers of patients with Alzheimer's disease reported on their coping responses to a problem specifically related to their caring for an individual with Alzheimer's disease or a related dementia. Catanzaro, Horaney, and Creasey's (1995) participants were individuals aged 65 years or older. In addition to negative relations between NMR expectancies and avoidant coping and depressive symptoms, Catanzaro et al. also found that when NMR expectancies were statistically controlled, active coping was positively related to depressive symptoms.

Mearns and Mauch (1998) studied coping among police officers, a population at high risk for stress-related problems. They assessed symptoms of anger and general distress. Those police officers with stronger beliefs in their mood regulation abilities reported using more active coping strategies and experiencing less anger and physical and psychological distress independent of their coping responses. In addition, the relation between job stress and distress depended on the strength of the officers' NMR expectancies. High NMR expectancies buffered individuals from distress even when they were experiencing high levels of stress, whereas those with low NMR expectancies were much more vulnerable to experiencing distress related to stressful events.

Similarly, Catanzaro (1993) found that NMR expectancies and anxiety sensitivity combined to predict distress: High levels of distress were reported by individuals with weak NMR expectancies and strong anxiety sensitivity, whereas the least distress was reported by those with strong NMR expectancies and low levels of anxiety sensitivity. This suggests that strong NMR expectancies might mitigate the risk of anxiety disorders associated with anxiety sensitivity.

Mearns and Bautista (1996) examined NMR expectancies as predictors of a specific domain of coping: coping with a moral transgression. As expected, NMR expectancies were negatively associated with general guilt feelings. Individuals with strong NMR expectancies reported using more active coping strategies to deal with moral transgressions independent of their level of trait guilt: They believed they could do something to relieve guilt and acted accordingly.

Catanzaro and Laurent (1996) investigated relations among NMR expectancies, family support, coping dispositions, and drinking behavior among adolescents. NMR expectancies were negatively correlated with the use of drinking as a coping mechanism, which in turn was associated with problem drinking (e.g., Cooper, Frone, Russell, & Mudar, 1995; Evans & Dunn, 1995; Laurent, Catanzaro, & Callan, 1997). Consistent with other studies, NMR expectancies were positively correlated with dispositional active coping and negatively correlated with dispositional avoidant coping. (The term *dispositional coping* refers to cross-situational tendencies to use certain coping strategies. This contrasts with *situational coping*, which refers to responses to a specific stressor.) It is interesting to note that adolescents with stronger NMR expectancies also reported weaker beliefs that alcohol has tension-reducing effects—an alcohol-related response expectancy that predicts greater and more problematic drinking (see chap. 10 in this book).

Flett, Blankstein, and Obertinsky (1996) examined the cross-sectional relations among NMR expectancies, dispositional coping, depressive symptoms, and affective intensity (i.e., the intensity with which people typically experience both positive and negative emotions; Larsen & Diener, 1985). The NMR scale was modestly negatively correlated with affective intensity, and relations with dispositional coping replicated other studies. Flett et al. (1996) did not examine relations of affective intensity and NMR expectancies with coping and depressive symptoms independently of each other. However, Catanzaro (1997) used their published correlations to show that (a) the NMR scale was correlated with depressive symptoms and dispositional coping independent of affective intensity and (b) the correlation between affective intensity and depressive symptoms was not independent of the NMR scale. Thus, although affective intensity and NMR expectancies are each associated with distinct coping dispositions, NMR expectancies are more potent predictors of the effectiveness of coping than is affective intensity. This finding follows from social learning theory: NMR expectancies should be more strongly related to mood regulation and recovery because they specifically address the perceived effectiveness of coping attempts.

In summary, all eight studies reviewed in this section indicate that NMR expectancies are associated with coping responses and adaptation across a wide range of the life span and in a variety of life contexts. These associations are independent of broad aspects of personality and temperament (e.g., trait guilt, Big Five dimensions, and affective intensity) and of contextual factors that influence coping (e.g., recent stress). Growing evidence indicates that NMR expectancies at least partially determine the effectiveness of coping responses. All of these researchers, however, examined simple cross-sectional relationships, leaving open questions having to do with causal direction. The question remains: Are weak NMR expectancies merely symptomatic of inadequate coping skills or dysphoric mood? Or do they reflect a distinct construct that has a causal impact on coping and depressive symptoms?

Longitudinal Studies

In several longitudinal studies, researchers examined NMR expectancies as predictors of coping responses and depression over time. First, reasoning that romantic relationships are an important source of stress for college students, Mearns (1991) conducted three studies examining NMR expectancies as predictors of college students' coping with and depression after the ending of a romantic relationship. In the first study, NMR scale scores were negatively correlated with retrospective reports of depression during the first week after the breakup and with current depression at the time of the study. Even with current depression statistically controlled, the NMR scale scores still correlated with initial depression.

Study 2 followed individuals from Study 1 whose relationship breakup had occurred in the previous 2 months. NMR expectancies predicted more active coping with the relationship breakup but not change in depression from the "current" assessment in Study 1. Study 3 took place 6 months after Study 1. Individuals from Study 1 who had since experienced the end of a romantic relationship were assessed. The NMR scale predicted subsequent active coping efforts, initial depressive symptoms after the end of the romantic relationship, and current depressive symptoms at the time of Study 3. More important, the NMR scale predicted changes in depression over the 6-month interval.

Catanzaro and Greenwood (1994) assessed a sample of college students at two times, separated by 6–8 weeks. They measured NMR expectancies, situational coping, and depressive and physical symptoms. Cross-sectional analyses at both Times 1 and 2 replicated the results of Kirsch et al. (1990). More important, Time 1 NMR expectancies prospectively predicted Time 2 active and avoidant coping responses, even after controlling for Time 1 coping. Also changes in NMR scale scores from Time 1 to Time 2 were correlated with changes in depressive symptoms over the same time frame. People who reported becoming more confident in their mood regulation abilities also reported becoming less depressed.

Catanzaro and Horlock (1996) focused on two questions: (a) Is the prospective relation between NMR expectancies and coping independent of initial levels of symptoms? and (b) Are situational coping responses predictive of subsequent changes in symptoms? Participants were assessed three times, with a 2- to 3-week interval between each assessment. As did other researchers, Catanzaro and Horlock found that NMR expectancies were positively correlated with a variety of active behavioral and cognitive coping responses and negatively correlated with depressive symptoms at each assessment. In addition, the relations between NMR expectancies and active situational coping responses—assessed 2–3 weeks later—were independent of depressive symptoms measured concurrently with NMR expectancies.

Catanzaro, Wasch, Kirsch, and Mearns (1999) reported two studies that used structural equation modeling to evaluate the direct and indirect effects of NMR expectancies on coping and symptoms over time, independent of other coping-related personality variables. In Study 1, NMR expectancies predicted situational avoidant coping responses that were assessed 4–6 weeks later, independent of dispositional avoidant coping. NMR expectancies also prospectively predicted depressive symptoms independent of coping and initial levels of symptoms. In Study 2, NMR expectancies were concurrently and prospectively associated with depressive symptoms independent of dispositional optimism and pessimism (Scheier & Carver, 1985).

In summary, in eight studies researchers examined cross-sectional relations among NMR expectancies, coping responses, and symptoms and five prospective studies (which also provided cross-sectional data). The relations of NMR scale scores with coping and symptoms found in these studies are summarized in Table 3.1.

NMR expectancies were consistently positively associated with active attempts to cope with problems. Somewhat less consistently, they were negatively associated with attempts to avoid, deny, or disengage from stressors. The cross-sectional relations between NMR expectancies and a variety of symptoms, especially depression, were even more robust. These relations were found even when a number of relevant covariates, including coping

TABLE 3.1
Relations of Negative Mood Regulation Expectancies With Coping and Symptoms

Study	Sample	Covariates	Coping measures	β	Symptom measures	β
		Cross-sectional data				
Kirsch et al. (1990)	472 undergraduates	Easy-going disposition Self-confidence Negative life events Family support	HDL active[a] HDL avoidant[a]	.25*** −.12**	HDL Depression HDL Somatic Checklist	−.36*** −.12*
Mearns (1991) Study 1	583 undergraduates	Relationship characteristics HDL depression	—	—	HDL Depression 1 week after relationship ended[b]	−.17**
Brashares & Catanzaro (1994)	73 female family caregivers	Daily hassles Alzheimer's hassles	HDL Active[a,c] HDL Avoidant[a,c]	(.18) −.29**	HDL Depression Caregiver burden	−.51*** −.14
Catanzaro & Greenwood (1994) Time 1	222 undergraduates	Negative life events	HDL Active[a] HDL Avoidant[a]	.27*** −.28***	HDL Depression HDL Somatic Checklist	−.36*** −.17*
Time 2		Daily hassles	HDL Active[a] HDL Avoidant[a]	.32*** −.32***	HDL Depression HDL Somatic Checklist	−.42*** −.25**
Catanzaro, Horaney, et al. (1995)	96 older individuals	Revised daily hassles	COPE Active factor[d,e] COPE Cognitive factor[d,e] COPE Avoidant factor[d,e] COPE Ventilation factor[d,e]	(.14) (.08) −.22* (−.04)	HDL Depression	−.31**
Mearns & Bautista (1996)	77 undergraduates	Trait guilt	COPE Active[d,f,g] COPE Emotion-Focused[d,f,h] COPE Avoidant[d,f,i]	.32** .19 −.15	—	—

Table continues

TABLE 3.1 (Continued)

Study	Sample	Covariates	Coping measures	β	Symptom measures	β
Catanzaro & Horlock (1996, Time 1)	190 undergraduates	LES	—	—	HDL Depression	-.36***
Catanzaro and Laurent (1996)	210 high school students	Family environment[i]	COPE scales[d]	-.30 to .31[k]	—	—
Catanzaro (1997)	153 female undergraduates	Affective intensity BDI[l]	CISS Task-Oriented CISS Emotion-Oriented CISS Social Diversion CISS Distraction	.26** -.35*** .32***	BDI[l]	-.22*
Mearns & Mauch (1998)	56 police officers	Police stress survey	COPE Active[f,m,n] COPE Emotion-Focused[f,m,o] COPE Avoidant[f,m,p]	.17 .37** .14	Anger BSI General Distress	-.32** -.31**
Catanzaro et al. (1999) Study 1, Time 1 (T1)	250 undergraduates	Negative life events COPE Avoidant[q,p] Optimism (LOT) Pessimism (LOT)	COPE Avoidant[d,p]	.03 -.08	BDI (T1) SAI (T1) BDI (T1) ASC (T1)	-.29*** -.39*** -.23*** -.27*
Catanzaro et al. (1999) Study 2, Time 1	353 female undergraduates 155 male undergraduates	Optimism (LOT) Pessimism (LOT)	— —		BDI (T1) ASC (T1)	-.23*** -.05
Prospective data						
Mearns (1991, Study 2) Follow-Up 1	114 undergraduates	HDL Depression[r] HDL Depression 1 week after relationship ended[b]	HDL Active[s] HDL Avoidant[s]	.23* -.08	HDL Depression BDI	N/A N/A
Follow-Up 2			—	—	HDL Depression BDI	N/A N/A

Mearns (1991, Study 3)	78 undergraduates	HDL Depression (T2)[r]	HDL Active[a,s]	.31*		—
		HDL Depression (T5)[b]	HDL Avoidant[a,s]	.05		—
		Relationship variables	—	—	HDL Depression[b]	-.25**
		HDI Depression[r] (n = 47)	—	—	HDI Depression[b]	-.32**
Catanzaro & Greenwood (1994) Time 2 (T2) NMR	222 undergraduates	Daily Hassles	HDL Active[a]	.21***	HDL Depression	-.21***
		HDL Active[a]	HDL Avoidant[a]	-.20**	HDL Somatic Checklist	-.12*
		HDL Avoidant[a]				
		HDL Depression (T1)				
		HDL Somatic Checklist (T1)				
Time 1 NMR		Daily hassles	HDL Active[a]	.17**	HDL Depression	-.08
		HDL Active[a]	HDL Avoidant[a]	-.15**	HDL Somatic Checklist	-.09
		HDL Avoidant[a]				
		HDL Depression (T1)				
		HDL Somatic Checklist (T1)				
Catanzaro & Horlock (1996) Time 1–Time 2	190 undergraduates	HDL Depression (T1)	COPE scales[t]	-.10 to .32[q]	HDL Depression (T2)	(-.02)
		Unpleasant events (T2)				
		Type of problem				
Time 2–Time 3		HDL Depression (T2)	—		HDL Depression (T3)	-.08
		COPE scales[t] (T2)				
		Unpleasant events (T3)				
Catanzaro et al. (1999) Study 1, Time 2	250 undergraduates	Negative life events	COPE Avoidant[d,p]	-.11*	BDI (T2)	-.12*
		COPE Avoidant[q,p]			SAI (T2)	-.11
		BDI (T1)				
		SAI (T1)				

Table continues

TABLE 3.1 (Continued)

Study	Sample	Covariates	β	Coping measures	β	Symptom measures	β
Catanzaro et al. (1999) Study 2, Time 2	353 female under-graduates	Optimism (LOT) Pessimism (LOT) BDI (T1) ASC (T1)	—	—	—	BDI (T2) ASC (T2)	−.10*** −.04
	155 male under-graduates	Optimism (LOT) Pessimism (LOT) BDI (T1) ASC (T1)	—	—	—	BDI (T2) ASC (T2)	−.10*** −.02

Note. Covariates are the variables entered with the Generalized Expectancies for Negative Mood Regulation (NMR) Scale scores in simultaneous regression examining independent correlates of coping or symptoms. In general, coping measures were also covariates in the prediction of symptoms. Beta coefficients are the standardized relations between NMR scale scores and coping or symptoms independent of all other covariates. Beta coefficients reported in parentheses were not reported in original articles but were not available. N/A = not available; HDL = health and daily living form (Moos, Cronkite, Billings, & Finney, 1983); BDI = Beck Depression Inventory (Beck, Ward, Mendelson, Mock, & Erbaugh, 1961); CISS = Coping Inventory for Stressful Situations (Endler & Parker, 1990); ASC = Adolescent Symptom Checklist (Garrick, Ostrov, & Offer, 1988); LES = Life Experiences Survey (Sarason, Johnson, & Siegel, 1978); LOT = Life Orientation Test (Scheier & Carver, 1985); SAI = State Anxiety Inventory (Spielberger, Gorsuch, & Lushene, 1970), — = variable was not included in the study.

*$p < .05$. **$p < .01$. ***$p < .001$.

[a]Including items added by Kirsch et al. (1990). [b]Retrospective report. [c]Situational coping with a problem related to caregiving. [d]Situational version. [e]Scores generated by principal-components analysis in this sample of the 13 COPE scales plus two exploratory scales (Alcohol and Drug Disengagement and Humor). [f]Additive composite based on correlations obtained in this sample. [g]COPE scales of Active, Planning, Suppression of Competing Activities, Restraint Coping, Positive Reinterpretation, Acceptance, Turning to Religion, and Behavioral Disengagement (reversed). [h]COPE scales of Seeking Instrumental Support, Seeking Emotional Support, Ventilation, and Humor. [i]COPE scales of Denial, Mental Disengagement, and Alcohol–Drug Disengagement. [j]Family Environment scales of Dimensions Cohesion, Expressiveness, Conflict, Independence, Achievement Orientation, Intellectual–Cultural Orientation, Active–Recreational Orientation, Moral–Religious Emphasis, Organization, and Control. [k]BDI scores were controlled in regressions examining independent correlates of coping dispositions but were also examined as criteria in regressions examining independent correlates of depressive symptoms. [l]Range of betas for 15 COPE scales (see the text for statistically significant relations with the NMR scale). [m]Dispositional version adapted for coping with a moral transgression. [n]COPE scales of Active, Planning, Suppression of Competing Activities, Restraint Coping, Positive Reinterpretation, Acceptance, Turning to Religion, and Humor. [o]COPE scales of Seeking Instrumental Support, Seeking Emotional Support, and Ventilation. [p]COPE scales of Behavioral Disengagement, Denial, Mental Disengagement, and Alcohol–Drug Disengagement. [q]Dispositional version. [r]Measured in Study 1. [s]Situational coping with the end of a romantic relationship. [t]Situational coping with either an academic or interpersonal problem.

responses, were controlled. Prospectively, NMR expectancies appear to be most strongly related to depressive symptoms.

NMR Expectancies and Dynamics of Negative Mood States

Recent researchers have begun to more directly address variables related to negative mood states and recovery from them. Catanzaro (1996) administered the NMR scale to a large group of college students on the first day of a semester. He later assessed their levels of anxiety and depressive symptoms just before they took an examination at the end of the semester. The effect of state anxiety on examination performance depended on the individual's level of NMR expectancies. More anxiety was associated with poorer performance only for those individuals who had reported relatively weak NMR expectancies earlier in the semester. These findings suggest that distress has adverse effects mostly on individuals who lack confidence in their ability to alleviate or manage their negative moods.

Catanzaro and Harger (1993) reasoned that generalized NMR expectancies ought to be associated with individuals' beliefs about how they will feel when confronted by problems. That is, given that expected mood generally predicts experienced mood, high generalized NMR expectancies should generate specific expectancies for more positive mood states in particular situations. Therefore, Catanzaro and Harger presented college students who had previously reported strong or weak NMR expectancies with three different relationship problems. For each, they reported how they would expect to feel that night and the following morning. The first report was of expected emotional reactions, whereas the second represented expected emotional recovery.

NMR expectancies predicted both specific expected emotions and expected emotional recovery. Compared with low scorers, those with high NMR scale scores expected to feel less negative affect. More important, high and low NMR scale scorers expected different patterns of recovery for different problems. All participants expected declines in negative affect except low NMR scale scorers responding to a challenge. They expected an increase in negative affect, despite the relatively positive nature of challenging events (cf. Lazarus & Folkman, 1984). Individuals with strong NMR expectancies expected to feel better the day after a stressful challenge.

Smith and Petty (1995) provided evidence from two experiments that stronger NMR expectancies are associated with more positive cognitions after a laboratory induction of negative mood. In Study 1, the overall positivity of stories produced to a Thematic Apperception Test card was significantly higher for high NMR scale scorers than for low scorers. Furthermore, mood congruency effects on cognition were found for low NMR scale scorers, but mood incongruency was observed for high scorers. Similar results were found in Study 2, which examined the positivity of autobiographical memories. The results of these two studies indicate that individuals with strong NMR expectancies actively generate mood-incongruent cognitions when in a negative mood.

The results of studies examining coping and distress suggest that NMR expectancies play an important role in the self-regulation of mood states, but we do not know of any that have examined the process by which mood change is effected during a specific stressful event. In contrast, the studies described in this section provide clearer evidence that NMR expectancies prospectively predict aspects of this process. Stronger NMR expectancies predict less disruption of examination performance by anxiety, more positive expected emotions in response to stress, better expected emotional recovery from stress, and more positive cognition after exposure to a negative mood induction. Research is still needed to examine the role of NMR expectancies in real-time recovery from upsetting events.

THEORETICAL MECHANISMS

Expected and Experienced Mood States

Research on expected emotional states and NMR expectancies conforms strongly to findings regarding other response expectancies (Kirsch, 1985, 1990, 1997). Several plausible accounts could explain how mood-related expectancies have self-confirming effects. First, these expectancies could alter interpretation of memories (Klaaren et al., 1994). Second, they could directly facilitate affective experience (Catanzaro, 1989; Klaaren et al., 1994). Third, they could bias attention to those stimuli most consistent with the expected state. For example, it is well documented that anxious and panic-prone individuals (who expect anxiety) are hypersensitive to threat-related stimuli (Barlow, 1988; Beck & Emery, 1985; Clark & Ehlers, 1993).

NMR Expectancies and Coping Preferences and Responses

Generalized expectancies for negative mood regulation are conceptualized within Rotter's (1954, 1978, 1982) social learning theory. In this framework, the probability of a behavior is determined by the expectancy that the behavior will lead to reinforcing consequences and the subjective value of those consequences. We assume that in most social situations, the termination or alleviation of a negative mood will be highly valued; thus, when individuals expect that they have the means to make themselves feel better, they will use those means. Also they will be less likely to use avoidant strategies, which merely delay the need to solve problems or regulate moods. Research consistently shows that high NMR scale scorers exhibit more active and less avoidant coping.

Social learning theory also posits that in any particular situation, generalized expectancies are only one influence on situational expectancies, which serve as a proximal link between generalized expectancies and specific behaviors. Mearns (1991) noted that situational NMR expectancies should function as secondary appraisals (Lazarus & Folkman, 1984). Therefore, examining the links among generalized NMR expectancies, situational appraisals, and coping responses will elucidate how generalized expectancies influence coping in specific stressful encounters.

NMR Expectancies, Mood, and Emotional Symptoms

NMR expectancies are hypothesized to affect mood in two ways. First, as response expectancies, they are self-confirming. Thus, researchers consistently observe a relation between NMR expectancies and depressive symptoms independent of actual coping behavior. Having a belief that one can alleviate a negative mood in and of itself reduces unpleasant affect. Second, there is the effect on mood that is mediated by coping responses. NMR expectancies are associated with engaging in coping responses that have a salutary impact on mood, either directly through emotion-focused coping or indirectly through eliminating or solving distressing problems.

The self-confirming effect of mood regulation expectancies can also be understood within models of mood effects on memory. Because negative mood regulation expectancies appear to function as a long-term cognitive bias toward anticipating positive mood-related outcomes, the encoding specificity principle proposed by Tulving and Thompson (1973) may help explain their self-confirming effect. According to Tulving and Thompson (1973), "what is stored is determined by what is perceived, how it is encoded, [and] what is stored determines what retrieval cues are effective in providing access to what is stored" (p. 353). Thus, NMR expectancies as a positive cognitive bias may cause storage and retrieval of memories to be more positive.

A great deal of evidence has accumulated in the past 2 decades that mood biases memory (Bower, 1981; Matt, Vazquez, & Campbell, 1992), social judgments (e.g., Forgas, 1995), social comparisons (e.g., Wheeler & Miyake, 1992), self-ratings of health and well-being (e.g., Salovey & Birnbaum, 1989), judgments about the risk of future negative and positive events (e.g., Johnson & Tversky, 1983; W. F. Wright & Bower, 1992), and personal standards and minimal goals (e.g., J. Wright & Mischel, 1982). To explain such effects, Bower (1981) proposed a network model of memory in which each distinct emotion is represented by a specific memory node. Activation of nodes by stimuli or associated cognitions spreads through a network of associative pathways. When an emotion node is activated, excitation will spread to nodes with which the emotion is associated. This spreading activation primes mood-congruent categories, making it more likely that one will focus on mood-congruent material, recall mood-congruent memories, and make mood-congruent interpretations of events. These proposed processes explain how a mood, and therefore a way of seeing the world, can perpetuate itself. Similar views have been elements of personality theories at least since Adler (1927).

Motivated by inconsistent findings (Eich, 1995) and by evidence that mood-congruency effects can be dampened or eliminated with attention-focusing manipulations (e.g., Hertel & Rude, 1991), alternative explanations for mood-congruent cognition have been proposed. Two influential accounts are mood as information (Schwarz & Clore, 1988) and resource allocation (Ellis & Ashbrook, 1988). The mood-as-information model posits that individuals use their moods to guide interpretation of events (e.g., "I feel bad; therefore, this must be a bad experience"). The resource allocation model posits that mood—particularly negative mood—consumes large amounts of cognitive resources that would otherwise enhance recall if they were available (cf. Kahneman, 1973). When someone is depressed, cognitive resources are directed toward the dysphoric mood state, increasing memory for dysphoria-consistent information.

The effects of NMR expectancies might be mediated by any of these cognitive mechanisms. Strong NMR expectancies should be associated with interpreting a negative mood as information signaling an opportunity to regulate mood rather than an overwhelming problem. Alternatively, strong NMR expectancies should be associated with more accessible mood regulatory strategies, requiring fewer attentional resources to generate material incongruent with a negative mood, including optimistic situational expectancies.

In the absence of studies directly comparing these models, we suggest that the effect of NMR expectancies would be best explained by Bower's (1981) cognitive network model because generalized expectancies can be represented as memory structures (cf. Mischel & Shoda, 1995). In this approach, NMR expectancies would be represented as a network of nodes linked with associative networks for active coping responses, memories of successful experiences with mood regulation, and nodes for positive mood states. Activation of these networks would also suppress activation of nodes associated with negative moods. An exciting direction for future research will be to compare the alternative models of mood and memory as explanations for the self-confirming effects of NMR expectancies on mood and cognition.

NMR Expectancies and Physical Health

NMR expectancies are associated with better physical health, at least as reported on questionnaires (Catanzaro & Greenwood, 1994; Kirsch et al., 1990; Mearns & Mauch, 1998). There are several possible pathways by which expectancies influence health. The first way is through the facilitation of behaviors promoting good health (O'Leary, 1985, 1992). Individuals with strong NMR expectancies engage in more active coping behaviors, which in turn promote health. These behaviors can also influence changes in sleeping, eating habits, and alcohol or drug use (O'Leary, 1990), thereby influencing health indirectly.

The second way that NMR expectancies may affect health is through an impact of these expectancies on the immune system. Experiencing life stress, engaging in repressive coping (i.e., holding one's feelings in stoically and engaging in denial), and experiencing negative moods all can suppress immune functioning; in contrast, relaxation training (one form of mood regulation) can improve immune functioning (Cohen, 1996; Cohen, Tyrell, & Smith, 1991, 1993; O'Leary, 1990; Stone et al., 1993). Through NMR expectancies' influence on coping, negative moods, and mood recovery, they can also influence immune response.

The association between NMR expectancies and negative mood states represents a possible mediated link between weak NMR expectancies and symptoms of ill health because the negative emotions caused by low NMR expectancies might affect immune system functioning through direct chemical action (Rabin, Cohen, Ganguli, Lyle, & Cunnick, 1989). Although we know of no studies that examine relations between NMR expectancies and immunosuppression under stress, others demonstrate that increasing self-efficacy and coping mastery enhances immune responses (Wiedenfeld et al., 1990).

SUMMARY AND CONCLUSIONS

Growing evidence suggests that response expectancies for mood states, like other response expectancies, have self-confirming properties. Furthermore, individuals who strongly believe that they can regulate their negative moods engage in more adaptive and effective coping responses; report less anger, depression, anxiety, guilt, and physical illness; are less susceptible to the detrimental effects of anxiety on performance; and show mood-incongruent cognition after a negative mood induction.

There are several implications of these findings for treatment. First, as noted by Kirsch et al. (1990) and Catanzaro and Greenwood (1994), psychologists helping people cope with stress should ensure that their clients believe in the effectiveness of new coping responses suggested in the course of treatment. Second, the findings concerning the self-perpetuation of mood and mood-related expectancies on cognition underscore the need for therapists to disrupt these negative mood cycles and initiate benign positive cycles. Many commonly used therapeutic strategies are intended to have this effect. For example, when cognitive–behavioral therapists help depressed clients explore explanations for life events that are less depressogenic than their usual explanations (e.g., Beck, Rush, Shaw, & Emery 1979), they are in part establishing new associations and expectancies (cf. Rotter, 1978).

In general, it is possible that one mechanism for the effect of so-called "nonspecific" factors in psychotherapy, such as therapists' communicating warm support and fostering a sense of hope, is that they facilitate the expectation of more positive moods in distressed individuals. If such effects were to generalize to important social situations, they would also likely have a positive impact on the person's social world, given that dysphoric individuals are at risk for social rejection (e.g. Joiner, Alfano, & Metalsky, 1992). Although our specific suggestions are speculative at this point, we believe that instilling positive mood and mood-related expectancies, including NMR expectancies, is an important expectancy-mediated mechanism for nonspecific treatment effects (cf. Kirsch, 1990).

Further research on mood-related expectancies is still needed to elucidate the processes by which expected mood states influence later mood states. The ultimate question will be, What are individuals with stronger NMR expectancies doing when they are upset that allows them to feel better, cope more effectively, and think more positively? Answering this question should provide critical information about the development and treatment of dysphoric mood states.

REFERENCES

Adler, A. (1927). *Understanding human nature*. New York: Greenberg.

Barlow, D. H. (1988). *Anxiety and its disorders: The nature and treatment of anxiety and panic*. New York: Guilford Press.

Beck, A. T., & Emery, G. (1985). *Anxiety disorders and phobia: A cognitive perspective*. New York: Basic Books.

Beck, A. T., Rush, A. J., Shaw, B. F., & Emery, G. (1979). *Cognitive therapy of depression*. New York: Guilford Press.

Beck, A. T., Ward, C. H., Mendelson, M., Mock, J., & Erbaugh, J. (1961). An inventory for measuring depression. *Archives of General Psychiatry, 4*, 561–571.

Bower, G. H. (1981). Mood and memory. *American Psychologist, 36*, 129–148.

Brashares, H. J., & Catanzaro, S. J. (1994). Mood regulation expectancies, coping responses, depression, and burden among female caregivers to dementia patients. *Journal of Nervous and Mental Disease, 182,* 437–442.

Bryant, F. B. (1989). A four-factor model of perceived control: Avoiding, coping, obtaining, savoring. *Journal of Personality, 57,* 773–797.

Catanzaro, S. J. (1989). Effects of enhancement expectancies on expectancy and minimal goal statements. *Journal of Psychology, 123,* 91–100.

Catanzaro, S. J. (1991). Adjustment, depression, and minimal goals: The moderating effect of performance feedback. *Journal of Personality, 59,* 243–261.

Catanzaro, S. J. (1993). Mood regulation expectancies, anxiety sensitivity, and emotional distress. *Journal of Abnormal Psychology, 102,* 327–330.

Catanzaro, S. J. (1994). Discrimination of mood regulation expectancies from dysphoria: Confirmatory factor analytic findings. *Assessment, 1,* 53–58.

Catanzaro, S. J. (1996). Negative mood regulation expectancies, emotional distress, and examination performance. *Personality and Social Psychology Bulletin, 22,* 1023–1029.

Catanzaro, S. J. (1997). Mood regulation expectancies, affect intensity, and dispositional coping preferences as correlates of depressive symptoms: A conceptual analysis and empirical reanalysis. *Personality and Individual Differences, 23,* 1065–1069.

Catanzaro, S. J., & Greenwood, G. (1994). Expectancies for negative mood regulation, coping, and dysphoria among college students. *Journal of Counseling Psychology, 41,* 34–44.

Catanzaro, S. J., & Harger, J. (1993, June). Mood regulation expectancies and anxiety sensitivity independently affect expected emotions under stress [Summary]. *Proceedings and Abstracts of the Annual Meeting of the American Psychological Society, 5,* 74.

Catanzaro, S. J., Horaney, F., & Creasey, G. (1995). Hassles, coping, and depressive symptoms in an elderly community sample: The role of mood regulation expectancies. *Journal of Counseling Psychology, 42,* 259–265.

Catanzaro, S. J., & Horlock, B. A. (1996, July). Mood regulation expectancies predict situational coping responses, but not changes in depression [Summary]. *Proceedings and Abstracts of the Annual Meeting of the American Psychological Society, 8,* 111.

Catanzaro, S. J., & Laurent, J. (1996). [Associations among mood regulation expectancies, perceived family environment, coping preferences, alcohol-related expectancies, drinking motives, and self-reported drinking among adolescents]. Unpublished raw data, Illinois State University, Normal.

Catanzaro, S. J., Laurent, J., Mearns, J., & Krogen, S. R. (1995, May). Expectancies for negative mood regulation among school-aged children: Initial scale development and validation [Summary]. *Proceedings and Abstracts of the Annual Meeting of the Midwestern Psychological Association, 67,* 117.

Catanzaro, S. J., & Mearns, J. (1990). Measuring generalized expectancies for negative mood regulation: Initial scale development and implications. *Journal of Personality Assessment, 54,* 546–563.

Catanzaro, S. J., Wasch, H. H., Kirsch, I., & Mearns, J. (1999). *Coping-related expectancies and dispositions as prospective predictors of coping responses and symptoms*. Manuscript in preparation, Illinois State University, Normal.

Clark, D. M., & Ehlers, A. (1993). An overview of the cognitive theory and treatment of panic disorder. *Applied and Preventive Psychology, 2*, 131–139.

Cohen, S. (1996). Psychological stress, immunity, and upper respiratory infections. *Current Directions in Psychological Science, 5*, 86–90.

Cohen, S., Tyrell, D., & Smith, A. P. (1991). Psychological stress and susceptibility to the common cold. *New England Journal of Medicine, 325*, 606–612.

Cohen, S., Tyrell, D., & Smith, A. P. (1993). Negative life events, perceived stress, negative affect, and susceptibility to the common cold. *Journal of Personality and Social Psychology, 64*, 131–140.

Cooper, M. L., Frone, M. R., Russell, M., & Mudar, P. (1995). Drinking to regulate positive and negative emotions: A motivational model of alcohol use. *Journal of Personality and Social Psychology, 69*, 990–1005.

Eich, E. (1995). Searching for mood dependent memory. *Psychological Science, 6*, 67–75.

Ellis, H. C., & Ashbrook, P. W. (1988). Resource-allocation model of the effects of depressed mood states on memory. In K. Fiedler & J. Forgas (Eds.), *Affect, cognition, and social behavior* (pp. 25–43). Göttingen, Germany: Hogrefe.

Endler, N. S., & Parker, J. D. A. (1990). Assessment of multidimensional coping: Task, emotion, and avoidance strategies. *Psychological Assessment, 6*, 50–60.

Evans, D. M., & Dunn, N. J. (1995). Alcohol expectancies, coping responses and self-efficacy judgments: A replication and extension of Cooper et al.'s 1988 study in a college sample. *Journal of Studies on Alcohol, 56*, 186–193.

Flett, G. L., Blankstein, K. R., & Obertinsky, M. (1996). Affect intensity, coping style, mood regulation expectancies, and depressive symptoms. *Personality and Individual Differences, 20*, 221–228.

Forgas, J. P. (1995). Mood and judgment: The affect infusion model (AIM). *Psychological Bulletin, 117*, 39–66.

Fradkin, B., & Firestone, P. (1986). Premenstrual tension, expectancy, and mother–child relations. *Journal of Behavioral Medicine, 9*, 245–259.

Franko, D., Powers, T. A., Zuroff, D. C., & Moskowitz, D. S. (1985). Children and affect: Strategies for self-regulation and sex differences in sadness. *American Journal of Orthopsychiatry, 55*, 210–219.

Garrick, T., Ostrov, E., & Offer, D. (1988). Physical symptoms and self-image in a group of normal adolescents. *Psychosomatics, 29*, 73–80.

Greenwood, G. L. (1990). *A social learning perspective on the tension reduction theory: Alcohol and affect*. Unpublished master's thesis, Illinois State University, Normal.

Gross, J. J., & Muñoz, R. F. (1995). Emotion regulation and mental health. *Clinical Psychology: Science and Practice, 2*, 151–164.

Hertel, P. T., & Rude, S. S. (1991). Depressive deficits in memory: Focusing attention improves subsequent recall. *Journal of Experimental Psychology: General, 120,* 301–309.

Holeyman, B. K. (1995). *Similarity as a predictor of intimate couple satisfaction.* Unpublished master's thesis, California State University, Fullerton.

Johnson, E. J., & Tversky, A. (1983). Affect, generalization, and the perception of risk. *Journal of Personality and Social Psychology, 45,* 20–31.

Joiner, T. E., Jr., Alfano, M. S., & Metalsky, G. I. (1992). When depression breeds contempt: Reassurance-seeking, self-esteem, and rejection of depressed college students by their roommates. *Journal of Abnormal Psychology, 101,* 165–173.

Kahneman, D. (1973). *Attention and effort.* Englewood Cliffs, NJ: Prentice Hall.

Kirsch, I. (1985). Response expectancy as a determinant of experience and behavior. *American Psychologist, 40,* 1189–1202.

Kirsch, I. (1990). *Changing expectations: A key to effective psychotherapy.* Pacific Grove, CA: Brooks/Cole.

Kirsch, I. (1997). Response expectancy theory and application: A decennial review. *Applied and Preventive Psychology, 6,* 69–80.

Kirsch, I., Mearns, J., & Catanzaro, S. J. (1990). Mood regulation expectancies as determinants of depression among college students. *Journal of Counseling Psychology, 37,* 306–312.

Klaaren, K. J., Hodges, S. D., & Wilson, T. D. (1994). The role of affective expectations in subjective experience and decision-making. *Social Cognition, 12,* 77–101.

Larsen, R. J., & Diener, E. (1985). A multitrait–multimethod examination of affect structure: Hedonic level and emotional intensity. *Personality and Individual Differences, 6,* 631–636.

Laurent, J., Catanzaro, S. J., & Callan, M. C. (1997). Stress, alcohol-related expectancies, and coping preferences: A replication of Cooper et al. (1992) with adolescents. *Journal of Studies on Alcohol, 58,* 644–651.

Lazarus, R. S., & Folkman, S. (1984). *Stress, appraisal, and coping.* New York: Springer.

Matt, G. E., Vazquez, C., & Campbell, W. K. (1992). Mood congruent recall of affectively toned stimuli: A meta-analytic review. *Clinical Psychology Review, 12,* 227–255.

McCrae, R. R., & Costa, P. T., Jr. (1987). Validation of a five-factor model of personality across instruments and observers. *Journal of Personality and Social Psychology, 52,* 81–90.

Mearns, J. (1991). Coping with a break-up: Negative mood regulation expectancies and depression following the end of a romantic relationship. *Journal of Personality and Social Psychology, 60,* 327–334.

Mearns, J., & Bautista, S. M. (1996). *Negative mood regulation expectancies predict guilt and coping with moral transgressions.* Unpublished manuscript, California State University, Fullerton.

Mearns, J., & Mauch, T. (1998). Negative mood regulation expectancies predict anger among police officers, and buffer the effects of job stress. *Journal of Nervous and Mental Disease, 186,* 120–125.

Mischel, W., & Shoda, Y. (1995). A cognitive–affective system theory of personality: Reconceptualizing situations, dispositions, dynamics, and invariance in personality structure. *Psychological Review, 102,* 246–268.

Moos, R. H., Cronkite, R. C., Billings, A. G., & Finney, J. W. (1983). *Health and daily living form manual.* (Available from Social Ecology Laboratory, Department of Psychiatry and Behavioral Sciences, Stanford University School of Medicine, Stanford, CA 94305)

Olasov, B., & Jackson, J. (1987). Effects of expectancies on women's reports of moods during the menstrual cycle. *Psychosomatic Medicine, 49,* 65–78.

O'Leary, A. (1985). Self-efficacy and health. *Behavior Research and Therapy, 23,* 437–451.

O'Leary, A. (1990). Stress, emotion, and human immune function. *Psychological Bulletin, 108,* 363–382.

O'Leary, A. (1992). Self-efficacy and health: Behavioral and stress-physiological mediation. *Cognitive Therapy and Research, 16,* 229–245.

Phares, E. J. (1972). A social learning theory approach to psychopathology. In J. B. Rotter, J. E. Chance, & E. J. Phares (Eds.), *Applications of a social learning theory of personality* (pp. 436–469). New York: Holt, Rinehart & Winston.

Rabin, B. S., Cohen, S., Ganguli, R., Lyle, D. T., & Cunnick, J. E. (1989). Bidirectional interaction between the central nervous system and immune system. *CRC Critical Reviews in Immunology, 9,* 279–312.

Reiss, S., Peterson, R. A., Gursky, D. M., & McNally, R. J. (1986). Anxiety sensitivity, anxiety frequency, and the prediction of fearfulness. *Behaviour Research and Therapy, 24,* 1–8.

Rotter, J. B. (1942). Level of aspiration as a method of studying personality: II. Development and evaluation of a controlled method. *Journal of Experimental Psychology, 31,* 410–422.

Rotter, J. B. (1954). *Social learning and clinical psychology.* New York: Prentice Hall.

Rotter, J. B. (1966). Generalized expectancies for internal versus external control of reinforcement. *Psychological Monographs, 80*(1, Whole No. 609).

Rotter, J. B. (1978). Generalized expectancies for problem solving and psychotherapy. *Cognitive Therapy and Research, 2,* 1–10.

Rotter, J. B. (1982). *The development and application of social learning theory.* New York: Praeger.

Salovey, P., & Birnbaum, D. (1989). Influence of mood on health-related cognitions. *Journal of Personality and Social Psychology, 57,* 539–551.

Sarason, I. G., Johnson, J. H., & Siegel, J. M. (1978). Assessing the impact of life changes: Development of the Life Experiences Survey. *Journal of Consulting and Clinical Psychology, 46,* 932–946.

Scheier, M. F., & Carver, C. S. (1985). Optimism, coping, and health: Assessment and implications of generalized outcome expectancies. *Health Psychology, 4,* 219–247.

Schwarz, N., & Clore, G. (1988). How do I feel about it? The informative function of affective states. In K. Fiedler & J. Forgas (Eds.), *Affect, cognition, and social behavior* (pp. 44–62). Göttingen, Germany: Hogrefe.

Smith, S. M., & Petty, R. E. (1995). Personality moderators of mood congruency effects on cognition: The role of self-esteem and negative mood regulation. *Journal of Personality and Social Psychology, 68,* 1092–1107.

Spielberger, C. A., Gorsuch, R. L., & Lushene, R. E. (1970). *Manual for the State–Trait Anxiety Inventory.* Palo Alto, CA: Consulting Psychologists Press.

Stone, A. A., Bovbjerg, D. H., Neale, J. M., Napoli, A., Valdimarsdottir, H., Cox, D., Hayden, F. G., & Gwaltney, J. M. (1993). Development of common cold symptoms following experimental rhinovirus infection is related to prior stressful life events. *Behavioral Medicine, 8,* 115–120.

Tate, J. C., Stanton, A. L., Green, S. B., Schmitz, J. M., Le, T., & Marshall, B. (1994). Experimental analysis of the role of expectancy in nicotine withdrawal. *Psychology of Addictive Behaviors, 8,* 169–178.

Tulving, E., & Thompson, D. M. (1973). Encoding specificity and retrieval process in episodic memory. *Psychological Review, 80,* 352–373.

Watson, D., Clark, L. A., & Tellegen, A. (1988). Development and validation of brief measures of positive and negative affect: The PANAS scales. *Journal of Personality and Social Psychology, 54,* 1063–1070.

Wheeler, L., & Miyake, L. (1992). Social comparison in everyday life. *Journal of Personality and Social Psychology, 62,* 760–774.

Wiedenfeld, S. A., O'Leary, A., Bandura, A., Brown, S., Levine, S., & Raska, K. (1990). Impact of perceived self-efficacy in coping with stressors on components of the immune system. *Journal of Personality and Social Psychology, 59,* 1082–1094.

Wilson, T. D., Lisle, D. J., Kraft, D., & Wetzel, C. G. (1989). Preferences as expectation-driven inferences: Effects of affective expectations on affective experience. *Journal of Personality and Social Psychology, 56,* 519–530.

Wright, J., & Mischel, W. (1982). Influence of affect on cognitive social learning person variables. *Journal of Personality and Social Psychology, 43,* 901–914.

Wright, W. F., & Bower, G. H. (1992). Mood effects on subjective probability assessment. *Organizational Behavior and Human Decision Processes, 52,* 276–291.

4

EXPECTANCIES AND MEMORY: INFERRING THE PAST FROM WHAT MUST HAVE BEEN

EDWARD R. HIRT, STEVEN JAY LYNN, DAVID G. PAYNE, ELISA KRACKOW, AND SEAN M. McCREA

Expectancies have been shown to exert a powerful influence on many aspects of information processing. Expectancies guide perception, so that people tend to focus on events that are congruent with their expectations (Anderson & Pichert, 1978; Chapman & Chapman, 1967; Cohen, 1981). Expectancies also guide interpretations of perceived events (Darley & Gross, 1983; Duncan, 1976; Lord, Ross, & Lepper, 1979). Information consistent with expectations is accepted as valid, whereas disconfirming evidence is often discounted and dismissed. Indeed, the influence of expectancies at both the attention and interpretation stages of information processing has proved to be consistent and robust: Expectancy-consistent information has a distinct advantage during encoding. Moreover, both of these influences lead people to perceive greater confirmation of their expectancies than is objectively warranted.

In this chapter, we focus on the effects of expectations on another stage of information processing: retrieval from memory. Many of the expectancies that affect encoding are stimulus expectancies. That is, they are expectancies about what will be found out there in the world. In contrast, the expectancies that affect retrieval are more likely to be response expectancies (Kirsch, 1985). They are expectations that people have about what is contained in their own memories. Although stimulus expectancies have been found to affect the perception of external events, the effects of response expectancies on subjective experience are ubiquitous (see Kirsch, 1997, for a review), as exemplified by the powerful effects of placebos (see chap. 12 in this book).

Given the ubiquity of response expectancy effects, one might expect them to affect memory processes as well. However, in contrast to the robustness and consistency of the effects on expectancies at the encoding and interpretation of information, the effects of expectancies on memory have been more controversial. Although Bartlett (1932) and Allport and Postman (1947) suggested that individuals tend to reconstruct information in a manner consistent with their expectancies, later researchers challenged these results. Furthermore, a number of studies (Rothbart, Evans, & Fulero, 1979; Wyer, Srull, Gordon, & Hartwick, 1982; Zadny & Gerard, 1974) were conducted that compared the effects of expectations at encoding and retrieval (by providing participants with expectations either before or after they encoded information). The results of these studies indicate that the expectancy effects were much stronger when presented before encoding than when presented after encoding. Moreover, several studies show no effects in the after (i.e., postencoding) conditions, leading many researchers to question the extent to which expectations actually influence memory for past information independent of differences in the initial encoding of the information. In this chapter, we provide a review of recent evidence from several different lines of research that suggests that expectancies do exert a powerful influence on memory after encoding.

This chapter is divided into four sections. In each section, we consider several different sources of expectancies, all of which have been shown to affect memory. In the first section, we review evidence from work on schema theory that suggests that expectations presented after encoding lead to biased reconstruction of past information. The dominant view in this section is that people often generate expectancies on the basis of past knowledge and experience and that these expectations influence how people remember the past. In the second section, we discuss evidence from work indicating that the expectations people hold about the way memory works and operates affect their memory for past information. Specifically, we review evidence regarding the role of metamemory assumptions and the difficulties people have in determining the source of various memories. In the third section, we consider evidence that expectancies that are externally provided (in the form of suggestions and presuppositions) can also bias recall. Of particular importance in this section is the recent work on false memory syndrome and the susceptibility of individuals to suggestions of the occurrence of various past events (e.g., sexual abuse, being lost in a shopping mall) that may or may not have actually occurred. In the final section, we consider the implications of this evidence, focusing particularly on issues regarding the underlying processes by which expectancies have their effects on memory and the inevitability and controllability of these expectancy effects.

SCHEMATIC EFFECTS ON MEMORY

Schemas are organized knowledge structures stored in memory that are developed through experience. Basically, schemas represent summaries and abstractions derived from prior experience. For example, most people have developed a schema for eating at a restaurant. In general, this event is characterized by a standard order of events. First, people are seated at a table, are given menus from which they order their food, wait while their food is prepared, eat the food, and pay for the food before they leave. There is even a standard sequence in ordering. Drinks are ordered first, followed by appetizers, soup or salad, entrees, and finally dessert or after-dinner drinks. Research indicates that people have schemas for activities (e.g., chess, football), events (e.g., weddings, graduations), individuals or groups of people (e.g., stereotypes), and social roles (e.g., occupations).

More important, schemas serve the useful function of providing people with a frame of reference from which to perceive new experiences. People enter new situations with expectations that are based on their schemas. When people go into a restaurant, they anticipate and expect things to follow the typical sequence of events. If the waiter asked them if they want dessert first, they would think that this was bizarre because it is not consistent with their restaurant schema or script. Schemas have critical implications for all phases of information processing. Schemas guide people's attention and perception in situations, directing their attention to the most important and relevant aspects of behavior. Schemas facilitate the encoding process (i.e., the process of interpreting and attaching meaning to perceived events). Schemas allow people to infer missing information. When someone describes a wedding he or she recently attended, he or she typically focuses only on the unique aspects of this particular event (e.g., it was held outdoors in a park, there were 12 people in the bridal party) because the speaker can assume that the audience can infer the rest (i.e., that things followed the standard sequence, unless otherwise specified). Finally, schemas serve as useful retrieval cues for later recall of information. In this section, we focus on the implications of schematic expectations for memory and the potential accuracy of memory.

Many researchers in social and cognitive psychology have examined schematic effects on memory. Historically, the seminal work of Bartlett (1932) is considered the first illustration of the biasing effects of schematic expectations on recall. Bartlett gave participants an unusual and unfamiliar text, a Native American folktale titled "The War of the Ghosts," and asked them to recall the story as accurately as possible. He found that participants often distorted the story to fit with their expectations. Similarly, Allport and Postman (1947) showed participants a picture depicting a scene on a subway in which a White man was wielding a razor at a well-dressed Black man as other bystanders looked on. Participants were asked to recount the scene depicted in the picture to others. The authors found that after repeated tellings, participants tended to recall that the Black man as the one wielding the razor, presumably because their stereotype of Blacks had biased their memory. Finally, Snyder and Uranowitz (1978) presented participants with a detailed case study of a woman named Betty K. After reading this information, some participants were told that Betty K. was currently living either a heterosexual or a lesbian lifestyle. On a subsequent recognition test, they found that participants distorted their memory of the original information (e.g., her dating habits, her relationship with her father) to be more in line with their current schema (i.e., her current lifestyle). Indeed, the results of all these studies support the notion that individuals reconstruct the past to fit their schematic expectations.

Such findings paint a pessimistic view of the potential accuracy of memory. Only to the extent that the past serendipitously happened to fit one's expectations would memory for the past be accurate (Dooling & Christiaansen, 1977; Spiro, 1980). However, arguments from several sources raise serious questions about the validity of these conclusions. First, several studies show that individuals can often display remarkably accurate (even verbatim) memory for past information (Bekerian & Bowers, 1983; Hasher & Griffin, 1978; McCloskey & Zaragoza, 1985). Thus, it is clear that researchers' conceptualization of schematic processes must be able to account for situations of accuracy as well as inaccuracy.

Second, there is evidence that individuals sometimes show preferential memory for information that is inconsistent with their expectations or prevailing schema (see Stangor & McMillan, 1992, for a review). Indeed, these studies show that when people enter situations with strong expectations, they often do not selectively focus on consistent information; instead, they focus their attention on the inconsistent information to explain away the inconsistency and justify it with their preexisting expectations (Hastie & Kumar, 1979). Under conditions in which one is motivated and able to engage in such inconsistency resolution processes (von Hippel, Sekaquaptewa, & Vargas, 1996), memory for inconsistent information is often better than memory for consistent information because of the greater cognitive effort expended at encoding (Srull, Lichtenstein, & Rothbart, 1985).

Third, a number of researchers have criticized the studies demonstrating schematic reconstruction of the past on both empirical and methodological grounds. Mandler and Johnson (1977) questioned Bartlett's (1932) materials as being unrepresentative of normal prose, and others have simply failed to replicate these results (Gauld & Stephenson, 1967; Zangwill, 1972). Bellezza and Bower (1981) and Clark and Woll (1981) criticized the recognition test used by Snyder and Uranowitz (1978), arguing that it did not correct for response biases under uncertainty. They demonstrated that participants who did not remember a particular fact tended to show schema-consistent guessing; indeed, when they corrected for these response biases using a signal-detection procedure, they found that participants' memory for the original information was not impaired as a result of receiving the lifestyle schema. As a result, several reviews of the literature (Alba & Hasher, 1983; Higgins & Bargh, 1987) questioned not only the inevitability of schematic reconstruction of the past but claimed that there was insufficient evidence to support the view that reconstructive or schematic postencoding effects reliably occur.

Recent work by Ross and his colleagues (Conway & Ross, 1984; Ross, 1989), however, provides more conclusive evidence that expectancies distort memory of the past. Imagine the following scenario: A young woman has chosen to enroll in a study skills improvement course. For several months, she religiously attends the classes. After the course, she shows only negligible improvement in her grades, but she still recalls that her past study skills were far worse than they are presently (Conway & Ross, 1984). In such a scenario, individuals use their expectancies of change to bias their memory of the past. Clearly, people who participate in self-help courses expect to improve. Thus, despite the fact that many of these courses result in no objective change in performance, people report that they feel much better off than they were before, consistent with their expectancy of improvement. Conversely, there are situations in which people expect to see decline. McFarland, Ross, and Giltrow (1992) found that older adults tended to recall their standing on certain attributes (e.g., physical strength, energy level, memory for details) to have been better in the past than it was currently, consistent with their expectancies of decline.

Arguably, though, the most prevalent expectation in most interpersonal contexts is one of stability over time (cf. Hamilton & Sherman, 1996). In most circumstances, people believe that their attitudes or beliefs have been relatively constant over time. Thus, even in situations in which participants' attitudes had been recently altered by an attitude change procedure, Ross, McFarland, and Fletcher (1981) found that participants recalled their past attitudes as being the same as their current (and newly changed) attitudes, consistent with their expectancy of stability.

On the basis of this work, Ross and Conway (1986) proposed a model of personal recall. According to this model, when people cannot directly access a past memory, they use a two-step process to attempt to recall the past. First, they consult their present status or standing on the attribute in question. The present, which is more salient and available to people, serves as a benchmark or anchor from which the past can then be inferred. Second, they invoke their response expectancies of stability or change. The expectancy then guides the reconstructive process such that the individual will recall an expectancy-congruent past. Thus, if one believes that one has improved between the present and the past (i.e., in wisdom or maturity), one will infer the past as being worse than the present ("Back then, I was a fool"); if one believes that one has declined over time (e.g., in flexibility or agility), one will infer the past as better than the present ("I used to have a 40-in. [101.6-cm] vertical jump").

More important, this model emphasized the role that response expectancies play in the reconstruction of the past. Indeed, Ross garnered an impressive amount of support for the predictions of this model (Conway & Ross, 1984; McFarland, Ross, & DeCourville, 1989; McFarland et al., 1992; Ross, 1989; Ross et al., 1981). Furthermore, Hirt (1990) directly tested the process by which expectancies lead to biased memory for the past. In his studies, Hirt gave participants academic information about a male student, which included his midterm examination scores. After a brief delay, he manipulated participants' expectancies such that some participants expected the student's grades to improve, decline, or remain stable. Participants' were then given the student's final examination scores (the "present") and were asked to recall the past (midterm) scores. The results indicate that participants used the present as a benchmark from which to recall the past; when these final scores were manipulated but all were given the same midterm scores (Hirt, 1990, Study 1), participants recalled higher midterm scores when the final scores were higher than when the final scores were lower. In addition, participants' recall of the past was significantly biased by their expectancies of change. Participants expecting improvement recalled lower midterm scores than did participants expecting stability or expecting a decline in performance. Thus, it appears that participants do indeed infer the past from the present, using their expectancies to adjust their recall of the past.

However, this model did not adequately address the fact that people can sometimes be highly accurate in their recall of the past. According to this view, recall will always be distorted in an expectancy-congruent manner. Hirt (1990) proposed his own model of reconstructive memory in which individuals are conceptualized as integrating information from three sources at retrieval: (a) the present or outcome, which serves as an anchor;

(b) the expectancy about the relationship between the past and the present; and (c) the episodic memory trace of the original information. Thus, this model builds on Ross and Conway's (1986) model but incorporates the fact that individuals also integrate input from the memory trace of the original information in their recall of the past. A critical implication of this model is that accurate recall can occur in two ways. First, recall should be accurate to the degree that one's outcome matches one's expectancy. Indeed, Hirt, Erickson, and McDonald (1993) conducted a study in which they provided participants with mixed feedback, such that half the scores were consistent and half were inconsistent with the induced expectancy. They found that participants were relatively accurate in their recall of the expectancy-consistent scores but also found expectancy-congruent distortion of the expectancy-inconsistent information. Second, recall can be accurate to the extent that participants give greater relative weight to the memory trace and reduced weight to the expectancy at retrieval. Thus, the relative weighting that individuals give to the memory trace versus the expectancy will also determine the accuracy of recall.

What factors determine the relative weighting given to the expectancy as opposed to the memory trace at retrieval? Hirt and his colleagues identified a number of moderating factors. Clearly, one important factor is the salience or accessibility of these two sources of information. Hirt et al. (1993) argued that in most of the studies demonstrating schematic reconstruction effects (e.g., Hirt, 1990; Snyder & Uranowitz, 1978), the biasing schema or expectancy was presented right before retrieval; thus, the expectancy was far more accessible at the time of recall than was the memory trace of the original information. To test this notion, Hirt et al. (1993) varied the timing at which participants received the expectancy information. Some participants received this information immediately after the original information, whereas others received it at different delays afterward (and thus closer in time to the time of retrieval). Their results indicated that the effects of the expectancy on recall were strongest when it was presented temporally closer to the time of recall. Furthermore, when the expectancy was presented immediately after the original information and had no distinct advantage in accessibility over the memory trace, no expectancy-congruent distortion of the past was obtained. Thus, it appears that the relative accessibility of these two sources of information plays a critical role in their relative weighting at retrieval.

Similarly, the strength of the original memory trace has been shown to be another pivotal factor in the relative weighting of these components at retrieval. Hirt, McDonald, and Erickson (1995) manipulated the encoding instructions given to participants as they read the initial information. Some participants were given recall set instructions (e.g., "Try to memorize the information"), whereas other participants were given impression set instructions (e.g., "Try to form a general impression of the target person") or comprehension set instructions (e.g., "Try to focus on the grammaticality of the passage"). These manipulations have been shown to influence the relative strength of the memory trace, at least with respect to the memory for the details of the original information (cf. Lichtenstein & Srull, 1987). The results indicated that recall-set participants showed remarkably accurate recall for the original information, even after a 2-day delay; moreover, the recall of these participants was unaffected by their expectancy, suggesting that they gave little or no weight to the expectancy at retrieval. Impression-set and especially comprehension-set participants, however, displayed expectancy-congruent distortion in their recall of the past in both immediate and delayed recall conditions, suggesting that the weaker memory traces formed under these conditions forced participants to weight the expectancy more heavily at retrieval.

A final and particularly intriguing factor shown to influence the relative weighting of the expectancy versus the memory trace is the participant's motivation at retrieval. Kunda (1990) distinguished between two major classes of motivational goals: (a) accuracy goals, in which one desires to arrive at accurate conclusions, and (b) directional goals, in which one desires to arrive at a particular (desired) conclusion. When individuals are motivated by accuracy goals, they should give greater weight to the original memory trace and expend greater effort attempting to access this information from memory. However, when accuracy goals are absent, individuals tend to be "cognitive misers" (cf. Fiske & Taylor, 1991), expending little effort in attempting to accurately recall the past. Hirt (1990, Study 3) manipulated participants' accuracy goals by providing some participants with a cash incentive for accurate recall. Participants given the accuracy incentive displayed greater accuracy and less expectancy-congruent distortion in recall, suggesting that they gave greater weight to the memory trace at retrieval.

In other circumstances, people are motivated to see particular outcomes. For example, when one goes to his or her dermatologist and has a biopsy done, one is motivated to have the results come back negative, indicating that there is no evidence of cancer. A great deal of research demonstrates that people motivated to maintain certain beliefs tend to engage in selective information processing to justify their desired conclusions (Ditto & Lopez, 1992; Pyszczynski & Greenberg, 1987; Sanitioso, Kunda, & Fong, 1990). McDonald and Hirt (1997) argued that biased reconstruction of the past may be another mechanism by which people might justify a desired conclusion. In their research, they manipulated participants' liking for the target person by having participants watch a videotape of him interacting with another student (in an interview scenario). In some cases he acted in a friendly and positive manner, whereas in other cases he acted in a neutral or in a completely rude and inappropriate manner. Participants' expectancies about the target's academic performance were induced, such that some participants expected him to improve, whereas others expected him to decline. Their logic was as follows: On the basis of the just-world hypothesis (Lerner, 1980), participants should want to see good things happen to a liked target but bad things happen to a disliked target. Thus, participants were expected to want to see improvement for the likable target and decline for the unlikable target. Under conditions in which participants' expectancies matched their liking (motivation) for the target, they should give considerable weight to their expectancies in their recall of his past performance. However, under conditions in which participants' expectancies mismatched their liking for the target (e.g., liked target–expect decline, disliked target–expect improvement), participants should give little or no weight to the expectancy because it will lead them to an undesired conclusion.

The results of McDonald and Hirt's (1997) experiments support these hypotheses. Participants showed a great amount of expectancy-congruent distortion in the match conditions, indicating that they gave considerable weight to their expectancies at retrieval. Moreover, by doing so, match participants were able to justify their desired beliefs about the target; match participants believed that the liked target improved and projected that he should continue to improve, whereas they believed the disliked target declined and should continue to decline in the future. Mismatch participants, however, showed little evidence of expectancy-congruent distortion in their recall of the past, suggesting that these participants failed to give significant weight to the expectancy at retrieval. Thus, these data suggest that participants' motivations or desires to see particular outcomes influence the relative weight given to the expectancy at retrieval. To the extent that most of people's expectancies in the real world tend to be in the service of their motives and desires (e.g., stereotypes), these results imply that people are often motivated to see their expectancies fulfilled and that biased reconstruction of the past may be one avenue by which they maintain their belief in the validity of these expectancies.

In summary, more recent research provides support for the notion that schematic expectancies can strongly influence memory for the past (Hirt, McDonald, & Markman, 1998). The bulk of the evidence suggests that individuals tend to distort recall in an expectancy-congruent manner, a process that has notable implications for the maintenance of schemas and their corresponding expectancies. Although individuals do sometimes recall events that are blatantly inconsistent with their prevailing expectancies (cf. Hamilton, Katz, & Leirer, 1980), the evidence examining the effects of expectancies at retrieval finds that consistent information is better recalled, as the schematic expectations provide the individual with retrieval cues that facilitate better memory for this information.

METACOGNITIVE ASSUMPTIONS AS A
SOURCE OF EXPECTATIONS

Another source of response expectancies that has been shown to exert a powerful influence on memory derives from people's metacognitive assumptions about how the mind works. Consistent with the general constructivist view of memory, recent research emphasizes the critical role that people's beliefs about memory play in what they remember. According to this view, remembering is not the result of finding a memory trace (a "storehouse" metaphor) but is instead an inference based on internal and situational cues (Kelley & Jacoby, 1990). In particular, metacognitive beliefs concerning how memory functions serve to identify internal cues that may be useful when attempting to reconstruct the past.

Identifying the Source of Memories

Have you ever awoken after a particularly vivid dream wondering whether the events depicted in your dream really happened or whether it was just a dream? How do you make this discrimination? Marcia Johnson and her colleagues (Johnson, Hashtroudi, & Lindsay, 1993; Johnson & Raye, 1981; Lindsay & Johnson, 1989) investigated the ways in which individuals engage in the process of source monitoring, that is, the process by which people identify the origins of memories, knowledge, or beliefs. Johnson et al. distinguished between internally and externally generated sources: Internally generated sources included things such as imagination, fantasies, and confabulation, whereas externally generated sources included actual perceived events as well as information obtained from outside sources (e.g., others' recollections, newspaper stories).

Johnson and Raye (1981) identified a number of characteristics that are believed to separate memories for real and imagined events. Compared with memories for imagined events, memories for perceived events tend to include more perceptual information (e.g., sound, color), contextual information (e.g., spatial, temporal), semantic detail, and affective information (e.g., emotional reactions) and less information about cognitive operations (e.g., records of organizing, elaborating, retrieving, or identifying). It is interesting to note that Johnson and her colleagues found that participants used these sorts of cues to infer the likely source of a memory. For example, a memory with a great deal of visual and spatial detail would most often be judged as something that was actually perceived (Johnson, Foley, Suengas, & Raye, 1988). Thus, people clearly have expectations about the differences between memories from these different sources and attempt to match features of the retrieved memory to these "schemas" that represent particular sources. By and large, the use of this decision strategy is reasonable and leads to accurate source monitoring. However, in situations in which the perceptual clarity of the memory for an imagined event is high (as with a vivid dream) or situations in which few details can be recalled for a perceived event (e.g., due to distraction, stress, or other impairments), individuals could have a difficult time making this discrimination, resulting in confusion and a greater propensity for errors in source monitoring.

Another important metacognitive assumption used to guide inferences of where and how knowledge was obtained is the feeling of familiarity. Individuals believe that feelings of familiarity serve as a reliable indicator of past experience with a target. Indeed, in a now-classic set of experiments, Jacoby, Kelley, Brown, and Jasechko (1989) demonstrated how feelings of familiarity function as internal cues for such inferences. In Phase 1, participants read a list of nonfamous names. In Phase 2, participants made fame judgments for a list containing both Phase 1 nonfamous names, new nonfamous names, and famous names. Before Phase 2, participants were told that the names they had seen in Phase 1 were all nonfamous. Although participants did a good job of correctly identifying the Phase 1 names as nonfamous on an immediate test, their performance on a delayed test indicated that participants tended to erroneously recall the Phase 1 nonfamous names as famous (relative to new nonfamous names), suggesting that participants were using their feelings of familiarity as a basis for inferences about the fame of the individual. It is as if participants say to themselves, "I remember seeing or hearing that name before; it must be somebody famous." As a result, participants incorrectly attribute the memory of the name to past experience rather than to prior exposure during the experiment.

More important, many recognition memory tasks simply require individuals to indicate whether an item is "old" or "new." In such tasks, people use their feelings of familiarity as a basis of responding, with familiar items judged as old and unfamiliar items judged as new. However, the research of Jacoby et al. (1989) indicates that feelings of familiarity may be biased by contextual factors; unless individuals are aware of the source of such bias (e.g., prior exposure), their responses using such a heuristic may be highly inaccurate.

Clearly, the experience of familiarity or recollection may often be used as a basis for inferring that a stimulus has been encountered before. One particularly intriguing area in which such errors in source monitoring errors have been investigated is eyewitness testimony. Work by Loftus and her colleagues (Loftus, 1979; Loftus, Miller, & Burns, 1978; Wells & Loftus, 1984) demonstrates that people are susceptible to misleading suggestions about recently witnessed events. In these studies, participants first watched an event and were later asked a series of questions about it. Some of the questions contained misleading suggestions about event details. Later, participants were given a forced-choice recognition test about event details.

Some of these questions asked about details for which participants were presented with misleading suggestions. Their results indicate a strong tendency for participants to respond with the alternative consistent with the misleading suggestion rather than the correct response (i.e., the alternative consistent with the actually presented event), suggesting that the misleading suggestion was more familiar and accessible at the time of test (because of recency) and thus participants tended to misattribute the source of this recollection to the actual event. Other research shows that these memory errors are particularly likely to occur when participants incidentally visualize (e.g., Durso & Johnson, 1980; Zaragoza, 1991) or imagine the misleading information (Johnson, Foley, & Leach, 1988). These results appear to be a manifestation of a failure at source monitoring; indeed, studies that have explicitly given participants source monitoring instructions to focus on the modality that they received an item of information (i.e., a picture, verbal narrative, or both) resulted in fewer memory errors (Lindsay & Johnson, 1989; Zaragoza & Koshmider, 1989). However, when participants are not explicitly instructed to consider source information, source confusion errors are prevalent.

Metacognitive Assumptions and Absence of Recollective Experience

Up to this point, we focused on the inferences individuals make when they have a sense of familiarity or a clear recognition experience. Under such circumstances, an important inference that the individual must make is the source of that recollective experience—a task that is often difficult and results in source confusion errors of many types. However, one might ask what happens when there is the absence of a recollective experience. Recent work by Strack and his colleagues (Strack & Bless, 1994; Strack & Forster, 1998) indicates that metacognitive knowledge about the determinants of one's own experience is used to make inferences about the reasons for this absence of a recollection. It could be that the absence of a recollective experience is due to the fact that the stimulus was not presented; alternatively, it could be that the individual simply does not remember perceiving the stimulus, but it might have actually been presented. How does one make such a determination?

Strack and Forster (1998) argued that two components of metacognitive knowledge play a role. The first metacognitive assumption is that attention precedes encoding. That is, people assume that if a stimulus is not noticed or attended to, it will not be encoded or subsequently remembered. The second metacognitive assumption is that information that is more familiar or more easily assimilated with past knowledge can be more efficiently encoded and stored. That is, things that are unfamiliar to people (e.g., words spoken in another language) will not be effectively encoded or subsequently remembered. Each of these assumptions can then be used as a basis for inferring the diagnostic value of the presence or absence of a recollective experience. For example, consider the first metacognitive assumption about the role of attention. Imagine that a man is asked to decide whether the guy next to him at a ballgame was wearing a baseball cap. Although he might have no recollection, he would likely not feel confident answering *no* because the lack of a recollective experience could be due to either the fact (a) that the person was not wearing a cap or (b) he may not have even noticed it because lots of people around him were wearing caps. Contrast this with a situation in which he is asked whether the guy next to him at a ballgame was wearing a top hat and tuxedo. The absence of a recollective experience in this case would lead him to confidently respond *no* because he assumed that he "would have remembered that if he had seen it." The assumption that this event would have certainly attracted his attention and thus would have been remembered leads him to make a confident inference about the diagnostic value of an absence of a recollective experience. In short, the expectancy of being able to remember events that are highly unusual is an important determinant of inferences about whether an unremembered event did or did not occur.

Strack and Bless (1994) tested this notion in a series of studies. Participants were presented with a series of slides of 30 tools and five objects that did not belong to this category. Because the majority of stimuli were tools, it was assumed that the nontools would be particularly salient and would be assumed to draw attention in this situation. Participants were then given a recognition test (*yes* or *no* to the question of whether the item was presented in the slides) in which they were presented with the original set of items as well as a number of distractors (some of which were tools and some nontools). Their predictions focused on recognition performance for the (nonpresented) distractors. For these items, participants should have no recollective experience of having seen these items. The extent to which participants correctly rejected these distractors (by saying *no*) versus falsely recognizing them as having been previously presented (by saying *yes*) was the critical measure. The results indicated that the salient nontools were confidently and accurately rejected, whereas approximately a third of the nonsalient distractor tools were falsely recognized. Thus, it appears that participants assumed that the absence of a recollective experience of a salient distractor item convinced them that it had not been presented for they believed that they "would have remembered it, had it been presented"; however, for the nonsalient distractor items, participants were not confident that they would have noticed or remembered the item and thus were much more prone to make errors and falsely recognize these items.

In subsequent experiments, Strack and Bless (1994) provided participants with another source by which to infer whether an item had been presented previously. Research by Loftus (1979) and others shows that language can create expectations that influence assessments of whether a target has been encountered previously. This research shows that individuals are more likely to infer the presence of some past detail when the test item uses a definite article ("Did you see the X?") as opposed to an indefinite article (Did you see a[n] X?"). Conversational norms indicate that the definite article clearly implies that the item was present and asks the individual if he or she recalls seeing it, whereas the indefinite article leaves open the possibility that the item may or may not have been present. Strack and Bless provided participants with test items using either definite or indefinite articles and tested their recognition performance for presented or distractor salient and nonsalient items. As before, participants correctly rejected the salient distractors. Furthermore, for these items, participants were unaffected by whether the test item contained a definite or indefinite article. However, for the nonsalient distractors, participants were strongly affected by the type of article and were more likely to falsely recognize items tested using definite articles than those tested using indefinite articles. Thus, it appears that for nonsalient items, participants do not see the absence of a recollective experience as diagnostic and use other sources of information (e.g., the expectation created by the phrasing of the question) as a basis of inferring whether the item had been previously presented.

With regard to the second metacognitive assumption (i.e., some conditions facilitate encoding and retention more than others), recent work by Forster and Strack (1998) provides evidence that participants' expectations about the likelihood of successful encoding and storage affect memory performance. Participants learned lists of words that they later would be asked to recall under two conditions: music and no music. However, participants' metacognitive expectations about the effects of music on learning were manipulated in this study, such that half the participants were told that music enhanced learning and the other half that music inhibited learning. Again, participants were given a recognition test for presented and distractor words that belonged to the set of items learned with or without music. Their results indicate that participants falsely recognized distractor items of the category of words learned with music when they believed that music would inhibit learning than when they believed that music would enhance learning. This finding is consistent with the notion that participants expected to have a difficult time remembering words learned with music when told that it inhibited learning; thus, the absence of a recollective experience was not deemed diagnostic that the item was not presented, resulting in a higher incidence of false recognitions. Participants anticipating that music facilitates learning, however, deemed the absence of a recollective experience as highly diagnostic and correctly rejected the distractor items.

Indeed, these results attest to the powerful role that metacognitive assumptions play in memory performance. However, many people still question the importance of these memory errors. Given that the researchers above have tended to use forced-choice recognition tests, it could be argued that participants are encouraged to respond even when they are highly uncertain. Thus, an important question to be considered is whether these responses reflect guessing under uncertainty or true distortions of memory. Metamemory researchers (e.g., Nelson & Narens, 1990) have addressed this issue by proposing different paradigms from which to study the phenomenological characteristics of these memories. One influential memory paradigm was devised by Tulving (1985). Tulving's methodology requires that participants distinguish between two states of awareness about the past: remembering and knowing. When this procedure is applied to a recognition test, participants are told first to judge each item as old (i.e., previously presented) or new (i.e., nonstudied) and then to make an additional judgment for each item judged to be old, specifically whether they *remember* or *know* that the item occurred on the studied list. A *remember experience* is defined as one in which the participant can mentally relive the experience of the item (e.g., recalling the voice or other aspects of the presentation of the word, recalling its neighbors, etc.). A *know judgment* is made when participants are confident that the item occurred on the list but are unable to reexperience or recall the circumstances of its presentation. Thus, remember judgments reflect a mental reliving of the experience, whereas know judgments do not. Applying this distinction, it would be interesting to see whether the recognition errors demonstrated by Strack and his colleagues (Strack & Bless, 1994; Strack & Forster, 1998) result in actual remember experiences or whether they simply reflect know judgments resulting from metamemory assumptions.

In a compelling set of studies, Roediger and McDermott (1995) tested this hypothesis. They used a standard list learning paradigm following a procedure borrowed from Deese (1959). Deese tested memory for word lists in a single trial free-recall paradigm. However, a unique feature of these lists of words was that the words were all associated with a single, nonpresented item. For example, participants might study a list including the words *thread, pin, eye, sewing, sharp, point, pricked, thimble, haystack, pain, hurt,* and *injection*, all of which are primary associates of the critical nonpresented item *needle*. Deese found that such lists reliably induced participants to produce the critical nonpresented word as an intrusion in immediate free-recall tests. Roediger and McDermott replicated this result and found that people falsely recalled the critical nonpresented word as having been on the list more than half (55%) the time (Roediger & McDermott, 1995, Study 2). Using Tulving's (1985) procedure, Roediger and McDermott had participants complete a recognition test and provide remember and know judgments to each of the items. It is interesting to note that they found that participants were more than willing to indicate that they "remembered" the critical nonpresented items. In fact, they made remember judgments for these falsely recognized items at about the same rate (58%) as they made remember judgments for items that were included on the list.

These findings are surprising insofar as it is not possible for participants to mentally relive the process of experiencing an event that never occurred. Yet participants in these studies were in many cases certain that the critical nonpresented items were actually presented. Subsequently, Payne, Elie, Blackwell, and Neuschatz (1996) found that participants went so far as to claim that they remembered who had said the critical nonpresented words (in this experiment, there were two experimenters who alternated reading the words on the lists). Participants also claimed to remember other details about the presentation of nonpresented words, such as when in the list the items were presented (Read, 1996) and whether the items were presented in a visual or auditory modality (Payne, Lampinen, & Cordero, 1996). Moreover, participants' confidence ratings for their recognition of these critical nonpresented items were uniformly high (60% were given the highest confidence rating on the scale, according to Payne, Lampinen, & Cordero, 1996, Experiment 2). Warnings given to participants about the thematic relatedness of the words and the possibility of false recall and recognition did not significantly reduce or eliminate the effect (Neuschatz, Payne, & Lampinen, 1997). Thus, these errors suggest that individuals were convinced that these critical nonpresented words were on the list and that the false memories produced by this procedure are as "real" to the participants as their memories for the actually presented items.

These latter studies of false memories attest to the power of expectations based on metamemory assumptions to influence memory. Participants presumably generate the critical nonpresented word as they process the items on the list because it is so strongly associated with the other items on the list. Immediately afterward, however, they are unable to distinguish their internally generated memory for the critical nonpresented word from their memory for the actually presented items, resulting in a persistent false memory effect. This research clearly implies that people's ability to successfully engage in source monitoring is compromised when they have such strongly associated nonpresented items. However, do all false memories have this same clarity and persistence? The answer is certainly not. Indeed, the extent to which people can successfully distinguish the source of their memories will continue to be an interesting area for future research.

SUGGESTIONS, EXPECTATIONS, AND FALSE MEMORIES

The idea that memory is reconstructive, imperfect, and shaped by expectancies, needs, and beliefs lies at the heart of current controversies about false memories. The controversy about the extent to which memory is prone to errors versus faithful to the historical record has provoked considerable debate about the veracity of eyewitness reports and whether histories of sexual or physical abuse recounted in psychotherapy are valid or are instead false constructions based on response expectancies, beliefs, and suggestive therapeutic interventions.

Concerns about false memories and the scope of suggestive influences in psychotherapy appear warranted: Survey research (Poole, Lindsay, Memon, & Bull, 1995) shows that as many as 75% of 145 doctoral therapists randomly sampled from the National Register of Health Service Providers in Psychology reported that they had used suggestive techniques such as guided imagery and hypnosis to help clients remember child sexual abuse. Considerable research indicates that suggestion effects are mediated by response expectancy (see chap. 16 in this book). It is thus imperative that researchers come to understand the degree to which memory is malleable and the conditions or circumstances in which suggestive influences are likely to engender false memories. In this section, we present evidence that externally provided expectancies in the form of suggestions, presuppositions, and the like bias recall. In so doing, we examine the effects of interviewer bias, event plausibility and decision-making processes, and the role of specialized techniques in instilling false memories.

Interviewer Bias and Demands for Recall

Bruck and Ceci (1997) maintained that "interviewer bias is the central driving force in the creation of suggestive interviews" (p. 75) that engender false memories in children. Interviewer bias occurs when the interviewer's sole focus is on gathering confirmatory evidence for a particular hypothesis, such as that a child was abused or mistreated. Bruck and Ceci reported that in suggestibility studies of interviewer bias, children have been led to falsely report a variety of far-fetched events such as that a scientist put something "yucky" in their mouths, a doctor inserted a spoon into their genitals, and a man kissed their friends on the lips and removed some of the children's clothes.

Interviewer bias effects are by no means limited to young children. In fact, even relatively small variations in interviewer behavior have a substantial impact on the age of recall of college students' early memories. Two years of age is an important memory milestone insofar as workers in the field (see Malinoski, Lynn, & Sivec, 1998) generally agree that the phenomenon of infantile amnesia makes it highly unlikely that memories recovered at or before this age will be accurate. In Lynn and Malinoski's (1997) research on memories that cross the threshold of infantile amnesia, college students were asked four times to report on their earliest memories under different expectancy conditions. In one condition (low expectancy), the questions were phrased in a highly permissive manner, with statements such as "If you don't remember, it's alright." In a second condition (high expectancy), participants were led to expect that they should be able to recall earlier memories on each trial (i.e., "Tell me when you get an earlier memory"). This small change in wording resulted in a difference of average recall of nearly 1 year across groups (the low-expectancy earliest memory mean was 3.45 years vs. 2.28 years for high expectancy). Furthermore, by the end of the interview, fully 43% of participants in the high-expectancy condition reported a memory at or before the age of 24 months, compared with 20% of participants in the low-expectancy group.

In a second study (Malinoski & Lynn, in press), interviewers asked college students to report on their earliest memory. When participants could no longer provide additional recall, they were asked to close their eyes, see themselves "in their mind's eye" as a toddler or infant, and "get in touch" with memories of long ago. Expectancies about early memories were manipulated by informing participants that most young adults can retrieve memories of early events including their 2nd birthday if they "let themselves go" and try hard to visualize, focus, and concentrate. Interviewers then asked for participants' memories of their 2nd birthday, after which they received additional instructions to visualize, concentrate, and focus on even earlier memories. Participants were complimented and reinforced for reporting increasingly early memories.

The mean age of the initial reported memory was 3.70 years, with only 11% of participants reporting initial earliest memories at or before 24 months of age. However, after receiving the visualization instructions, 59% of the participants reported a memory of their 2nd birthday. After the birthday memory was solicited, interviewers pressed participants for even earlier memories. The mean age of the earliest memory reported was 1.60 years, fully 2 years less than their initial memory report.

One of the most interesting findings was that 78% of the sample reported at least one memory that occurred at 24 months of age or earlier. Furthermore, 56% of the participants reported a memory between birth and 18 months of age, 33% reported a memory that occurred at 12 months of age or younger, and 18% reported at least one memory of an event that occurred at 6 months of age or younger, well outside the boundary of infantile amnesia. Finally, 4% of the sample provided memory reports from the 1st week of life. In conclusion, participants reported increasingly implausible memories in keeping with induced expectancies about what they should be able to recall.

Can Complex Memories for False Events be Instated?

A growing body of studies indicate that providing direct suggestions for events that did not occur can evoke rich and detailed false memories.

One group of researchers (Loftus, Coan, & Pickrell, 1996; Loftus & Pickrell, 1995) manipulated participants' expectancies about events that occurred when they were 4–6 years old by having siblings, parents, or other older relatives supply information about three events that had actually happened and one event that was false (i.e., getting lost in a shopping mall). One to 2 weeks later, participants were asked to recall as much detail as possible about each of the events. Six (25%) of the 24 participants claimed to have at least some memory for the false event.

Hyman, Husband, and Billings (1995) investigated whether false memories of relatively unusual events, such as attending a wedding reception and having spilled a punch bowl on the parents of the bride, could be implanted. By the third time participants were interviewed and repeatedly asked about past events, 25% of the participants recalled one of the three false events that occurred at 2, 6, or 10 years of age. Hyman et al. also found that more than one third of the participants who discussed relevant background knowledge consistent with the event (e.g., having gone to a wedding) reported false memories, whereas only 2 of 21 participants who did not discuss relevant background information recalled a false event. In all likelihood, accessing schematic knowledge, associations, and imaginings pertinent to the event-to-be-remembered strengthens expectations about the occurrence of a particular memory, whether it is true or false.

Two recent studies using a different paradigm demonstrate that complex, vivid, and detailed memories can be evoked by structuring expectations and motivating individuals to access memories congruent with induced expectations. Spanos, Burgess, Burgess, Samuels, and Blois (in press) informed participants that their test results revealed that they had a personality type ("high positive cognitive monitors") associated with an insightful, intuitive cognitive style established in the first few days after birth as a probable result of their being born in hospitals with swinging colored mobiles that facilitated eye coordination and visual exploration. After these expectations were established, participants received either a hypnotic or a nonhypnotic procedure aimed at retrieving memories of the day after their birth. False memories of infancy were generated in 87% of the 78 age-regressed individuals. Nearly half (49%) of the participants who reported infancy memories classified them as real memories. Many of the memories reported contained details such as bars on cribs, doctors and nurses wearing masks, and bright lights. It is interesting to note that participants who were not hypnotized (95%) were slightly more likely to report infancy experiences than hypnotized participants (79%).

In a subsequent study, DuBreuil, Garry, and Loftus (1998) replicated the procedure of Spanos et al. (in press) for developing memories of the 1st day of life and extended their research by including a comparison group of individuals informed that they fit the profile described by Spanos et al.

because of spiral disks that were hung in their classrooms on the 1st day of kindergarten to stimulate eye movements and visual exploration. As in the initial investigation, DuBreuil et al. found that the majority of participants (80%) reported memories associated with the target age, and approximately 60% of the participants who were age regressed to infancy reported memories of the mobile, with some of the memories being rich and detailed. In contrast, 25% of the participants who were age regressed to kindergarten claimed that they could recall the spiral disk. Taken together, the results of these studies imply that when expectancies are structured by a credible source to imply that certain "hidden" events occurred and credible procedures that reinforce those expectancies are used to "uncover" the events, an appreciable percentage of participants will report that the suggested events indeed occurred (Loftus, 1997).

Metamemory, Suggestion, and False Memories

As we noted earlier, memory is the end product of decision and inferential processes: Pseudomemories result when participants mistakenly decide that a suggested event occurred when in fact it did not. The principle of discrepancy detection (Hall, Loftus, & Tousignant, 1984) states that misleading information is most likely to bias participants when they do not detect discrepancies between postevent information and memory for an original event.

As an extension of the principle of discrepancy detection, when the contents of suggestions conflict with expectancies and memories for events that participants are certain did not take place, such suggestions are unlikely to elicit pseudomemory reports. Recall that in their "lost in the mall" research, Loftus and Pickrell (1995) were able to show that 25% of the adult participants accepted the false memory suggestion, a rate that was approximated (15%) by Pezdek, Finger, and Hodge (1997) in an attempted replication. However, when Pezdek et al. provided information to participants that they received a rectal enema, none of the individuals accepted the suggestion, which sharply conflicted with their expectancies and memories about what occurred in their past. According to Pezdek et al. (1997),

> it should be easier to plant false memories of sexual abuse during childhood with people for whom sexual contact with an adult during their childhood is more plausible than with people for whom sexual contact with an adult during their childhood is less plausible. (p. 441)

However, as Butler and Spiegel (1997) pointed out, familiarity with an event such as child abuse may be acquired by a variety of means, including the media and vicarious learning of the experience.

Our discussion implies that regardless of whether a person reports that a suggested event occurred may well vary with respect to the nature of the event and the expectancy of its actual occurrence. Research in the area of hypnotic pseudomemories supports the hypothesis (Lynn, Weekes, & Milano, 1989; McCann & Sheehan, 1987) that events (e.g., phone ringing in the room) that are publicly verifiable, memorable, and in the person's direct field of experience are associated with relatively low pseudomemory rates (0%–25%). In contrast, when events have a high base rate of occurrence (and a concomitant high expectation of future occurrence) in everyday life and are not particularly distinctive (e.g., a door slamming during sleep or in the hallway the previous week, a car backfiring), pseudomemory rates ranging from 39% to 81% have been reported (see Lynn, Myers, & Malinoski, 1997).

It is possible that these research findings can be extrapolated to other contexts. Thus, if therapists convey to their clients that a history of sexual abuse is a high-base-rate event that could account for the symptomatology manifested (e.g., depression, relationship problems) and that the event could well have been repressed (a low perceived likelihood of remembering the event), then an increased pseudomemory risk may eventuate. Furthermore, if a client were able to visualize suggested events with particular vividness or intensity, then the imagined events may well assume "realistic" characteristics (see Belli & Loftus, 1993; Johnson et al., 1993; and Zaragoza & Lane, 1994) and lead to the attribution that the events did occur independent of their historical accuracy. Several studies document an "imagination inflation" effect in which repeatedly imagining an action ranging from a simple one (e.g., breaking a toothpick; Garry, Manning, Loftus, & Sherman, 1996) to a complex one (e.g., going to a hospital with a mousetrap on one's finger; Ceci, Crotteau, Smith, & Loftus, 1994) increases the likelihood that individuals will mistakenly assume that they had performed the action.

Hypnosis and Suggestive Interview Techniques

Given that imaginal exposure to seemingly nonplausible events can blur the distinction between fantasy and reality, it is not surprising that techniques such as hypnosis, which involve imagining suggested events and are widely believed to enhance accurate memories (see Lynn, Lock, Myers, & Payne, 1997), increase false memory risk. In a recent review of the literature, Lynn et al. (1997) argued that hypnosis should not be used to recover historically accurate memories in psychotherapy. Whereas memories elicited during hypnosis are not always inaccurate and although hypnosis can sometimes yield a greater number of memories, meta-analyses (Steblay & Bothwell, 1994) indicate that hypnosis results in more recall errors, more uncued errors, and more false memories in response to leading questions. Moreover, hypnosis increases unwarranted confidence in remembered events, although the effect is not always evident and is not invariably strong (cf. Lynn, Lock, et al., 1997).

Given that participants enter hypnosis situations with strong beliefs that hypnosis will improve their memory, such expectancies may be difficult to "undo," particularly when the hypnosis protocol contains misleading suggestions. This line of reasoning was supported by Green, Lynn, and Malinoski's (1998) "warning" study in which they manipulated expectancies about hypnosis by providing one group of participants ("warned") with negative expectancies that hypnosis can lead to false memories, whereas another group of participants received no expectancy altering information. During hypnosis, all participants were given the suggestion that they had been awakened by a noise during a night of the previous week. Before receiving this suggestion, all the participants indicated that they had slept through the night.

Warned participants who received negative expectancies were less likely to accept the suggestion during hypnosis: Thirty-eight percent of the warned participants did so, versus 75% of the unwarned participants. Hence, expectancy information reduced false memories during hypnosis. However, an analysis of the participants who accepted the suggestion during hypnosis showed that expectancy information had no effect on their posthypnotic pseudomemories: Among this group, 75% of those who had been warned and 58% of those who had not been warned stated after hypnosis that the noise had actually occurred (i.e., reported a pseudo-memory). After extensive questioning, during a final confidential assessment, 58% of the warned participants who had accepted the noise suggestion during hypnosis reported a false memory, compared with 50% of the unwarned participants. Furthermore, warned participants were just as confident in their false memories as were unwarned participants.

In another study (Burgess & Kirsch, in press), high- and low-hypnotizable students were shown slides of 40 line drawings and were asked to recall them six times. Two thirds of the students were hypnotized and received a hypermnesia suggestion for Trials 3 and 4. Half of these participants were provided with positive expectancies that hypnosis enhances memory, whereas the other participants were provided with negative expectancies (warned) that hypnosis can lead to the production of false memories. Hypnotizable students who received positive expectancy information displayed an increase in confident errors during hypnosis and retained these false memories after hypnosis. It is interesting to note that warnings mitigated this effect during hypnosis and eliminated this effect after hypnosis. Although hypnosis did not result in an increase in accurate memories compared with control participants, expectancy information did appear to moderate the false memory effect in this investigation.

The influence of prehypnotic expectancies on implausible memories has been extended to the contents of hypnotically elicited reports, such as claims of having a "past life." In a series of studies, Spanos, Menary, Gabora, DuBreuil, and Dewhirst (1991) found that many highly hypnotizable participants reported past life identities when given suggestions to age regress to a time when they lived a previous life. It is interesting to note that participants' past life reports varied as a function of induced expectancies about the nature of past life experiences. Specifically, participants' reports varied in accordance with the information they received about whether past life identities were likely to be of a different sex and race from themselves, whether past life identities were likely to live in an exotic culture, and whether past life identities were likely to have endured childhood abuse that was common in earlier historical periods.

Taken together, the research reviewed indicates that response expectancies can play an important role in pseudomemory and implausible memory formation, although the expectancy that hypnosis can engender false memories appears to have the greatest impact (i.e., in terms of reducing false memories) in the absence of highly specific, misleading, and perhaps ultimately confusing suggestions, as were administered by Green et al. (1998).

WHAT DO THESE EXPECTANCY EFFECTS INDICATE ABOUT PSYCHOLOGISTS' MODELS OF MEMORY? IMPLICATIONS AND FUTURE DIRECTIONS

On the basis of the evidence reviewed in this chapter, it is clear that response expectancies exert a powerful role in shaping people's memories. Expectancies derived from a variety of different sources, such as people's own prior knowledge and schemas, metacognitive assumptions, or explicit suggestions, color the way they remember events from the past. Expectancy consistent information is selectively recalled, and inconsistent information is distorted in an expectancy-congruent fashion. Moreover, expectancies can lead people to remember events that did not occur or to make erroneous inferences about the source of a recollection. These findings have important implications for how memory is conceptualized.

Over the years, memory research has been dominated by different metaphors for the memory system (see Payne & Blackwell, 1998, for a more detailed discussion). The predominant metaphor used to explain memory has been a storehouse metaphor that assumes that records of events are kept within the storehouse. Remembering is viewed as the act of locating these records within the storehouse. However, the findings we have discussed are difficult to explain within a simple storehouse model of memory and are more consistent with a view of memory as a constructive process. Recently, Payne and Blackwell (1998) proposed a perception–reperception model of memory that likens the "retrieval" process to reperceiving the stimulus event. This model builds on arguments made by Roediger (1996) that many memory errors can be viewed as memory illusions. One of the primary advantages of reframing memory errors as memory illusions is that it changes how these behaviors are viewed. Memory errors are no longer considered a failure of accurate retrieval; instead, they are an outgrowth of the normal processes by which people interpret the world around them. As with visual illusions, people's active interpretation of the internal representations that arise from their sensory and perceptual processes can sometimes lead them to recall events that did not actually occur.

Indeed, an important question for future research is the inevitability of these false memory effects. Many researchers (particularly those who adhere to the storehouse metaphor of memory) believe that these effects are largely due to poor motivation. According to this view, manipulations providing incentives for accuracy should increase the effort expended at retrieval, resulting in less reliance on expectancies and other shortcuts and in greater recall accuracy. However, as we have seen, such manipulations have been largely unsuccessful in improving memory accuracy. Thus, it does not appear that a lack of effort plays a major role in false memory effects.

Alternatively, other researchers have argued that false memories result when participants have a lower threshold for responding. Using a signal-detection theory analogy, one could argue that people who report false memories are simply those individuals who have a lower criterion or threshold for reporting on a memory test that a presented item was "old." According to this view, manipulations that lead individuals not to guess or to use a higher threshold in responding should reduce the incidence of false memories. The results of studies taking this approach have proved far more promising (Gardiner, Richardson-Klavehn, & Ramponi, 1997; Koriat & Goldsmith, 1996). Encouraging participants to monitor and control their guessing during recognition tests leads to greater response accuracy. Indeed, it is clear that in a number of situations in which false memories tend to occur, there are suggestions to lower one's threshold for responding. For example, many therapists give clients explicit suggestions that certain events (e.g., sexual abuse) may have occurred in their past and encourage the individuals to lower their inhibitions for reporting related events and memories. Furthermore, the effectiveness of warning manipulations in reducing the incidence of false memory effects suggests that people can indeed be more careful and can distinguish between the sources of various recollections more effectively when encouraged to do so.

However, beyond threshold effects, another contributing force to these false memory effects results from people's general tendency to search for confirming evidence. Research on hypothesis testing has documented people's robust tendency to search for information consistent with our current hypothesis (Devine, Hirt, & Gehrke, 1990; Skov & Sherman, 1986;

Trope & Liberman, 1996), a phenomenon called a "positive test strategy" by Klayman and Ha (1987). Similarly, people tend to engage in biased search processes through memory for evidence consistent with their expectations (cf. Sanitioso et al., 1990) and to interpret retrieved information in a manner congruent with their expectancies (cf. McDonald & Hirt, 1997). Thus, even if individuals are able to monitor and control their retrieval efforts, it is still likely that response expectancies can influence and distort reported memories.

A final issue to consider is the fact that many of these false memories arise from repeatedly being asked to recall a particular event. It appears that such memories, once reconstructed and reperceived, take on a life of their own. Repeatedly recalling a false event—especially vivid and highly imaginable events—may blur the distinction between imagined and actually perceived events (Johnson et al., 1993), making the source monitoring process all the more difficult. Indeed, these findings are reminiscent of the responses that many individuals have to doctored footage used in various media. Anyone who saw the movie *Forrest Gump* can recall the scene in which Forrest was shown shaking hands with President Kennedy. Although viewers know that this event did not actually occur, the ability of the movie makers to create a scene that mirrors reality so closely is eerily frightening. Such footage blurs the distinction between what is real and what is fiction. Similarly, the work reviewed in this chapter highlights the fact that the distinction between memories of actually perceived events and reconstructions and confabulations is blurry and gives rise to many instances of false or erroneous memories. However, these memory illusions serve to illustrate the interpretative nature of people's memory processes and the need for models that can account for these dynamic aspects of recollection.

REFERENCES

Alba, J. W., & Hasher, L. (1983). Is memory schematic? *Psychological Bulletin, 93,* 203–231.

Allport, G. W., & Postman, L. J. (1947). *The psychology of rumor.* New York: Holt.

Anderson, R. C., & Pichert, J. W. (1978). Recall of previously unrecallable information following a shift in perspective. *Journal of Verbal Learning and Verbal Behavior, 17,* 1–12.

Bartlett, F. C. (1932). *Remembering: A study in experimental and social psychology.* Cambridge, England: Cambridge University Press.

Bekerian, D. A., & Bowers, J. M. (1983). Eyewitness testimony: Were we misled? *Journal of Experimental Psychology: Learning, Memory, and Cognition, 9,* 139–145.

Bellezza, F. S., & Bower, G. H. (1981). Person stereotypes and memory for people. *Journal of Personality and Social Psychology, 41,* 856–865.

Belli, R. F., & Loftus, E. (1993). Recovered memories of childhood abuse: A source monitoring perspective. In S. J. Lynn & J. W. Rhue (Eds.), *Dissociation: Theoretical and clinical perspectives* (pp. 415–434). New York: Guilford Press.

Bruck, M., & Ceci, S. J. (1997). The suggestibility of young children. *Current Directions in Psychological Science, 6,* 75–78.

Burgess, C. A., & Kirsch, I. (in press). Expectancy information as a moderator of the effects of hypnosis on memory. *Contemporary Hypnosis.*

Butler, L. D., & Spiegel, D. (1997). Trauma and memory. *Review of Psychiatry, 16,* 13–53.

Ceci, S. J., Crotteau, M., Smith, E., & Loftus, E. F. (1994). Repeatedly thinking about non-events. *Consciousness and Cognition, 3,* 388–407.

Chapman, L. J., & Chapman, J. P. (1967). Genesis of popular but erroneous diagnostic observations. *Journal of Abnormal Psychology, 72,* 193–204.

Clark, L. F., & Woll, S. B. (1981). Stereotype biases: A reconstructive analysis of their role in reconstructive memory. *Journal of Personality and Social Psychology, 41,* 1064–1072.

Cohen, C. E. (1981). Person categories and social perception: Testing some boundaries of the processing effects of prior knowledge. *Journal of Personality and Social Psychology, 40,* 441–452.

Conway, M., & Ross, M. (1984). Getting what you want by revising what you had. *Journal of Personality and Social Psychology, 47,* 738–748.

Darley, J. M., & Gross, P. G. (1983). A hypothesis-confirming bias in labeling effects. *Journal of Personality and Social Psychology, 44,* 20–33.

Deese, J. (1959). On the prediction of occurrence of particular verbal intrusions in immediate recall. *Journal of Experimental Psychology, 58,* 17–22.

Devine, P. G., Hirt, E. R., & Gehrke, E. M. (1990). Diagnostic and confirmation strategies in trait hypothesis testing. *Journal of Personality and Social Psychology, 58,* 952–963.

Ditto, P. H., & Lopez, D. F. (1992). Motivated skepticism: Use of differential decision criteria for preferred and nonpreferred conclusions. *Journal of Personality and Social Psychology, 63,* 568–584.

Dooling, D. J., & Christiaansen, R. E. (1977). Episodic and semantic aspects of memory for prose. *Journal of Experimental Psychology: Human Learning and Memory, 3,* 428–436.

DuBreuil, S. C., Garry, M., & Loftus, E. F. (1998). Tales from the crib. In S. J. Lynn & K. M. McConkey (Eds.), *Truth in memory* (pp. 137–162). New York: Guilford Press.

Duncan, S. L. (1976). Differential social perception and attribution of intergroup violence: Testing the lower limits of stereotyping in Blacks. *Journal of Personality and Social Psychology, 34,* 590–598.

Durso, F. T., & Johnson, M. K. (1980). The effects of orienting tasks on recognition, recall, and modality confusion of pictures and words. *Journal of Verbal Learning and Verbal Behavior, 19,* 416–429.

Fiske, S. T., & Taylor, S. E. (1991). *Social cognition* (2nd ed.). New York: McGraw-Hill.

Forster, J., & Strack, F. (1998). Subjective theories about encoding may influence recognition: Judgmental regulation in human cognition. *Social Cognition, 16,* 78–92.

Gardiner, J. M., Richardson-Klavehn, A., & Ramponi, C. (1997). On reporting recollective experiences and "direct access on memory systems." *Psychological Science, 8,* 391–394.

Garry, M., Manning, C., Loftus, E. F., & Sherman, S. J. (1996). Imagination inflation. *Psychonomic Bulletin and Review, 3,* 208–214.

Gauld, A., & Stephenson, G. M. (1967). Some experiments relating to Bartlett's theory of remembering. *British Journal of Psychology, 58,* 39–49.

Green, J. P., Lynn, S. J., & Malinoski, P. (1998). Hypnotic pseudomemories, prehypnotic warnings, and the malleability of suggested memories. *Applied Cognitive Psychology, 12,* 431–444.

Hall, D. F., Loftus, E. F., & Tousignant, J. P. (1984). Postevent information and changes in recognition for a natural event. In G. Wells & E. Loftus (Eds.), *Eyewitness testimony: Psychological perspectives* (pp. 124–141). Cambridge, England: Cambridge University Press.

Hamilton, D. L., Katz, L. B., & Leirer, V. O. (1980). Cognitive representation of personality impressions: Organizational processes in first impression formation. *Journal of Personality and Social Psychology, 39,* 1050–1063.

Hamilton, D. L., & Sherman, S. J. (1996). Perceiving persons and groups. *Psychological Review, 103,* 336–355.

Hasher, L., & Griffin, M. (1978). Reconstructive and reproductive processes in memory. *Journal of Experimental Psychology: Human Learning and Memory, 4,* 318–330.

Hastie, R., & Kumar, P. (1979). Person memory: Personality traits as organizing principles in memory for behaviors. *Journal of Personality and Social Psychology, 37,* 25–38.

Higgins, E. T., & Bargh, J. A. (1987). Social cognition and social perception. *Annual Review of Psychology, 38,* 369–425.

Hirt, E. R. (1990). Do I see only what I expect? Evidence for an expectancy-guided retrieval model. *Journal of Personality and Social Psychology, 58,* 937–951.

Hirt, E. R., Erickson, G. A., & McDonald, H. E. (1993). The role of expectancy timing and outcome consistency in expectancy-guided retrieval. *Journal of Personality and Social Psychology, 65,* 640–656.

Hirt, E. R., McDonald, H. E., & Erickson, G. A. (1995). How do I remember thee? The role of encoding set and delay in reconstructive memory processes. *Journal of Experimental Social Psychology, 31,* 379–409.

Hirt, E. R., McDonald, H. E., & Markman, K. D. (1998). Expectancy effects in reconstructive memory: When the past is just what we expected. In S. J. Lynn & K. M. McConkey (Eds.), *Truth in memory* (pp. 62–89). New York: Guilford Press.

Hyman, I. E., Jr., Husband, T. H., & Billings, F. J. (1995). False memories of childhood experiences. *Applied Cognitive Psychology, 9,* 181–197.

Jacoby, L. L., Kelley, C., Brown, J., & Jasechko, J. (1989). Becoming famous overnight: Limits on the ability to avoid unconscious influences of the past. *Journal of Personality and Social Psychology, 56,* 326–338.

Johnson, M. K., Foley, M. A., & Leach, K. (1988). The consequences for memory of imagining in another person's voice. *Memory & Cognition, 16,* 337–342.

Johnson, M. K., Foley, M. A., Suengas, A. G., & Raye, C. L. (1988). Phenomenal characteristics of memories for perceived and imagined autobiographical events. *Journal of Experimental Psychology: General, 117,* 371–376.

Johnson, M. K., Hashtroudi, S., & Lindsay, D. S. (1993). Source monitoring. *Psychological Bulletin, 114,* 3–28.

Johnson, M. K., & Raye, C. L. (1981). Reality monitoring. *Psychological Review, 88,* 67–85.

Kelley, C. M., & Jacoby, L. L. (1990). The construction of subjective experience: Memory attributions. *Mind and Language, 5,* 49–68.

Kirsch, I. (1985). Response expectancy as a determinant of experience and behavior. *American Psychologist, 40,* 1189–1202.

Kirsch, I. (1997). Response expectancy theory and application: A decennial review. *Applied and Preventive Psychology, 6,* 69–79.

Klayman, J., & Ha, Y.-W. (1987). Confirmation, disconfirmation, and information in hypothesis testing. *Psychological Review, 94,* 211–228.

Koriat, A., & Goldsmith, M. (1996). Monitoring and control processes in the strategic regulation of memory accuracy. *Psychological Review, 103,* 490–517.

Kunda, Z. (1990). The case for motivated reasoning. *Psychological Bulletin, 108,* 480–498.

Lerner, M. (1980). *The belief in a just world: A fundamental delusion.* New York: Plenum.

Lichtenstein, M., & Srull, T. K. (1987). Processing objectives as a determinant of the relationship between recall and judgment. *Journal of Experimental Social Psychology, 23,* 93–118.

Lindsay, D. S., & Johnson, M. K. (1989). The eyewitness suggestibility effect and memory for source. *Memory & Cognition, 17,* 349–358.

Loftus, E. F. (1979). *Eyewitness testimony.* Cambridge, MA: Harvard University Press.

Loftus, E. F. (1997). Memory for a past that never was. *Current Directions in Psychological Science, 6,* 60–65.

Loftus, E. F., Coan, J. A., & Pickrell, J. E. (1996). Manufacturing false memories using bits of reality. In L. Reder (Ed.), *Implicit memory and metacognition* (pp. 195–220). Mahwah, NJ: Erlbaum.

Loftus, E. F., Miller, D. G., & Burns, H. J. (1978). Semantic integration of verbal information into visual memory. *Journal of Experimental Psychology: Human Learning and Memory, 4,* 19–31.

Loftus, E. F., & Pickrell, J. E. (1995). The formation of false memories. *Psychiatric Annals, 25,* 720–725.

Lord, C. G., Ross, L., & Lepper, M. (1979). Biased assimilation and attitude polarization: The effects of prior theories on subsequently considered evidence. *Journal of Personality and Social Psychology, 37,* 2098–2109.

Lynn, S. J., Lock, T., Myers, B., & Payne, D. (1997). Recalling the unrecallable: Should hypnosis be used for memory recovery in psychotherapy? *Current Directions in Psychological Science, 6,* 79–83.

Lynn, S. J., & Malinoski, P. T. (1997). *Early memory reports as a function of low and high situational influence.* Unpublished manuscript, Ohio University, Athens.

Lynn, S. J., Myers, B., & Malinoski, P. (1997). Hypnosis, pseudomemories, and clinical guidelines: A sociocognitive perspective. In D. Read & S. Lindsay (Eds.), *Recollections of trauma: Scientific studies and clinical practice* (pp. 305–336). New York: Plenum.

Lynn, S. J., Weekes, J. R., & Milano, M. (1989). Reality versus suggestion: Pseudomemory in hypnotizable and simulating participants. *Journal of Abnormal Psychology, 98,* 75–79.

Malinoski, P. T., & Lynn, S. J. (in press). The plasticity of very early memory reports: Social pressure, hypnotizability, compliance, and interrogative suggestibility. *International Journal of Clinical and Experimental Hypnosis.*

Malinoski, P., Lynn, S. J., & Sivec, H. (1998). The assessment, validity, and determinants of early memory reports: A critical review. In S. J. Lynn & K. McConkey (Eds.), *Truth in memory* (pp. 109–136). New York: Guilford Press.

Mandler, J. M., & Johnson, N. S. (1977). Remembrance of things parsed: Story structure and recall. *Cognitive Psychology, 9,* 111–151.

McCann, T., & Sheehan, P. W. (1987). The breaching of pseudomemory under hypnotic instruction: Implications for original memory retrieval. *British Journal of Experimental and Clinical Hypnosis, 4,* 101–108.

McCloskey, M., & Zaragoza, M. (1985). Misleading postevent information and memory for events: Arguments and evidence against memory impairment hypotheses. *Journal of Experimental Psychology: General, 114,* 1–16.

McDonald, H. E., & Hirt, E. R. (1997). When expectancy meets desire: Motivational effects in reconstructive memory. *Journal of Personality and Social Psychology, 72,* 5–23.

McFarland, C., Ross, M., & DeCourville, W. (1989). Women's theories of menstruation and biases in recall of menstrual symptoms. *Journal of Personality and Social Psychology, 57,* 522–531.

McFarland, C., Ross, M., & Giltrow, M. (1992). Biased recollections in older adults: The role of implicit theories of aging. *Journal of Personality and Social Psychology, 62,* 837–850.

Nelson, T. O., & Narens, L. (1990). Metamemory: A theoretical framework and new findings. *Psychology of learning and motivation, 26,* 125–173.

Neuschatz, J. S., Payne, D. G., & Lampinen, J. M. (1997). *Effects of warnings on the production of false memories.* Manuscript submitted for publication.

Payne, D. L., & Blackwell, J. M. (1998). Truth in memory: Caveat emptor. In S. J. Lynn & K. M. McConkey (Eds.), *Truth in memory* (pp. 32–61). New York: Guilford Press.

Payne, D. L., Elie, C. J., Blackwell, J. M., & Neuschatz, J. S. (1996). Memory illusions: Recalling, recognizing, and recollecting events that never occurred. *Journal of Memory and Language, 35,* 261–285.

Payne, D. L., Lampinen, J. M., & Cordero, M. L. (1996, November). *Remembrances of things not passed: Further evidence concerning false memories.* Paper presented at the 37th Annual Meeting of the Psychonomic Society, Chicago.

Pezdek, K., Finger, K., & Hodge, D. (1997). Planting false childhood memories: The role of event plausibility. *Psychological Science, 8,* 437–441.

Poole, D. A., Lindsay, D. S., Memon, A., & Bull, R. (1995). Psychotherapy and the recovery of memories of childhood sexual abuse: U.S. and British practitioners' opinions, practices, and experiences. *Journal of Consulting and Clinical Psychology, 68,* 426–437.

Pyszczynski, T., & Greenberg, J. (1987). Toward an integration of cognitive and motivational perspectives on social inference: A biased hypothesis-testing model. *Advances in Experimental Social Psychology, 20,* 297–340.

Read, J. D. (1996). From a passing thought to a false memory in 2 minutes: Confusing real and illusory events. *Psychonomic Bulletin & Review, 3,* 105–111.

Roediger, H. L. (1996). Memory illusions. *Journal of Memory and Language, 35,* 76–100.

Roediger, H. L., & McDermott, K. B. (1995). Creating false memories: Remembering words not presented in lists. *Journal of Experimental Psychology: Learning, Memory, and Cognition, 21,* 803–814.

Ross, M. (1989). Relation of implicit theories to the construction of personal histories. *Psychological Review, 96,* 341–357.

Ross, M., & Conway, M. (1986). Remembering one's own past: The construction of personal histories. In R. M. Sorrentino & E. T. Higgins (Eds.), *Handbook of motivation and cognition* (Vol. 1, pp. 122–144). New York: Guilford Press.

Ross, M., McFarland, C., & Fletcher, G. J. O. (1981). The effect of attitude on recall of personal histories. *Journal of Personality and Social Psychology, 40,* 627–634.

Rothbart, M., Evans, M., & Fulero, S. (1979). Recall for confirming events: Memory processes and the maintenance of social stereotyping. *Journal of Experimental Social Psychology, 15,* 343–355.

Sanitioso, R., Kunda, Z., & Fong, G. T. (1990). Motivated recruitment of autobiographical memory. *Journal of Personality and Social Psychology, 59,* 229–241.

Skov, R. B., & Sherman, S. J. (1986). Information gathering processes: Diagnosticity, hypothesis-confirming strategies, and perceived hypothesis confirmation. *Journal of Experimental Social Psychology, 22,* 93–121.

Snyder, M., & Uranowitz, S. W. (1978). Reconstructing the past: Some cognitive consequences of person perception. *Journal of Personality and Social Psychology,* 941–950.

Spanos, N. P., Burgess, C. A., Burgess, M. F., Samuels, C., & Blois, W. O. (in press). Creating false memories of infancy with hypnotic and nonhypnotic procedures. *Applied Cognitive Psychology.*

Spanos, N. P., Menary, E., Gabora, N. J., DuBreuil, S. C., & Dewhirst, B. (1991). Secondary identity enactments during hypnotic past-life regression: A sociocognitive perspective. *Journal of Personality and Social Psychology, 61,* 308–320.

Spiro, R. J. (1980). Accommodative reconstruction in prose recall. *Journal of Verbal Learning and Verbal Behavior, 19,* 84–95.

Srull, T. K., Lichtenstein, M., & Rothbart, M. (1985). Associative storage and retrieval processes in person memory. *Journal of Experimental Psychology: Learning, Memory, and Cognition, 11,* 316–345.

Stangor, C., & McMillan, D. (1992). Memory for expectancy-congruent and expectancy-incongruent information: A review of the social and social developmental literatures. *Psychological Bulletin, 111,* 42–61.

Steblay, N. M., & Bothwell, R. K. (1994). Evidence for hypnotically refreshed testimony: The view from the laboratory. *Law and Human Behavior, 18,* 635–651.

Strack, F., & Bless, H. (1994). Memory for non-occurrences: Metacognitive and presuppositional strategies. *Journal of Memory and Language, 33,* 203–217.

Strack, F., & Forster, J. (1998). Self-reflection and recognition: The role of metacognitive knowledge in the attribution of recollective experience. *Personality and Social Psychology Review, 2,* 111–123.

Trope, Y., & Liberman, A. (1996). Social hypothesis testing: Cognitive and motivational mechanisms. In E. T. Higgins & A. W. Kruglanski (Eds.), *Social psychology: Handbook of basic principles* (pp. 239–270). New York: Guilford Press.

Tulving, E. (1985). Memory and consciousness. *Canadian Journal of Psychology, 26,* 1–12.

von Hippel, W., Sekaquaptewa, D., & Vargas, P. (1996). On the role of encoding processes in stereotype formation. *Advances in Experimental Social Psychology, 27,* 177–254.

Wells, G. L., & Loftus, E. F. (Eds.). (1984). *Eyewitness testimony: Psychological perspectives.* Cambridge, England: Cambridge University Press.

Wyer, R. S., Srull, T. K., Gordon, S. E., & Hartwick, J. (1982). Effects of processing objectives on the recall of prose material. *Journal of Personality and Social Psychology, 43,* 674–688.

Zadny, J., & Gerard, H. B. (1974). Attributed intentions and informational selectivity. *Journal of Experimental Social Psychology, 10,* 34–52.

Zangwill, O. L. (1972). Remembering revisited. *Quarterly Journal of Experimental Psychology, 24,* 123–138.

Zaragoza, M. S. (1991, June). *Source misattributions in eyewitness memory.* Paper presented at the third annual convention of the American Psychological Society, Washington, DC.

Zaragoza, M. S., & Koshmider, J. W., III. (1989). Misled participants may know more than their performance implies. *Journal of Experimental Psychology: Learning, Memory, and Cognition, 15,* 246–255.

Zaragoza, M. S., & Lane, S. M. (1994). Source misattributions and the suggestibility of eyewitness memory. *Journal of Experimental Psychology: Learning, Memory, and Cognition, 20,* 934–945.

5

EXPECTANCY AND FEAR

NANCY E. SCHOENBERGER

The central element of normal fear is the perception of danger. As such, fear is a highly adaptive response to the threat of personal harm because it motivates people to take the actions necessary to avoid or escape from danger. For example, the fear produced by the smell of smoke in a home motivates people to evacuate the house. However, much of the fear and anxiety that people experience is unrelated to the danger of a situation. By definition, phobic anxiety is an excessive or unreasonable reaction to a particular situation (American Psychiatric Association, 1994). A person may know intellectually that taking a commercial plane flight is much safer than traveling by automobile and yet still refuse to get on an airplane because of an extreme fear of flying. Anxiety disorders, including specific phobias, social phobia, panic disorder, and agoraphobia, result in personal suffering and incapacitation for people who experience them and are a major focus of clinical intervention. In this chapter, I focus on the role of expectancies in the experience of fear and on the implications for treatment. Although the primary emphasis is on phobic anxiety, the theoretical models presented are also applicable to less severe manifestations of fear and anxiety.

ANXIETY EXPECTANCY

In recent years, there has been a move away from conditioning theories of anxiety and greater interest in cognitive explanations (Beck, Emery, & Greenberg, 1985; Kirsch, 1985; Reiss & McNally, 1985). Kirsch's theory of response expectancy began with the notion that anxiety expectancies are the driving force behind phobic anxiety and that they distinguish phobic anxiety from normal fear. Anxiety expectancy is the anticipation of one's autonomic anxiety reaction to a particular situation. Like other response expectancies, anxiety expectancies are self-confirming and motivate behavior (Kirsch, 1997). People who predict greater anxiety in response to a stimulus are more likely to experience greater anxiety once in the feared situation and to avoid or escape from it if possible.

Anxiety expectancy is a belief about the occurrence of anxiety, a purely internal experience. As such, it is different from other outcome expectancies that involve the anticipation of external events. A good student may expect to receive an A on an upcoming examination, but the expectation alone will not cause the grade to be given. Although the student can attempt to increase the probability of success by studying hard, other factors such as the difficulty of the test, distractions in the testing environment, and mental alertness at the time of the test can influence the outcome. Such extraneous factors do not influence the link between anxiety expectancy and fear. Like other response expectancies, anxiety expectancy is thought to have a direct effect on subjective experiences without mediation by any external influences or other psychological variables. The expectancy of anxiety is sufficient to produce subjective feelings of fear on exposure to a situation. The experience of fear is aversive to many people. Therefore, it is not surprising that the anticipation of fear can directly produce such feelings. Because anxiety expectancy and fear both occur within an individual, the link between the two can occur independently from external events. Thus far, I know of no mediating variables that have been identified for this effect. However, other expectancy theories propose that anxiety expectancy alone is insufficient to explain fear and avoidance behavior and that other variables must be considered.

The results of several research studies demonstrate a relationship between anxiety expectancy and experienced fear and fear behavior. In most cases, anxiety expectancy was measured by asking participants to rate on an interval scale the degree of anxiety they expected to experience in a specific feared situation. Table 5.1 shows zero-order correlations of anxiety expectancy with fear reported during exposure to the fear stimulus and with avoidance behavior. The magnitude of the relationships was highly significant across studies for people with animal phobias (Kirsch, Tennen, Wickless, Saccone, & Cody, 1983; Schoenberger, Kirsch, & Rosengard,

TABLE 5.1
Relationships Among Anxiety-Related Variables

	Anxiety expectancy	
Study and assessment time	Experienced fear	Avoidance behavior
Kirsch et al. (1983)		
Pretreatment	.46**	−.73***
Posttreatment	.78***	−.73***
Schoenberger et al. (1991)	.60***	−.56***
Assessment		
Schoenberger et al. (1997)		
Pretreatment	.32*	—[a]
Posttreatment	.65***	—[a]
Southworth & Kirsch (1988)		
Pretreatment	.49**	—[b]
Posttreatment	.76***	—[b]
Telch, Brouillard, et al. (1989)		
Assessment	—[c]	.89***
Valentiner et al. (1993)		
Assessment (second of two trials)	.79***	−.54***
Williams et al. (1984)		
Pretreatment	.75***	−.66***
Posttreatment	.64***	−.78***
Williams et al. (1985)		
Pretreatment	.51***	−.51***
Posttreatment	.73***	−.80***
Follow-up	.86***	−.86***

Note. The direction of correlations depended on measures used. For all correlations, greater anxiety expectancy was related to greater fear and avoidance.
*$p < .05$. **$p < .01$. ***$p < .001$.
[a]Measured anxiety-related behaviors rather than avoidance. [b]The method of measuring expected fear in this study precluded assessment of the association between anxiety expectancy and behavior. [c]Correlation not reported.

1991), claustrophobia (Valentiner, Telch, Ilai, & Hehmsoth, 1993), panic disorder with and without agoraphobia (Craske, Rapee, & Barlow, 1988; Southworth & Kirsch, 1988; Telch, Brouillard, Telch, Agras, & Taylor, 1989), public speaking anxiety (Schoenberger, Kirsch, Gearan, Montgomery, & Pastyrnak, 1997), and height and driving phobias (Williams, Dooseman, & Kleinfeld, 1984; Williams, Turner, & Peer, 1985). Across studies, anxiety expectancy was the only variable that consistently correlated with the degree of fear experienced when the effects of other variables were partialed out. Similar results were observed in the relationship with behavior, although they were not as strong.

The methodology of some studies of panic disorder does not lend itself to correlational analysis. Kenardy, Fried, Kraemer, and Taylor (1992) assessed the precursors of spontaneous panic attacks in a sample of women with panic disorder. Measures completed hourly and at the time of panic attacks included anxiety level, sense of control, sense of danger, somatic symptoms, and prediction of the likelihood of panic in the next hour.

When data from the hour preceding panic attacks were compared with "control hours" (i.e., the same time of day on the days before and after an attack), the only difference that emerged was for the likelihood of panic ratings. The increased likelihood of panic was the only predictor of a subsequent panic attack. This finding confirms response expectancy theory in that increased anxiety expectancy preceded panic attacks but increased feelings of anxiety did not. Therefore, it is unlikely that increased expectancy was related to increased perception of anxiety symptoms.

Other researchers have developed individual behavioral tests for people with panic disorder and moderate-to-severe avoidance (Craske et al., 1988). Craske et al. assessed a number of variables as determinants of avoidance behavior and found that only the expected probability of panic and the expected level of fear tolerance significantly predicted whether participants completed, escaped, or avoided the feared situations. Similarly, results of a study of patients with panic disorder show that panic expectancy in agoraphobic situations predicted the severity of agoraphobia but that the severity and frequency of panic did not (Cox, Endler, & Swinson, 1995). Thus, there is robust evidence that the expectancy for feeling anxious in a situation is a stronger predictor of incidence, severity of panic, and avoidance than are other variables. In view of these findings, it seems ironic that in the *Diagnostic and Statistical Manual of Mental Disorders* (4th ed.; American Psychiatric Association, 1994) the recurrence of unexpected panic attacks is listed as an essential feature of panic disorder.

OTHER COGNITIVE VARIABLES

Danger Expectancy

The perception of personal threat is the central factor in normal fear, and expected danger has been examined with regard to phobic anxiety and avoidance. Beck, Emery, and Greenberg (1985) proposed that danger expectancy motivates avoidance behavior because the perception of danger becomes irrationally high with increasing proximity to the stimulus for people with phobias. This explanation seems limited, however, because phobic avoidance begins when the perceived danger is lowest, according to this theory, long before people are near the feared stimulus (Williams & Watson, 1985). For example, people who fear traveling through tunnels meticulously plan vacations months in advance to avoid feared roads or train routes.

Only a few researchers have investigated the impact of danger expectancy on avoidance behavior in feared situations. A study of height phobia confirms the effect of danger expectancy as rated at a distance from the feared situation (Williams et al., 1985). Ratings of danger expectancy made on the ground were significantly correlated with subsequent approach behavior, both immediately after treatment and at follow-up 1 month later. Thus, perceived danger was not observed to increase with proximity to the feared stimulus, but even danger expectancies made outside the feared situation predicted future behavior.

Williams and Watson (1985) tested Beck's (Beck et al., 1985) theory in a study of severe height phobia. For each floor of a 10-story building, participants rated the likelihood of falling while looking over the balcony railing. These ratings were made at three locations: standing on the ground, 6 ft (1.83 m) from the railing, and at the railing. After treatment, all three ratings of danger expectancy predicted participants' subsequent willingness to approach the balcony railings. Beck's theory received partial support, in that ratings of danger made at the railing were significantly greater than the others.

This finding of greater perceived danger at closer proximity to the feared situation was not confirmed in a group of people who were fearful of snakes (Schoenberger et al., 1991). Participants were briefly exposed to the snake before making their initial ratings of danger expectancy to ensure that they understood the nature of the approach tasks. Nonetheless, they perceived the snake as less threatening on closer approach. Initial ratings of danger expectancy were substantially related to subsequent approach behavior.

Danger expectancy has been compared with anxiety expectancy in the prediction of approach behavior and the marked fear in people with a fear of snakes (Schoenberger et al., 1991), claustrophobic situations (Valentiner et al., 1993), and height (Williams et al., 1985). In those studies, danger expectancy was significantly correlated with behavior and with self-reported fear, as was anxiety expectancy, and the magnitude of the correlations was comparable. Thus, both expectancies predicted subent fear and behavior. However, the correlation between the two expectancy measures was high, indicating a substantial amount of overlapping variance.

Despite the high correlations between anxiety expectancy and danger expectancy, the two constructs can be differentiated empirically. Gursky and Reiss (1987) examined the distinction between anxiety expectancy and danger expectancy by constructing scales to measures these constructs for fears of flying, heights, and public speaking. When subjected to factor analysis, danger expectancy and anxiety expectancy items loaded on two distinct factors for each fear examined, even though correlations between the expectancy measures ranged from .59 for fear of flying to .67 for fear of public speaking.

It is not surprising to find large correlations between anxiety expectancy and danger expectancy. When one expects to be in danger, it makes sense that one would also expect to be anxious. Furthermore, much, if not all, of the consequent fear and avoidance would be due to the expected harm rather than the expected fear. A person would fear and avoid an airplane flight that was expected to be bombed by terrorists. That person would also expect to feel extreme fear if on that flight. Nevertheless, it is the perception of the threat, rather than the expectation of fear, that leads the person to avoid the flight and to experience fear if it cannot be avoided. For this reason, Schoenberger et al. (1991) proposed that the degree of fear and avoidance that is predicted by the variance shared by danger expectancy and anxiety expectancy should be attributed to the effects of danger expectancy, with that portion of the variance in anxiety expectancy interpreted as being epiphenomenal.

Evidence that anxiety expectancy is not merely epiphenomenal has been reported in at least three studies. In a sample of participants with a marked fear of snakes, anxiety expectancy remained highly correlated with both fear and behavior when danger expectancy was controlled, but the correlations of danger expectancy with fear and behavior were near zero when anxiety expectancy was controlled (Schoenberger et al., 1991). In a claustrophobic sample, each expectancy was significantly related to behavioral approach when the other was partialed out, and only anxiety expectancy was a significant predictor in similar analyses of self-reported fear (Valentiner et al., 1993). Finally, anxiety expectancy predicted variance in self-reported fear and avoidance beyond what was explained by danger expectancy in a sample of people with height phobia (Kirsch, 1990, with an analysis of data reported by Williams et al., 1985).

In those studies, the expectancy of danger emerged as being distinct from anxiety expectancy and appeared to motivate avoidance behavior in fearful people, although anxiety expectancy was a stronger predictor of both fear and avoidance. With anxiety expectancy controlled, the predictive power of expected danger was unreliable. In contrast, correlations of anxiety expectancy with fear and behavior were highly significant, even with danger expectancy held constant. These data lend strong support to the hypothesized causal effects of anxiety expectancy.

Anxiety Sensitivity

Reiss and McNally (1985) developed a theoretical model to explain avoidance behavior based on the concepts of anxiety expectancy, danger expectancy, and anxiety sensitivity. Anxiety sensitivity is conceptualized as an individual-differences variable indicating the extent to which anxiety is experienced as aversive. Reiss (1991) later elaborated the model to include expectancy and sensitivity for negative social evaluation. Reiss's model can be expressed as follows: fear behavior (i.e., avoidance) = (Danger expectancy × Danger sensitivity) + (Anxiety expectancy × Anxiety sensitivity) + (Expectancy of negative social evaluation × Sensitivity to negative social evaluation). One's expectancies for danger, anxiety, and negative social evaluation interact with one's sensitivities to these experiences to influence avoidance behavior, and each interaction exerts an independent effect. Consider the interaction between anxiety expectancy and anxiety sensitivity. According to this model, anxiety sensitivity alone is not sufficient to motivate the avoidance of a situation; it is also necessary that one expect to experience anxiety. However, expected anxiety is predicted to be a stronger determinant of avoidance for people who have high anxiety sensitivity.

The Anxiety Sensitivity Index (ASI) consists of 16 items related to possible negative consequences of anxiety and has good internal consistency and good test–retest reliability (Reiss, Peterson, Gursky, & McNally, 1986; Telch, Shermis, & Lucas, 1989). Results of a validity study (Reiss et al., 1986) show that a group of people with agoraphobia scored significantly higher on the ASI than did people with other anxiety disorders ($p < .001$), who in turn, had significantly higher scores than college students ($p < .001$), providing support for the criterion validity of the ASI. A behavioral validation (Maller & Reiss, 1987) shows that participants with high scores on the ASI exhibited more anxiety in response to anxiety-relevant questions than to anxiety-irrelevant questions when compared with low scorers on the ASI. Anxiety sensitivity has been shown to be distinct from measures of anxiety. In factor analysis, items from the ASI loaded on a factor distinct from fearfulness items (Peterson & Heilbronner, 1987; Reiss, Peterson, & Gursky, 1988), and the ASI predicted variance in fearfulness when the effects of state and trait anxiety were controlled (McNally & Lorenz, 1987; Reiss et al., 1986).

Further investigation confirms that anxiety sensitivity varies across anxiety disorders. A large sample that included people with panic disorder, generalized anxiety disorder, simple phobia, obsessive–compulsive disorder, social phobia, simple phobia, and posttraumatic stress disorder were given the ASI (Taylor, Koch, & McNally, 1992). Participants with panic disorder had significantly greater anxiety sensitivity than did all other groups, except those with posttraumatic stress disorder; unlike other diagnostic groups, people diagnosed with simple phobia did not have higher ASI scores than the norms for nonclinical controls (cf. Taylor, Koch, & Crockett, 1991). These differences remained in analyses with trait anxiety as a covariate, indicating that differences in anxiety sensitivity across groups cannot be explained by differences in anxiety. Anxiety sensitivity appears to be especially central to panic disorder and relatively less important in simple phobias.

Valentiner et al. (1993) tested the predictions of an older model of Reiss and McNally's (1985) expectancy theory, which includes anxiety sensitivity and anxiety expectancy but not expectancies and sensitivities for danger and negative social evaluation. They hypothesized that (a) the interaction between anxiety expectancy and anxiety sensitivity would predict claustrophobic behavior with other variables in the model partialed out and (b) anxiety sensitivity alone would not predict claustrophobic behavior when other variables were controlled. Results of the study confirm these predictions. The interaction between anxiety expectancy and sensitivity significantly predicted behavior, but neither anxiety sensitivity nor the interaction term significantly predicted self-reported fear when other variables were controlled.

In addition to interacting with anxiety expectancy to motivate avoidance behavior in situations that are already feared, anxiety sensitivity may be a risk factor for the development of panic disorder (McNally, 1990; Reiss, 1991). Heightened anxiety sensitivity has been observed to precede the experience of a panic attack (Donnell & McNally, 1990). Among college students scoring at least 1 SD above the mean on the ASI, two thirds had never experienced a panic attack. Thus, increased anxiety sensitivity does not appear to result from experiences with anxiety. Furthermore, Maller and Reiss (1992) found that scores on the ASI predicted the frequency and intensity of panic attacks experienced 3 years later. These findings are suggestive and merit further evaluation.

Negative Evaluation Sensitivity

Reiss (1991) proposed that expectancy for and sensitivity to negative evaluation interact to predict fear and avoidance. The Fear of Negative Evaluation Scale (Watson & Friend, 1969) is a measure of sensitivity to negative evaluation. This scale has been administered in several studies of anxiety, primarily to identify salient differences among anxiety disorders or to measure treatment outcome. People with generalized social phobia generally score higher on fear of negative evaluation than do people with discrete social phobia (Brown, Heimberg, & Juster, 1995; Holt, Heimberg, & Hope, 1992; Tran & Chambless, 1995). Higher Fear of Negative Evaluation Scale scores also distinguish people with social phobias from those with simple phobias, but they do not discriminate social phobias from other major anxiety disorders (Oei, Kenna, & Evans, 1991; Turner, McCanna, & Beidel, 1987). Decreased fear of negative evaluation has resulted from treatment for people with social phobias (Mattick, Peters, & Clarke, 1989), avoidant personality disorder (Renneberg, Goldstein, Phillips, & Chambless, 1990), public speaking anxiety (Schoenberger et al., 1997), and social anxiety (Schelver & Gutsch, 1983). These findings indicate that sensitivity to negative evaluation is an important feature of many anxiety disorders and can be modified by treatment. However, its interaction with expectancy for negative evaluation as a determinant of fear has not, to my knowledge, been evaluated.

Self-Efficacy

Bandura (1977, 1988) articulated an expectancy theory of anxiety in which perceived self-efficacy for control over a prescribed situation is the primary determinant of fear and behavior. Feelings of inefficacy are predicted to result in fear and avoidance, whereas expectations of successful coping are not. According to this theory, anxiety expectancy and danger expectancy are also determined by self-efficacy. People expect to be anxious and in danger only to the extent that they feel unable to manage the situation adequately.

Although self-efficacy in feared situations was defined in terms of perceived coping ability, measures of self-efficacy in studies of fear have generally involved participants' ratings of their ability to perform fearful tasks on a behavioral hierarchy (Bandura, Adams, & Beyer, 1977; Bandura, Reese, & Adams, 1982; Kirsch et al., 1983; Williams et al., 1984; Williams, Kinney, & Falbo, 1989; Williams & Rappoport, 1983; Williams et al., 1985; Williams & Watson, 1985). Kirsch (1982) argued that operationalizing self-efficacy as perceived ability is accurate for skill-oriented situations but that it must be reinterpreted when applied to anxiety-laden tasks. Snake-fearful participants rated self-efficacy for a hierarchy of snake approach tasks and for a series of motor skill tasks. For the first item on the snake hierarchy that participants stated they could not complete and for the most difficult item, they were offered a hypothetical incentive beginning at $5 and increasing, stopping when they stated that they could perform the task given such an incentive. They were then asked whether they could perform corresponding items on the motor skill hierarchy for the incentive that they had accepted on the snake hierarchy. All participants indicated that they would be able to hold a snake in front of their faces if the incentive were large enough, but increased incentive caused little change in the self-efficacy of motor skill. Specifically, most participants altered their self-efficacy for approaching a snake for hypothetical incentives of $20 or less, but 54% did not change their self-efficacy ratings on the motor skill task, regardless of the incentive.

Kirsch (1982, 1985) interpreted these findings to mean that statements of inability to perform a behavior on the snake hierarchy were really statements of unwillingness to perform the behavior, given the adverse consequences expected by participants. In reality, much smaller incentives have produced changes in the perceived self-efficacy and behavior of snake-fearful people. Valins and Ray (1967) induced 75% of the participants who had refused to touch a snake to perform the behavior for incentives as small as $1–$2. In a different snake-fearful sample (Schoenberger et al., 1991), half the participants were given a verbal exhortation emphasizing the importance of maximizing performance on a behavioral approach test. These participants rated self-efficacy significantly higher and performed significantly more feared behaviors than did participants who did not receive the incentive. One would expect that people with more severe anxiety disorders would require larger incentives to increase their approach behavior. However, these data are sufficient to demonstrate that self-efficacy ratings made for fear-inducing situations can be increased with incentives. Therefore, it is unreasonable to conclude that these measures of self-efficacy actually tap perceived ability. Rather, in fear-inducing situations, these types of self-efficacy ratings should be interpreted as ratings of behavioral intention (Kirsch, 1986, 1990; see also chap. 1 in this book).

Kirsch (1990) proposed that in fearful situations, anxiety expectancy predicts self-efficacy (when measured as behavioral intention), which in turn influences behavior. People with high anxiety expectancy for a situation intend to avoid it and subsequently do so whenever possible. Studies comparing self-efficacy and anxiety expectancy as determinants of fear and behavior in fearful samples generally show that both variables significantly predict subjective fear and avoidance behavior (Kirsch et al., 1983; Schoenberger et al., 1991; Williams et al., 1984, 1985, 1989; Williams & Rappoport, 1983). Greater anxiety expectancy is related to greater subjective fear and avoidance, and the same is true of low self-efficacy. Anxiety is the strongest predictor of fear, in that it is significantly correlated with subjective fear when the effects of self-efficacy are partialed out, but the partial correlations of self-efficacy and fear are usually nonsignificant when anxiety expectancy is controlled. Conversely, self-efficacy is the most powerful predictor of behavior in most instances. Because anxiety expectancy and self-efficacy are measured before the assessment of behavior and fear in fearful situations, these studies suggest that anxiety expectancy and self-efficacy have a causal effect on subsequent fear and behavior.

A different pattern of results emerges when self-efficacy is operationalized as coping ability. In a study of people with agoraphobia (Telch, Brouillard, et al., 1989), self-efficacy was measured as confidence in executing coping behaviors, such as controlling one's breathing, in feared situations and not as the ability to complete the behavioral tasks. Anxiety expectancy was measured by the predicted chance of panic in each situation. The correlation of expected panic and agoraphobic avoidance, with self-efficacy and eight other predictor variables partialed out, was .84 ($p <$ .001). The partial correlation of coping self-efficacy and agoraphobic avoidance was .03.

In summary, anxiety expectancy and self-efficacy for behavioral approach are both strong predictors of fear and avoidance behavior. Anxiety expectancy is the better predictor of fear, and self-efficacy for approach is the better predictor of behavior. In contrast, the effects of coping self-efficacy on behavior appear to be mediated by anxiety expectancy.

The expectancy model presented in Figure 5.1 integrates hypotheses generated by each of the theories discussed earlier (i.e., Bandura, 1977; Beck et al., 1985; Kirsch, 1985, 1997; Reiss, 1991). Arrows intersecting lines in the figure indicate the operation of moderator variables. Thus, experienced fear is a multiplicative function of expected negative outcomes and the person's sensitivity to those outcomes. Approach behavior, but not subjective fear, is mediated by approach self-efficacy. Because self-efficacy is strongly affected by outcome expectancies (e.g., incentives), it is interpreted as an intention or willingness to approach (see Maddux, chap. 1, this volume). Consistent with the data reviewed earlier, the effects of coping self-efficacy are mediated by a negative outcome expectancy, specifically expected anxiety.

Some of hypothesized relations have been well supported by research findings, whereas others are purely theoretical at this point. As reviewed in earlier sections, anxiety expectancy has emerged repeatedly as a strong predictor of experienced fear, and a few studies show this effect to be moderated by anxiety sensitivity. Danger expectancy exerts a direct effect on fear and affects the level of anxiety expectancy. Reiss and McNally's (1985) model predicts that danger sensitivity moderates the effects of danger expectancy, but this hypothesis has not been empirically tested. Similarly, the predicted interaction between negative evaluation sensitivity and negative evaluation expectancy requires evaluation.

In the prediction of approach behavior, self-efficacy for approach me-

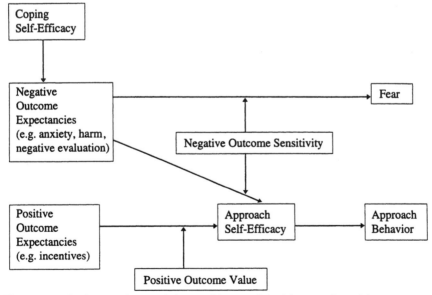

Figure 5.1. An integrative social–cognitive model of fear and avoidance.

diates the effects of other variables. Approach self-efficacy reflects one's intention to approach a feared object, and behavioral intentions have been shown to be immediate determinants of behavior (Ajzen & Fishbein, 1980). Incentives such as money can increase one's willingness to approach a feared object, although they do not alter the amount of fear experienced. Approach self-efficacy is also strongly influenced by anxiety expectancy, which appears to be the most central of the expectancy constructs depicted here. Schoenberger et al. (1991) reported that the effect of danger expectancy on approach self-efficacy was mediated by anxiety expectancy. People who expected to be in greater danger expected to feel more anxiety and, as a result of their anxiety expectancy, intended to avoid the feared stimulus. Expectancy for negative evaluation is predicted to operate in a similar fashion. Compared with approach self-efficacy, coping self-efficacy has received little attention. However, the effects of coping self-efficacy appear to be mediated by anxiety expectancy; the more confidence one has for coping in a situation, the less anxiety one expects to experience.

IMPLICATIONS

Treatment

According to response expectancy theory, decreasing the anticipation of fear should result in decreased fear experiences and an increased willingness to enter situations that were previously avoided. Changes in anxiety expectancy have been related to improvement in treatment. Measures of change in anxiety expectancy and reported fear are highly correlated. A correlation of .63 was reported for a sample of people with agoraphobia (Southworth & Kirsch, 1988) and .56 for a group of participants with public speaking anxiety (Schoenberger et al., 1997).

In addition, expectancy for change in anxiety has been shown to be a determinant of improvement after treatment for anxiety-related problems (Kirsch et al., 1983; Schoenberger et al., 1997). In these two studies, expectancy for anxiety change was measured before the beginning of treatment by asking participants to rate the amount of anxiety they expected to experience during feared situations following treatment. These predictions were highly correlated with experienced fear at posttreatment assessment in the sample with snake phobia. In the group with public speaking anxiety, correlations between predicted anxiety at posttreatment and a measure of change in anxiety failed to reach significance, possibly because of the small sample size in this study.

Southworth and Kirsch (1988) more directly illustrated the role of expectancy in the treatment of agoraphobia. They provided the same in vivo exposure treatment to all participants, but for half of them it was described only as an evaluation procedure, whereas the other participants were told that it was a part of the treatment. Treatment with therapeutic expectancy instructions produced greater change in both expectancy and behavior than did the treatment with assessment expectancy instructions. Participants in the former were able to travel farther from home and improved more rapidly.

Expectancy modification has also proved effective in the treatment of speech anxiety (Kirsch & Henry, 1977) and snake phobia (Kirsch et al., 1983), for which highly credible control treatments produced significant change in fear and avoidance, comparable with that observed after standard systematic desensitization. The control treatments involved discussing events unrelated to the target fear and included compelling rationales developed to convince participants that the treatments would be effective. It is possible that nonspecific factors, such as having a supportive relationship with a therapist, may have contributed to the effectiveness of these treatments. However, without a convincing treatment rationale, these factors produce substantially less change (Southworth & Kirsch, 1988; also see McReynolds, Barnes, Brooks, & Rehagen, 1973). These data point to the importance of expectancy in treatment outcome. The modification of anxiety expectancy should not be regarded as a nonspecific effect. Because anxiety expectancy has been identified as a cause of fear and avoidance, decreasing it is an important goal of treatment.

A number of therapeutic techniques may serve to decrease anxiety expectancy. Cognitive–behavioral techniques such as systematic desensitization, in vivo exposure, and cognitive restructuring are particularly effective because they provide compelling experiential feedback of improvement to clients. Experiential feedback is important because this perception is directly related to decreases in anxiety expectancy (Kirsch, 1990). In vivo exposure is particularly important because it provides the opportunity for people to learn that the reality of the situation is not as fearful as they expected. Feedback acquired through direct experience is more powerful than that obtained vicariously through imagery or verbal persuasion. In vivo experience produces greater change in expectancies (Wickless & Kirsch, 1989) and attitudes (Fazio & Zanna, 1981), which in turn influence changes in behavior.

Observations made by Rachman and Bichard (1988) suggest that treatment is not necessary for people to receive the benefits of exposure. They described a number of studies in which a wide variety of people were observed to overpredict the amount of fear that they subsequently experienced. The level of anxiety expectancy became more accurate with more experience in a given situation. People who overpredicted fear had experiences that disconfirmed their prediction, and they subsequently expected less fear. In such cases, feedback was a naturally occurring process. However, even for overpredictors without anxiety disorders, exposure alone was insufficient to maintain changes in anxiety expectancy over time because a single episode of underprediction could result in extended periods of increased anxiety expectancy (Rachman & Bichard, 1988). In addition, many people who expect to be extremely anxious do not have the opportunity for even one disconfirming experience because they avoid all feared situations. For example, some people with severe snake phobia avoid opening the S volume of an encyclopedia because it may contain a picture of a snake (Kirsch et al., 1983), and the fear of having a panic attack keeps people with agoraphobia confined to their homes. For these reasons, spontaneous remission of anxiety disorders is not prevalent, despite the phenomenon of an overprediction of fear.

In treatment settings, exposure sessions can be structured to ensure that expectancies for fear are disconfirmed by experiences of anxiety reduction, and treatment can be organized so that clients receive interventions that make exposure sessions easier for them. Some clients with extremely high anxiety expectancies refuse to enter the exposure phase of treatment unless some decrease in anxiety expectancy is first effected. Anxiety expectancy can be reduced before exposure sessions by increasing clients' skills for coping with their anxiety in feared situations. This can be accomplished by using techniques such as relaxation training, imagery, and cognitive restructuring.

Once anxiety expectancy is reduced somewhat, clients are more willing to engage in in vivo exposure, and they experience less fear when they do so because they have already learned some skills for controlling their feelings of anxiety. Treatments for phobias specifically designed to increase clients' mastery over feared situations have produced significant decreases in anxiety expectancy as well as improvements in reported fear and avoidance behavior (Williams et al., 1984, 1985, 1989).

Hypnosis is an effective adjunct to many treatments (Kirsch, Montgomery, & Sapirstein, 1995; Rhue, Lynn, & Kirsch, 1993), and adding it to a cognitive–behavioral treatment for public speaking anxiety has been shown to enhance treatment outcomes (Schoenberger et al., 1997). Furthermore, some of the data in the Schoenberger et al. (1997) study indicate that much of the potentiating effect of hypnosis was mediated by expectancy. Hypnosis increased participants' expectancies for improvement, and changes in expectancy were significantly and substantially associated with changes on most measures of anxiety. These data suggest that adding hypnosis to treatment protocols will increase effectiveness, except for clients with negative attitudes toward hypnosis (also see Kirsch, 1993).

Treatments that target change in anxiety expectancy may fail to produce desired changes to the extent that danger expectancy is unaddressed. For cases in which the perception of danger is irrationally high (e.g., having a heart attack during an episode of panic or being injured by a garter snake), cognitive restructuring can be used to challenge the accuracy of clients' assumptions. If perceptions of danger are unrealistic because of a lack of exposure to feared objects or situations, gradual exposure should decrease danger expectancies. Decreases in anxiety expectancy, as well as fear and avoidance, should accompany reduction in danger expectancy.

Treatment can also serve to reduce anxiety sensitivity. Scores on the ASI declined in one sample of people with agoraphobia after a 10- to 12-week group treatment that included education, cognitive restructuring, exposure, and medication as needed (McNally & Lorenz, 1987). After treatment, patients in McNally and Lorenz's study were comparable in anxiety sensitivity with a nonclinical control group. The ASI measures the extent to which respondents are distressed by experiences of anxiety. Some of these items (e.g., "When I cannot keep my mind on a task, I worry that I might be going crazy") appear to be irrational beliefs that may have been altered by cognitive restructuring, thus contributing to reduced scores. Decreasing anxiety sensitivity may not be necessary for successful treatment as long as anxiety expectancy is reduced; expectancy theory predicts (Reiss, 1991) and some findings confirm (Valentiner et al., 1993) that anxiety sensitivity is not related to fear or avoidance as long as the levels of anxiety expectancy is low. However, if anxiety sensitivity is a risk factor for the development of anxiety disorders, then decreasing it should help to prevent relapse after treatment.

Cognitive–behavioral treatments are widely accepted as being effective in the treatment of anxiety disorders. Given the robust findings regarding the importance of anxiety expectancy in maintaining and reducing fear and avoidance, the success of such treatments may be attributed, in large part, to their ability to reduce anxiety expectancy. For this reason, every effort should be made to optimize therapeutic outcome expectancies, and hypnosis can provide one effective means for so doing. Treatment can help increase clients' ability to control their anxiety reactions, and tentative expectations for change can be validated in exposure situations resulting in less fear and avoidance in the future.

Research

The finding that anxiety expectancy predicts the experience of anxiety and avoidance behavior has been well established for a wide range of anxiety disorders. Studies also provide support for the hypothesized role of anxiety sensitivity as it interacts with anxiety expectancy and for the predictive power of self-efficacy as a determinant of approach and avoidance. However, the effects of the other variables, specifically danger sensitivity and expectancy for and sensitivity to negative social evaluation, have received little attention. A comprehensive test of the elaborated model, including anxiety expectancy and sensitivity, is merited. It may be that danger expectancy is more important in some anxiety disorders and that fear of negative evaluation is more crucial in others. Concerns that one will be injured by a snake, fall from a balcony, or suffocate during a panic attack involve the perception of personal threat, although the expectancy for danger is excessive for the situation. However, the fears of people with social phobias are more related to concerns about being embarrassed and judged harshly than they are to physical danger. To my knowledge, such ideas have not yet been empirically tested. The relationship between anxiety and self-efficacy also requires investigation. Perceived coping ability may be highly important in the maintenance and treatment of anxiety disorders and merits further attention.

CONCLUSION

Of the variables considered in cognitive theories of fear, anxiety expectancy is the strongest predictor of subsequent feelings of anxiety across a variety of diagnostic groups and a wide range of severity of anxiety-related problems. Danger expectancy appears to be an important factor in some anxiety disorders, but anxiety expectancy has an impact on fear and behavior that is independent of perceptions of danger. To my knowledge, expectancy for negative social evaluation, which is hypothesized to be especially important in social phobias, has not been evaluated.

Although danger expectancy, negative evaluation expectancy, and anxiety expectancy are all types of outcome expectancies, there are important differences among them. Danger expectancy and negative evaluation expectancy involve fears of external outcomes such as a plane crash or being laughed at during a speech, whereas anxiety expectancy pertains to a subjective experience. Therefore, only anxiety expectancy can exert a direct influence to engender the expected outcome. Anxiety sensitivity is especially relevant in panic disorder and agoraphobia, but the data consistently indicate that it is also a major component of other anxiety disorders. The level of anxiety sensitivity interacts with anxiety expectancy, so that expectancy is a more powerful predictor of fear and avoidance among people who are particularly distressed by the experience of anxiety symptoms.

Treatments that include techniques to increase clients' ability to cope with their anxiety in feared situations are highly effective for people with anxiety disorders. Thus, it is likely that coping self-efficacy is an important determinant of fear and avoidance. This hypothesis has yet to be adequately evaluated, however, because most current measures of self-efficacy assess people's willingness to perform feared behavior rather than their perceived ability to cope with anxiety-provoking situations. The one study that examined perceived coping ability in anxiety disorders shows that coping self-efficacy was a significant predictor of agoraphobic avoidance but that this effect was mediated by anxiety expectancy (Telch, Brouillard, et al., 1989).

The research on anxiety expectancy has important clinical implications. Decreases in anxiety expectancy are associated with decreased anxiety and increased approach behavior over the course of treatment. The effectiveness of cognitive–behavioral treatments for anxiety is likely related to their ability to decrease anxiety expectancy, and the development of new treatments should include expectancy modification as a primary goal. As noted earlier, hypnosis is one means of enhancing expectancy effects, but additional procedures need to be developed, especially for clients with negative attitudes toward hypnosis.

REFERENCES

Ajzen, I., & Fishbein, M. (1980). *Understanding attitudes and predicting social behavior*. Englewood Cliffs, NJ: Prentice Hall.

American Psychiatric Association. (1994). *Diagnostic and statistical manual of mental disorders* (4th ed.). Washington, DC: Author.

Bandura, A. (1977). Self-efficacy: Toward a unifying theory of behavioral change. *Psychological Review, 84*, 191–215.

Bandura, A. (1988). Self-efficacy conception of anxiety. *Anxiety Research, 1*, 77–98.

Bandura, A., Adams, N. E., & Beyer, J. (1977). Cognitive processes mediating behavior change. *Journal of Personality and Social Psychology, 35*, 125–139.

Bandura, A., Reese, L., & Adams, N. E. (1982). Microanalysis of action and fear arousal as a function of differential levels of perceived self-efficacy. *Journal of Personality and Social Psychology, 43*, 5–21.

Beck, A. T., Emery, G., & Greenberg, R. L. (1985). *Anxiety disorders and phobias: A cognitive perspective*. New York: Basic Books.

Brown, E. J., Heimberg, R. G., & Juster, H. R. (1995). Social phobia subtype and avoidant personality disorder: Effect on severity of social phobia, impairment, and outcome of cognitive behavioral treatment. *Behavior Therapy, 26*, 467–486.

Cox, B. J., Endler, N. S., & Swinson, R. P. (1995). An examination of levels of agoraphobic severity in panic disorder. *Behaviour Research and Therapy, 33*, 57–62.

Craske, M. G., Rapee, R. M., & Barlow, D. H. (1988). The significance of panic-expectancy for individual patterns of avoidance. *Behavior Therapy, 19*, 577–592.

Donnell, C. D., & McNally, R. J. (1990). Anxiety sensitivity and panic attacks in a nonclinical population. *Behaviour Research and Therapy, 28*, 83–85.

Fazio, R. H., & Zanna, M. P. (1981). Direct experience and attitude-behavior consistency. *Advances in Experimental Social Psychology, 14*, 161–202.

Gursky, D. M., & Reiss, S. (1987). Identifying danger and anxiety expectancies as components of common fears. *Journal of Behavior Therapy and Experimental Psychiatry, 18,* 317–324.

Holt, C. S., Heimberg, R. G., & Hope, D. A. (1992). Avoidant personality disorder and the generalized subtype of social phobia. *Journal of Abnormal Psychology, 101,* 318–325.

Kenardy, J., Fried, L., Kraemer, H. C., & Taylor, C. B. (1992). Psychological precursors of panic attacks. *British Journal of Psychiatry, 160,* 668–673.

Kirsch, I. (1982). Efficacy expectations or response predictions: The meaning of efficacy ratings as a function of task characteristics. *Journal of Personality and Social Psychology, 42,* 123–136.

Kirsch, I. (1985). Response expectancy as a determinant of experience and behavior. *American Psychologist, 40,* 1189–1202.

Kirsch, I. (1986). Self-efficacy and expectancy: Old wine with new labels. *Journal of Personality and Social Psychology, 49,* 824–830.

Kirsch, I. (1990). *Expectancy modification: A key to effective therapy.* Belmont, CA: Brooks-Cole.

Kirsch, I. (1993). Cognitive–behavioral hypnotherapy. In J. W. Rhue, S. J. Lynn, & I. Kirsch (Eds.), *Handbook of clinical hypnosis* (pp. 151–171). Washington, DC: American Psychological Association.

Kirsch, I. (1997). Response expectancy theory and application: A decennial review. *Applied and Preventive Psychology, 6,* 69–79.

Kirsch, I., & Henry, D. (1977). Extinction versus credibility in the desensitization of speech anxiety. *Journal of Consulting and Clinical Psychology, 45,* 1052–1059.

Kirsch, I., Montgomery, G., & Sapirstein, G. (1995). Hypnosis as an adjunct to cognitive–behavioral psychotherapy: A meta-analysis. *Journal of Consulting and Clinical Psychology, 63,* 214–220.

Kirsch, I., Tennen, H., Wickless, C., Saccone, A. J., & Cody, S. (1983). The role of expectancy in fear reduction. *Behavior Therapy, 14,* 520–533.

Maller, R. G., & Reiss, S. (1987). A behavioral validation of the Anxiety Sensitivity Index. *Journal of Anxiety Disorders, 1,* 265–272.

Maller, R. G., & Reiss, S. (1992). Anxiety sensitivity in 1984 and panic attacks in 1987. *Journal of Anxiety Disorders, 6,* 241–247.

Mattick, R. P., Peters, L., & Clarke, J. C. (1989). Exposure and cognitive restructuring for social phobia: A controlled study. *Behavior Therapy, 20,* 3–23.

McNally, R. J. (1990). Psychological approaches to panic disorder: A review. *Psychological Bulletin, 108,* 403–419.

McNally, R. J., & Lorenz, M. (1987). Anxiety sensitivity in agoraphobics. *Journal of Behavior Therapy and Experimental Psychiatry, 18,* 3–11.

McReynolds, W. T., Barnes, A. R., Brooks, S., & Rehagen, N. J. (1973). The role of attention-placebo influences in the efficacy of systematic desensitization. *Journal of Consulting and Clinical Psychology, 41,* 86–92.

Oei, T. P., Kenna, D., & Evans, L. (1991). The reliability, validity and utility of the SAD and FNE scales for anxiety disorder patients. *Personality and Individual Differences, 12,* 111–116.

Peterson, R. A., & Heilbronner, R. (1987). The Anxiety Sensitivity Index: Construct validity and factor analytic structure. *Journal of Anxiety Disorders, 1,* 117–121.

Rachman, S., & Bichard, S. (1988). The overprediction of fear. *Clinical Psychology Review, 8,* 303–312.

Reiss, S. (1991). Expectancy model of fear, anxiety, and panic. *Clinical Psychology Review, 11,* 141–153.

Reiss, S., & McNally, R. J. (1985). The expectancy model of fear. In S. Reiss & R. R. Bootzin (Eds.), *Theoretical issues in behavior therapy* (pp. 107–121). New York: Academic Press.

Reiss, S., Peterson, R. A., & Gursky, D. M. (1988). Anxiety sensitivity, injury sensitivity, and individual differences in fearfulness. *Behaviour Research and Therapy, 26,* 341–345.

Reiss, S., Peterson, R. A., Gursky, D. M., & McNally, R. J. (1986). Anxiety sensitivity, anxiety frequency and the prediction of fearfulness. *Behaviour Research and Therapy, 24,* 1–8.

Renneberg, B., Goldstein, A. J., Phillips, D., & Chambless, D. L. (1990). Intensive behavioral group treatment of avoidant personality disorder. *Behavior Therapy, 21,* 363–377.

Rhue, J. W., Lynn, S. J., & Kirsch, I. (Eds.). (1993). *Handbook of clinical hypnosis.* Washington, DC: American Psychological Association.

Schelver, S. R., & Gutsch, K. U. (1983). The effects of self-administered cognitive therapy on social-evaluative anxiety. *Journal of Clinical Psychology, 39,* 658–666.

Schoenberger, N. E., Kirsch, I., Gearan, P., Montgomery, G., & Pastyrnak, S. L. (1997). Hypnotic enhancement of a cognitive behavioral treatment for public speaking anxiety. *Behavior Therapy, 28,* 127–140.

Schoenberger, N. E., Kirsch, I., & Rosengard, C. (1991). Cognitive theories of human fear: An empirically derived integration. *Anxiety Research, 4,* 1–13.

Southworth, S., & Kirsch, I. (1988). The role of expectancy in exposure-generated fear reduction in agoraphobia. *Behaviour Research and Therapy, 26,* 113–120.

Taylor, S., Koch, W. J., & Crockett, D. J. (1991). Anxiety sensitivity, trait anxiety, and the anxiety disorders. *Journal of Anxiety Disorders, 5,* 293–311.

Taylor, S., Koch, W. J., & McNally, R. J. (1992). How does anxiety sensitivity vary across the anxiety disorders? *Journal of Anxiety Disorders, 6,* 249–259.

Telch, M. J., Brouillard, M., Telch, C. F., Agras, W. S., & Taylor, C. B. (1989). Role of cognitive appraisal in panic-related avoidance. *Behaviour Research and Therapy, 27,* 373–383.

Telch, M. J., Shermis, M. D., & Lucas, J. A. (1989). Anxiety sensitivity: Unitary personality trait or domain-specific appraisals? *Journal of Anxiety Disorders, 3,* 25–32.

Tran, G. Q., & Chambless, D. L. (1995). Psychopathology of social phobia: Effects of subtype and avoidant personality disorder. *Journal of Anxiety Disorders, 9,* 489–501.

Turner, S. M., McCanna, M., & Beidel, D. C. (1987). Validity of the Social Avoidance and Distress and Fear of Negative Evaluation Scales. *Behaviour Research and Therapy, 25,* 113–115.

Valentiner, D. P., Telch, M. J., Ilai, D., & Hehmsoth, M. M. (1993). Claustrophobic fear behavior: A test of the expectancy model of fear. *Behaviour Research and Therapy, 31,* 395–402.

Valins, S., & Ray, A. A. (1967). Effects of cognitive desensitization on avoidance behavior. *Journal of Personality and Social Psychology, 7,* 345–350.

Watson, D., & Friend, R. (1969). Measurement of social-evaluative anxiety. *Journal of Consulting and Clinical Psychology, 33,* 448–457.

Wickless, C., & Kirsch, I. (1989). The effects of verbal and experiential expectancy manipulations on hypnotic susceptibility. *Journal of Personality and Social Psychology, 57,* 762–768.

Williams, S. L., Dooseman, G., & Kleinfeld, E. (1984). Comparative effectiveness of guided mastery and exposure treatments for intractable phobias. *Journal of Consulting and Clinical Psychology, 52,* 505–518.

Williams, S. L., Kinney, P. J., & Falbo, J. (1989). Generalization of therapeutic changes in agoraphobia: The role of perceived self-efficacy. *Journal of Consulting and Clinical Psychology, 57,* 436–442.

Williams, S. L., & Rappoport, A. (1983). Cognitive treatment in the natural environment for agoraphobics. *Behavior Therapy, 14,* 299–313.

Williams, S. L., Turner, S. M., & Peer, D. F. (1985). Guided mastery and performance desensitization treatments for severe acrophobia. *Journal of Consulting and Clinical Psychology, 53,* 237–247.

Williams, S. L., & Watson, N. (1985). Perceived danger and perceived self-efficacy as cognitive determinants of acrophobic behavior. *Behavior Therapy, 16,* 136–146.

6

EXPECTATION AND DESIRE IN PAIN AND PAIN REDUCTION

DONALD D. PRICE AND JAMES J. BARRELL

The focus of this chapter is on the cognitive factors of expectancy and desire and their relationship to the sensory-discriminative and affective-motivational components of pain and to the reduction of these components by placebo administration. The *sensory-discriminative dimension* refers to the capacity to experience the qualitative and quantifiable features of sensations associated with nociceptive stimuli, whereas the *affective-motivational dimension* refers to both the moment-by-moment unpleasantness associated with these sensations as well as the negative emotions associated with reflection about the implications of having a persistent pain condition (i.e., suffering). Both immediate unpleasantness and suffering occur in the context of clinical pain, whereas only immediate unpleasantness occurs in most forms of experimental pain. However, expectancy and desire have salient roles in mediating or moderating immediate unpleasantness, pain-related suffering, and possibly the sensory dimension of pain.

The chapter is organized into four parts. In the first, evidence for the role of expectancy and desire in pain is reviewed and includes a consideration of studies of both experimental pain and clinical pain. The importance of separately assessing the influence of expectancy and desire on the different dimensions of pain experience, sensory and affective, is emphasized. In the second part, the roles of desire for pain relief and expectation of pain relief are discussed as critical factors in placebo analgesia. These factors are contrasted and compared with the explanation that classical conditioning most optimally accounts for placebo analgesia. In the third, expectancy is discussed in the larger context of a desire–expectation model of emotions to further explain the psychological mechanisms by which expectancy could influence pain and placebo responses. According to the desire–expectation model, the factors of desire and significance, along with their variants, approach and avoidance goals, are shown to interact with expectancy to determine specific levels of positive or negative affective feeling. Moreover, these interactions are related to some fundamental emotions commonly associated with pain-related affect. Consideration is given to how the desire–expectation model of human emotions can help explain the effects of cognitive factors on experiential aspects of pain and pain relief. Finally, the implications of the desire–expectation model for research and treatment of pain are briefly discussed.

EVIDENCE THAT DESIRE AND EXPECTATION ARE INTEGRAL TO PAIN-RELATED EMOTIONS

The affective dimension of pain is based on experienced meanings and is thereby related to the cognitive-evaluative dimension of pain (Buytendyck, 1961; Melzack & Casey, 1968; Price, 1988; Wade, Dougherty, Archer, & Price, 1996; Wade, Dougherty, Hart, Rafii, & Price, 1992; Wade, Price, & Hamer, 1990). These meanings are directed toward the painful sensations, the context in which they occur, and the implications for impending harm. Thus, part of the unpleasantness of pain is related to the perception of threat, a perception that represents an integration from several sources. For example, the perception of being stung by a bee includes an integration of visual, auditory, and nociceptive inputs. These inputs are immediately checked against one's past associations and integrated into an overall perception of threat (Price & Harkins, 1992). This overall perception is likely to lead to a desire to escape or avoid further harm and is manifested, at least in part, by expectations regarding future harm or pain. Although the factors of desire and expectation may be implicit in one's experience, they are likely to have a salient influence in the emotions that accompany acute pain. Thus, affective feelings associated with pain use some of the same principles that underly emotions in general. As Buytendyck (1961) pointed out, an adequate explanation of pain depends on an adequate theory of human emotions. The role of desire and expectation in pain, particularly that of pain-related affect, can be understood in the context of the meanings of pain experience.

Meanings of Pain

Similar to many types of biological threat, pain contains both immediate and long-term implications. Cognitive appraisals of these implications constitute the link between the sensory features of pain and emotional feelings and their expressions. Cognitive appraisals, in turn, are often associated with specific desires and expectations. Thus, the understanding of the role of desire and expectation in pain affect must begin with a discussion of the meanings that are common to the experience of pain.

Both empirical studies of experiential factors of pain and consideration of the experience of pain itself indicate that there are two stages of pain-related emotional feeling (Price, 1988; Price & Harkins, 1992). The first is the *immediate affective stage of pain*, comprised of the moment-by-moment unpleasantness, distress, and annoyance that closely covaries with the intensity of the painful sensation and its accompanying arousal. Pain-related sensations can not only be intense and persisting but also can be perceived as spreading, penetrating, and sometimes summating. They are experienced as an invasion of both the body and consciousness because their intensity and qualities are perceived as intense, penetrating, or both. Therefore, a frequent meaning given to painful sensations is that of *intrusion*, a meaning that requires little reflection and occurs somewhat but not entirely automatically. It is the meaning conveyed by someone who says, "It bothers me because it hurts!" Thus, similar to states of nausea, dizziness, intense thirst, and intense hunger, part of the affective dimension of pain is closely linked to the nature of the sensations themselves. This being the case, both neural and psychological processes related to pain-related sensation can be conceived of as important causal links in the production of pain-related emotional disturbance. The close link between acute forms of pain-related sensation and immediate pain unpleasantness has been a source of confusion among psychologists, some of whom have questionned whether there are indeed separately measurable dimensions of pain experience. Psychophysical studies clearly demonstrate that pain-related sensation and immediate pain-related unpleasantness or disturbance represent two separate dimensions of pain that demonstrate reliably different relationships to nociceptive stimulus intensity, which can be separately influenced by various psychological factors (Price, 1988; Price & Harkins, 1992; Rainville, Feine, Bushnell, & Duncan, 1992).

Part of the confusion may stem from the fact that although pain-related sensation intensity and pain unpleasantness closely covary under controlled laboratory conditions, pain unpleasantness can be shown as powerfully and selectively modulated by contextual factors, such as the degree of threat present within the experimental setting. As pointed out earlier, the immediate emotional disturbance associated with an acute pain episode is often part of a more integrated perception of threat that is accompanied by a desire to eliminate the source of pain and expectations about how this can be done. As such, one would expect that the intensity of immediate pain unpleasantness could be modulated by expectations.

A second stage of pain-related affect is based on more reflective cognitive processes (Buytendyck, 1962; Price, 1988). These involve more elaborate meanings related to the perception of the longer term implications of painful sensations and their accompanying arousal. These implications are based on three potential meanings. First, the painful condition is *interrupting* something, such as one's ability to function or to live a meaningful life. Second, the painful condition and its accompanying domination of consciousness are a *burden* that one must *endure over time*. Finally, the painful sensation may mean that something *harmful might happen or has happened.*

The meaning of intrusion in the first stage of pain-related affect and the meanings of interruption, enduring, and concern for the future in the second stage of pain-related affect are directed at the painful sensations, the context in which they occur, and the implications of avoiding harm. Each of these meanings, in turn, is easily related to a desire to avoid or remove the intrusion, interruption, burden, or negative future consequences. Numerous contextual factors that relate to information about the nature of the painful condition and about the potential means of avoiding or removing the pain and its associated negative consequences converge to determine one's level of expectation that pain and its associated negative consequences will or can be removed. As such, it would appear that emotional feelings that accompany the first and second stages of pain-related affect are determined to an extent by desires and expectations in the same way that many common human emotions are determined by these two factors (Price & Barrell, 1984; Price, Barrell, & Barrell, 1985). The following discussion provides empirical support for this possibility.

Influence of Expectancy on the Affective Dimension of Experimental Pain

Evidence that desires and expectations are integral components of the pain experience comes from studies of experimental pain in which manipulations are explicitly directed at changing expectation. In one such study, a psychophysical analysis was made of experiential factors that influence the affective but not sensory discriminative dimension of heat-induced pain (Price, Barrell, & Gracely, 1980). Trained participants made cross-modality matching judgments of both pain sensation intensity and unpleasantness. Nonnoxious (35–42°C) and noxious (45–51°C) skin temperature stimuli (5-s duration) were randomly interspersed during each experimental session. Changes in expectations of receiving painful stimulation were induced by preceding half of all the noxious stimuli by a warning signal.

The mean responses of the participants clearly indicate that noxious temperatures were experienced as being less unpleasant when preceded by a warning signal. In contrast, pain sensation magnitudes, evoked by the same stimulus temperatures, were completely unaffected by the warning signal. Moreover, the selective lowering of pain unpleasantness by the warning signal was greatest toward the lowest end of the noxious temperature range (i.e., 45°C) and was minimal or ineffective at the highest end of the stimulus range (i.e., 51°C). Apparently, participants prefer knowing that the next stimulus will be painful as compared with being taken by surprise. The uncertainty of knowing whether the next stimulus will be painful is likely to produce anxiety. However, if the intensity of stimulation is high (i.e., 51°C), then it makes little difference whether someone is warned.

This interpretation of the anti-anxiety effects of a warning signal is supported by other experiments in which anxiety associated with experimental pain was reduced, either with an anti-anxiety drug or placebo saline. Gracely, McGrath, and Dubner (1976) demonstrated that 5 mg of intravenous diazepam, a common tranquilizer, significantly reduced affective descriptor responses to painful electrocutaneous shock without altering sensory descriptor responses. Similar to the expectancy manipulation of providing a warning signal, the reductions were greatest for low-intensity noxious stimuli. In another study by Gracely (1979), a highly similar pattern was found for intravenous saline placebo injections. The results of all of these studies can be parsimoniously explained as a selective lowering of pain unpleasantness by a reduction in anxiety. Part of pain unpleasantness is the anxiety associated with anticipating and receiving a noxious stimulus. Anxiety represents a state of wanting to avoid negative consequences combined with an experienced uncertainty of avoiding them (Barrell, Madieros, Barrell, & Price, 1985; Price et al., 1985). Regardless of whether anxiety is reduced by a drug or a cognitive manipulation that modifies expectation, the result is that of selectively reducing pain unpleasantness, with the largest effects occurring for mildly painful intensities.

Expectations about the qualitative nature of pain sensations also have been shown to selectively influence pain affect. Johnson (1973) found that participants who received a description of the painful sensations produced by ischemia of the forearm had lowered levels of distress compared with participants who received only a description of the procedure. Similar to Price et al. (1980), pain sensation intensities were unaffected by this difference in description. Thus, it is apparent that different kinds of expectations, either about the time of the occurrence of pain or the types of sensations that will occur, can alter experienced unpleasantness without changing the intensity of experimentally induced painful sensation.

The role of expectancy in experimental pain also has been examined within the context of social learning theory. A study using various cognitive manipulations for coping with experimental pain examined perceived self-efficacy and pain expectancy as potential mediators of pain perception and pain tolerance (Baker & Kirsch, 1991). Results show that pain tolerance was predicted by perceived self-efficacy, which in turn was predicted by pain expectancy and the provision of incentives. Pain perception was strongly influenced by pain expectancy, but it was unrelated to self-efficacy. Ohlwein, Stevens, and Catanzaro (1996), using an experimental paradigm and approach similar to that of Baker and Kirsch, likewise found that response expectancy had a stronger relationship to pain responses than did self-efficacy. However, they did not replicate the finding that self-efficacy mediated the effects of response expectancy on pain tolerance. Although the mediating effect of self-efficacy remains to be clarified, a consistent finding across both studies is that expectations about pain intensity were somewhat predictive of perceived pain intensity itself. A limitation common to both studies is that sensory and affective dimensions of pain were not separately evaluated. Therefore, the question needs to be reexamined for both pain dimensions.

Researchers who attempted to modify either experimental or clinical pain intensity by manipulations designed to change expectancy have found either weak or negligible effects, as indicated in a meta-analysis by Fernandez and Turk (1989). In their analysis of 9 studies comparing positive expectancy manipulations with no-treatment control conditions, they found a mean weighted effect size of 0.03, which was not reliably different from zero. This analysis had a fail-safe sample size of 67, which was above the criterion. Furthermore, when they analyzed 12 studies that compared expectancy manipulations with other cognitive strategies such as pain acknowledgment, neutral imaging, pleasant imagery, and external attention, the mean weighted effect size was 0.35, which was significantly different at the .05 level. This analysis had a fail-safe sample size of 133, which was well above criterion. Other interesting findings of this analysis were that 10 of the 12 studies showed that expectancy manipulations were the least effective in reducing pain and that, in general, expectancy controls were less effective than any of the other cognitive strategies. A distinct limitation of nearly all of these studies, however, is that the independent variable was that of a manipulation or instruction designed to persuade participants to develop a positive expectation rather than a measure of expectation itself. Another limitation of the studies in this meta-analysis is that the pain measures were nearly always crude, simplistic measures of only pain threshold, pain tolerance, or simple pain rating scales that did not also assess affective dimensions of pain. Therefore, whereas the weight of all of these studies indicates weak or negligible effects of expectancy manipulations on pain intensity, it is not at all clear that direct effects of actual expectations have such weak effects. In fact, data published after Fernandez and Turk's (1989) meta-analysis indicate that experiential manipulations of expectancy have stronger effects than verbal manipulations (Montgomery & Kirsch, 1997; Voudouris, Peck, & Coleman, 1990).

In summary, on the basis of results of experimental pain studies, it is apparent that expectations about different aspects of pain and about the contextual conditions in which pain occurs influence pain differently. Expectations about when the pain will occur and what it means once it does occur may have relatively selective effects on the unpleasantness or immediate emotional disturbance associated with pain. Expectations about pain sensation intensity itself appear to have a modest influence on perceived pain intensity. Finally, manipulations designed to produce a positive expectation appear to have the weakest effect on pain intensity, although it is difficult to reach a definitive conclusion about this possibility because of the questionable pain measures used in most available studies.

Influence of Expectancy on the Affective Dimension of Clinical Pain

In general, the factors of desire for relief and expectation would appear to have a greater influence on pain-related affect in the case of clinical pain because the implications of having clinical pain in general are likely to be perceived as being more open ended and threatening than experimental pain. Unfortunately, there have been few explicit attempts to directly assess the role of expectancy in clinical pain. Nevertheless, such a role is strongly supported by at least indirect evidence that is largely consistent with the idea that a significant component of clinical pain affect is that of anxiety. Thus, in one study it was hypothesized that affective ratings of clinical pain would be higher in patients whose pain was likely to be associated with a serious threat to health or life than in patients whose pain was likely to be less threatening (Price, Harkins, & Baker, 1987). Cancer pain patients and labor pain patients were chosen as representative of the former and latter, respectively. As a corollary to this hypothesis, it was proposed that women in labor who focused mainly on the birth of their child would have lower ratings of pain unpleasantness than women who focused mainly on pain or on avoiding pain. Sensory and unpleasantness ratings of experimental pain were also compared with those of various types of clinical pain.

Labor pain patients and cancer pain patients used separate visual analogue scales (VASs) to rate their levels of pain sensation intensity and degree of unpleasantness that occurred at different times during their clinical condition. Cancer pain patients were distinguished by the fact that their VAS unpleasantness ratings were higher than their VAS sensory ratings, whereas the reverse was true for labor pain patients. Furthermore, significant differences in pain VAS affect ratings were observed among labor pain patients as a function of whether the patient focused primarily on pain or avoiding pain as compared with focusing on having the baby. Patients who focused primarily on having the baby, an approach goal, rated the unpleasantness of their pain as being approximately half that of patients who focused primarily on pain or avoiding pain. This difference occurred for each stage of labor. In contrast, no significant differences in pain sensation intensity VAS ratings occurred between patients with these two orientations at any stage of labor.

The combination of all these results indirectly indicates that goals, desires, and expectations about outcomes strongly influence emotional feelings associated with different clinical pain conditions. The influence of these factors is most apparent when there are divergent psychological orientations within a clinical pain condition. Thus, the unpleasantness brought about by the implications of cancer pain, including that of impending deterioration, death, or both, appears to add to that which is directly related to the pain sensations. One of the implications of having labor pain, however, is that the birth of a baby is imminent. The positive emotional consequence of this implication appears to offset the unpleasantness of labor pain to some degree. This interpretation is further supported by the much greater degree of labor pain unpleasantness among women who focus on avoiding pain compared with those who focus on the birth of the baby. Part of what constitutes pain unpleasantness is the implication of the pain condition. The implication, in turn, is related to a goal, desire, and expectation associated with that goal.

EVIDENCE FOR THE INVOLVEMENT OF DESIRE AND EXPECTATION IN PLACEBO ANALGESIA

If desire and expectancy have a role in clinical and experimental pain, then it is reasonable to surmise that both factors are also important in the psychological mechanisms of pain reduction. Thus, in conditions in which patients experience a strong need to be relieved of pain, (a) they have expectations that pain relief will occur as a result of a treatment, (b) the treatment reproduces in some way a previously effective treatment, or (c) pain reduction may result from psychological factors. This is known as the *placebo analgesic response*. In this section, we discuss the possible contributions of classical conditioning, expectation of pain relief, and desire for pain relief on placebo analgesia.

The potential assessment of the influence of these factors on placebo analgesia must take into consideration the problems inherent in determining the relative magnitude of placebo effects in both experimental and clinical contexts. Although there is considerable literature indicating that placebo manipulations can reduce both experimental and clinical pain

(Jospe, 1978), there is still some confusion about the extent to which placebos reduce sensory and affective dimensions of pain and about the relative size of placebo analgesic effects (see Price & Fields, 1997b, for a more complete discussion of this topic). Clinical studies designed to control for placebo analgesic effects rarely measure placebo effects because a natural history control group is rarely included in such studies. This limitation is a major source of confusion about the nature and prevalence of placebo analgesia. The assessment of the mean magnitude of a placebo analgesic effect in a group of patients can usually be carried out by comparing a group in a no-treatment condition with a group that receives the placebo treatment condition. Because few studies of placebo analgesia include an untreated comparison group or condition, little knowledge exists with regard to the magnitude, time course, or frequency of occurrence of placebo effects. Among studies of placebo analgesia in which experimental pain is used, the assessments of magnitude of placebo analgesia are generally more reliable because stable baseline pain intensities (i.e., "natural histories") are more controllable. The magnitudes of placebo analgesic effects in studies of experimental pain are generally much smaller than those alleged for clinical pain. However, this difference may be partly attributable to a decline in clinical pain intensity over time (Jospe, 1978). Finally, among studies of placebo analgesia in which experimental pain is used, those that measure both sensory and affective dimensions are even more rare. Thus, in the discussion that follows, emphasis is on those studies for which the stability of baseline pain or natural history was taken into account, studies in which sensory and affective dimensions of pain are measured, or both.

Potential Role of Classical Conditioning

A major hypothesis considers the efficacy of placebo analgesia to be a function of classical conditioning. Indeed, several psychologists have independently proposed this idea (Korcyn, 1978; Watkins & Mayer, 1982; Wickramasekera, 1985). Wickramasekera (1985) suggested that active ingredients in agents that reduce pain (morphine, aspirin, etc.) can serve as unconditioned stimuli (UCSs), whereas neutral stimuli associated with the diminution of unpleasant symptoms (due to spontaneous remission or delivery of an active drug) or with the onset of therapeutic action of an active ingredient for therapeutic effects can serve as conditioned stimuli (CSs). CSs can come to be associated with the therapeutic agent and its efficacy, such as syringes, authoritative-appearing health care professionals, elaborate medical equipment, and so on. Consistent with the classical conditioning hypothesis, a landmark human study clearly show that prior experience with an effective analgesic drug enhances the analgesic effectiveness of a subsequent placebo (Laska & Sunshine, 1973). In Laska and

Sunshine's study, placebo given as a second treatment was more effective as an analgesic when it followed a more potent analgesic. Their results support learning, even classical conditioning, as a major factor in placebo analgesia.

Problems With the Classical Conditioning Hypothesis

There have been several challenges to explaining placebo effects on the basis of classical (Pavlovian) conditioning. In particular, Kirsch (1990) pointed out that various studies of placebo effects disconfirm several criteria used to decide whether a phenomenon can be attributed to classical conditioning: (a) Conditioning trials with tranquilizers weaken rather than produce the predicted strengthened placebo effect; (b) contrary to the criterion that the magnitude of placebo effect should be directly related to the strength of the active tranquilizer, it is inversely related; (c) placebo effects are often not specific to the pharmacological properties of the active drug (e.g., alcohol, caffeine) but depend heavily on context and suggestion; (d) placebos often fail the extinction test, as in the case of placebo treatment for panic disorder; and (e) placebo effects sometimes can be stronger (not weaker) than the effects of an active drug. However, except for the demonstration of extinction, all of the criteria for classical conditioning were fulfilled by Laska and Sunshine's (1973) study. Moreover, Fedele, Marchinin, Acaia, Garagiola, and Tiengo (1989) demonstrated a loss of analgesic effectiveness of placebo with repeated administration (i.e., extinction). The exceptions cited by Kirsch (1990) may be unique to certain kinds of studies in which psychologically therapeutic effects are measured (e.g., reductions in panic or anxiety) or to instances in which a drug induces arousal or sedation (i.e., caffeine or alcohol), and the specific effects observed, such as increased motor performance, could be attributed largely to contextual factors and suggestion. These considerations may have less application to placebo analgesia, at least to its sensory-discriminative dimension.

Do Cognitive Factors Contribute to Placebo Responses?

The study of cognitive factors has the potential to increase the understanding of how learning influences the placebo effect and how factors not directly related to classical conditioning influence placebo responses. First, conditioning stimuli (e.g., syringes, doctors in white coats) and conditioned responses (e.g., pain relief) may well have concomitant dimensions within human experience. For example, CSs occurring during the visit to the doctor and during the prescription and ingestion of medication, such as pills and syringes, become associated with active pharmacological agents (i.e., UCSs) as well as with the reduction in pain (unconditioned responses) and indicate that relief and healing are imminent.

Second, although the consideration of experiential factors extends and supports the role of learning and even classical conditioning in placebo analgesia, it also helps to resolve some of the limitations and inconsistencies of older stimulus substitution models of classical conditioning as an explanation for placebo analgesia. Although there is ample evidence that prior exposure to an effective treatment enhances placebo effects, it is questionable whether such prior exposure is necessary for a placebo response. Because of the important roles that meanings, attributions, imagery, and information have in mediating beliefs, desires, and expectations, it is plausible that the placebo response is more directly controlled by these cognitive factors than by the immediate and direct association of a specific treatment with pain reduction as required for classical conditioning (i.e., CSs and UCSs). An illustrative hypothetical example would be a patient receiving an unknown pain medicine for the first time from the family doctor. The patient's life experiences with doctors in general, trust in this specific doctor based on past medical conditions other than pain, and nature of the communication between the doctor and this patient all may codetermine this patient's level of expectation that this specific (and unknown) pain medicine will provide significant pain relief.

Indeed, consideration of the nature of suggestions inherent in placebo manipulations strongly indicate that cognitive factors operate to influence and even determine the nature and magnitude of the placebo response. The suggestion in placebo analgesia is typically that pain relief is being provided by an outside authoritative source (e.g., pain medicine prescribed by a knowledgeable professional). Implicit in the overall suggestion inherent in a placebo analgesic manipulation is the credibility of this outside authoritative agent. Thus, a tacit assumption in the administration of placebo analgesic agents is that patients will develop an expectation of pain relief provided by the agent administered.

Role of Expectation

The possible role of expectation in placebo responses is supported both by alternative models of learning (Mowrer, 1960; Reiss, 1980; Rescorla, 1988) and evidence that it plays a critical role in the placebo response. Classical conditioning itself may lead to the acquisition of expectancies; thus, Reiss (1980) argued that "what is learned in Pavlovian conditioning is an expectation regarding the occurrence or nonoccurrence of a UCR [unconditioned response] onset or a change in UCR magnitude or duration" (p. 390). In fact, contemporary theories of Pavlovian classical conditioning emphasize the role of expectancies (Rescorla, 1988). However, although classical conditioning is one way to change one's expectation, other types of learning can contribute. For example, expectation can reflect knowledge about the therapeutic agent, the circumstances under which it is administered, and the condition to be treated. Classical conditioning could result in increased knowledge about the efficacy of the therapeutic agent by producing a memory of past effects. However, as indicated by the hypothetical example given earlier, expectation could also be critically influenced by information that is independent of one's previous direct experience with a specific therapeutic agent. For that matter, one could even read a book about the agent's therapeutic efficacy. In either case, increased information indicating an agent's effectiveness could increase one's expectation of relief.

What all of this implies for placebo analgesia is that expectation for relief may cause a placebo response without prior exposure to a similiar-appearing therapeutic agent, although such exposure does increase expectation (e.g., Laska & Sunshine, 1973). This possibility is supported by several studies that indirectly show that expectation exerts a considerable influence in the production of placebo effects. Lasagna, Laties, and Dohan (1958) analyzed postoperative patients who responded to placebos and to analgesic drugs. They concluded that a positive placebo response indicates a psychological set in which pain relief is anticipated. Unfortunately, neither the early studies of placebo analgesia by Beecher (1955, 1959) nor most of the recent studies of placebo analgesia directly assess the role of expectation. Although Nash and Zimring (1969) focused on the effects of placebo on short-term memory and not pain, they specifically studied the role of expectation in 100 patients. They compared the effects of two drugs versus placebo and found that the two drugs had no effect that differentiated them from placebo. However, there was a strong correlation between the measured expectation and the placebo effect. Although both correlations were statistically reliable, the correlation was stronger for subjectively experienced change in the performance of memory tests ($r = .36$) than for objective tests of performance ($r = .23$).

Despite the commonly asserted claim that expectation is a critical factor in placebo analgesic effects, its role has not been consistently demonstrated in experiments explicitly designed to assess its relative contribution, particularly in analgesic studies. In particular, the effects of expectation on placebo analgesia were not convincingly distinguished from those of conditioning in the first two studies designed to compare conditioning with expectancy. In the first, Voudouris et al. (1990) compared the effects of *conditioning* (exposure to a pain-reducing treatment) and *explicit expectation* (verbal suggestions for pain reduction) manipulations within the same experiment on placebo analgesia. The conditioning manipulation consisted of providing participants with an experience of cream-induced analgesia by surreptitiously lowering painful stimulation intensity after administering the "analgesic cream." There were four groups in the study:

Group 1 received a combined expectancy and conditioning manipulation; Group 2 received expectancy treatment alone; Group 3 received conditioning alone; Group 4, a control group, received neither treatment. All participants' VAS ratings of pain were compared with and without a placebo cream using iontophoretic pain stimulation. The results showed an enhanced placebo effect from conditioning but not verbally induced expectancy and no interaction between the two different types of manipulations. The authors suggested that conditioning may be a more powerful factor than verbal expectancy in inducing a placebo response.

Although the Voudouris et al. (1990) study was the first attempt that we know of to assess the differential role of conditioning and expectancy in evoking placebo analgesia, there were several problems specifically related to the expectancy manipulation and its assessment. First, the expectancy manipulation itself is questionable because it consisted of simply providing different consent forms for the expectancy groups and the conditioning-alone group, one stating that they would receive a powerful analgesic and the other stating that they were in a control group. Whether this approach was actually effective among the university students who participated, given their possible level of knowledge of psychology experiments, is open to question. Second, their expectancy manipulation check was simplistic, consisting of an analysis of responses to only a single question (embedded in a series of other irrelevant questions) asking whether they had expected the cream to be effective. Finally, they asked this question only once, before the conditioning manipulation. Thus, the effect of conditioning on expectancy was never assessed. As is appropriate given these problems, the authors indicated that their results by no means excluded the role of expectation in evoking placebo responses. Rather they suggested that expectations may be more strongly shaped by previous experience (e.g., that provided by conditioning) than by verbal persuasion. The authors admitted that it would have been more revealing to have actually directly assessed the expectation levels of participants who received only conditioning rather than to have simply assumed that expectation was successfully increased only by their expectancy manipulation. Direct measures of expectation using continuous scales or questionnaires with multiple questions about expectation clearly need to be incorporated into studies of placebo effects. These measures may account for more of the variance in placebo effects than the manipulations intended to produce changes in expectations.

The second study that fails to distinguish the effects of conditioning from expectancy was an attempt to replicate the main results of Voudouris et al. (1990). de Jong, van Baast, Arntz, and Merkelbach (1996) showed that "mere verbal persuasion was not sufficient to elicit placebo-induced pain reduction" (p. 27), a conclusion similar to that arrived at by Voudouris et al. However, this is much different from claiming that expectations of pain relief are not sufficient to elicit placebo-induced pain reduction or that conditioning is more effective than verbal expectancy. The data of de Jong et al. do not support either of these two potential claims for several reasons. To give just two, all of their experimental effects, including that of conditioning, were weak and expectations of low pain were in fact significantly associated with low pain intensities across all participants and conditions of the experiment. A more useful approach would be to introduce an experimental manipulation that dissociates the factor of expectancy, for example, from that of conditioning. This is precisely the approach taken by Montgomery and Kirsch (1997). They tested opposing models of classical conditioning (the stimulus substitution variant) and expectancy using an experimental paradigm similar to that used by Voudouris et al. and providing two conditions of UCS–CS pairings. These two conditions included informing one group of participants about the lowering of painful stimulus intensity and not informing the other group. The uninformed group was thereby provided with an experience of cream-induced analgesia during conditioning and, as expected, demonstrated placebo analgesia in the subsequent test trials. In contrast, the group that was informed of a reduction of stimulus intensity during the conditioning trials had both lowered expectations of analgesia and no overall analgesia (i.e., placebo effect) during test trials. Furthermore, although conditioning trials significantly enhanced placebo responding, this effect was eliminated by adding the participants' expectancy values to the regression equation, indicating that the effect of pairing trials on placebo response was mediated completely by expectancy (Baron & Kenny, 1986). Finally, the magnitude of the placebo effect increased significantly over 10 extinction trials, a result opposite to that predicted by a stimulus substitution model of classical conditioning.

This experiment is important because it demonstrates that conditioning is not sufficient for placebo effects and provides evidence that is consistent with the hypothesis that a high expectation of a therapeutic effect is necessary for placebo effects. Indeed, this experiment provides multiple lines of evidence against the stimulus substitution model of classical conditioning and for the mediating role of expectancy. Thus, according to Baron and Kenny (1986),

> to establish mediation, the following conditions must hold: First, the independent variable must affect the mediator. . . . Second, the independent variable must be shown to affect the dependent variable. . . . Third, the mediator must affect the dependent variable. . . . Perfect mediation holds if the independent variable has no effect when the mediator is controlled. (p. 1178)

By these criteria, Montgomery and Kirsch (1997) established that the effect of conditioning on responses to placebo is mediated perfectly by expectancy, consistent with contemporary theories of classical conditioning.

Perhaps the most intriguing and unexpected result of Montgomery and Kirsch's (1997) study is that not only did the placebo effect fail to extinguish but it also actually increased across the 10 extinction trials. This pattern of results is inconsistent with a stimulus substitution model of classical conditioning and is consistent with an informational model of classical conditioning. If placebo produces a powerful effect the first time it is given, then the perception of placebo as pain relief is bolstered and strengthens the effect of subsequent placebo treatments. In Montgomery and Kirsch's study, pain stimulation without placebo produced a progressive increase in reported pain with repeated trials and the possibility was raised that the magnitude of the placebo effect is proportional to the magnitude of pain without the placebo. The magnitude of pain may in turn relate to a second factor in placebo analgesia: the perceived need or desire for pain relief.

Role of Desire for Relief

An approach similar to that used to analyze expectancy needs to be taken to evaluate the additional role of motivation or desire for pain relief. Placebo effects are commonly observed in circumstances in which it is likely that participants not only expect therapeutic effects but also strongly want these effects to occur. Although the desire for relief, or motivation, which is not quite the same thing, has been directly or indirectly implicated in the placebo response, less explicit recognition has been given to this factor than to expectation. Evaluation of the role of desire for pain relief in placebo analgesia could be accomplished in part by systematically varying the degree of pain or degree of threat presented in an experiment or by using the natural variability of patients' desire for pain relief in clinical settings. The interrelationship between expectation and desire for relief also needs to be evaluated.

Although direct evidence for the mediating role of a desire for relief has yet to be obtained, the possible contribution of this factor in placebo analgesia is supported by some indirect evidence. First, there is evidence that the magnitude of placebo analgesia is influenced by the degree of threat present in the context in which placebo treatments are given. Presumably, the degree of threat would contribute to desire for pain relief. On the basis of comparisons of placebo analgesic effects across studies of different types of pain, both Beecher (1955, 1959) and Jospe (1978) asserted that the magnitudes of analgesic responses to an explicit placebo manipulation are in general much greater in studies of clinical pain than in studies of experimental pain. Although both authors based this assertion on a considerable number of studies, a serious limitation in this comparison is that the natural history of the participants' pain is rarely taken into account in clinical studies. However, among studies using experimental pain, for which assessments of the natural history, baseline reliability, or both are available, placebo analgesic effects are larger for those forms of experimental pain that are of longer duration, more stressful, or both (Jospe, 1978). These types of experimental pain are more likely to simulate the psychological conditions of most acute clinical pains. Thus, although placebo treatments produce large reductions in experimental pains that continuously increase in intensity over several minutes, such as ischemic limb pain (Grevert, Albert, & Goldstein, 1983), they have no effects on brief pains produced by 5-s heat stimuli applied to the skin (Price et al., 1985) or 1-s electrical stimuli applied to the tooth pulp (Gracely, 1979).

Second, although the role of desire for pain relief has not been directly assessed in research on placebo analgesia, the desire for symptom change was assessed in a study of placebo manipulations suggesting possible sedative or stimulant effects. Jensen and Karoly (1991) assessed separate contributions of motivation and expectancy to placebo responses. According to those authors, the term *motivation* referred to the degree to which the participants wanted to experience a symptom change and *expectancy* was the participants' expectations of symptom change. They manipulated both of these variables by separate instructions and then later checked (through participant self-ratings) to determine whether either or both variables had been influenced. Thus, the study was a 2 × 2 factorial design that contained four groups (high motivation and high expectancy, etc.). They found that motivation accounted for a significant amount of variance in placebo responses, which included perceived sedation in the case of placebo tranquilizers or perceived arousal in the case of placebo stimulants.

To date, many researchers who have sought to explain the psychological basis of the placebo analgesic effect have focused on a single factor, such as anxiety, expectancy, hope, or faith in the treatment. On the basis of the studies and considerations elaborated earlier, we propose that three factors need to be explicitly tested for their possible contribution to placebo analgesia: (a) a classical conditioning effect that occurs without the participant's conscious awareness of the CS–UCS association, (b) a desire for a given treatment or agent to significantly relieve pain, and (c) the level of expectation that pain will be significantly relieved by such treatment or agent. Although we think that classical conditioning is a major determinant of the magnitude of the placebo effect, we propose that what is learned during classical conditioning is an explicit or implicit expectation that a given set of conditions will lead to pain relief.

A THEORETICAL BASIS FOR MECHANISMS OF PAIN MODULATION BY DESIRE AND EXPECTATION

We provided evidence for the possibility that both pain and placebo analgesic responses are strongly influenced by the desire for pain relief and expectancy. However, questions remain concerning how these two factors influence pain and pain relief. In this section, we discuss possible general mechanisms by which these factors could mediate pain and placebo analgesia. One possibility is that desire and expectation are integral components of pain affect and reduction in pain affect by placebo administration. The other is that the desire for pain relief and expectancy produce a response bias that is reflected in changes in the way people report pain ratings, pain thresholds, or pain tolerance without an actual change in the strength of pain-related signals in ascending pathways for pain. The third is that the desire for pain relief and expectancy somehow are associated with brain mechanisms that trigger descending modulation of the pain-related signal. In the following discussion, we focus on these possibilities.

Desire for Pain Relief and Expectancy Are Direct Components of Pain and Pain Reduction

Desire for pain reduction and expectancy could be integral components of pain and placebo analgesia if two conditions were fulfilled: (a) the desire for pain relief and expectancy were components of the pain-related affect itself and (b) placebo administration directly influenced pain affect through changes in these two factors. As discussed earlier, there is empirical support for the role of these two factors in pain affect. The mechanism by which these two factors affect pain and placebo responses could be clarified if it could be shown that desire and expectation are components of emotions in general and hence in emotions that operate during pain.

Evidence that desire and expectation are integral factors in at least some common emotions comes from the studies of Price and Barrell (1984; Price et al., 1985) and from an earlier theoretical formulation of Barrell and Neimeyer (1975). Price and Barrell (1984) found that the intensities of at least some common types of emotional feelings can be explained on the basis of two major factors: how much people desire something to happen or not happen and their level of expectation that it will happen or has happened. Neither of these two factors appears to be specifically emotional in themselves, yet they are integral to many ordinary emotions. Both qualitative and quantitative evidence has provided support for this two-factor model.

This desire–expectation model could help to explain emotions that occur during pain, particularly if pain-related emotions are codetermined by desire and expectation in the same way as emotions in general. For example, placebo administration could reduce pain unpleasantness by either decreasing the desire for pain relief (independently of reducing pain sensation intensity) or increasing expectations of pain relief. This could occur under some circumstances in which placebo effects involve only a reduction in anxiety and therefore a selective reduction in the affective dimension of pain. Anxiety represents a combination of the desire to avoid negative consequences coupled with an uncertain expectation of avoiding those consequences (Barrell et al., 1985; Price & Barrell, 1980; Price et al., 1985). These two factors constitute the anxiety that is associated with acute clinical pain and some forms of experimental pain. To the extent that patients increase their expectations that a given treatment or agent will reduce their pain, their anxiety decreases when they receive the treatment or when they know they are going to receive a treatment. This reduction in anxiety would be expected to reduce the overall unpleasantness associated with pain (Price, 1988). In this way, the direct perception of the placebo agent as meaning a reduction in pain unpleasantness, pain distress, or pain-related anxiety is an integral part of the placebo response itself. A selective anti-anxiety effect could occur if the patient were led to expect that the therapeutic agent would make the pain less threatening, bothersome, or distressing but not necessarily less intense (e.g., "I am going to give you something to make it easy to experience the procedure").

The results of one study have shown a selective effect of a placebo on the affective dimension of pain. As pointed out earlier, Gracely (1979) found that saline placebo reduced affective but not sensory ratings of experimental pain and that this effect was greater toward the low end of the nociceptive stimulus range, a pattern of effect similar to that produced by an anxiety-reducing agent (Gracely et al., 1976) and by cognitive manipulations likely to reduce anxiety (Price et al., 1980). Indeed, it may be that the combined factors of desire for relief and uncertainty of relief may at least partly account for the association between the placebo response and anxiety (Bootzin, 1985; Evans, 1985).

Desire for and Expectations of Pain Relief Produce a Response Bias

The explanation of a general placebo mechanism that reduces only pain-related affect is at variance with evidence for placebo mechanisms that reduce both pain intensity and pain affect. Furthermore, there is evidence that placebo-induced reductions in pain may include multiple components and that not all placebo manipulations are selective for pain affect. Thus, the results of some studies have shown placebo effects on sensory-intensive aspects of pain (Grevert & Goldstein, 1985; Levine, Gordon, Bornstein, & Fields, 1979; Levine, Gordon, & Fields, 1978), and others have shown placebo effects on both sensory and affective dimensions of pain (Montgomery & Kirsch, 1996).

Montgomery and Kirsch's (1996) study also provides further evidence that the psychological mediation of placebo analgesic effects involves much more specific mechanisms than the simple reduction of anxiety or other global effects on emotions. Montgomery and Kirsch demonstrated that the application of a placebo in the guise of a topical anesthetic produced reduction in pain only at the body site at which the placebo anesthetic agent was administered. Controlled mechanical pain stimuli were administered simultaneously to treated and untreated fingers for one group of participants and sequentially for another. For both groups, a reduction in pain occurred only on the finger that was treated with the placebo anesthetic, thereby indicating a highly specific mechanism. This result suggests that not all placebos are mediated by global mechanisms such as anxiety reduction or endogenous release of opioid hormones. Such specificity in response would be consistent with a highly specific response expectancy on the part of the participant (Kirsch, 1990). Other aspects of their results include the finding that the effects were relatively small (about 12%–15%) and uniform across intensity and unpleasantness dimensions. The combined results indirectly suggest a second general mechanism for placebo analgesia: the development of a response bias.

This latter possibility has been tested more directly using signal-detection theory. Clark (1969) demonstrated that the administration of a placebo described as a strong analgesic increased the criterion for labeling a stimulus intensity as painful (also considered a measure of response bias) without changing the capacity to distinguish among different levels of painful stimulus intensity. Unfortunately, we know of no other studies of placebo analgesia that have a bearing on the possibility that placebo analgesia is mediated by response bias. Nevertheless, such a possibility is consistent with but not confirmatory of the hypothesis that placebo analgesic responses are mediated by the development of a highly specific response expectancy. Kirsch (1997) has provided the alternative explanation that response expectancies, defined as the anticipation of nonvolitional responses, are capable of eliciting the expected response in much the same way that intentions elicit voluntary behaviors (cf. Ajzen & Fishbein, 1980). However, it is not clear how Kirsch's proposal differs from the hypothesis that specific expectations and desires lead to the development of a response bias or perceptual bias.

Compliance with demand characteristics of the experimental or clinical situation can also be conceptualized as a type of response bias that could mediate apparent placebo analgesic responses. In such cases, patient-participants would reduce their ratings of pain after a placebo treatment in response to both their desire to please the person administering the treatment and their expectation that reduction of pain ratings would do so.

Desire for and Expectations of Pain Relief Trigger Descending Control of Pain Signals

The possibility for this mechanism is indicated by some evidence that placebo analgesia is mediated physiologically by endogenous opioid systems.

Although still somewhat controversial, the evidence consists of demonstrations that placebo-induced reductions in experimental and clinical pain can be reversed or antagonized by naloxone, an opioid antagonist (Grevert et al., 1983; Levine et al., 1978, 1979). If the desire for and expectations of pain relief are both necessary for placebo analgesia and if placebo effects are mediated physiologically by endogenous opioid control systems, then brain states associated with such desires and expectations may be sufficient to trigger opioid descending control systems. If so, then the reduction in pain would represent a true antinociceptive effect (i.e., a reduction in the ascending signal for pain) and not just a production of a response bias or a general selective change in affective state. Moreover, the reduction would occur in both the sensory and affective dimensions of pain because it is known that descending modulatory effects on pain reduce both of these dimensions and not just pain affect (see Fields & Basbaum, 1994; Fields & Price, 1996; and Price, 1988, for reviews).

These three general mechanisms (i.e., a direct change in affective state, response bias, and activation of descending control mechanisms) all share the common idea that desire and expectation are proximate psychological mediators of pain-related affect or placebo-induced pain reduction (or at least reports of pain reduction). However, from the foregoing discussion, it is apparent that desires and expectations may be targeted toward different responses or aspects of future experience. Thus, the desire and expectation may be focused on the avoidance of negative consequences associated with the pain condition, on the avoidance of the pain sensation itself, or even on the avoidance of disappointing the person who administers the therapeutic agent.

The possibility must be considered that there are multiple types of responses to placebo analgesic manipulations because of multiple types of desires and expectations that can be developed. Clearly, different desires and expectations could be induced in participants of studies by the way placebo suggestions are framed, and even the same placebo instructions could lead some people to desire and expect reductions in unpleasantness and others to desire and expect reductions in both pain sensation intensity and unpleasantness. Furthermore, some people may expect global changes, whereas others may expect highly specific locations or types of therapeutic effects and still others may simply desire and expect to please the person administering the therapeutic agent. This diversity in the types of placebo responses is indirectly supported by studies of hypnotic analgesia in which these same general possibilities were proposed to explain variations in changes in pain reports and behavior after hypnotic analgesic interventions (Barber & Adrian, 1982; Kiernan, Dane, Phillips, & Price, 1995; Price & Barber, 1987).

Despite the potential diversity in the types of desires and expectations that may mediate different types of placebo responses, the desire–

expectation model may provide the most parsimonious model of factors that mediate placebo responses. It may partly account for the diversity in the types of emotional, perceptual, and behavioral responses to placebo manipulations. Indeed, the multiplicative desire–expectation model that has been established for human emotions can be related to Expectancy × Value theories (Rotter, 1954, 1966, 1972; Tolman, 1955). To the extent that one can conceptualize placebo responses in terms of changes in emotions, changes in the tendency to respond, or learned changes in pain responsiveness, the potential application of a desire–expectancy model to all of these possible variants of placebo analgesic response appears promising and testable.

IMPLICATIONS OF THE DESIRE–EXPECTATION MODEL FOR FUTURE PAIN RESEARCH AND TREATMENT

We have suggested that desire and expectation are integral components of many common human emotions and that human emotional feelings are in turn integral components of pain experience. We have also suggested that the desire for and expectations of pain relief may be proximate mediators of placebo analgesia and have indicated some general psychological mechanisms through which these two factors could exert their influence. This analysis of potential mechanisms brings us to considerations about how the desire–expectation model could be applied in studies of pain and placebo analgesia in general and in studies that attempt to distinguish their psychological mechanisms in particular. A strategy could be developed in which the measurement of desire for pain relief and expectations of pain relief could be interfaced with measurements of the multiple dimensions of pain. Such a strategy could provide a means of determining the extent to which the desire for pain relief or expectations of pain relief or both account for changes in sensory-intensive or affective components of pain after a placebo manipulation. One could, for example, determine whether an additive or multiplicative model of the desire–expectation interaction accounts for more of the variance in placebo responses (Price & Fields, 1997a). The question of whether an additive or multiplicative model of these factors best accounts for the variance in placebo effects is both testable and heuristic. If critical levels of both desire and expectation are necessary for placebo effects and if these factors interact to an extent that is much greater than that predicted by the sum of their values, then a multiplicative model could apply. It would be interesting if a desire–expectation model shown to be applicable to human emotions would also apply to placebo effects. The nature of this interactive effect of desire and expectation on placebo responses might also differ according to whether the participant's desired therapeutic effect represents an avoidance or approach goal, similar to human emotions. Thus, the effects of placebo on the usual type of desire for pain relief and avoidance of further pain may require higher levels of expectation than that required for placebo effects associated with a general desire to reduce pain to achieve better health, an approach goal.

So far, the means of demonstrating the effects of conditioning or expectation on placebo analgesia has been to provide explicit instructions or experimental manipulations intended to increase a patient's expectation that a treatment will produce pain relief. However, in all such studies, the manipulations themselves constitute the independent variables of the experiment. Measures of expectation or motivation have been used to determine whether the manipulations were effective, not as independent variables themselves. Nash and Zimring's (1969) study, which focused on memory but not pain, showed significant correlations between placebo effects and expectation ratings. We do not know of anyone who has reported using direct rating or questionnaire response measures of either desire or expectation as independent variables in a study of placebo analgesia. However, if these two factors mediate placebo analgesia, then it should be possible to measure and assign them as independent variables in placebo studies.

Just as there are multiple psychological dimensions or factors that contribute to placebo responses, the placebo responses themselves are likely to be composed of multiple dimensions. Pain has both a sensory-discriminative and an affective-motivational dimension. The strategy discussed earlier for characterizing the critical psychological factors that mediate placebo analgesia could be interfaced with one that assesses how these factors influence the different dimensions of pain. The potential strength of this strategy requires that accurate, sensitive, and valid methods of pain measurement be used. This may be accomplished by using pain measurement methods that fulfill criteria for ideal pain measurement (Gracely & Dubner, 1981; Price, 1988). Direct magnitude scaling of sensory and affective dimensions of pain would seem essential, especially if placebo effects differentially influence these two dimensions. The use of more sophisticated scaling methods would obviate many of the deficiencies of category and other assessment methods as they relate to the assessment of placebo effects. This approach, in which desire and expectancy and multiple dimensions of pain are measured, could be used to further characterize the various psychological mechanisms of pain-related affect and placebo analgesia. For example, the mechanisms by which desire and expectation mediate placebo analgesia could be determined by whether the effects of the placebo manipulation were selective for the affective dimension of pain, whether the effects were that of production of a response bias (signal-detection theory), or whether the effects resulted from a decrement in the strength of the pain signal itself. The latter mechanism could be confirmed or ruled out by providing a measure of the early processing of the pain signal, such as that provided by simultaneous measurement of electrically evoked pain and nociceptive spinal reflexes. If both are simultaneously reduced by a placebo treatment, then evidence is provided for a reduction in the pain signal at the early stages of processing. This specific approach has proved useful in demonstrating that hypnotic analgesia works in part by diminishing the strength of the sensory signal for pain (Kiernan et al., 1995).

The possibility of a refined analysis of placebo effects within studies has far-reaching scientific and medical implications (Price & Fields, 1997b; Wall, 1994). Researchers' present limited capacity to ascertain, measure, and control for placebo effects is at the heart of complex and difficult questions about pharmacological therapies for pain as well as many non-pharmacological therapies, particularly those related to surgery, hypnosis, electrical stimulation, and "alternative medical treatments." If it is true that the magnitudes of the desire for and expectations of a specific therapeutic effect account for the large majority of the variance in the placebo effect, then measures of such factors could be incorporated into studies in which it is extremely difficult to provide a flawless placebo control treatment condition. In this way, their measurement in analgesia studies could serve as an important adjunct if not a substitute for questionable control treatment conditions. This possible improvement could be applied not only to studies of alternative treatments such as acupuncture but also to any study in which the active analgesic treatment can be subjectively distinguished from its placebo control. We think this improvement could apply to the vast majority of analgesic studies.

REFERENCES

Ajzen, I., & Fishbein, M. (1980). *Understanding attitudes and predicting social behavior.* Englewood Cliffs, NJ: Prentice Hall.

Baker, S. L., & Kirsch, I. (1991). Cognitive mediators of pain perception and tolerance. *Journal of Personality and Social Psychology, 61,* 504–510.

Barber, J., & Adrian, C. (1982). *Psychological approaches to the management of pain.* New York: Brunner/Mazel.

Baron, R. M., & Kenny, D. A. (1986). The moderator–mediator variable distinction in social psychological research: Conceptual, strategic, and statistical considerations. *Journal of Personality and Social Psychology, 51,* 1173–1182.

Barrell, J. J., Madieros, D., Barrell, J. E., & Price, D. D. (1985). Anxiety: An obstacle to performance. *Journal of Humanistic Psychology, 25,* 106–122.

Barrell, J. J., & Neimeyer, R. (1975). A mathematical formula for the psychological control of suffering. *Journal of Pastoral Counseling, 10*(17), 60–67.

Beecher, H. K. (1955). The powerful placebo. *Journal of the American Medical Association, 159,* 1602–1606.

Beecher, H. K. (1959). *Measurement of subjective responses: Quantitative effects of drugs*. New York: Oxford University Press.

Bootzin, R. R. (1985). The role of expectancy in behavior change. In L. White, B. Turskey, & G. E. Schwartz (Eds.), *Placebo: Theory, research, and mechanisms* (pp. 196–210). New York: Guilford Press.

Buytendyck, F. J. J. (1961). *Pain*. London: Hutchinson.

Clark, W. C. (1969). Sensory decision theory analysis of placebo effect on the criterion for pain and thermal sensitivity (d'). *Journal of Abnormal Psychology, 74*, 361–371.

de Jong, P. J., van Baast, R., Arntz, A., & Merkelbach, H. (1996). The placebo effect in pain reduction: The influence of conditioning experiences and response expectancies. *International Journal of Behavioral Medicine, 3*, 14–29.

Evans, F. J. (1985). Expectancy, therapeutic instructions, and the placebo response. In L. White, B. Turskey, & G. E. Schwartz (Eds.), *Placebo: Theory, research, and mechanisms* (pp. 215–228). New York: Guilford Press.

Fedele, L., Marchinin, M., Acaia, B., Garagiola, U., & Tiengo, M. (1989). Dynamics and significance of placebo response in primary dysmenorrhea. *Pain, 36*, 43–47.

Fernandez, E., & Turk, D. C. (1989). The utility of cognitive coping strategies for altering pain perception: A meta-analysis. *Pain, 38*, 123–135.

Fields, H. L., & Basbaum, A. I. (1994). Endogenous pain control mechanisms. In P. D. Wall & R. Melzack (Eds.), *Textbook of pain* (3rd ed., pp. 243–260). London: Churchill Livingston.

Fields, H. L., & Price, D. D. (1996). Toward a neurobiology of placebo analgesia. In A. Harrington (Ed.), *Placebo: Probing the self-healing brain* (pp. 93–116). Cambridge, MA: Harvard University Press.

Gracely, R. H. (1979). Psychophysical assessment of human pain. In J. J. Bonica, J. C. Liebeskind, & D. G. Albe-Fessard (Eds.), *Advances in pain research and therapy* (Vol. 3, pp. 805–824). New York: Raven Press.

Gracely, R. H., & Dubner, R. (1981). Pain assessment in humans—A reply to Hall. *Pain, 11*, 109–120.

Gracely, R. H., McGrath, P., & Dubner, R. (1976). Validity and sensitivity of ratio scales of sensory and affective verbal pain descriptors: Manipulation of affect by diazepam. *Pain, 2*, 19–29.

Grevert, P., Albert, L. H., & Goldstein, A. (1983). Partial antagonism of placebo analgesia by naloxone. *Pain, 16*, 129–143.

Grevert, P., & Goldstein, A. (1985). Placebo analgesia, naloxone, and the role of endogenous opioids. In L. White, B. Turskey, & G. E. Schwartz (Eds.), *Placebo: Theory, research, and mechanisms* (pp. 332–350). New York: Guilford Press.

Jensen, M. P., & Karoly, P. (1991). Motivation and expectancy factors in symptom perception: A laboratory study of the placebo effect. *Psychosomatic Medicine, 53*, 144–152.

Johnson, J. E. (1973). Effects of accurate expectations about sensations on the sensory and distress component of pain. *Journal of Personality and Social Psychology, 27,* 261–275.

Jospe, M. (1978). *The placebo effect in healing.* Lexington, MA: Lexington Books.

Kiernan, B. D., Dane, J. R., Phillips, L. H., & Price, D. D. (1995). Hypnotic analgesia reduces R-III nociceptive reflex: Further evidence concerning the multifactorial nature of hypnotic analgesia. *Pain, 60,* 39–47.

Kirsch, I. (1990). *Changing expectations: A key to effective psychotherapy.* Pacific Grove, CA: Brooks/Cole.

Kirsch, I. (1997). Expectancy and conditioning in placebo analgesia: Related or independent mechanisms? *Pain Forum, 6,* 57–58.

Korcyn, A. D. (1978). Mechanism of placebo analgesia. *Lancet, 2,* 1304–1305.

Lasagna, L., Laties, V. G., & Dohan, J. L. (1958). Further studies on the "pharmacology" of a placebo administration. *Journal of Clinical Investigation, 37,* 533–537.

Laska, E., & Sunshine, A. (1973). Anticipation of analgesia a placebo effect. *Headache, 1,* 1–11.

Levine, J. D., Gordon, N. C., Bornstein, J. C., & Fields, H. L. (1979). Role of pain in placebo analgesia. *Proceedings of the National Academy of Sciences, 76,* 3528–3531.

Levine, J. D., Gordon, N. C., & Fields, H. L. (1978). The mechanism of placebo analgesia. *Lancet, 2,* 654–657.

Melzack, R., & Casey, K. L. (1968). Sensory, motivational, and central control of determinants of pain. In D. R. Kenshalo (Ed.), *The skin senses* (pp. 423–439). Springfield, IL: Charles C Thomas.

Montgomery, G. H., & Kirsch, I. (1996). Mechanisms of placebo pain reduction: An empirical investigation. *Psychological Science, 7,* 174–176.

Montgomery, G. H., & Kirsch, I. (1997). Conditioned placebo effects: Stimulus substitution or expectancy change. *Pain, 72,* 107–113.

Mowrer, O. H. (1960). *Learning theory and behavior.* New York: Wiley.

Nash, N. N., & Zimring, F. M. (1969). Prediction of reaction to placebo. *Journal of Abnormal Psychology, 74,* 569–573.

Ohlwein, A. L., Stevens, M. J., & Catanzaro, S. J. (1996). Self-efficacy, response expectancy, and temporal context: Moderators of pain tolerance and intensity. *Imagination, Cognition, and Personality, 16,* 3–23.

Price, D. D. (1988). *Psychological and neural mechanisms of pain.* New York: Raven Press.

Price, D. D., & Barber, J. J. (1987). An analysis of factors that contribute to the efficacy of hypnotic analgesia. *Journal of Abnormal Psychology, 96,* 46–51.

Price, D. D., Barrell, J. E., & Barrell, J. J. (1985). A quantitative–experiential analysis of human emotions. *Motivation and Emotion, 9,* 19–38.

Price, D. D., & Barrell, J. J. (1980). An experiential approach with quantitative methods: A research paradigm. *Journal of Humanistic Psychology, 20,* 75–95.

Price, D. D., & Barrell, J. J. (1984). Some general laws of human emotion: Inter-relationships between intensities of desire, expectation, and emotional feeling. *Journal of Personality, 52,* 389–409.

Price, D. D., Barrell, J. J., & Gracely, R. H. (1980). A psychophysical analysis of experiential factors that selectively influence the affective dimension of pain. *Pain, 8,* 137–179.

Price, D. D., & Fields, H. L. (1997a). The contribution of desire and expectation to placebo analgesia: Implications for new research strategies. In A. Harrington (Ed.), *Placebo: Probing the self-healing brain* (pp. 117–137). Cambridge, MA: Harvard University Press.

Price, D. D., & Fields, H. L. (1997b). Where are the causes of placebo analgesia? An experiential behavioral analysis. *Pain Forum, 6,* 44–52.

Price, D. D., & Harkins, S. W. (1992). The affective–motivational dimension of pain: A two stage model. *Journal of the American Pain Society, 1,* 229–239.

Price, D. D., Harkins, S. W., & Baker, C. (1987). Sensory–affective relationships among different types of clinical pain and experimental pain. *Pain, 28,* 297–307.

Rainville, P., Feine, J. S., Bushnell, M. C., & Duncan, G. H. (1992). A psychophysical comparison of sensory and affective responses to four modalities of experimental pain. *Somatosensory and Motor Research, 9,* 265–277.

Reiss, S. (1980). Pavlovian conditioning and human fear: An expectancy model. *Behavior Therapy, 11,* 380–396.

Rescorla, R. A. (1988). Pavlovian conditioning: It's not what you think it is. *American Psychologist, 43,* 151–160.

Rotter, J. B. (1954). *Social learning: Clinical psychology.* Englewood Cliffs, NJ: Prentice Hall.

Rotter, J. B. (1966). Generalized expectancies for internal versus external control of reinforcement. *Psychological Monographs, 80*(1, Whole No. 609).

Rotter, J. B. (1972). *Applications of social learning theory of personality.* New York: Holt, Rinehart & Winston.

Tolman, E. C. (1955). Principles of performance. *Psychological Review, 62,* 315–326.

Voudouris, N. J., Peck, C. L., & Coleman, G. (1990). The role of conditioning and expectancy in the placebo response. *Pain, 43,* 121–128.

Wade, J. B., Dougherty, L. M., Archer, C. R., & Price, D. D. (1996). Assessing the stages of pain processing: A multivariate analysis. *Pain, 68,* 157–168.

Wade, J. B., Dougherty, L. M., Hart, R. P., Rafii, A., & Price, D. D. (1992). A canonical correlation analysis of the influence of neuroticism and extroversion on chronic pain, suffering, and pain behavior. *Pain, 51,* 67–74.

Wade, J. B., Price, D. D., & Hamer, R. M. (1990). An emotional component analysis of chronic pain. *Pain, 40,* 303–310.

Wall, P. D. (1994). The placebo and the placebo response. In P. D. Wall & R. Melzack (Eds.), *Textbook of pain* (pp. 1297–1308). London: Churchill Livingstone.

Watkins, L. R., & Mayer, D. J. (1982). Organization of endogenous opiate and nonopiate pain control systems. *Science, 216,* 1185–1192.

Wickramasekera, I. (1985). A conditioned response model of the placebo effect: Predictions from the model. In L. White, B. Turskey, & G. E. Schwartz (Eds.), *Placebo: Theory, research, and mechanisms* (pp. 255–287). New York: Guilford Press.

7

RESPONSE EXPECTANCY AND SEXUAL DYSFUNCTION IN WOMEN

EILEEN M. PALACE

Research on sexual arousal is not commensurate with knowledge of other emotional processes. Three decades of research have been directed at identifying the interrelations between cognitive and physiological response components in human emotion. Cognitive response includes subjective appraisals and expectancies about one's own subjective and physiological responses. Since Schachter and Singer's (1962) two-factor theory of emotion and Valins's (1966, 1967) reformulated cognitive theory, extensive research has been devoted to clarifying cognitive and physiological processes in the mediation of emotions such as fear and anxiety. In contrast, investigation of the relationship between cognitive and physiological processes in sexual arousal has just begun. Little is known about the basic mechanisms that mediate sexual arousal, and in particular, there is a notable discrepancy in the availability of medical and psychological research findings and interventions for women as compared with men. Treatment programs based on theoretical assumptions are widely used despite a lack of empirical knowledge of the mechanisms that control sexual response.

Researchers and clinicians require the ability to make valid and reliable diagnostic decisions and to develop effective interventions for preventing and alleviating sexual dysfunction based on empirically derived knowledge of the following fundamental question: What is sexual dysfunction? The difficulty with the identification or treatment of sexual dysfunction is based on limited knowledge of a more fundamental question: What is sexual function? Put another way, What are the differences that distinguish sexually functional and dysfunctional responses? This question may be asked more specifically as follows: What are the *components* that mediate sexual response and the *processes* in which these mechanisms mediate sexual arousal?

In this chapter, I address this question. Empirical knowledge of the key response components and how they interact to mediate sexual arousal (i.e., identification of the mechanisms and processes of sexual arousal) will allow researchers and clinicians to (a) define the construct of sexual arousal (i.e., what are the response components and how do they interact to comprise sexual arousal?); (b) differentiate sexual function and dysfunction (i.e., what are the differences in response components and how do they mediate different outcomes?); (c) identify an etiological model of sexual dysfunction (i.e., how do these mechanisms interact to reverse the process and yield a lack of response); (d) determine valid and reliable assessment methods (i.e., what tools can be used to identify these mechanisms and processes); and (e) develop effective, empirically based treatment methods for the alleviation of sexual dysfunction (i.e., how can these mechanisms be modified to reverse the dysfunctional process). Identification of these processes in sexual arousal has direct implications for identifying the nature of these processes in the mediation of other types of emotion processing.

In this chapter, I present (a) new empirical findings on cognitive and physiological response patterns and processes of sexual response in sexually functional and dysfunctional women; (b) a new empirically derived process model of mechanisms of sexual arousal; (c) an intervention that, from preliminary research, has been found to reverse dysfunctional processes; and (d) implications for new approaches to promote mental and physical sexual health for women.

COGNITIVE AND PHYSIOLOGICAL COMPONENTS OF SEXUAL RESPONSE

Three lines of research have provided insights to critical components of female sexual response. These focus on (a) identification of response components and patterns that differentiate sexually functional and dysfunctional women, (b) synchrony or concordance of these response components, and (c) comparison of general autonomic reactivity in sexually functional and dysfunctional women.

Cognitive and Physiological Differences in Sexually Functional and Dysfunctional Women

Palace and Gorzalka (1992) examined response components and patterns in sexually functional and dysfunctional women by comparing their physiological and cognitive sexual responses to a range of sexual stimuli.[1,2] Erotic stimulus conditions included (a) a silent black-and-white, "homemade-quality" videotape that showed a nude heterosexual couple engaging in foreplay; (b) a silent color videotape made for educational or therapeutic purposes that showed a nude heterosexual couple engaging in foreplay and intercourse; and (c) a commercially produced film designed for adult entertainment that showed an attractive heterosexual couple engaging in multiple sexual activities and positions. This videotape contained a wide range of sexual stimuli (e.g., color, sound, sexual activities, and verbal interactions).

Palace and Gorzalka (1992) found that sexually dysfunctional women exhibited less genital arousal than sexually functional women in all three erotic stimulus conditions within 30 s.[3] Furthermore, analyses of subjective ratings revealed that dysfunctional women consistently reported less sexual arousal and lower expectations about their ability to become aroused than sexually functional women during all three erotic stimulus conditions. These findings show that subjective or cognitive experience and physiological arousal (i.e., genital vasocongestion) are primary components of

---

[1]Sexual dysfunction in this program of research includes heterogeneous disturbances across the sexual response cycle: Sexual desire disorders are characterized by an absence or decline in interest in sexual activity with a mate or other partner, in sexual dreams and fantasies, and in reactions to people of the opposite and same sex. Sexual arousal disorders are characterized by an inability to achieve and maintain lubrication, vasocongestion, or other physiological signs of arousal or a decreased subjective sense of pleasure during sexual activity. Orgasm disorders include an absence of or delay in the ability to achieve orgasm. Sexual pain disorders include dyspareunia, or pain during intercourse that is not caused by insufficient lubrication, and vaginismus, an involuntary spasm of the musculature of the outer third of the vagina that makes penetration difficult or impossible.

[2]Physiological arousal in these studies was measured by a vaginal photoplethysmograph (Sintchak & Geer, 1975), which, when DC coupled, measures vaginal blood volume (VBV). The photoplethysmograph is a small acrylic, tampon-shaped device with a light-emitting diode and phototransistor. When inserted into the vagina, the phototransistor is affected by indirect light reflected back to the vaginal wall during changes in vasocongestion. VBV reflects location-specific changes in the direction, rate, and magnitude of vaginal blood flow during engorgement.

[3]Note that the system of data collection and reduction I developed for this program of research provided the first continuous digital measurement and graphic representation of VBV in women through direct analogue to digital transfer of 1/10,000 mV changes in VBV at 5 times/s across the entire stimulus. These 0.20-s samples are then reduced across groups to yield 5 means/s of VBV response (e.g., in this study, seventy-two hundred 0.20-s means across women). This system presents not a single case example of a polygraph record but a "continuous average" across sexually functional and dysfunctional women. It provides not only more highly refined analyses, but more important, also the first visual, nontheoretical graph of early stages of the sexual response cycle and the first graphic display of group differences in genital response lability. The new system is used for all data presented in this program of research, including those shown in Figures 7.1, 7.2, and 7.3.

sexual response that reliably discriminate dysfunctional from functional arousal patterns. Women with sexual dysfunctions exhibit significantly lower levels of genital and subjective arousal within 30 s of responding to sexual stimuli. Moreover, these women have more negative expectations about their ability to become aroused and more negative expectations about their body's appearance and ability to perform sexually.

Desynchrony of Cognitive and Physiological Sexual Response

Contrary to research findings with men (Heiman & Rowland, 1983; Rosen & Beck, 1988; Steinman, Wincze, Sakheim, Barlow, & Mavissakalian, 1981), genital and subjective responses are not necessarily concordant for women (Morokoff & Heiman, 1980; Palace & Gorzalka, 1990, 1992; Steinman et al., 1981; Wincze, Hoon, & Hoon, 1976). For men, there is a high degree of similarity between penile response and subjective ratings of how aroused they feel. For women, however, physical response and subject arousal are independent; that is, they may be feeling aroused but not have an accompanying physical response or experience vasocongestion and lubrication but not feel sexually interested. However, Sakheim, Barlow, Beck, and Abrahamson (1984) found that when sexually functional men watched erotic films while naked and with a board placed over their laps, like women, there was not a high correlation between subjective and physiological responses. This finding suggests that, for men, attention to erection facilitates further physiological arousal. Visual and tactile awareness of genital arousal provides important feedback for men's subjective appraisals of their sexual arousal. Because women have a less obvious physiological feedback system (e.g., vaginal vasocongestion vs. erection), some women may experience more difficulty attending to or labeling bodily cues, thereby yielding a discrepancy between subjective and physiological arousal. These factors may be compounded by socialization factors that further mediate women's attention to and acknowledgment of genital cues.

General Autonomic Differences in Sexually Functional and Dysfunctional Women

Data suggest (Palace & Gorzalka, 1990, 1992) that women with sexual dysfunctions display less *genital response lability* and less *general autonomic reactivity* to environmental stimuli. That is, not only do these women have less vaginal response to sexual stimuli, but they also demonstrate decreased general autonomic activity (e.g., heart rate, respiration, muscle activity) and decreased vaginal response to other types of environmental stimuli (e.g., anxiety-eliciting film stimuli and neutral film stimuli of scenes in Antarctica). It is almost as if the homeostatic balance for these women is lower or dampened, resulting in less autonomic and less vaginal reactivity to all types of external stimuli. Women with sexual dysfunctions are therefore not simply less attentive to bodily cues of sexual arousal, but they actually have less *general*, as well as *genital*, physiological response to which to attend. Of course, these findings do not necessarily infer a genetic etiology. Sociocultural scripts, expectations, and social learning for women may facilitate the unlearning or habituation of genital responsivity and alter autonomic arousability.

To summarize, findings from this program of research reveal that women with heterogeneous sexual dysfunctions show significantly (a) lower physiological (genital) response to sexual stimuli and less genital response lability to other types of environmental stimuli; (b) lower subjective ratings of sexual arousal and more negative expectations about their ability to become aroused; (c) less general autonomic reactivity to environmental stimuli; and (d) desynchrony between cognitive and physiological sexual response. These findings raise the next question: What are the processes by which these components interact to cause sexually functional or dysfunctional response, and how can it be modified?

COGNITIVE AND PHYSIOLOGICAL PROCESSES THAT MEDIATE SEXUAL RESPONSE

Physiological Mechanisms and the Role of Increased Autonomic Arousal

To increase physiological sexual response, researchers have examined the effects of increasing general autonomic arousal (e.g., heart rate, respiration, muscle activity) through anxiety-eliciting films (Palace & Gorzalka, 1990). Leading researchers in the area (e.g., Kaplan, 1974, 1988; Masters & Johnson, 1970; Wolpe, 1958, 1982) claim that anxiety, characterized by sympathetic nervous system (SNS) activation, causes sexual dysfunction by disrupting parasympathetic nervous system functioning. Wolpe (1982) concluded that sexual arousal and anxiety are incompatible, reciprocally inhibitory responses. Barlow (1986, 1988) proposed a model based on research with men that suggested that for dysfunctional men and women, anxiety inhibits sexual arousal by facilitating the efficiency with which they distract themselves from sexual stimuli by focusing on nonerotic cues. On the basis of these assumptions, anxiety-reducing and relaxation techniques, presumed to enhance sexual arousal by decreasing SNS response, are widely used in the treatment of sexually dysfunctional men and women. However, the autonomic processes that control sexual response in women are unknown (Schneiden & Rees, 1985).

Research findings challenge traditional assumptions about the role of anxiety and demonstrate that for sexually functional men and women, anxiety has a facilitatory effect on sexual arousal. In studies with men, anxiety has been operationally defined as crossing a fear-arousing suspension bridge (Dutton & Aron, 1974), viewing an anxiety-evoking film segment (Wolchik et al., 1980), receiving the threat of a shock contingent on the size of erection (Barlow, Sakheim, & Beck, 1983), and receiving performance demand instructions to self-monitor and maintain an erection (Heiman & Rowland, 1983). All of these anxiety-arousing manipulations enhanced genital sexual arousal. Similarly, P. W. Hoon, Wincze, and Hoon (1977b) demonstrated that sexual arousal is enhanced in sexually functional women when they are exposed to an anxiety-evoking rather than relaxation-inducing film stimulus before exposure to sexual stimuli. Until recently, the effects of anxiety arousal on sexual responding had not been tested with dysfunctional women.

Figure 7.1 shows the physiological data for Palace and Gorzalka's (1990) study for sexually functional and dysfunctional women across the last 80 s of a neutral or anxiety-eliciting preexposure stimulus followed by 180 s of an erotic stimulus. Note that the anxiety-eliciting films were action-adventure content and were piloted to ensure that they elicited significant increases in autonomic arousal (i.e., both physiological and subjective increases in heart rate, respiration, and muscle activity). They contained no violent or sexual material and had female character leads.

As can be seen in Figure 7.1, anxiety preexposure significantly enhanced the rate and magnitude of genital arousal for both sexually functional and dysfunctional women. This effect was consistent across 100% of a heterogeneous sample of sexually dysfunctional women that included women who were experiencing low desire, low arousal, primary and secondary inorgasmia, and dyspareunia, and 2 women with a history of sexual abuse.

Contrary to the etiological assumptions of more than 30 years that anxiety inhibits sexual response, these findings provide evidence that autonomic control of sexual arousal may involve primarily *sympathetic* (as opposed to parasympathetic) activation, and that some of Masters and Johnson's (1970) traditional assumptions and widely used anxiety-reduction techniques may be counterproductive to eliciting sexual arousal. These findings suggest an alternate explanation for the effects of anxiety: Anxiety (increased autonomic arousal) may enhance sexual arousal because of generalized sympathetic activation, which directly provides a "jump start" or preparedness for sexual arousal. When sexual cues are provided, this enhanced SNS response activates specific genital responses. For those women whose general autonomic reactivity is low, SNS activation provides a means of physiological preparedness that serves to facilitate genital response. It is as though the homeostatic balance for these women is "cranked up" by the autonomic jump start; so that when sexual cues are present, it is easier for them to respond.

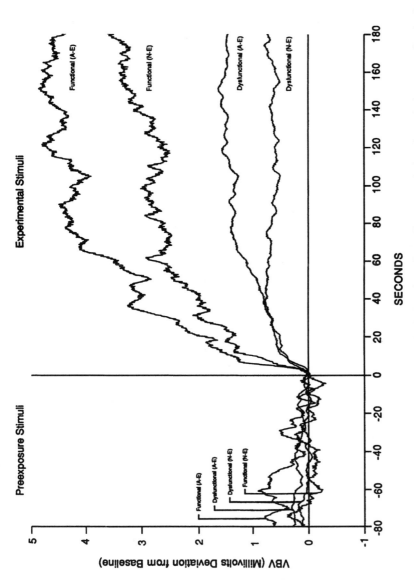

Figure 7.1. Mean vaginal blood volume (VBV) in millivolts deviation from baseline for sexually dysfunctional and functional women during anxiety-erotic (A-E) and neutral-erotic (N-E) conditions. Continuous VBV response is shown by thirteen hundred 0.20-s means across women for each group (5,200 means). From "The Enhancing Effects of Anxiety on Arousal in Sexually Dysfunctional and Functional Women," by E. M. Palace and B. B. Gorzalka, 1990, *Journal of Abnormal Psychology, 99,* p. 407. Copyright 1990 by the American Psychological Association. Reprinted with permission.

It is important to clarify that it is not anxiety itself that is the active component in enhancing sexual arousal. Rather, increased general autonomic arousal (i.e., increased heart rate, respiration, muscle activity) characteristic of SNS activation is the active mechanism in the autonomic control of sexual response (Palace, 1995a, 1995b, 1996; Palace & Gorzalka, 1990). Anxiety was used to elicit sympathetic activity in these studies, but it can be elicited by other means such as laughter, anger, and bicycle riding. I use the terms *increased autonomic arousal* and *sympathetic activation* interchangeably in this chapter to refer to the general physiological increase in heart rate, respiration, and muscle activity elicited by these films.

Cognitive Mechanisms and the Role of Genital Feedback

Recall that women with sexual dysfunctions have lower physiological responses and more negative cognitions (i.e., lower expectations about their ability to become aroused and lower perceived arousal) than sexually functional women. Increasing general autonomic arousal was an effective technique to address the low physiological genital component (Palace & Gorzalka, 1990). To increase the response expectancy component, Palace (1995b) used the false feedback paradigm from emotion theory research. Traditionally, false feedback has been used to induce research participants to infer that they have responded physiologically in a manner contrary to their expectations. In this case, women were shown a false polygraph chart of their vaginal blood volume (VBV) responses that depicted a large increase in sexual response during an erotic stimulus (i.e., inaccurate feedback of a heightened genital response). I refer to this intervention as *positive-false feedback*.

Palace's (1995b) study was designed to answer a series of questions that would identify the processes and mechanisms by which cognitive and physiological components interact to mediate sexual arousal and can be modified to reverse dysfunctional processes. Taken together, the findings suggest that the interaction between a physiological tendency for low autonomic response and negative response expectancy produce a negative feedback loop of dysfunctional sexual response. Accordingly, strategies to enhance physiological response via increasing general autonomic arousal (autonomic arousal-eliciting films) and to modify negative cognitions via false feedback of a heightened genital response (positive-false feedback) may reverse the negative dysfunctional cycle and initiate a positive cognitive–physiological feedback loop of sexual arousal. Answers to each of six empirical questions would map, in a linear progression, the cognitive–physiological process:

1. Does increased autonomic arousal enhance physiological sexual arousal?

2. Does positive-false VBV feedback modify response expectancies of sexual arousal?

3. Does positive-false VBV feedback modify actual physiological sexual response?

4. If expectations are modified, how do they affect actual physiological sexual response?

5. Does positive-false VBV feedback modify the subsequent subjective experience of sexual arousal?

6. What are the combined effects of increased autonomic arousal and positive-false VBV feedback on cognitive and physiological sexual response?

To investigate these questions, Palace (1995b) compared the physiological and subjective responses of 64 women with sexual dysfunctions in four conditions: an autonomic arousal-evoking or neutral-control pre-exposure videotape stimulus paired with an erotic videotape stimulus (autonomic arousal-erotic [A-E] or neutral-erotic [N-E]) and positive-false VBV feedback or no feedback. Subjective measures of arousal were assessed after each of two erotic stimulus conditions and the feedback conditions.

The results of Palace's (1995b) study answered each of the six questions that map the cognitive–physiological process. First, it provided two between-groups replications of Palace and Gorzalka's (1990) within-subjects finding that for women with sexual dysfunctions, increased autonomic arousal enhances genital arousal (see Figure 7.2, Stimulus Series 1). Second, positive-false feedback of genital vasocongestion increased expectations of sexual arousal. Third, positive-false feedback increased actual genital response (see Figure 7.2, Stimulus Series 2). This effect was consistent across 100% of the women in the false feedback conditions. Fourth, and most interesting, a direct positive feedback loop of sexual arousal was found, in which women who significantly increased their expectations of sexual arousal after false feedback directly increased their actual genital response within 30 s. That is, cognitive change directly influenced physical change. For more than 50% of the women whose expectations increased, they increased their physiological response to match the "false" feedback. Fifth, positive-false VBV feedback further increased the subsequent subjective experience of sexual arousal (i.e., perceived physiological change further increased subsequent cognitions about how aroused they felt). Finally, increased autonomic arousal combined with false feedback interacted to elicit the greatest increase in expectations and actual genital response. In both cases, the responses of the dysfunctional women in this group became comparable to those of sexually functional women within 3 min. Note that this effect was found for a heterogeneous group of women with sexual dysfunctions that included desire, arousal, and orgasm phase disorders and coital pain disorders.

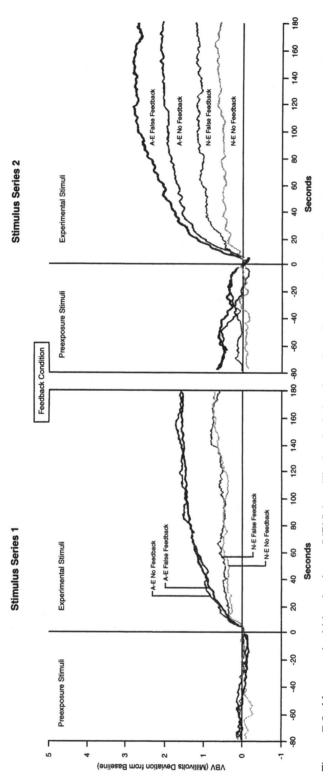

Figure 7.2. Mean vaginal blood volume (VBV) in millivolts deviation from baseline sampled at 5 times/s for matched groups of sexually dysfunctional women during autonomic arousal-erotic (A-E) or neutral-erotic (N-E) stimuli at Stimulus Series 1 (before) and Stimulus Series 2 (after) positive-false VBV feedback or no feedback. Continuous VBV response is shown by thirteen hundred 0.20-s means across women for each group (10,400 means). From "Modification of Dysfunctional Patterns of Sexual Response Through Autonomic Arousal and False Physiological Feedback," by E. M. Palace, 1995b, *Journal of Consulting and Clinical Psychology, 63,* p. 610. Copyright 1995 by the American Psychological Association. Reprinted with permission.

Although highly effective, the use of positive-false feedback is restricted to laboratory analog research and requires the use of deception. Research was needed to identify techniques to provide feedback to alter negative expectations in clinical practice and to assess the durability and generalizability of the effects. The most obvious solution was to examine the effects of accurate feedback, or biofeedback, of genital responses.

Biofeedback of vaginal vasocongestion has not been found to be an effective technique to increase sexual arousal (E. F. Hoon, 1980; P. W. Hoon, Wincze, & Hoon, 1977a). Research findings suggest that sexually functional women can exert voluntary control of vaginal vasocongestion (Cerny, 1978; E. F. Hoon, 1980) but that biofeedback alone does not facilitate genital or subjective sexual arousal (Cerny, 1978; E. F. Hoon, 1980; P. W. Hoon et al., 1977a). This finding is not surprising given that accurate feedback of a low sexual response validates negative expectations and thereby strengthens dysfunctional responses. However, because autonomic arousal increases genital responses (Palace, 1995b; Palace & Gorzalka, 1990), increased autonomic arousal *paired* with biofeedback should increase physiological response and give women *positive-accurate* and reinforcing feedback. To replace false feedback with accurate biofeedback for the purposes of clinical intervention, this hypothesis was tested by Palace (1996).

Palace's (1996) study was designed to (a) examine the effects of VBV biofeedback (vs. false feedback) combined with autonomic arousal in increasing sexual arousal and reversing the dysfunction process; (b) complete the mapping of the cognitive–physiological feedback loop by identifying, in a linear progression, the relation between cognitive and physiological processes in sexual arousal over repeated trials; and (c) assess the durability and effectiveness of this new technique over time.

Palace (1996) compared women with sexual dysfunctions in three conditions: accurate VBV feedback (biofeedback), positive-false feedback, or no feedback, each paired with autonomic arousal. Autonomic arousal-eliciting stimuli consisted of three matched and counterbalanced films that depicted impending danger and were found in pilot studies to increase general autonomic activity. Participants were shown four 6-min stimulus series: a 3-min neutral stimulus followed by a 3-min sexually arousing stimulus (N-E) and three 3-min autonomic arousal-eliciting stimuli followed by a 3-min sexual arousing stimulus (A-E1, A-E2, and A-E3). As seen in Figure 7.3, during Session 1 (N-E) the neutral stimulus was followed by an erotic stimulus to provide a baseline measure of sexual response. During Session 2, the autonomic arousal stimulus was followed by an erotic stimulus to compare the effects of adding the physiological treatment component (autonomic arousal). Following A-E1, feedback was added to compare the effects of adding the cognitive treatment component (feedback). A-E2 and A-E3 were added to compare the additive effects of these combined techniques over time and to trace the feedback loop of physiological

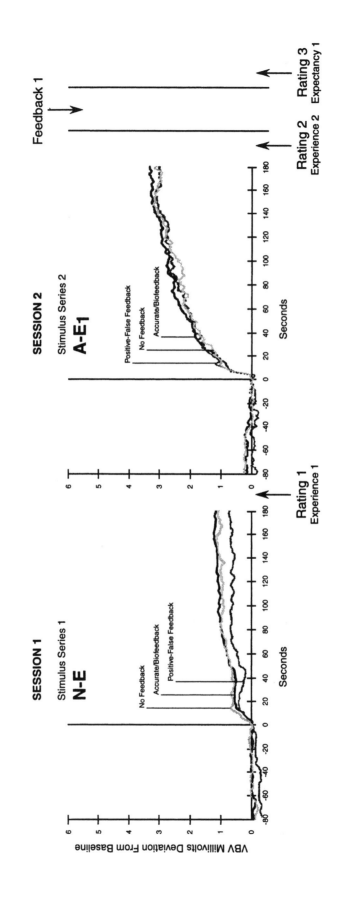

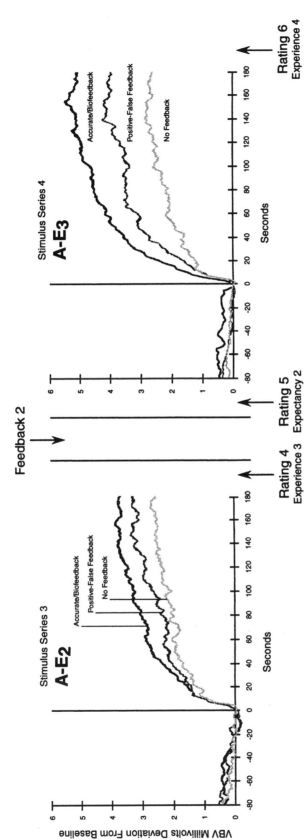

Figure 7.3. Mean vaginal blood volume (VBV) in millivolts deviation from baseline sampled at 5 times/s for matched groups of sexually dysfunctional women during four stimulus series: a neutral-erotic (N-E) stimulus and three autonomic arousal-erotic stimuli (A-E1, A-E2, and A-E3) for the accurate feedback (biofeedback), positive-false VBV feedback, and no-feedback groups. Continuous VBV response is shown by thirteen hundred 0.20-second means across women for each group (15,600 means). From "A New Model and Treatment Approach for Sexual Arousal and Response in Women," by E. M. Palace, 1996.

change on cognitive response as well as cognitive change on subsequent physiological response. Note that after the erotic stimulus, participants rated their sexual arousal, received feedback, and rated their expected arousal to the next presentation. This sequence occurred four times, that is, each participant saw the stimulus combination four times and rated not only their experience of arousal but also their expectancy about their subsequent ability to become aroused across all four stimulus conditions.

Figure 7.3 shows the results of all four stimulus series in order to compare groups across time as the physiological and cognitive techniques are added. Comparison of N-E and A-E1 shows the dramatic effect of autonomic arousal in increasing sexual arousal across all three groups within 30 s. Note that this is the sixth time I have replicated the finding of autonomic arousal increasing sexual arousal. A-E2 shows the effect of adding the feedback conditions: After the first round of feedback, notice that the groups begin to split, with the no-feedback group remaining at the same level, the positive-false feedback and the biofeedback groups significantly increasing, and the biofeedback group showing the greatest change. After the second round of feedback and the third autonomic arousal stimulus (A-E3), again notice that the groups continue to diverge in the same pattern, with the no-feedback group remaining at the same level and the false feedback and biofeedback groups showing the greatest change. When combined with automatic arousal, VBV biofeedback was more effective than positive-false feedback in enhancing cognitive and physiological sexual responses. Autonomic arousal combined with biofeedback increased genital and subjective arousal to levels comparable to sexually functional women within 3 min. This effectiveness of autonomic arousal combined with biofeedback was also durable. This technique showed significantly increased effectiveness in enhancing sexual arousal across three sequential trials of erotic stimuli. That is, increased autonomic arousal combined with VBV biofeedback significantly increased in a positive spiral: physiological sexual response, expectations of sexual arousal, subsequent genital response, the subjective experience of sexual arousal, future expectations of sexual arousal, subsequent physiological response, and subsequent experience, to levels comparable to sexually functional women within 3 min. These levels of physiological arousal and subjectively rated arousal and expectancy continued to increase throughout the duration of the trials.

Identification of the response components of sexual arousal and the mechanisms by which these components interact to mediate sexual arousal has multifaceted etiological and treatment implications for women's health. First, these findings identify mechanisms by which cognitive and physiological response components mediate sexual arousal and provide an empirically derived mapping of cognitive–physiological processes of arousal. Second, this has major implications for developing a new cognitive–

physiological treatment approach for sexual dysfunction. Third, and more broadly, the model has implications for understanding mind–body linkages in emotion processing. Finally, the model has implications for new behavioral medicine approaches to treatment, in which changes in cognitions and behavior are used to change physical problems and improve mental and physical health for women.

A COGNITIVE–PHYSIOLOGICAL PROCESS MODEL OF SEXUAL AROUSAL AND RESPONSE

The findings from this program of research provide a process model of the cognitive–physiological pathway for sexual response in women. It provides a mapping of cognitive–physiological processes of arousal and identifies mechanisms by which cognitive and physiological response components form an interactive feedback loop to mediate sexual arousal.

Sexual dysfunction may be explained as the interaction between a physiological tendency for low autonomic response and negative cognitive expectancy, which produce a negative feedback loop of dysfunctional sexual responses. A process flow between bodily symptoms and subjective reactions to these symptoms occurs when low physiological response (e.g., less general and genital physiological response) decreases subjective expectations of sexual arousal and, reciprocally, low expectations (e.g., lack of awareness, attention, or misinterpretation of physical cues) further inhibit physiological response. This negative feedback loop between low physiological response and negative expectations produces a learning curve that exacerbates a cognitive predisposition, a physiological predisposition, or both and reciprocally facilitates the habituation and extinction of sexual arousal and response. Accordingly, enhancing physiological response through increasing general autonomic arousal and changing negative expectancy via genital feedback of a new higher response provides both the physical jump start and the subsequent visual verification to reverse the negative dysfunction cycle and initiate a positive cognitive–physiological feedback loop of sexual arousal.

The process model of sexual arousal is an *additive model*, not a compensatory model in which increasing the cognitive intervention can replace the physiological. Rather, optimal sexual functioning results from the summation of these cognitive and physiological techniques. To demonstrate this, I review the effects of the cognitive and physiological components as they were progressively added in the program of research. In a constructive treatment strategy approach, each consecutive study has replicated each previous finding before adding a new component. A process flow diagram (see Figure 7.4) of the effects of each treatment component on cognitive and physiological response is provided that shows the results of the empirical findings (Palace, 1995a, 1995b, 1996; Palace & Gorzalka, 1990, 1992).

Autonomic arousal alone is highly effective in enhancing subsequent physiological sexual response. Figure 7.4a shows a process flow diagram of the results for sympathetic activation alone (A-E no feedback group; Palace, 1995b). This enhancing effect of autonomic arousal on sexual arousal has been replicated six times in this program (Palace, 1995b, 1996; Palace & Gorzalka, 1990) using both within-subjects and between-subjects designs and across heterogeneous samples of women with sexual dysfunctions including desire, arousal, and orgasm phase disorders; coital pain disorders; and histories of sexual abuse. Interestingly, autonomic arousal was also successful in increasing expectations of sexual arousal. It was not, however, immediately effective in increasing subsequent genital responses or perceptions of sexual arousal. This is because autonomic arousal without genital feedback cannot provide information to reinforce attention to and correct labeling of these new genital sensations. In this way, the polygraph chart showing a high vaginal vasocongestive response is similar to the information provided to men by seeing erection. Without this information, women in the no-feedback groups lacked the reinforcement provided by visual verification that they had responded physically and labeled their sensations accurately. This study provides evidence that for both women and men (Sakheim et al., 1984), visual attention to vasocongestion elicits significantly greater physiological and subjective sexual arousal. The additive function of feedback is therefore to provide information that both facilitates and reinforces positive labeling of genital responses elicited by autonomic arousal.

Positive-false feedback increases expectations of sexual arousal and in turn directly increases actual physiological responses and subjective perceptions. Figure 7.4b shows a process flow diagram of the results for positive-false feedback alone (N-E false feedback group; Palace, 1995b). This pathway between cognition and physiological responses is extremely rapid, as demonstrated by the finding that irrespective of stimulus condition, positive changes in expectation were accompanied by significant increases in genital responses within 30 s of exposure to an erotic stimulus (Palace, 1995b, 1996). If accurate feedback were provided to sexually dysfunctional women without sympathetic activation, however, low physiological response would exacerbate the dysfunctional processes by validating negative expectations. Sympathetic activation is therefore important because, by increasing genital responses, positive-false feedback can be replaced by positive-true feedback (i.e., accurate feedback of a heightened response).

The combined effects of autonomic arousal and positive-false VBV feedback surpass the effects of either autonomic arousal or false feedback alone. Figure 7.4c shows a process flow diagram of the results for combining sympathetic activation and positive-false feedback (A-E false feedback

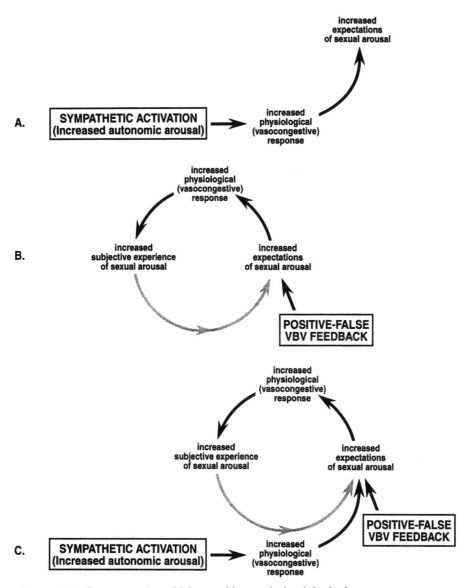

Figure 7.4. Processes by which cognitive and physiological response components interact to mediate sexual arousal. Process flow diagrams show the results for each condition in Palace's (1995b) study. a: Process by which increased autonomic arousal enhances sexual arousal (autonomic arousal-erotic [A-E], no-feedback group). b: Process by which positive-false vaginal blood volume (VBV) feedback enhances sexual arousal (neutral-erotic [N-E], false-feedback group). c: Process by which autonomic arousal combined with false VBV feedback (A-E, false-feedback group [indicated in bold]) reverses the dysfunctional process and initiates a positive feedback loop of sexual arousal. From "A Cognitive–Physiological Process Model of Sexual Arousal and Response," by E. M. Palace, 1995a, *Clinical Psychology: Science and Practice, 2,* 378. Copyright 1995 by the American Psychological Association. Reprinted with permission.

group; Palace, 1995b). Women in the A-E false feedback group (Palace, 1995b) demonstrated an increase in physiological sexual responses, a positive change in expectations, and subsequently a further increase in genital responses. Note that within 3 min of exposure to an erotic stimulus, these sexually dysfunctional women achieved levels of genital arousal comparable to sexually functional women.

Palace's (1996) study demonstrates that, when paired with sympathetic activation, accurate feedback replaces the usefulness of false feedback and in fact surpasses its effects. Figure 7.5 shows a process flow diagram of the results for combining sympathetic activation and biofeedback (the accurate/biofeedback group; Palace, 1996). Most importantly, Figure 7.5 shows the completed cognitive–physiological process flow model of sexual arousal and responses for women. This figure is a diagram of the data presented in Figure 7.3 (Palace, 1996) and the findings replicated in stepwise progression in this program of research (Palace, 1995a, 1995b, 1996; Palace & Gorzalka, 1990, 1992). The combination of physiologically based intervention to enhance autonomic arousal, and a cognitively based interven-

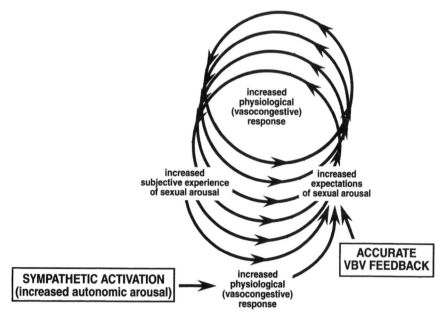

Figure 7.5. A cognitive–physiological process model of sexual arousal and response. Process flow diagram shows the empirical results of Palace's (1996, Figure 3) study and the cumulative findings replicated across studies in the program of research (Palace, 1995a, 1995b, 1996; Palace & Gorzalka, 1990, 1992). The process by which increased autonomic arousal combined with accurate vaginal blood volume (VBV) feedback reverses the dysfunction process and initiates a positive feedback loop of sexual arousal. From "A New Model and Treatment Approach for Sexual Arousal and Response in Women," by E. M. Palace, 1996.

tion to change expectancies and facilitate labeling of actual genital cues, was the most effective and durable method of modifying dysfunctional responses. Increased autonomic arousal combined with VBV biofeedback significantly increased in a linear progression (a) physiological (vasocongestive) sexual response, (b) expectations of sexual arousal, (c) subsequent genital response, (d) the subjective experience of sexual arousal, (e) future expectations of sexual arousal, (f) physiological response (for the third time), and (g) subsequent experience to levels comparable to sexually functional women within 3 min. This is faster than what the newest drugs can do for men. Notice also that this effect is durable: The cognitive–physiological process is empirically traced twice around the feedback loop and shows an upwardly increasing spiral of heightened sexual arousal.

A COGNITIVE–PHYSIOLOGICAL TREATMENT FOR DYSFUNCTIONAL SEXUAL RESPONSE

The cognitive–physiological model of arousal identifies mechanisms that prevent, and therefore may be modified to produce, sexual health for women. Specifically, strategies directed at enhancing physiological response and modifying negative cognitions via the pairing of autonomic arousal and genital feedback may reverse the dysfunctional cycle and initiate a positive cognitive–physiological feedback loop of sexual arousal.

Research provides support for the view that autonomic arousal-eliciting stimuli facilitate sexual arousal through the direct instigation of generalized SNS activation. When sexual stimuli are subsequently present, this enhanced autonomic reactivity activates specific genital responses. A. T. Beck (cited in Marmor, 1987) pointed out that when individuals are in a heightened state of affective arousal, they are more susceptible to therapeutic intervention. He argued that the most effective techniques of cognitive and behavior therapy involve arousing anxiety to achieve an increased state of reactivity. In other words, increased autonomic arousal may facilitate the acquisition of a learned response. For women with sexual dysfunctions, it may be that increasing autonomic responsivity therefore not only increases the capacity for heightened genital response but that it also facilitates learning and thereby a more rapid extinction of conditioned negative response patterns. Feedback of genital vasocongestion provides observable and positive physical cues to validate and reinforce the experience elicited by autonomic arousal. In other words, it is the combined effects of jump starting physical response and providing feedback for cognitive awareness of that change that increases genital and subjective response.

A new cognitive–physiological treatment approach for sexual dysfunction consists of strategies to increase genital responses through increased autonomic arousal through physical activity or exercise (Palace & Gorzalka, 1990) combined with strategies to increase cognitive expectancy through genital biofeedback. This technique uses the feedback loop by providing an initial jump start or preparedness for physiological sexual arousal, followed by information to increase the ability to interpret positively reinforcing genital feedback. The interaction of these cognitive and physiological techniques interrupts dysfunctional cognitive and physiological processes and initiates a positive cognitive–physiological feedback loop of heightened sexual arousal (see Figure 7.5). Although the efficacy of such a program awaits treatment–outcome evaluation, the rehearsal of new cognitive responses to new physiological sensations has been shown to increase response synchrony, initiate a positive feedback loop between subjective and physiological arousal, and possibly provide a rapid and durable treatment for the alleviation of sexual dysfunction in women. Recall that in the laboratory, this technique was effective in increasing physical and subjective sexual arousal to levels comparable to sexually functional women in 3 min.

COGNITIVE–PHYSIOLOGICAL APPROACHES TO WOMEN'S HEALTH: IMPLICATIONS FOR BEHAVIORAL MEDICINE

Finally, these findings have implications for rapid and potentially durable, noninvasive behavioral medicine approaches to the treatment of other common types of physiological and medical disorders for women. Findings from this program of research show a direct pathway where changes in response expectancies (Kirsch, 1985) have an immediate impact on actual physiological processes. Similarly, Rubinow (1992) found that contextual variables such as expectancy may cause differential sensitivity to gonadal steroids in premenstrual syndrome. Individual differences in physiological vulnerability to premenstrual syndrome are therefore affected by physiological factors. That is, social experience and learning (i.e., operant and classical conditioning) that change behavior, alter neuroanatomical structure and function (e.g., Squire, 1987), and change thoughts and behavior effect physiological and biological plasticity. Therefore, instead of surgery or pharmaceutical techniques, "behavioral" medicine can change behavior and cognitions to treat physical problems. Response expectancies are critical targets for behavioral medicine because their direct mind–body link between cognitive and physiological functioning provides the availability for causing change in physical functioning without the use of traditional medical intervention. These include new behavioral medicine approaches not only for sexual dysfunction but also anxiety disorders and depression as well as cardiovascular disorders, infertility, and cancer (Palace, in press).

CONCLUSIONS

This program of research identifies a process flow model of the mechanisms where cognitions and physiological response interact in a reciprocal feedback loop. This model identifies mechanisms that produce sexual arousal for sexual functioning and prevent it in the etiology of sexual dysfunction and provides a new treatment approach for the prevention and alleviation of health-related problems for women.

Sexual arousal is elicited by the interaction of increased autonomic arousal and positive expectancy, which produces a positive feedback loop. Sexual dysfunction is explained as a process flow between bodily symptoms and subjective reactions to these symptoms, in which low autonomic response and negative expectancy reverse the process in a downward spiral of dysfunctional sexual responses. This negative feedback loop between low physiological response and negative expectations may produce a learning curve that exacerbates a cognitive predisposition, a physiological predisposition, or both and reciprocally facilitates the habituation and extinction of sexual arousal and responses.

Accordingly, overlaying the process model is a treatment that uses the cognitive–physiological interaction to intercept and reverse the dysfunctional process. Enhancing physiological responses via increasing general autonomic arousal and changing negative expectancy via genital feedback of a new higher response provides both the physical instigation and the subsequent visual reinforcement to reverse the negative dysfunctional cycle and initiates a positive cognitive–physiological feedback loop of sexual arousal. This cognitive–physiological approach increased expectations, actual physiological responses, and reported sexual arousal to levels comparable to sexually functional women within 3 min. As a clinical application of the process model, a new cognitive–physiological "arousal-retraining" approach combines increased general autonomic arousal and cognitive expectation through exercise and genital biofeedback.

The finding that positive changes in thought processes increase actual physiological processes within 30 s has direct implications for understanding processes that mediate human emotion. The model identifies a potential common mind–body pathway not only for sexual functioning but also for other emotional processes, such as anger, depression, and reactions to stress.

This cognitive–physiological or mind–body pathway also provides direct implications for new health psychology and behavioral medicine approaches for the prevention and alleviation of psychological and medical disorders. This model suggests options for rapid and potentially durable, noninvasive behavioral medicine approaches to the treatment of common types of psychological and medical disorders for women, where, instead of traditional medical techniques, changes in behavior and cognitions are used to change physical problems. United research efforts are needed to instigate programs to facilitate understanding women's sexual health requirements, to pursue new approaches to improve the quality of health care, and ultimately to promote mental and physical sexual health for women. Identification of the interrelationship between response expectancies and physiological response components in emotion processing may replace traditional mind–body dichotomies with integrated behavioral medicine techniques for improved biobehavioral approaches to mental and physical sexual health for women.

REFERENCES

Barlow, D. H. (1986). Causes of sexual dysfunction: The role of anxiety and cognitive interference. *Journal of Consulting and Clinical Psychology, 54*, 140–148.

Barlow, D. H. (1988). *Anxiety and its disorders: The nature and treatment of anxiety and panic.* New York: Guilford Press.

Barlow, D. H., Sakheim, D. K., & Beck, J. G. (1983). Anxiety increases sexual arousal. *Journal of Abnormal Psychology, 92*, 49–54.

Cerny, J. A. (1978). Biofeedback and the voluntary control of sexual arousal in women. *Behavior Therapy, 9*, 847–855.

Dutton, D. G., & Aron, A. P. (1974). Some evidence for heightened sexual attraction under conditions of high anxiety. *Journal of Personality and Social Psychology, 30*, 510–517.

Heiman, J. R., & Rowland, D. L. (1983). Affective and physiological sexual response patterns: The effects of instructions on sexually functional and dysfunctional men. *Journal of Psychosomatic Research, 27*, 105–116.

Hoon, E. F. (1980). Biofeedback-assisted sexual arousal in females: A comparison of visual and auditory modalities. *Biofeedback and Self-Regulation, 5*, 175–191.

Hoon, P. W., Wincze, J. P., & Hoon, E. F. (1977a). The effects of biofeedback and cognitive mediation upon vaginal blood volume. *Behavior Therapy, 8*, 694–702.

Hoon, P. W., Wincze, J. P., & Hoon, E. F. (1977b). A test of reciprocal inhibition: Are anxiety and sexual arousal in women mutually inhibitory? *Journal of Abnormal Psychology, 86*, 65–74.

Kaplan, H. S. (1974). *The new sex therapy: Active treatment of sexual dysfunctions.* New York: Brunner/Mazel.

Kaplan, H. S. (1988). Anxiety and sexual dysfunction. *Journal of Clinical Psychiatry, 49*(Suppl. 10), 21–25.

Kirsch, I. (1985). Response expectancy as a determinant of experience and behavior. *American Psychologist, 40*, 1189–1202.

Marmor, J. (1987). The psychotherapeutic process: Common denominators in diverse approaches. In J. K. Zeig (Ed.), *The evolution of psychotherapy* (pp. 266–282). New York: Brunner.

Masters, W. H., & Johnson, V. E. (1970). *Human sexual inadequacy*. Boston: Little, Brown.

Morokoff, P. J., & Heiman, J. R. (1980). Effects of erotic stimuli on sexually functional and dysfunctional women: Multiple measures before and after sex therapy. *Behaviour Research and Therapy, 18,* 127–137.

Palace, E. M. (1995a). A cognitive–physiological process model of sexual arousal and response. *Clinical Psychology: Science and Practice, 2,* 370–384.

Palace, E. M. (1995b). Modification of dysfunctional patterns of sexual response through autonomic arousal and false physiological feedback. *Journal of Consulting and Clinical Psychology, 63,* 604–615.

Palace, E. M. (1996, September). *A new model and treatment approach for sexual arousal and response in women.* Paper presented at the Women's Health Conference on Psychosocial and Behavioral Factors in Women's Health: Research, Prevention, Treatment, and Service Delivery in Clinical and Community Settings, American Psychological Association, Washington, DC.

Palace, E. M. (Ed.). (in press). *Improving women's health: A behavioral medicine approach.* New York: Oxford University Press.

Palace, E. M., & Gorzalka, B. B. (1990). The enhancing effects of anxiety on arousal in sexually dysfunctional and functional women. *Journal of Abnormal Psychology, 99,* 403–411.

Palace, E. M., & Gorzalka, B. B. (1992). Differential patterns of arousal in sexually functional and dysfunctional women: Physiological and subjective components of sexual response. *Archives of Sexual Behavior, 21,* 135–159.

Rosen, R. C., & Beck, J. G. (1988). *Patterns of sexual arousal: Psychophysiological processes and clinical applications.* New York: Guilford Press.

Rubinow, D. R. (1992). The premenstrual syndrome: New views. *Journal of the American Medical Association, 268,* 1908–1912.

Sakheim, D. K., Barlow, D. H., Beck, J. G., & Abrahamson, D. J. (1984). The effect of an increased awareness of erectile cues on sexual arousal. *Behaviour Research and Therapy, 22,* 151–158.

Schachter, S., & Singer, J. E. (1962). Cognitive, social and physiological components of the emotional state. *Psychological Review, 69,* 379–399.

Schnieden, H., & Rees, J. M. H. (1985). Pharmacological aspects of sexual dysfunction caused by drugs of abuse. In M. Segal (Ed.), *Psychopharmacology of sexual disorders* (pp. 99–113). London: Libbey.

Sintchak, G., & Geer, J. H. (1975). A vaginal plethysmograph system. *Psychophysiology, 12,* 113–115.

Squire, L. R. (1987). *Memory and brain.* New York: Oxford University Press.

Steinman, D. L., Wincze, J. P., Sakheim, D. K., Barlow, D. H., & Mavissakalian, M. (1981). A comparison of male and female patterns of sexual arousal. *Archives of Sexual Behavior, 10,* 529–547.

Valins, S. (1966). Cognitive effects of false heart-rate feedback. *Journal of Personality and Social Psychology, 4,* 400–408.

Valins, S. (1967). Emotionality and information concerning internal reactions. *Journal of Personality and Social Psychology, 6,* 458–463.

Wincze, J. P., Hoon, E. F., & Hoon, P. W. (1976). Physiological responsivity of normal and sexually dysfunctional women during erotic stimulus exposure. *Journal of Psychosomatic Research, 20,* 445–451.

Wolchik, S. A., Beggs, V. E., Wincze, J. P., Sakheim, D. K., Barlow, D. H., & Mavissakalian, M. (1980). The effects of emotional arousal on subsequent sexual arousal in men. *Journal of Abnormal Psychology, 89,* 595–598.

Wolpe, J. (1958). *Psychotherapy by reciprocal inhibition.* Stanford, CA: Stanford University Press.

Wolpe, J. (1982). *The practice of behavior therapy* (3rd ed.). Elmsford, NY: Pergamon Press.

8

EXPECTANCY AND ASTHMA

SAMANTHA C. SODERGREN AND MICHAEL E. HYLAND

Asthma is a disease of variable airway obstruction caused by inflammation of the airways (leading to thickening of the airway walls) and bronchoconstriction (i.e., the muscles in the airways contract). Changes in inflammation are relatively slow, whereas bronchoconstriction can be rapid. Expectancy research in asthma focuses on comparatively rapid changes in the airways, and it is therefore the bronchoconstriction that is the most important pathological process to this topic of research. In normal (i.e., nonasthmatic) airways, a small amount of bronchoconstriction occurs to certain triggers or irritants, such as smoke. In the asthmatic individual, this bronchoconstriction is exaggerated, and the tendency to bronchoconstrict is potentiated by the inflammation of the airways. Bronchoconstriction in asthma is an accentuation of a normal process, and the asthmatic response merges with the normal response in people with mild asthma. Thus, mildly asthmatic people, whose airway inflammation is abolished by the control exerted by inhaled steroids, may show a pattern of bronchoconstriction that is not much different from nonasthmatic people. This point is relevant to the data reviewed here because if asthmatic individuals' symptoms are well controlled, their airways are not that different from nonasthmatic people.

Asthmatic individuals have "twitchy" airways in the sense that their airways constrict more easily to asthma triggers (triggers are anything that can elicit bronchoconstriction). The triggers vary among patients, but the most common ones are listed here. First, any small airborne particles can act as an asthma trigger, including smoke, exhaust fumes, and the dander that is shed from animals, particularly cats, dogs, and horses. Some asthmatic people have an allergic reaction (rather than an irritant reaction), particularly to animal dander, and will show a marked bronchoconstriction. Asthmatic individuals having an allergic reaction are referred to as *extrinsic asthmatics*, and those who have no clear allergic response are called *intrinsic asthmatics*. Second, cold air or a change in air temperature can act as a trigger; for example, exercise can cause bronchoconstriction. Finally, psychological states cause bronchoconstriction, particularly negative emotional states associated with interpersonal conflict and anxiety. Asthmatic people who report that emotion precipitates their attacks are known as *emotionally triggered asthmatics*. In addition to the well-known effect of emotion on asthmatic airways, expectations produced by suggestion, hypnosis and relaxation can also affect bronchoconstriction, and it is these expectancy effects that are reviewed in this chapter.

EXPECTANCY RESEARCH IN ASTHMA

The earliest example of an expectancy effect in asthma that we know of was reported by Mackenzie (1886), who described the case of a patient who was allergic to roses (actually, a rare occurrence) and who, on seeing an artificial rose, developed marked bronchoconstriction. Other incidences in which "meaningful" stimuli could cause bronchoconstriction were reported by Dekker and Groen (1956). These early case reports preceded the first experimental study of expectancy effects in asthma by Luparello, Lyons, Bleecker, and McFadden (1968). In that study, participants with asthma inhaled an inert substance that was described to them as a potent bronchoconstrictor, and airways obstruction was then measured. This and subsequent experimental expectancy studies vary in three main ways: the type of expectancy manipulation, the type of physical manipulation, and the type of lung function measurement taken to assess airways obstruction.

Type of Expectancy Manipulation

In the majority of studies, researchers have used a verbal suggestion as the type of expectancy manipulation. For example, patients may be told that they are about to inhale a potent bronchodilator or bronchoconstrictor. Patients are certainly likely to be familiar with pharmacological bronchodilators (e.g., albuterol, marketed under various brand names such as Ventolin) because these are used in "relieving" asthma medicines. Patients are also likely to be familiar with bronchoconstrictors such as pollen, cigarette smoke, and exercise, which precipitate asthma attacks. In addition, patients may have been assessed using a metacholine challenge test, a test in which patients inhale a bronchoconstricting substance. Other researchers have used manipulations that may involve, in one way or another, the person developing an expectancy. Patients may be hypnotized into experiencing an asthma attack, certain emotional states (e.g., fear and anxiety), or a state of relaxation. Hypnosis is attractive as a manipulation because of its rapid onset and offset, and it tends to be highly focused. Research indicates that the effects of hypnosis are mediated by expectancy (Kirsch, 1990). Relaxation may have effects that are independent of expectancy. Alternatively, relaxation techniques may generate expectancies of one kind or another because many patients realize that stress (i.e., lack of relaxation) can act as a bronchoconstrictor. Relaxation techniques usually focus on breathing and abdominal exercises and on reducing the levels of negative emotional states. Relaxation may be used to reduce bronchoconstriction after inhalation of bronchoconstricting substances or substances presented as bronchoconstrictors.

There are two types of expectancies: The airways will either constrict or they will dilate. These two expectancies are not equivalent in terms of underlying physiology. A relaxed airway can constrict; a partially constricted airway can constrict even more. However, a relaxed airway cannot dilate. Thus, for relaxation to occur, there must be some constriction already present, and given our earlier comment that well-controlled mild asthmatic individuals may not be much different from nonasthmatic individuals, it follows that some asthmatic people may have little scope for bronchodilation after a suggestion.

Type of Physical Manipulation

Many asthma expectancy studies require individuals to inhale a specified substance. Irrespective of the suggestion, this substance may actually be inert, or it may be pharmacologically active either as a bronchoconstrictor or as a bronchodilator. Thus, dilating or constricting instructions may be coupled with either a bronchodilator, a bronchoconstrictor, or an inert substance. Inert substances are typically either saline or room air, but doubt has been expressed about whether inert substances have a neutral effect on the airways. Pastorello et al. (1987) observed a bronchoconstrictive response to saline in the absence of any suggestion. It is possible that the inhalation of saline has a cooling effect on the airways, leading to bronchoconstriction. In support of this hypothesis, Lewis, Lewis, and Tattersfield (1983) demonstrated removal of the bronchoconstrictive effect by performing inhalations at 37 °C and 100% relative humidity.

Method of Measuring Lung Function

Although lung function measurement is straightforward in principle, in practice there are a number of measures of obstruction as well as measures of other types of lung function, such as lung volume. The use of the whole-body plethysmograph provides several somewhat similar measures of obstruction, such as airway resistance (Ra/Raw) and specific airway conductance (sGaw), as well as providing a measure of airway volume (thoracic gas volume [vtg/TGV]). From a psychological perspective, an important feature of this technique is that the whole body is placed within a sealed container with the head protruding, and therefore the measurement procedure may have a psychological impact. Stein (1962) showed that merely being encased in a whole-body plethysmograph can trigger asthma symptoms. Nevertheless, despite its evident inconvenience, the whole-body plethysmograph provides a physiologically accurate form of assessment.

A second method is forced oscillation, which provides measures of respiratory resistance, respiratory rate, and tidal volume. In this method, the person breathes into a tube while oscillatory waves are fed into the airstream, and the effect on these oscillatory waves provides a measure of resistance.

Spirometry and peak flow measurement are similar in that individuals are asked to blow as hard as they can into a tube. This method is therefore effort dependent. Although spirometry and peak flow measurement are easy and convenient to perform, the potential for psychological factors affecting the measurement is a possible criticism in expectancy studies. Spirometry provides measures of obstruction called forced expiratory volume in the first second (FEV1) and maximal midexpiratory flow (MMEF) as well as measures of lung volume vital capacity (VC) and forced vital capacity (FVC). Peak flow measurement provides a measure of peak expiratory flow rate (PEFR).

Finally, the metacholine challenge test assesses airway reactivity (i.e., the severity of asthma). In this test, metacholine of increasing concentration is inhaled until a specified drop in FEV1 is achieved.

SUMMARY OF STUDIES

The studies reviewed in this chapter vary in terms of (a) the use of expectancy manipulation (i.e., whether constriction or relaxation is suggested); (b) the physical manipulation (i.e., whether the substance is active or inert); and (c) the type of measurement involved. Many researchers have used a combination of several different parameters (e.g., they used more than one type of measurement or expectancy manipulation).

Fourteen studies combined an inert substance with a dilating or constricting suggestion (see Table 8.1). Ten studies showed respiratory changes consistent with the suggestion. In the remaining 4 studies, the effect of suggestion was either not apparent or was only slightly apparent. Overall, there seemed to be no difference in the efficacy of dilating or constricting suggestions. Thus, the overall evidence supports the hypothesis that suggestion can affect the airways when combined with a neutral substance.

Tables 8.2 and 8.3 show the same results, but this time for studies in which a constricting or dilating substance was combined with suggestion. Not surprisingly, suggestions consistent with the pharmacological agent had an effect in the predicted direction. Four studies showed that suggestion could have some effect in the opposite direction of the pharmacological agent. That is, a bronchodilating suggestion provided some protection (but not complete protection) against a bronchoconstricting substance, and a bronchoconstricting suggestion attenuated the therapeutic effect of a bronchodilating substance. In addition, two studies included a neutral suggestion in which the pharmacological agent was described as having no effect on airway function. Philipp, Wilde, and Day (1972) found that the neutral suggestion increased patients' tolerance to a bronchoconstricting substance. However, Lewis et al. (1983) were not able to attenuate the therapeutic effect of a bronchodilator by describing it as a neutral substance.

Table 8.4 shows a summary of results of studies in which hypnosis was used in the manipulation of expectancy. The two hypnotic studies demonstrated that hypnosis can affect both bronchoconstriction and bronchodilation. Table 8.5 shows the results from relaxation studies, in which the intention was to use relaxation as a bronchodilator. Positive results were obtained in the three studies reviewed. However, although the other experimental manipulations are concerned with an immediate effect on pulmonary function, the therapeutic effect of relaxation can be measured over a longer period of time; for example, Vazquez and Buceta (1993) conducted evaluation sessions over a 12-month period.

POTENTIAL MEDIATING VARIABLES

The results just reviewed show that the majority of studies support the hypothesis that expectancy affects the airways in asthmatic people. However, not all the results are consistent with this hypothesis, and it is possible to examine them in terms of factors that may account for these differences. Although sample size varied in the different studies, this appears to have had little effect on the results. In addition to sample size, there are two groups of factors that may have affected the results: those relating to asthma and those relating to psychology and demographic factors.

TABLE 8.1
Studies in Which a Suggestion Is Coupled With an Inert Substance

Study	Sample	Measurement	Result	Notes
		Constricting suggestion		
Luparello et al. (1969)	40 Asthmatics, 40 controls	Raw	+	Positive only for asthmatics (19 of 40)
		vtg	+	
McFadden et al. (1969)	29 Asthmatics	Raw	+	Positive results for 15 of 29, replicated in 13 of 15
		vtg	+	
Weiss et al. (1970)	16 Asthmatic children	PEFR	−	Positive results only for 1 of 16
Philipp et al. (1972)	20 Asthmatics: 10 INs, 10 EXs	FEV1	+	Positive results for 6 of 10 INs and 3 of 10 EXs
		VC	+	
Strupp et al. (1974)	13 Asthmatics	RT	Both	4 of 13 responded positively
Spector et al. (1976)	9 Asthmatics	Raw	+	6 of 9 positive
		vtg	−	
		sGaw	+	6 of 9 positive
		FEV1	−	
		MMEF	−	
		FVC	−	
Horton et al. (1978)	22 Asthmatics	Raw	+	5 of 22 positive
		vtg	−	
Lewis et al. (1983)	30 Asthmatics, 12 normals	sGaw	+[a]	5 of 22 positive
		sGaw	+[a]	9 of 30 asthmatics responded positively
Neild and Cameron (1985)	25 Asthmatics	FEV1	+	Positive results for 10 of 25
Butler and Steptoe (1986)	12 Asthmatics	RT	+	
		Respiratory rate	+	
		Tidal volume	+	
Kotses et al. (1987)	30 Normals	FEV1	+	
Pastorello et al. (1987)	25 Asthmatics (emotionally triggered attacks)	RT	+[a]	Positive for 7 of 25
		FEV1	−	
Isenberg et al. (1992)	33 Asthmatics	FEV1	+	
		MMEF	−	
		FVC	+	

Study	Participants	Measure	Dilating suggestion
Luparello et al. (1968)	40 Asthmatics, 40 controls	Raw	+
		vtg	+
McFadden et al. (1969)	29 Asthmatics	Raw	+
		vtg	+
Godfrey & Silverman (1973)	44 Asthmatic children	PEFR	+ Positive for 20 of 44
Spector et al. (1976)	9 Asthmatics	Raw	+
		vtg	−
		sGaw	−
		FEV1	+
		MMEF	−
		FVC	−
Lewis et al. (1983)	30 Asthmatics, 12 normals	sGaw	−
Neild & Cameron (1985)	25 Asthmatics	FEV1	+
		RT	+
Butler & Steptoe (1986)	12 Asthmatics	Respiratory rate	+
		Tidal volume	+
		FEV1	+
Pastorello et al. (1987)	25 Asthmatics (emotionally triggered attacks)	FEV1	−
Isenberg et al. (1992)	33 Asthmatics	FEV1	−
		MMEF	−
		FVC	+

Note. INs = intrinsic asthmatics; EXs = extrinsic asthmatics; Raw = airway resistance; sGaw = specific airway conductance; vtg = thoracic gas volume; RT = respiratory resistance; FEV1 = forced expiratory volume in the first second; MMEF = maximum midexpiratory flow; FVC = forced vital capacity; PEFR = peak expiratory flow rate; + = positive results in the direction of the suggestion; − = negative results not in the direction of the suggestion.
[a]Effects independent of verbal suggestion.

TABLE 8.2
Studies in Which a Suggestion of Effect Is Coupled With a Constricting Substance

Study	Sample	Measurement	Result
Constricting suggestion			
Luparello et al. (1970)	20 Asthmatics	Raw	+
		vtg	+
Philipp et al. (1972)	20 Asthmatics:	VC	+
	10 INs, 10 EXs	FEV1	+
Spector et al. (1976)	9 Asthmatics	Raw	+
		vtg	−
		sGaw	+
		FEV1	−
		MMEF	−
		FVC	−
Dilating suggestion			
Luparello et al. (1970)	20 Asthmatics	Raw	+
		vtg	+
Neutral suggestion			
Philipp et al. (1972)	20 Asthmatics:	VC	+
	10 INs, 10 EXs	FEV1	+

Note. INs = intrinsic asthmatics; EXs = extrinsic asthmatics; Raw = airway resistance; sGaw = specific airway conductance; VC = lung volume vital capacity; vtg = thoracic gas volume; FEV1 = forced expiratory volume in the first second; MMEF = maximal midexpiratory flow; FVC = forced vital capacity; + = positive results in the direction of the suggestion; − = negative results not in the direction of the suggestion.

Asthma-Related Factors

Asthma Severity

It is difficult to assess the effect of asthma severity on expectancy responses because the majority of the studies reviewed did not specify asthma severity. Strupp et al. (1974) identified 4 of 13 mildly asthmatic individuals as being reactive to bronchoconstrictive suggestion. Nine of 20 moderately asthmatic individuals responded to a similar manipulation carried out by Philipp et al. (1972). Weiss, Martin, and Riley's (1970) study of 16 children with chronic severe asthma yielded negative results, with only one child responding; however, Weiss et al. argued that the chronic intractable nature of the children's asthma should have rendered them more susceptible to suggestion. Thus, there is no clear evidence to suggest that expectancy effects vary with asthma severity.

Airway Reactivity

Horton, Suda, Kinsman, Souhrada, and Spector (1978) and Pastorello et al. (1987) identified airway hyperreactivity, as measured by histamine

TABLE 8.3
Studies in Which a Suggestion of Effect Is Coupled With a Dilating Substance

Study	Sample	Measurement	Result	Notes
		Constricting suggestion		
McFadden et al. (1969)	29 Asthmatics	Raw	+	Positive results for both measures in 15 of 29
		vtg	+	
Luparello et al. (1970)	20 Asthmatics	Raw	+	
		vtg	+	
Strupp et al. (1974)	13 Asthmatics	RT	Both	
		Dilating suggestion		
Luparello et al. (1970)	20 Asthmatics	Raw	+	
		vtg	+	
Godfrey and Silverman (1973)	44 Asthmatic children	PEFR	+	
Strupp et al. (1974)	13 Asthmatics	RT	+	
Lewis et al. (1983)	30 Asthmatics, 12 normals	sGaw	+[a]	
		Neutral suggestion		
Lewis et al. (1983)	30 Asthmatics, 12 normals	sGaw	−	

Note. Raw = airway resistance; sGaw = specific airway conductance; vtg = thoracic gas volume; RT = respiratory resistance; PEFR = peak expiratory flow rate; + = positive results in the direction of the suggestion; − = negative results not in the direction of the suggestion.
[a]Effects independent of verbal suggestion.

TABLE 8.4
Studies Involving Hypnosis

Study	Sample	Hypnotic Suggestion	Measurement	Result	Note
Smith et al. (1970)	2 Asthmatics	Bronchonconstriction: fear, anger, asthma attack Relaxation	Raw calculated from transpulmonary pressure and gas flow by pneumotach	+	
Aronoff et al. (1975)	17 Asthmatic children	Bronchodilation	FVC	+	Positive for all children with FVC measurement.
			PEFR	+	Positive for 14 of 17 children with PEFR

Note. Raw = airway resistance; FVC = forced vital capacity; PEFR = peak expiratory flow rate; + = positive results in the direction of the hypnotic suggestion.

TABLE 8.5
Studies Involving Relaxation

Study	Sample	Measurement	Result	Notes
Philipp et al. (1972)	20 Asthmatics: 10 INs, 10 EXs	VC FEV1	+ +	Positive for 7 of 10 asthmatics with both measurements
Lehrer et al. (1986)	20 Asthmatics	Metacholine challenge test	+	Positive for large airway obstruction
Vazquez & Buceta (1993)	27 Asthmatic children with high trait anxiety, emotionally triggered attacks, or both	PEFR	+	Positive for children with emotionally triggered attacks

Note. INs = intrinsic asthmatics; EXs = extrinsic asthmatics; VC = lung volume vital capacity; FEV1 = forced expiratory volume in the first second; PEFR = peak expiratory flow rate; + = positive results in the direction of the manipulation.

and metacholine challenges, as an important correlate of bronchoconstrictive suggestibility. Thus, although comparative data in the different studies revealed no firm evidence to support the hypothesis that expectancy effects increase with disease severity, using airway reactivity as a measure of severity leads to the conclusion that increased twitchiness of the airways does lead to greater expectancy effects.

Intrinsic Versus Extrinsic Asthma

In two of the studies reviewed (Horton et al., 1978; Philipp et al., 1972), intrinsic and extrinsic asthmatic participants were compared. Philipp et al. (1972) found that intrinsic asthmatic participants were more susceptible to the effect of suggested bronchoconstriction and that they were more likely to profit from the therapeutic effects of relaxation techniques. Horton et al. (1978), however, failed to find a relationship between intrinsic–extrinsic asthma and bronchoconstrictive responses to suggestion.

Type of Pulmonary Assessment

Studies using whole-body plethysmograph, in particular to measure Raw and sGaw, seem to offer more positive outcomes than studies using peak flow meters and spirometry. This was illustrated in a study by Spector, Luparello, Kopetzky, Souhrada, and Kinsman (1976), in which only Raw and sGaw were sensitive to the effects of bronchoconstrictive suggestion, with vtg, FEV1, FVC, and MMEF failing to detect any pulmonary function changes. Of the six studies using whole-body plethysmograph, only one study (Lewis et al., 1983) produced negative results.

Type of Manipulation

We argued earlier that bronchoconstriction and bronchodilation expectancies rely on different physiological mechanisms and that it may be easier to induce bronchoconstriction than bronchodilation. However, the studies reviewed show that both types of expectancies are equally efficacious. Few opportunities were offered to evaluate the assertion of Lewis et al. (1983) that cooling of the airways, rather than suggestion, is responsible for observed pulmonary changes. However, Neild and Cameron (1985) reported bronchoconstriction even after attempting to control for the effect of airways cooling by heating the aerosol to 32 °C throughout. Two studies (Isenberg, Lehrer, & Hochron, 1992; Kotses, Rawson, Wigal, & Creer, 1987) also demonstrated bronchoconstriction after inhalation of room air, but the number of responsive asthmatic participants in the study of Isenberg et al. (1992) was particularly small. The manipulations reviewed appeared to be equal in terms of efficacy in inducing pulmonary changes.

Psychological and Demographic Factors

Gender

Philipp et al. (1972) found that female participants were slightly more suggestible than male participants. The remaining studies reviewed did not report any relationship between gender and response to expectancy manipulations.

Age

Weiss et al. (1970), using a sample of asthmatic children, failed to replicate the findings of Luparello et al. (1968), who used asthmatic adults. Weiss et al. speculated that age could have been a possible explanation. However, Weiss et al. dismissed this explanation for the differences in findings on the basis that there is ample evidence to suggest that the symptoms of asthmatic children are as open to psychological manipulation as are those of adults and that there is no evidence to imply that children are immune to the effects of suggestion.

Personality

The research of Isenberg et al. (1992) identified the following personality dimensions as important mediators of suggestibility: a general susceptibility to suggestion of bronchial change, perceived physical vulnerability, and anxiety. Horton et al. (1978) found that emotionally unstable asthmatic participants, according to physiological measurements such as blood pressure, were more likely to respond to bronchoconstrictive suggestion.

Emotionally Triggered Asthmatics

Pastorello et al. (1987) selected individuals with an emotional component to their asthma and found that they reacted to saline with bronchoconstriction even in the absence of suggestion. In Vazquez and Buceta's (1993) study, participants describing emotionally triggered attacks, rather than those with high levels of trait anxiety, benefited most from relaxation therapy. Another study involving relaxation performed by Lehrer, Hochron, McCann, Swartzman, and Reba (1986) also showed that relaxation therapy targets emotionally mediated asthma, with only the number of emotional precursors to an asthma attack decreasing more in the relaxation condition than in the placebo condition. Thus, there is evidence to suggest that emotionally triggered asthmatic people are more responsive to expectancy manipulations.

Health Locus of Control

Butler and Steptoe (1986) discovered that asthmatic participants with more pronounced bronchoconstrictive responses to suggestion were more likely to believe that their health depended on chance factors rather than on their own actions or those of powerful others.

CONCLUSIONS

Asthmatic individuals have more twitchy airways than do nonasthmatic individuals. The twitchiness or bronchoconstriction of the airways can be brought about by expectancy effects, but there is substantial variation in this effect between asthmatics. There is some evidence that the more asthmatic the person is (i.e., the more naturally twitchy the airways), the greater the likelihood of obtaining an effect. Although the original description of this phenomenon was one that would be consistent with a classical conditioning explanation (i.e., a patient reacts to an artificial rose), all the experimental studies are consistent with an expectancy-mediated effect (Kirsch, 1990). That is, the verbal suggestion of bronchoconstriction or dilation will have an effect regardless of the overt characteristics of the inhaled substance.

The size of the expectancy effect varies substantially among people with asthma, but it is not as great as for active pharmacological agents (Spector et al., 1976). Thus, when an active agent with no suggestion is compared with a neutral agent plus suggestion, the effect of the neutral agent plus suggestion is about two thirds that of the active agent (Godfrey & Silverman, 1973). Similarly, when an opposite suggestion is given to that actually being achieved by the pharmacological agent, the airway changes in the direction of the pharmacological agent, but the pharmacological effect is reduced by about one half (Luparello, Leist, Lourie, & Sweet, 1970). Nevertheless, expectations about bronchoconstriction or bronchodilation can have clinically relevant effects on asthmatic airways. Patients high in emotional instability, emotionally triggered asthma, feelings of anxiety, vulnerability, and lack of control over their health appear to be more responsive to suggestion.

Practical Implications

Expectancy effects have two different kinds of practical implication, one concerning the onset of asthma symptoms and the other relating to treatment.

Asthma Symptom Onset

It is well-known that asthma symptoms can be brought about by a variety of physical triggers as well as the psychological trigger of emotional upset. What is less well-known is that expectancy effects can also act as a psychological trigger, that the size of this effect varies, but that for some patients expectancy effects are large enough to be clinically relevant. Whenever a physical asthma trigger affects a patient, if the patient knows that the physical trigger is present, this knowledge can contribute to an expectancy effect. Thus, the bronchoconstricting effect of a physical asthma trigger may be increased when patients know that the trigger is present. In summary, expectancy effects contribute to asthma attacks.

Asthma Treatment

When patients take a bronchodilating inhaler as relief medication, the effects of the pharmacological treatment are likely to be enhanced by dilating expectations. In addition, patients may develop expectancies about particular inhalers and therefore resist change to other "equivalent" medicines that are not accompanied by the same expectancies. Albuterol, which is a common generic bronchodilating agent, comes with a variety of labels and inhaler devices. Ventolin is the trade name of albuterol, which is marketed by the original inventors of the compound, GlaxoWelcome (previously Allen & Hanburys), but exactly the same chemical entity is sold as a generic formulation because the product's patent has expired. Some patients resist being switched from Ventolin to the cheaper generic form, asserting that the latter is less effective. In fact, different ways of forming a vapor of the drug may cause physiological differences, but, in any case, differences in perceptions may arise because patients have developed a positive expectancy to their "old" drug.

On a final note, it may be that when asthma is being treated in the emergency room after an asthma attack, it might be helpful to tell patients "We are now going to give you a powerful bronchodilator," as this suggestion could possibly have a positive effect on outcome. Substantiating the usefulness of such a suggestion in emergency departments may, however, be difficult.

Directions for Further Research

The term *asthmatic* refers to people who may suffer from a variety of different related diseases and who certainly experience asthma in different ways. A consistent thread throughout the research reviewed earlier is that asthmatic individuals respond in different ways to the same expectancy manipulation. Indeed, one could question the meaningfulness of "mean scores" to describe expectancy response in a group of patients with asthma.

Therefore, it seems that a useful research direction would be to explore in greater detail why expectancy manipulations are more effective in some asthmatic patients than others. Specifically, two questions need to be addressed: First, are physiological parameters other than disease severity predictive of the level of response to expectancy manipulations? As reviewed earlier, for example, there is inconclusive evidence about whether intrinsic asthma produces results different from extrinsic asthma. Second, do psychological characteristics predict responses to expectancy manipulations? For example, are asthmatic patients who report that psychological stress acts as a bronchoconstrictor more or less likely to respond to an expectancy manipulation? Answers to these questions about individual differences should provide a better picture of whether expectancy manipulation can be a useful tool in asthma therapy.

REFERENCES

Aronoff, G. M., Aronoff, S., & Peck, L. (1975). Hypnotherapy in the treatment of bronchial asthma. *Annals of Allergy, 34,* 356–362.

Butler, C., & Steptoe, A. (1986). Placebo responses: An experimental study of psychophysiological processes in asthmatic volunteers. *British Journal of Clinical Psychology, 25,* 173–183.

Dekker, E., & Groen, J. (1956). Reproducible psychogenic attacks of asthma. *Journal of Psychosomatic Research, 1,* 58.

Godfrey, S., & Silverman, M. (1973). Demonstration by placebo response in asthma by means of exercise testing. *Journal of Psychosomatic Research, 17,* 293–297.

Horton, D. J., Suda, W. L., Kinsman, R. A., Souhrada, J., & Spector, S. L. (1978). Bronchoconstrictive suggestion in asthma: A role for airways hyperreactivity and emotions. *American Review of Respiratory Disease, 117,* 1029–1038.

Isenberg, S. A., Lehrer, P. M., & Hochron, S. (1992). The effects of suggestion on airways of asthmatic subjects breathing room air as a suggested bronchoconstrictor and bronchodilator. *Journal of Psychosomatic Research, 36,* 769–776.

Kirsch, I. (1990). *Changing expectancies: A key to effective psychotherapy.* Pacific Grove, CA: Brooks/Cole.

Kotses, H., Rawson, J. C., Wigal, J. K., & Creer, T. L. (1987). Respiratory airway changes in response to suggestion in normal individuals. *Psychosomatic Medicine, 49,* 536–541.

Lehrer, P. M., Hochron, S. M., McCann, B., Swartzman, L., & Reba, P. (1986). Relaxation decreases large-airway but not small-airway asthma. *Journal of Psychosomatic Research, 30,* 13–25.

Lewis, R. A., Lewis, M. N., & Tattersfield, A. E. (1983). Asthma and suggestion: Psychological or physical? *Agents and Actions, 13,* 71–79.

Luparello, T. J., Leist, N., Lourie, C. H., & Sweet, P. (1970). The interaction of psychological stimuli and pharmacologic agents on airway reactivity in asthmatic subjects. *Psychosomatic Medicine, 32,* 509–513.

Luparello, T., Lyons, H. A., Bleecker, E. R., & McFadden, E. R. (1968). Influences of suggestion on airway reactivity in asthmatic subjects. *Psychosomatic Medicine, 30,* 819–825.

Mackenzie, J. N. (1886). The production of "rose asthma" by an artificial rose. *American Journal of Medical Science, 91,* 45.

McFadden, E. R., Luparello, T., Lyons, H. A., & Bleecker, E. (1969). The mechanism of suggestion in the induction of acute asthma attacks. *Psychosomatic Medicine, 31,* 134–143.

Neild, J. E., & Cameron, I. R. (1985). Bronchoconstriction in response to suggestion: Its prevention by an inhaled anticholinergic agent. *British Medical Journal, 290,* 674.

Pastorello, E. A., Codecasa, L. R., Pravattoni, V., Zara, C., Incorvaia, C., Froldi, M., & Zanussi, C. (1987). The role of suggestion in asthma: I. Effects of inactive solution on bronchial reactivity under bronchoconstrictor or bronchodilator suggestion. *Annals of Allergy, 59,* 336–338.

Philipp, R. L., Wilde, G. J. S., & Day, J. H. (1972). Suggestion and relaxation in asthmatics. *Journal of Psychosomatic Research, 16,* 193–204.

Smith, M. N., Colebatch, H. J. H., & Clarke, P. S. (1970). Increase and decrease in pulmonary resistance with hypnotic suggestion in asthma. *American Review of Respiratory Disease, 102,* 236–242.

Spector, S. L., Luparello, J. L., Kopetzky, M. T., Souhrada, J., & Kinsman, R. A. (1976). Response of asthmatics to metacholine and suggestion. *American Review of Respiratory Disease, 113,* 43–50.

Stein, M. (1962). Etiology and mechanisms in the development of asthma. In J. H. Nodine & J. H. Moyer (Eds.), *Psychosomatic medicine* (pp. 149–156). Philadelphia: Lea & Febiger.

Strupp, H. H., Levenson, R. W., Manuck, S. B., Snell, J. P., Hinrichsen, J. J., & Boyd, S. (1974). Effects of suggestion on total respiratory resistance in mild asthmatics. *Journal of Psychosomatic Research, 18,* 337–346.

Vazquez, M. I., & Buceta, J. M. (1993). Effectiveness of self-management programs and relaxation training on the treatment of bronchial asthma: Relationships with trait anxiety and emotional behavioral triggers. *Journal of Psychosomatic Research, 37,* 71–81.

Weiss, J. H., Martin, C., & Riley, J. (1970). Effects of suggestion on respiration in asthmatic children. *Psychosomatic Medicine, 32,* 409–415.

III

SUBSTANCE EXPECTANCIES
AND SUBSTANCE ABUSE

9

EXPECTANCY AND BEHAVIORAL EFFECTS OF SOCIALLY USED DRUGS

M. VOGEL-SPROTT AND MARK T. FILLMORE

The term *expectancy* is commonly understood to refer to the anticipation of some type of future event. The possibility that expectations can
affect behavior has received considerable research attention in psychology
and has been broadly applied to explain a wide range of behavior. The
contemporary interest in drug-related expectancies reflects this general
trend. Many researchers have investigated expectancies that individuals
report about alcohol and other socially used or abused drugs (e.g., Brandon
& Baker, 1992; Goldman, Brown, & Christiansen, 1987; Jaffe, 1992;
Schafer & Brown, 1991). This research has primarily proceeded by gathering information on the kinds of drug-related expectancies individuals
report. The findings have shown that individuals have expectancies about
receiving drugs, their effects, and the consequences of those effects (e.g.,
Brown, 1993). Most of this research has focused on expectancies about
alcohol, and this work reveals that these expectancies differ among individuals. A particularly important observation is that heavier drinkers tend
to report expectancies of more favorable effects in a variety of social, be-

Preparation of this chapter was supported in part by grants from the Natural Sciences and
Engineering Research Council and the Alcoholic Beverage Medical Research Foundation.

havioral, and physical domains (e.g., Brown, 1993; Goldman et al., 1987). These findings are consistent with the view that drug expectancies may contribute to the development of drug abuse and relapse from treatment (e.g., Marlatt & Gordon, 1985).

Less attention has been paid to the important possibility that drug-related expectancies may also influence behavior under the drug. In this chapter we describe research that has examined this possibility. This work has relied on learning theory to investigate how drug-related expectancies are acquired, how they may influence behavior, and how these expectancies may be changed.

The expectancy concept was introduced in learning theory by Tolman (1932). Subsequent work by Bolles (1972, 1975, 1979) systematized the expectancy concept in learning theory by providing rules for inferring and defining an expectancy on the basis of associations between specific events. When one event always follows another, the presentation of one leads to an expectation of the other. In Bolles's analyses, expectancies were intervening cognitive variables that represented information about the relationship of a response to a stimulus outcome, or the relation between stimulus events. More recently, Kirsch (1985) extended the expectancy concept to include the relationship between a stimulus event and a subsequent response. Many learning experiments have identified events in a situation that permit the acquisition of different expectancies and have shown that they influence behavior. Much research now indicates that behavior is mediated by environmentally arranged relationships among a response, an outcome, and a stimulus context (e.g., Colwill & Rescorla, 1986; Rescorla, 1987, 1992).

In the next section, we explain how principles of associative learning are applied to a drug-taking situation to identify relationships between stimulus and response events that give rise to drug-related expectancies. By manipulating the events associated with expectancies in a situation, researchers can investigate their role in mediating drug-related behavior and can better understand the conditions under which drug-related expectancies may be acquired.

LEARNING ANALYSIS OF DRUG-RELATED EXPECTANCIES

For the purposes of our analysis, a drug-taking situation is assumed to involve relationships between environmental and drug stimuli, a response, and an outcome. Figure 9.1 illustrates these four types of events as an environmental cue for a drug (S), a drug stimulus (S^*_d), a response to the drug (R_d), and an outcome (S^*).[1] The events occur in a temporal

---

[1]Stimulus events accompanied by an asterisk identify stimuli that have some impact that is important to an individual. This symbolization follows that of Bolles (1972), who used the asterisk to identify biologically important stimuli, such as food or shock.

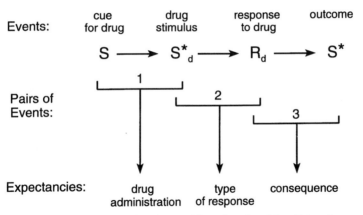

Events:

| cue for drug | drug stimulus | response to drug | outcome |

$$S \longrightarrow S^*_d \longrightarrow R_d \longrightarrow S^*$$

Pairs of Events:

1

2

3

Expectancies: drug administration   type of response   consequence

Figure 9.1. A learning model of a drug-taking situation identifying four events: cue for drug (S), drug stimulus (S^*_d), response to drug (R_d), and outcome (S^*). The model shows how successive pairs of these events provide three expectancies that concern drug administration, type of response, and its consequence.

sequence. Their repetition in a drug-taking situation provides an opportunity to associate three successive pairs of events to yield three expectancies.

The first pair consists of a stimulus (S) that precedes the drug stimulus (S^*_d). The $S–S^*_d$ association provides an opportunity to learn what stimuli predict the drug. When this information is acquired, the stimuli function as cues that signal the administration of the drug, and an individual may expect the drug when these cues are presented. For example, the presentation of a beer bottle or the scent of the beverage would predict the administration of alcohol. An individual's reaction to the presentation of cues for a drug has traditionally been attributed to the expectation of the drug. However, Figure 9.1 shows that the expectation of a drug is also a prerequisite for the occurrence of two other expectancies concerning the type of response and its consequence.

The second pair of events relate a drug stimulus (S^*_d) to a particular type of response to a drug (R_d). The widespread action of a drug allows it to affect many different responses. In the case of behavior, the particular type of response associated with a drug depends on the ongoing activity. Experiencing a drug effect on an activity provides an opportunity to learn what type of response occurs to the drug. Repeated pairings of these events contribute to the learning of the association and result in an expected response that closely corresponds to the effect that the drug has on the activity. For example, greater success in playing darts after drinking alcohol should lead an individual to expect that the drug improves this particular activity.

Figure 9.1 shows that the last pair of events consists of a response to the drug (R_d) and its outcome (S^*). A reliable association between these two events permits the acquisition of a third expectancy: the expected consequence of a response to a drug. The outcome of a response to a drug depends on the situation. As a result, a person may learn that a given response to a drug is associated with a particular outcome in one situation and an entirely different one in another setting. In theory, the resulting expected consequence should affect the response to a drug, making it more likely to be observed when a consequence is desirable and less likely when it is undesirable. For example, drinkers may expect alcohol to impair the motor skills involved in driving. However, drinkers who also expect that resisting this effect yields a more desirable consequence (safety) than displaying impairment (accidents) may increase their care and attention to driving and so should display less impairment than would otherwise be observed. Thus, the expected consequence can play an adaptive role, modifying the intensity of the response to a drug to maximize a favorable outcome.

Up to this point, our learning analysis has considered the role of the three expectancies in predicting the behavioral response to a drug. However, the analysis applies to placebo responses as well. Once a particular response to a drug is expected in a drug-taking situation, that response should also be observed when a placebo is substituted for the drug. This is because the placebo provides the expectation of receiving the drug that leads to the other two expectancies that influence the response. Responses to a placebo may be consistent with the behavioral effect of a drug, but sometimes they are opposite to the drug effect. The learning analysis indicates that a drug-opposite placebo response should be observed when an expected type of drug effect is accompanied by an expectation of unfavorable consequences for displaying the effect. For example, a drinker who expects that impaired performance under alcohol leads to undesirable consequences may attempt to compensate by resisting impairment. In this case, the display of a drug-opposite compensatory response would result in performance under a placebo that is better than normal because the impairing effect of the drug is absent.

In summary, the learning analysis identifies specific relationships between events in a drug-taking situation. These events allow the acquisition of expectations about the administration of the drug, the type of behavioral effect it exerts on a given activity, and the consequence of displaying the response in a particular situation. Studies of drug expectancies have shown that individuals commonly report these three expectancies. By identifying specific events that provide an opportunity to acquire these expectancies, the model highlights the complexity of a drug-taking situation by showing how these expectancies may be activated sequentially to influence the response to a drug or to a placebo. The expectation of receiving a drug, identified as the first expectancy in the model, has been the subject of much research. The novel contribution of the model is the identification of effects attributed to the other two expectancies. In the next two sections we describe research on two socially used drugs (i.e., alcohol and caffeine) that has tested the learning model by examining the influence of the expected type of response and its expected consequence on cognitive and psychomotor behavior.

EXPECTED TYPES OF RESPONSE

Many researchers have investigated the effect of a moderate dose of alcohol on the performance of a variety of psychomotor and cognitive activities (e.g., for a review, see Mitchell, 1985). These researchers have typically found that the performance of social drinkers tends to be impaired under alcohol, although the intensity of impairment differs somewhat among individuals. One factor contributing to individual differences in responses to alcohol may be expectancies about the effects of the drug. During the normal course of social drinking, an individual likely has many opportunities to experience some alcohol-induced impairment in cognitive and psychomotor activities. This relationship, identified in our learning analysis by S^*_d–R_d (see Figure 9.1), should lead a drinker to expect some impairment under alcohol. However, individuals are likely to differ in the particular activities performed under alcohol and in the intensity of the alcohol effects they experience. As a result, drinkers may differ in the degree of alcohol impairment they expect for a given activity. In theory, individual differences in the expected degree of impairment on a given task should predict the degree of impairment under alcohol. Those who expect more impairment should display poorer performance.

Several studies of male social drinkers have investigated the relationship between their expected and actual impairment under alcohol (Fillmore, Carscadden, & Vogel-Sprott, 1998; Fillmore & Vogel-Sprott, 1994, 1995c). Participants in these studies performed a laboratory task alone in a room where no feedback or other environmental consequence was associated with any response on the task. The expected type of response to alcohol was measured after participants were familiarized with the task. They rated the expected effect of alcohol (two beers drunk in 1 hr) on their task performance using a scale with endpoints of *extreme impairment* and *extreme improvement*. When participants subsequently received alcohol and performed the task, their impairment was measured by the pre- to postalcohol change in task performance. These expectancy and impairment measures served to test the relationship between the expected and actual degree of impairment.

These studies of cognitive and psychomotor performance have shown that individuals differ in their expectations about the degree to which alcohol will impair their task performance, and these differences predict the degree of impairment they display under alcohol (Fillmore et al., 1998; Fillmore & Vogel-Sprott, 1994, 1995c). In accord with the learning analysis, the impairment of information-processing and motor skills under alcohol increased as a function of expectations of greater impairment.

Several studies of expectancies about alcohol impairment have included groups of drinkers who received a placebo instead of alcohol (Fillmore et al., 1998; Fillmore & Vogel-Sprott, 1994, 1995c). The findings showed that those who expected greater impairment from alcohol performed more poorly under a placebo. Thus, just as expectancies about alcohol impairment were related to changes in behavior under the drug, these expectancies also were related to changes in response to a placebo when drinkers expected alcohol.

The relationship between expected and actual drug effects has also been extended to caffeine, a socially used stimulant in the form of coffee. Earlier research with placebo caffeine indicated that differences in performance under the placebo related to individual differences in the expected effects of the drug (Kirsch & Weixel, 1988). In our research (Fillmore, 1994; Fillmore & Vogel-Sprott, 1994), two groups of participants rated the effect they expected four cups of caffeinated coffee would have on their performance of a psychomotor task and subsequently performed the task under 2.93 mg/kg caffeine or placebo caffeine (i.e., decaffeinated coffee). The results showed that individual differences in the type and degree of effects expected from caffeine predicted the type of response displayed under the drug and the placebo. Caffeine tended to improve performance compared with placebo, but, in both cases, individuals who expected less improvement performed more poorly.

Most research on drug expectancies has been concerned with only one drug, but individuals may also combine drugs. For example, a social drinking occasion often concludes with caffeine in the form of coffee. The repeated experience of the behavioral effect of combining alcohol and caffeine should lead individuals to expect a particular effect $(S^*_d-R_d)$ from the drug combination. Research testing such expectancies has shown that social drinkers differed in the degree of impairment they expected from combining alcohol and caffeine and that these differences predicted their changes in psychomotor performance when they expected to receive both drugs (Fillmore & Vogel-Sprott, 1995b). The impairing effect of alcohol (0.56 g/kg) was reduced by caffeine (4.4 mg/kg), but those who expected more impairment from the combined drugs performed more poorly.

Other research has investigated conditions that should strengthen the relationship between the expected and actual behavioral effect of alcohol. An individual may hold expectations about the behavioral effect of alcohol before any personal use of alcohol (e.g., Christiansen, Goldman, & Inn, 1982). However, when social drinking commences, an individual's personal experience of the drug effect provides information that allows the acquisition of an expected type of effect that more closely corresponds to the person's own actual response to the drug. The degree to which this experience is repeated should depend in part on the length of time that a drinker has been using alcohol regularly. This possibility has been investigated in a study that classified social drinkers in terms of the length of time they had been using alcohol regularly (Fillmore & Vogel-Sprott, 1995a). "Novices" had been drinking socially for 20 months or less, and "experienced" individuals had been drinkers for 24 months or more. The respondents rated the degree to which alcohol was expected to impair their performance of a motor skill before they performed the task under alcohol (0.56 g/kg). The results showed that the experienced drinkers who expected more impairment performed more poorly under alcohol. In contrast, no relationship was found between novice drinkers' expected and actual impairment under alcohol. These findings indicate that some history of regular drinking is required before a relationship can be observed between drinkers' expected and actual behavioral effects of alcohol.

Relationships between expectancies and drug-related behavior are consistent with the assumption that expectancies mediate this behavior. However, this correlational evidence cannot rule out the possibility that some other factor is responsible for the expectancy–behavior relationship. To infer cause, researchers must manipulate the expectation about a drug effect to show that it alters drug-related behavior. One method of altering these expectancies is to provide an individual with new information about the effect of a drug on an activity. Several studies have used this procedure to manipulate the expected type of drug response.

In some experiments placebos have been used to test the behavioral effect of manipulating expectancies in the absence of any pharmacological drug effects (Fillmore, Mulvihill, & Vogel-Sprott, 1994; Fillmore & Vogel-Sprott, 1992). In these experiments, alcohol placebos and caffeine placebos were administered to different groups of participants. After they became familiar with a psychomotor task, two groups expecting caffeine received new information that led them to expect that caffeine would either enhance or impair their task performance. Similarly, those expecting alcohol received information that led them to expect that alcohol would either enhance or impair their performance. When the groups subsequently performed the task under their respective placebos, the expectancy manipulation was found to alter performance. The response of each group expecting caffeine was consistent with the type of effect it had been led to expect. The expectation of enhancement from caffeine resulted in better performance than the expectation of impairment. In contrast, the placebo response of each group expecting alcohol was contrary to the type of effect it had been led to expect. The group expecting enhancement performed more poorly, and the group expecting impairment showed drug-opposite improvement. In theory, the drug-opposite compensatory improvement displayed by the latter group would be attributed to the expectation of some favorable consequence for resisting impairment. This possibility was suggested by participants' reports of a greater desire to resist alcohol impairment than caffeine impairment. Thus, it may be that drinkers entered the experiment expecting that resisting alcohol impairment generally leads to more favorable consequences and maintained this expectation even though the test situation provided no environmental outcome for performance.

This explanation for compensatory improvement in performance observed in the studies of placebo alcohol has been tested in other research (Fillmore & Vogel-Sprott, 1996). It was reasoned that if participants in the experimental situation tend to expect that resisting alcohol impairment is desirable, they should also display compensatory performance under alcohol. Accordingly, when alcohol (0.56 g/kg) was administered, the participants led to expect impairment displayed a compensatory response (i.e., less impairment) compared with those who had not been led to expect impairment. Another interesting facet of this study was the evidence it provided to show that drinkers differed in the degree to which their expectancies could be manipulated to alter their behavior. Those who had been using alcohol regularly for a longer period of time were less susceptible to the expectancy manipulation and less likely to change their response to alcohol.

The research reviewed in this section was designed to assess the effect of the expected type of response to drug. To investigate this one expectancy, research was conducted in a drug-taking setting that provided no environmental outcome for any response to a task. In the next section, we describe research that has tested the influence of a third expectancy, the expected consequence of the response to a drug. This requires a different experimental design in which only the outcome of the response to a drug is manipulated.

EXPECTED CONSEQUENCES

The association between a response and its outcome provides an opportunity to learn what consequence to expect for a given response. Studies of learning have shown that altering the value of the outcome has a predictable impact on behavior (e.g., Dickinson & Balleine, 1995). The motivation for the response is attributed to the incentive value of the expected consequence. The occurrence of a response increases in a situation when it is reliably associated with some favorable outcome and decreases when the outcome is withheld. The learning model of expectancies in a drug-taking situation symbolizes these relationships as R_d-S^* and predicts that the occurrence of a particular behavioral response to a drug depends on the expected presence or absence of a favorable consequence.

A clear test of this hypothesis requires an experimental procedure in which all the participants expect and receive a drug and only the outcome of the response is manipulated. An example of this method, illustrated in terms of the model (see Figure 9.1), is one that holds constant the expectation of receiving a drug ($S-S^*_d$) and allows the expected type of response ($S^*_d-R_d$) to vary randomly among participants. The only factor that is systematically changed is the outcome associated with a particular response to a drug. When these outcomes differ, individuals learn to expect different consequences, and the acquisition of these expectancies should depend on the reliability of the response–outcome association in a drug-taking setting. This can be ensured by administering repeated drug doses in the same experimental situation. To control for repeated drug exposures, experimenters give all participants the same doses equally often.

This experimental procedure has been applied in a number of studies of the behavioral response to alcohol. Alcohol is one drug with effects that are often found to diminish with habitual use. This phenomenon is termed *tolerance*, and it is commonly attributed to a compensatory response that counteracts the drug effect (e.g., Kalant, 1987; Siegel, 1989). In behavior, tolerance is inferred from a reduction in the impairing effect of alcohol on performance. Although some instances of alcohol tolerance may be due to physiological changes induced solely by repeated drug exposure, the model of learned expectancies indicates that behavioral tolerance should be predicted by the expected consequence of the response to the drug. Specifically, behavioral tolerance should be evident when resisting alcohol impairment is expected to yield a favorable consequence. If no such consequence is expected, little or no tolerance should be displayed. Considerable research testing these hypotheses and their implications has been reviewed elsewhere (Vogel-Sprott, 1992), and an overview of the findings is presented here.

Participants in this research were social drinkers who were trained on a motor skill task before they attended a number of weekly drinking sessions in which they practiced the task under alcohol (0.62 g/kg). The occurrence of a compensatory response to counteract the alcohol-induced impairment was identified by performance that was equal to a participant's prior drug-free level of achievement. Positive reinforcement, in the form of money or verbal feedback, was administered whenever a compensatory response was displayed. This training provided an opportunity to learn to expect a favorable consequence for drug-compensatory performance (i.e., resisting alcohol impairment). The effect of this training has been compared with control treatments that provided equivalent task practice under repeated doses of alcohol when reinforcement was absent or administered randomly with respect to performance (e.g., Beirness & Vogel-Sprott, 1984). These control conditions provided no opportunity to acquire this expectancy. The results have consistently demonstrated that training with a favorable outcome for resisting impairment results in behavioral tolerance and that equivalent training without this specific response–outcome association has little effect on tolerance (Vogel-Sprott, 1992).

The findings are in line with the proposal that the learned expectation of some reward for resisting alcohol impairment leads to a compensatory reaction that counteracts the drug effect. Under alcohol, this effect is observed as behavioral tolerance. However, if alcohol is absent, the compensatory response should be observed directly and should operate to improve performance. In support of this prediction, participants who are trained to expect a favorable consequence for drug-compensatory performance under alcohol also show greater compensatory improvement under a placebo when the drug is expected (e.g., Sdao-Jarvie & Vogel-Sprott, 1991).

Other research has shown that tolerance can be extinguished by withholding the favorable outcome for drug-compensatory performance that drinkers had learned to expect (R. E. Mann & Vogel-Sprott, 1981). Because tolerance in this research extinguished even though alcohol doses continued to be repeated, the results indicate that a period of abstinence from alcohol is not necessary for behavioral tolerance to subside.

A learned response on one task is likely to generalize and transfer to another similar task (e.g., Domjan & Burkhard, 1986). Accordingly, when participants expected a rewarding consequence for resisting alcohol impairment on one motor skill task, their tolerance transferred to a second similar task performed for the first time under alcohol (Rawana & Vogel-Sprott, 1985). This research also showed that the expectation of the reward was crucial for transfer because little tolerance was displayed on the second task when no rewarding consequence was expected.

In these various experiments on behavioral tolerance to alcohol, researchers tested the hypothesis that the learned expectation of a favorable consequence for resisting alcohol impairment is the specific expectancy that enhances behavioral tolerance to alcohol. This was confirmed in studies in which drug exposures were controlled and this expectancy was manipulated. In general, the findings indicate that the behavioral tolerance of social drinkers may be better predicted by the expected consequences of behavior acquired during repeated doses of alcohol than by the physiological effects of the doses.

In contrast to research interest in factors contributing to behavioral tolerance to alcohol, little attention has been paid to the phenomenon of *sensitization*, which is an intensification of the behavioral effect of repeated doses of alcohol. However, the learning model predicts that sensitization to alcohol impairment should be produced as readily as tolerance and requires only that a drinker expects behavioral impairment to yield a favorable consequence. A series of studies has confirmed this hypothesis, showing that sensitization is displayed by drinkers trained to expect a favorable consequence for behavioral impairment under alcohol, whereas tolerance is displayed by others expecting the same consequence for drug-compensatory performance (Zack & Vogel-Sprott, 1995, 1997). Speaking loosely, it seems that drunk or sober behavior under alcohol depends on which behavior is expected to yield a favorable consequence.

This review of research on the third expectancy, identified as R_d–S* in the model, has provided evidence to show that it plays a role in mediating behavior when alcohol is expected and when it is actually received. Manipulating this expectancy by altering the outcome of the response to alcohol can predictably produce behavioral tolerance or sensitization to the drug. In the next section we consider some general implications of the evidence on the three-expectancy model.

IMPLICATIONS

In the research discussed in this chapter, a learning approach was adopted that broadens the perspective concerning factors that determine behavioral responses to drugs. Depressant drugs such as alcohol usually impair motor and cognitive performance, and stimulants like caffeine generally improve these activities. Although the pharmacological classification of a drug provides a general indicator of its effects, it does not account for differences in the response to a drug among individuals or within individuals in different situations. The research discussed in this chapter shows how a cognitive variable, expectancy, may explain such differences. The evidence has shown that drug-related expectancies depend on events in drug-taking situations and so can differ among individuals and across situations. In addition, these expectancies can affect the behavioral response displayed to a drug. Thus, interpersonal and intersituational differences in expectancies make it possible to account for differences in behavioral responses to a drug that could not otherwise be explained by its comparatively static pharmacological action. The learning model indicates the importance of considering not only the pharmacological effect of a drug but also the drug-related expectancies of an individual and the environmental conditions that give rise to these expectations.

There is no doubt that drugs exert pharmacological effects on behavior. However, an understanding of these effects must be considered in the context of the accompanying drug-related expectancies. The relative importance of drug-related expectancies in determining behavior likely depends on a number of factors. The findings presented in this chapter were based on socially used doses of alcohol and caffeine as well as their placebos. This evidence served to demonstrate the importance of expectancies in determining the behavioral responses when drug effects were moderate or absent. Evidence from moderate drug doses shows that the pharmacological effect on behavior can be modulated by an individual's drug-related expectancies. In some cases, these expectancies were shown to override the pharmacological effect of the drug, as in the case in which expected favorable consequences of resisting behavioral impairment produced tolerance to alcohol. However, higher drug doses that exert more intense pharmacological effects may overwhelm any influence of expectancies on behavior.

Drug use factors, such as the quantity and frequency of consumption, may also contribute to individual differences in response to a drug. However, the current alcohol or caffeine consumption of individuals who used these drugs socially failed to account for the variation in their responses to these drugs. It may be that evidence of a relationship between current consumption and response to a drug requires a wider range in consumption that includes high levels exceeding those reported by social users. It is also possible that the effect of typical drug consumption becomes evident only after a long period of time. In contrast to long-term drug use, the research reviewed in this chapter shows that expectancies influence drug responses at an early stage in the course of social drinking. Within a few years of regular alcohol use, social drinkers' expectations about behavioral impairment become more closely related to their actual impairment of an activity under the drug, and these expectancies are more resistant to change.

Although expectancies about a drug may initially be fairly task and situation specific, they may also generalize and transfer to other drug-taking situations to exert a broader influence on drug-related behavior. This possibility was found in a study on alcohol tolerance that transferred from one task to another when the situation provided the expected reward for compensating (Rawana & Vogel-Sprott, 1985). Another example discussed in this chapter concerns the compensatory placebo responses of social drinkers who reported a desire to resist alcohol impairment in a situation that provided no environmental outcomes for performance (Fillmore et al., 1994). Expectancies about the response to a drug and its consequence may also have more pervasive effects, possibly influencing what activities are undertaken. For example, social drinkers who expect alcohol to induce little impairment of a task, like driving a car, may be more inclined to engage in this activity after drinking. The relation of expectancies about drug effects and their consequences to risk taking and other types of behaviors may be important to understanding drug-related accidents.

The role of environmental events in determining expectancies has a number of important implications for interpreting individual differences in response to a drug. Differences in behavioral impairment to a challenge dose of alcohol have been considered as possible markers for the development of alcohol-related problems (e.g., Schuckit, 1994), and tolerance to its behavioral impairing effects is usually considered a symptom of drug abuse (American Psychiatric Association, 1994). Such interpretations assume that an individual's behavioral response to alcohol is a fairly stable attribute that is relatively constant across different drinking situations. However, research indicates that a social drinker can display impairment in one situation and tolerance in another depending on the expected behavioral effects and consequences. Such adaptability in response to a drug challenges the notion that drug responses are stable attributes of individuals.

Finally, the evidence on drug-related expectancies has implications for research in which placebos are used to control for the effect of expecting a drug. A comparison between placebo and drug groups is used to distinguish the pharmacological effect of a drug from the expectation of receiving it. However, this learned expectancy is just the first in a sequence that is followed by two others. These concern the type of response and its consequence, and each can influence the placebo response. Although the administration of a placebo is commonly considered to provide an adequate control for drug expectancies, it ensures only a common expectation of receiving a drug that leads to other expectancies whose behavioral effects are unknown and uncontrolled. Thus, it appears that individuals' expectations about the type of drug effect and its environmental consequences must be determined to provide an adequate interpretation of the response to a placebo.

CLINICAL CONSIDERATIONS

The theory and research reviewed in the chapter shows that three drug-related expectancies have to be considered to predict the behavioral response to a drug or to a placebo. These same expectancies have been implicated in many theories of the use and abuse of alcohol as well as other drugs (e.g., Brown, 1993). In this section, we consider the possible role of drug-related expectancies in the development of drug use and abuse.

Investigations of drug-related expectancies have shown that individuals report expectancies about receiving a drug, its effect, and its consequence. However, little is yet known about the role of each expectancy because investigators have not distinguished among these expectancies. Instead, researchers have focused on the finding that more favorable expectancies of all types are associated with greater drug use (e.g., Brown, 1993). These relationships are consistent with the assumption that expectancies may mediate behavior. In particular, favorable expectations may increase drug use and thus play a causal role in substance use and abuse. Additional circumstantial evidence has been provided by findings that indicate that favorable alcohol expectancies are related to high-risk status based on a family history of alcoholism and personality characteristics that may predispose individuals to early alcohol abuse (Brown & Munson, 1987; L. M.

Mann, Chassin, & Sher, 1987). Such evidence has raised the possibility that expectancies related to drug abuse may depend on genetic and biological factors as well as on environmental variables.

Important information on factors predisposing addictive drug use has been obtained from research on drug activation of neurological reward systems (Robinson & Berridge, 1993; Stewart, deWit, & Eikelboom, 1984; Wise & Bozarth, 1987). However, these researchers did not address individual differences in susceptibility to addictive drug use. Such information may be provided by investigations of drug-related expectancies that consider the environmental context in which drug taking occurs and the rich potential for learning expectancies based on predrug cues and outcomes of drug effects. Even though addictive drugs activate neurological reward systems common to all individuals, differences in their expectancies may contribute importantly to susceptibility for addiction.

It is difficult to test the causal role of expectancies as mediators of drug use and abuse in humans. However, some research with heavy social drinkers has shown that an educational program designed to reduce their favorable expectations about alcohol resulted in a reduction of their alcohol consumption (Darkes & Goldman, 1993). Consistent with other studies of drug use, these investigators do not distinguish between the expected effects of the drug and its expected consequences. It may be important to determine which expectancy has greater influence on drug use. Such information may be essential to addiction prevention and intervention programs that attempt to incorporate techniques to identify and change high-risk drug-related expectancies (e.g., Brown, 1993). A learning model of expectancies may offer some helpful guidance because it identifies different pairs of events that give rise to expectancies about the type of response and its consequence and indicates how each pair of events can be manipulated to alter these expectancies and change behavior in a drug-taking situation.

A learning analysis would predict that heavy repeated drug use should be most likely to occur when the expected type of response and its expected consequence are desirable. Their rehearsal each time a drug is taken should be particularly important in determining drug use because this practice may affect expectancies in a fashion analogous to that observed when a task is repeatedly performed. Repeated practice of a task under similar conditions leads to performance that is qualitatively different from that observed when a task is originally undertaken (e.g., Schneider & Shiffrin, 1977). Initially, an individual pays considerable attention to each stimulus and response component of the activity. Performance is slow, hesitant, and variable. With extended practice, performance stabilizes and the activity is completed rapidly with little awareness, attention, or effort. This transformation is referred to as the development of *automaticity* (e.g., Logan, 1988; Schneider, 1985). Automaticity has received much research attention and is considered to characterize most of the regularly occurring cognitive activities of humans. Practice, in the form of repeated drug use, may have a similar transforming effect on drug-related expectancies. When drug use begins or occurs in a new drug-taking situation, the acquisition of each expectancy may require some deliberate attention and appraisal of stimulus–response events. However, extended practice in similar drug-taking situations may integrate the set of expectancies so that they occur more swiftly, "automatically," with little conscious deliberation. This suggestion bears some parallel to the proposal that repeated drug-taking results in the development of an "automatic drug action schema" (Tiffany, 1990). According to this theory, cognitive expectancies are assumed to function automatically to govern the drug-taking routine, and craving, or urges, for the drug occurs when circumstances (e.g., a decision to remain abstinent) impede or change the habitual drug-taking activity.

The learning interpretation of drug-related expectancies is compatible with other conceptualizations in which drug-related expectancies are thought to be learned (e.g., Goldman, Brown, Christiansen, & Smith, 1991; Rather & Goldman, 1994; Stacy, Leigh, & Weingardt, 1994). In these studies, expectancies were viewed as being encoded memories of information about a drug, and their structure, storage, and retrieval were investigated. The research involves an inductive process based on exploring the relationships among measures of established expectancies. In the research described in this chapter, the investigators adopted a deductive approach that manipulated events to investigate the learning processes involved in acquiring or changing drug-related expectancies. Both approaches provide different information and contribute importantly to more fully understanding the role of expectancies in drug-related behavior.

REFERENCES

American Psychiatric Association. (1994). *Diagnostic and statistical manual of mental disorders* (4th ed.). Washington, DC: Author.

Beirness, D. J., & Vogel-Sprott, M. (1984). Alcohol tolerance in social drinkers: Operant and classical conditioning effects. *Psychopharmacology, 84,* 393–397.

Bolles, R. C. (1972). Reinforcement, expectancy and learning. *Psychological Review, 79,* 394–409.

Bolles, R. C. (1975). *Theory of motivation* (2nd ed.). New York: Harper & Row.

Bolles, R. C. (1979). *Learning theory* (2nd ed.). New York: Holt, Reinhart & Winston.

Brandon, T. H., & Baker, T. B. (1992). The Smoking Consequences Questionnaire: The subjective utility of smoking in college students. *Psychological Assessment, 3,* 484–491.

Brown, S. A. (1993). Drug effect expectancies and addictive behavior change. *Experimental and Clinical Psychopharmacology, 1,* 55–67.

Brown, S. A., & Munson, E. (1987). Extroversion, anxiety and the perceived effects of alcohol. *Journal of Studies on Alcohol, 48,* 272–276.

Christiansen, B. A., Goldman, M. S., & Inn, A. (1982). Development of alcohol-related expectancies in adolescents: Separating pharmacological from social learning influences. *Journal of Consulting and Clinical Psychology, 50,* 336–344.

Colwill, R. M., & Rescorla, R. A. (1986). Associative structures in instrumental learning. *Psychology of Learning and Motivation, 20,* 55–104.

Darkes, J., & Goldman, M. S. (1993). Expectancy challenge and drinking reduction: Experimental evidence for a mediational process. *Journal of Consulting and Clinical Psychology, 61,* 334–353.

Dickinson, A., & Balleine, B. (1995). Motivational control of instrumental action. *Current Directions in Psychological Science, 4,* 162–167.

Domjan, M., & Burkhard, B. (1986). Stimulus control of instrumental and classical conditioning. In M. Domjan (Ed.), *The principles of learning and behavior* (2nd ed., pp. 181–215). Monterey, CA: Brooks/Cole.

Fillmore, M. T. (1994). Investigating the behavioral effects of caffeine: The contribution of drug-related expectancies. *Pharmacopsychoecologia, 7,* 63–73.

Fillmore, M. T., Carscadden, J., & Vogel-Sprott, M. (1998). Alcohol, cognitive impairment and expectancies. *Journal of Studies on Alcohol, 59,* 174–179.

Fillmore, M. T., Mulvihill, L. E., & Vogel-Sprott, M. (1994). The expected drug and its expected effect interact to determine placebo responses to alcohol and caffeine. *Psychopharmacology, 115,* 383–388.

Fillmore, M., & Vogel-Sprott, M. (1992). Expected effect of caffeine on motor performance predicts the type of response to placebo. *Psychopharmacology, 106,* 209–214.

Fillmore, M., & Vogel-Sprott, M. (1994). Psychomotor performance under alcohol and under caffeine: Pharmacological and expectancy effects. *Journal of Experimental and Clinical Psychopharmacology, 2,* 319–328.

Fillmore, M. T., & Vogel-Sprott, M. (1995a). Behavioral effects of alcohol in novice and experienced drinkers: Alcohol expectancies and impairment. *Psychopharmacology, 122,* 175–181.

Fillmore, M. T., & Vogel-Sprott, M. (1995b). Behavioral effects of combining alcohol and caffeine: The contribution of drug-related expectancies. *Journal of Experimental and Clinical Psychopharmacology, 3,* 33–38.

Fillmore, M. T., & Vogel-Sprott, M. (1995c). Expectancies about alcohol-induced motor impairment predict individual differences in responses to alcohol and placebo. *Journal of Studies on Alcohol, 56,* 90–98.

Fillmore, M., & Vogel-Sprott, M. (1996). Evidence that expectancies mediate behavior under alcohol. *Journal of Studies on Alcohol, 57,* 598–603.

Goldman, M., Brown, S., & Christiansen, B. (1987). Expectancy theory: Thinking about drinking. In H. Blane & K. Leonard (Eds.), *Psychological theories of drinking and alcoholism* (pp. 181–226). New York: Guilford Press.

Goldman, M. S., Brown, S. A., Christiansen, B. A., & Smith, G. T. (1991). Alcoholism and memory: Broadening the scope of alcohol-expectancy research. *Psychological Bulletin, 110,* 137–146.

Jaffe, A. (1992). Cognitive factors associated with cocaine abuse and its treatment: An analysis of expectancies of use. In T. Kosten & H. Kleiber (Eds.), *Clinician's guide to cocaine addiction* (pp. 128–150). New York: Guilford Press.

Kalant, H. (1987). Tolerance and its significance for drug and alcohol dependence. In L. S. Harris (Ed.), *Problems of drug dependence* (NIDA Research Monograph No. 76, pp. 9–19). Washington, DC: U.S. Government Printing Office.

Kirsch, I. (1985). Response expectancy as a determinant of experience and behavior. *American Psychologist, 40,* 1189–1202.

Kirsch, I., & Weixel, L. J. (1988). Double-blind versus deceptive administration of a placebo. *Behavioral Neuroscience, 102,* 319–323.

Logan, G. D. (1988). Toward an instance theory of automatization. *Psychological Review, 95,* 492–527.

Mann, L. M., Chassin, L., & Sher, K. J. (1987). Alcohol expectancies and the risk for alcoholism. *Journal of Consulting and Clinical Psychology, 55,* 411–417.

Mann, R. E., & Vogel-Sprott, M. (1981). Control of alcohol tolerance by reinforcement in nonalcoholics. *Psychopharmacology, 75,* 315–320.

Marlatt, G. A., & Gordon, J. R. (Eds.). (1985). *Relapse prevention: Maintenance strategies in the treatment of addictive behaviors.* New York: Guilford Press.

Mitchell, M. C. (1985). Alcohol-induced impairment of central nervous system function: Behavioral skills involved in driving. *Journal of Studies on Alcohol, Suppl. 10,* 109–116.

Rather, B. C., & Goldman, M. S. (1994). Drinking-related differences in the memory organization of alcohol expectancies. *Experimental and Clinical Psychopharmacology, 2,* 167–183.

Rawana, E., & Vogel-Sprott, M. (1985). The transfer of alcohol tolerance, and its relation to reinforcement. *Drug and Alcohol Dependence, 16,* 75–83.

Rescorla, R. A. (1987). A Pavlovian analysis of goal-directed behavior. *American Psychologist, 42,* 119–129.

Rescorla, R. A. (1992). The associative basis of instrumental learning. *APS Observer, 5,* 6.

Robinson, T. E., & Berridge, K. C. (1993). The neural basis of drug craving: An incentive-sensitization theory of addiction. *Brain Research Reviews, 18,* 247–291.

Schafer, J., & Brown, S. A. (1991). Marijuana and cocaine effect expectancies and drug use patterns. *Journal of Consulting and Clinical Psychology, 59,* 558–565.

Schneider, W. (1985). Toward a model of attention and the development of automatic processing. In M. E. Posner & O. S. M. Martin (Eds.), *Attention and performance* (Vol. 11, pp. 475–492). Hillsdale, NJ: Erlbaum.

Schneider, W., & Shiffrin, R. M. (1977). Controlled and automatic human information processing: I. Detection, search and attention. *Psychological Review*, *84*, 1–66.

Schuckit, M. (1994). Low level of response to alcohol as a predictor of future alcoholism. *American Journal of Psychiatry*, *151*, 184–189.

Sdao-Jarvie, K., & Vogel-Sprott, M. (1991). Response expectancies affect the acquisition and display of behavioral tolerance to alcohol. *Alcohol*, *8*, 491–498.

Siegel, S. (1989). Pharmacological conditioning and drug effects. In A. J. Goudie & M. W. Emmett-Oglesby (Eds.), *Psychoactive drugs* (pp. 115–169). Clifton, NJ: Humana Press.

Stacy, A. W., Leigh, B. C., & Weingardt, K. R. (1994). Memory accessibility and association of alcohol use and its positive outcomes. *Experimental and Clinical Psychopharmacology*, *2*, 269–282.

Stewart, J., deWit, H., & Eikelboom, R. (1984). The role of unconditioned and conditioned drug effects in the self-administration of opiates and stimulants. *Psychological Review*, *91*, 251–268.

Tiffany, S. T. (1990). A cognitive model of drug urges and drug-use behavior: Role of automatic and nonautomatic processes. *Psychological Review*, *97*, 147–168.

Tolman, E. C. (1932). *Purposive behavior in animals and men*. New York: Century.

Vogel-Sprott, M. (1992). *Alcohol tolerance and social drinking: Learning the consequences*. New York: Guilford Press.

Wise, R. A., & Bozarth, M. A. (1987). A psychomotor stimulant theory of addiction. *Psychological Review*, *94*, 469–492.

Zack, M., & Vogel-Sprott, M. (1995). Behavioral tolerance and sensitization to alcohol in humans: The contribution of learning. *Experimental and Clinical Psychopharmacology*, *3*, 396–401.

Zack, M., & Vogel-Sprott, M. (1997). Drunk or sober? Learned conformity to a behavioral standard. *Journal of Studies on Alcohol*, *58*, 495–501.

10

EXPECTANCY MEDIATION OF BIOPSYCHOSOCIAL RISK FOR ALCOHOL USE AND ALCOHOLISM

MARK S. GOLDMAN, JACK DARKES, AND FRANCES K. DEL BOCA

Alcohol, a chemical, affects behavior, and drinking behavior influences physiology (Goldman & Rather, 1993). This apparent mind–body duality has stimulated research ranging from the biological to the sociocultural. Contrary to hopes that a central individual characteristic or mechanism might be discovered at one of these levels of explanation, research has shown that many variables influence alcohol use and alcoholism[1] and that these variables operate over an extensive time course. For example, early family environment may influence the consumption of alcohol much later in life. However, adequate theories require more than a description of covariation. So, for example, showing that alcoholic individuals share a

Portions of this work were supported by National Institute on Alcohol Abuse and Alcoholism Grant R37 AA08333. This chapter was condensed from a more comprehensive and fully referenced version due to page limitations. A copy of the full text is available from the authors.

[1]In this chapter, the term *alcohol use* refers to consumption at any level; the terms *alcohol abuse* and *dependence* are used in accordance with the usage in the fourth edition of the *Diagnostic and Statistical Manual of Mental Disorders* (American Psychiatric Association, 1994); and the terms *alcoholism* and *alcohol dependence* are used interchangeably.

genetic characteristic or a particular childhood family environment does not constitute an explanation; the processes underlying this influence must be articulated. The variables that have been linked to alcohol use and alcoholism are reviewed in this chapter to highlight the need for expectancy as a process that can integrate and causally link these diverse variables to alcohol use and alcoholism. The alcohol expectancy literature is then reviewed in this context.

BIOLOGICAL AND GENETIC VARIABLES

The first-degree relatives of alcoholic individuals are 2–7 times more likely to develop alcoholism than members of the general population (National Institute Alcohol Abuse and Alcoholism, 1997). This increased risk may be due to family environment or to the genetic transmission of particular biological characteristics. In this section we briefly review the biological characteristics most commonly linked to genetic influences. Later, we examine the processes that might connect these variables to problem drinking. In each case, readers should consider whether the putative variable would translate into excessive drinking if the individual did not in some fashion "know" (i.e., store information about) what alcohol was and have information about its presumed pharmacological effects.

In 1990, Blum et al. reported that many more alcoholic than nonalcoholic individuals had a particular allele (gene variant) within the chromosomal region for the D_2 dopamine receptor (DRD_2 locus). This finding was significant given the reported links among the dopaminergic system, drug seeking, and reinforcement (Wise & Bozarth, 1987). Additional research has not replicated the finding but has instead revealed methodological issues that future researchers must address (e.g., natural ethnic variations in such gene polymorphisms).

Genetically determined variations in alcohol metabolism have been associated with the degree of risk. These variations, which occur mostly among individuals of Chinese and Japanese descent, result in high levels of blood acetaldehyde after ingestion of even small amounts of alcohol, producing facial flushing, nausea, headaches, hypothermia, and general dysphoria. Nonetheless, Asian college students may still drink heavily because of social pressure despite the flushing response (Nakawatase, Yamamato, & Sasao, 1993).

Sons of alcoholics (SOAs) differ from sons of nonalcoholics in alcohol sensitivity (i.e., their subjective and physiological reactions to alcohol). Some researchers (e.g., Schuckit, 1988) have argued that SOAs are less sensitive to alcohol (i.e., more tolerant) and must consume more to achieve a noticeable subjective effect. Schuckit (1994) has also reported that the SOAs who are the least sensitive to alcohol were most likely to become alcoholic 10 years later. Conversely, others (e.g., Pihl, Peterson, & Finn, 1990) have proposed that SOAs are more sensitive and achieve greater stress relief from drinking. After considering the biphasic nature of alcohol's effects, still other researchers (Newlin & Thompson, 1990) have suggested that SOAs are both more sensitive to the positive effects associated with the ascending limb of the blood alcohol curve (BAC) and more tolerant of the negative effects associated with the descending limb (a differentiator model). Although support for each position has been in the literature, failures to replicate have also been reported, possibly because of varying doses, conditions of administration, and methods for assigning familial risk (Finn & Pihl, 1988).

Certain aspects of event-related potentials (ERPs) and other electro-encephalographic (EEG) characteristics have been implicated in alcoholism. The results of numerous studies (see Polich, Pollock, & Bloom, 1994, for a review) have suggested that children of alcoholics (COAs) show reduced P3 amplitude compared with controls, primarily in response to a difficult visual (not auditory) discrimination task. This diminished P3 amplitude may reflect persistent neuropsychological differences in COAs and a delay in neurodevelopment (Polich et al., 1994), and it may be inherited (Katsanis, Iacono, McGue, & Carlson, 1997). Although resting EEG differences between SOAs and the sons of nonalcoholics have been reported only inconsistently, SOAs have greater increases in alpha activity on the ascending limb of the BAC and a faster return to resting alpha levels on the descending limb (e.g., Bauer & Hesselbrock, 1993), a pattern that is consistent with the differentiator model (Newlin & Thompson, 1990).

Two biochemical markers have reliably differentiated both alcoholic individuals and those with a positive family history of alcoholism: decreased availability of serotonin and reduced monoamine oxidase (MAO) activity. Because MAO is involved in the breakdown of serotonin, these two findings may be linked. Both neurotransmitter characteristics have been associated with behavioral tendencies toward impulsivity, sensation seeking, and antisocial personality, although they may also result from recent alcohol use (Goldman, 1993) and smoking (Sher, Byland, Wallitzer, Hartmann, & Ray-Prenger, 1994). Nevertheless, the link between the two markers and problem behavior has suggested a connection to an early-onset, antisocial form of alcoholism (e.g., Cloninger, 1987).

PSYCHOLOGICAL AND ENVIRONMENTAL VARIABLES

Researchers have identified two primary personality patterns associated with alcoholism risk. The first is characterized by high positive affectivity (or behavioral activation) with low negative affectivity (or behavioral inhibition), impulsivity, hyperactivity, sensation seeking, behavioral undercontrol, and antisocial personality (e.g., Sher, 1991; Watson & Tellegen, 1985). Although these attributes antedate alcoholism onset (e.g., Zucker & Gomberg, 1986), excessive drinking is probably only one concomitant of this personality profile. That is, these traits are not specific to risk for alcoholism (e.g., Hesselbrock & Hesselbrock, 1992). The second pattern, characterized by high emotionality, negative affect, anxious or depressed personality, and high behavioral inhibition (e.g., Gray, 1982; Watson & Tellegen, 1985), has been only modestly linked to alcohol abuse (Swaim, Oetting, Edwards, & Beauvais, 1989).

The rates of alcohol use and alcoholism differ across every level of social organization, from the local community to the national level (e.g., Clark & Hilton, 1991). "Wet" drinking cultures, which incorporate alcohol use into daily life, have been distinguished from "dry" drinking cultures, which restrict alcohol use but tend to engage in binge drinking (i.e., infrequent, but high-quantity, consumption). Perhaps paradoxically, dry cultures support more problem drinking despite higher abstinence rates (Hilton, 1991).

Alcohol consumption also differs across gender, race, and ethnic groups (National Institute on Alcohol Abuse and Alcoholism, 1993) and among nationalities, both in their native countries and after immigration to the United States. Family and peer groups also affect drinking. For example, Baer, Stacy, and Lorimer (1991) found that college students consistently overestimate peer drinking, which may promote heavy drinking in this group.

PROCESS IMPLICATIONS OF IDENTIFIED RISK VARIABLES

When all of the steps by which these physical, psychological, or environmental risk characteristics might influence alcohol use and alcoholism are considered, the need for a cognitive (information-processing) component of the causal pathway becomes evident. None of these characteristics commandeer drinking in some automatic fashion. Hence, their influence must be exerted by altering the likelihood of drinking. Furthermore, this influence must span time periods ranging from as long as childhood to adulthood, to as short as the time between entering a bar and consuming alcohol. Acceptable theories must clearly articulate each step in this influence process or note that further steps must be delineated.

One commonality among many identified variables is that they alter the reinforcement value of drinking relative to that of other behaviors. Alcohol metabolic and sensitivity differences, and affective states, make the experience of alcohol use more or less reinforcing. Neurotransmitter differences that lead to problem behavior, and related personality characteristics, may render alcohol use more reinforcing (e.g., more sensations for the sensation seekers). Even if alcohol itself were not more reinforcing, the competitive influence of other reinforcers or the anticipation of aversive states may be diminished. Alternative reinforcers also may become less available; for example, ERP and EEG differences may be markers of cognitive dysfunctions that decrease the probability of success in conventional activities (e.g., school, job). Family, peer group, and cultural influences place individuals in contexts that socially reward drinking, either directly or vicariously. For example, adolescents who do poorly in school and who are sensation seekers might be exposed to (even pressured to engage in) alcohol use through their affiliation with other problem peers. However, the litmus test is the same: Would they drink, under such circumstances, if they did not in some fashion "know" (i.e., retain information about) what effects to expect from alcohol?

Recent formulations of classical and operant conditioning include information-processing assumptions (Bolles, 1972; Rescorla, 1988). Learned behavior reflects templates stored in memory (i.e., expectancies) that anticipate relationships between external events and between behavior and its consequences (Grossberg, 1995; Schultz, Dayan, & Montague, 1997). Hence, the entire memory system may be conceptualized as a kind of information-based "buffer" into which the influence of both biological–genetic and psychological–environmental risk factors is fed. Information that reflects the reinforcement value of alcohol acquired as a function of biological, psychological, and environmental risk variables may be stored as memory templates that, once acquired, can influence alcohol use and its associated behavioral patterns over widely varying time periods (see Figure 10.1). Because such templates anticipate the conditions under which particular behaviors are to be performed, they are called "expectancies." The processing of expectancies can occur at both deliberate (controlled) and automatic levels (see Kirsch, 1985; and Kirsch & Lynn, 1999).

EVIDENCE SUPPORTING A PROCESS VIEW OF EXPECTANCIES

A network of empirical findings supports the inference that expectancies play a causal (i.e., mediational or process) role in drinking (our PsycINFO search from 1984 to 1996, using *alcohol* and *expectancies* as key words, identified 445 studies). Six increasingly stringent levels of evidence can be offered: (a) correlations between measured expectancies and various drinking measures; (b) measurement of expectancies in children well before drinking begins; (c) demonstrations that expectancies predict drinking prospectively; (d) in keeping with the notion that expectancies reflect learning, the observation that not only do expectancies predict drinking but also that drinking experience influences expectancy acquisition; (e) find-

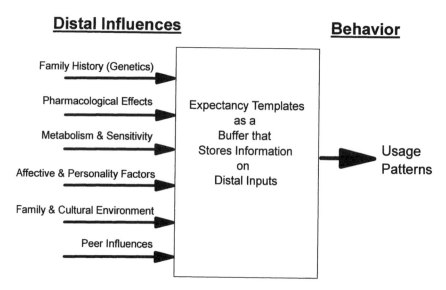

Distal Influences   **Behavior**

Family History (Genetics)

Pharmacological Effects

Metabolism & Sensitivity

Affective & Personality Factors

Family & Cultural Environment

Peer Influences

Expectancy Templates as a Buffer that Stores Information on Distal Inputs

Usage Patterns

Figure 10.1. Depiction of expectancy information serving as a memory "buffer" that mediates the influence of a variety of known antecedent influences on eventual drinking.

ings consistent with the statistical method for demonstrating mediation suggested by Baron and Kenny (1986); and (f) true experiments.

Correlations Between Expectancies and Drinking

The body of studies that show a relationship between expectancies and drinking is now so large that some researchers have called for a moratorium on simple correlational research in favor of the investigation of moderators of the expectancy–drinking relationship (McCarthy & Smith, 1996). We add to this a call for increased emphasis on process-oriented research. Several reviews of this material (e.g., Goldman, 1994; Goldman, Del Boca, & Darkes, in press) show that expectancies are among the strongest predictors of drinking. Researchers have used expectancy questionnaires of various types that have related measured expectancies to a variety of drinking measures (e.g., frequency, quantity, indexes of alcoholism and drinking problems) in age groups ranging from grade school-age children, to older adults, to alcoholic patients in treatment and in treatment follow-up. The expectancy–drinking relationship has been estimated by a range of statistical methods, from simple correlations to hierarchical linear modeling.

A recent meta-analytic review indicated that the average amount of variance in drinking accounted for by expectancies is 12% cross-sectionally and 4% over time (McCarthy & Smith, 1996). Some studies have accounted for 50% or more of the drinking variance when well-developed instruments and analysis techniques were used (e.g., Goldman, Greenbaum, & Darkes, 1997). McCarthy and Smith's (1996) meta-analysis indicated that questionnaire length was the major moderating influence on the size of the relationship between expectancies and alcohol use. Because expectancies presumably reflect information about drinking, it is no surprise that more items reflecting more alcohol effects might increase the relationship (as might the concomitant increase in reliability associated with an increase in items). Although the percentages of variance accounted for are sometimes reported to be much lower (Leigh, 1989a), we found no instances in our review of failures to find a statistically significant relationship. Recently, methods for measuring expectancies arising from cognitive psychology (including techniques understood to be both explicit and implicit) have also been reliably related to drinking (e.g., Palfai, Monti, Colby, & Rohsenow, 1997; Stacy, 1997). Clearly, the relationship is robust across participants, methods, and studies.

One potentially problematic aspect of this relationship arises from issues of possible contamination between the predictor (expectancy) and the criterion (drinking). Theory suggests that expectancies represent information about alcohol and its use acquired both vicariously and directly. Hence, expectancies should strengthen and diversify with experience. As a result, a relationship may be observed because the logically independent variables of expectancy and drinking are truly related or because the measurement of expectancy also indirectly measures accumulated drinking experience. This question is closely related to those raised by early behaviorists about the measurement of any hypothetical construct, particularly those assessed via verbal reports. As in other areas of science, the best support for a theory that uses unobservables is its effective organization and explanation of the data and the suggestion of new approaches and tests that would not be anticipated otherwise. Expectancy formulations have begun to meet this goal.

Cross-Sectional Designs

Expectancies have been detected in preschoolers (e.g., Zucker, Kincaid, Fitzgerald, & Bingham, 1996), grade school students (e.g., Dunn & Goldman, 1996), and high school students before they began to drink (Christiansen, Smith, Roehling, & Goldman, 1989). This suggests that expectancies can be acquired vicariously and before drinking, consistent with a causal process. As children become older and begin to drink, expectancies change from being primarily negative (e.g., unpleasant and antisocial outcomes) to primarily positive (e.g., sociability and arousal; Dunn & Goldman, 1996).

Longitudinal Designs

More persuasive of a causal influence are longitudinal studies that have investigated adolescents across the time span during which drinking is frequently initiated (Christiansen et al., 1989; Newcomb, Chou, Bentler, & Huba, 1988). As in cross-sectional studies, predrinking expectancies predicted drinking onset and later consumption level. Similar findings have also been reported over a time frame ranging into young adulthood (Stacy, Newcomb, & Bentler, 1991). The results of Stacy et al. (1991) further supported a causal role by showing that expectancies measured at a particular time predicted later drinking and drug use beyond the level predicted by these same behaviors at that initial time point.

The expectancies of alcoholic patients in treatment have predicted posttreatment outcomes. Connors, Tarbox, and Faillace (1993) found that expectancies decreased during an 18-month follow-up in individuals whose drinking declined. Jones and McMahon (1994) reported that individuals leaving treatment with the highest negative expectancies reduced their drinking the most.

Bidirectional Effects

Because expectancies should change as a function of drinking experience (see Goldman, 1994), changes in alcohol use should anticipate changes in expectancies. Smith, Goldman, Greenbaum, and Christiansen (1995) showed that, from early to midadolescence, higher social expectancy scores predicted more alcohol use 1 year later and that greater drinking at the second time point in turn predicted higher expectancy scores another year later. Covariance structural modeling (CSM) controlled for the spurious influence of autocorrelations, and results were cross-checked using hierarchical linear modeling. Sher, Wood, Wood, and Raskin (1996) used CSM to evaluate the sequencing of expectancies and drinking over 3 years beginning with college admission. Again, reciprocal effects were found, but declines in drinking predicted decreases in expectancies. Sher et al. noted that discerning such effects depended on the measurement interval; short time intervals masked effects because expectancy–drinking correlations over brief periods left little room beyond autoregressive effects.

These findings have implications for expectancy theory development. For most individuals, drinking increases into young adulthood and then decreases. Research tracking expectancies as drinking increased has shown them to elaborate and consolidate. Previous research, however, has not followed expectancies as drinking decreased. Therefore, a major question was whether expectancies would remain high, although drinking declined, during young adulthood or whether it would decrease with reductions in alcohol use. As suggested by Sher et al. (1996), expectancies might decrease because the enchantment with alcohol diminishes with repeated exposure (hence, as a consequence of alcohol experience). On the other hand, the emergence of other reward systems and their associated expectancies (e.g., school and career) might compete with expectations of reward from alcohol use, thereby influencing drinking prospectively (expectancies again anticipating alcohol use). At a process level, both effects are likely to occur reciprocally.

Mediational Models

Longitudinal statistical models can establish only temporal sequencing; inferences about process require more demanding designs. At the boundary between correlational designs and true experiments are tests of mediation using the design suggested by Baron and Kenny (1986). Such tests of alcohol expectancies have been carried out using both standard regression techniques and CSM.

Studies evaluating the role of expectancies have uniformly shown that they mediate other antecedent influences. This mediation is often partial, with the antecedent variable also having a direct effect (e.g., Darkes, Greenbaum, & Goldman, 1996b; Henderson, Goldman, Coovert, & Carnevalla, 1994). Antecedents at least partially mediated by expectancies include personality variables such as sensation seeking and risk based on peer and parental influences. The lack of total expectancy mediation is not surprising given that these antecedent influences place individuals in environments in which drinking is encouraged. Social encouragement may increase consumption without necessarily increasing expectancies.

True Experiments

The most persuasive evidence for mediation derives from experiments in which the random assignment of participants, manipulation of the hypothesized mediator, and appropriate control groups have been used to rule out the influence of alternative variables. The results of several studies support the inference that expectancies actively influence drinking, but in these studies the operational definition of expectancy must expand beyond questionnaire responses. In keeping with Tolman's (1932) conception of expectancies as memory contents, procedures designed by cognitive psychologists have been used recently to study expectancies. This expansion in operational definition does, however, raise the question of whether the same processes are being measured.

Early experimental studies have demonstrated a dissociation between the pharmacological effects of consuming alcohol and the psychological effects of being instructed by the experimenter that alcohol was consumed (e.g., the "balanced-placebo" design; Marlatt & Rohsenow, 1973). Although expectancies were presumably activated by this instructional set, they were not measured, and this design was criticized for failing to effectively mask the true nature of the beverages served (Knight, Barbaree, & Boland, 1986), particularly at higher doses (Lyvers & Maltzman, 1991). Nevertheless, this design has been defended (R. L. Collins & Searles, 1988), and its limitations cannot diminish the extensive documentation of placebo effects and their relationship to expectancies (see chap. 9 in this book).

A way station on the path to true experiments in which expectancies were more definitively operative were studies that manipulated cognitive factors in subject groups defined by preexisting drinking characteristics. For example, in Chenier and Goldman's (1992) study, heavier drinking college students completed more fragments of expectancy words in an environment that included alcohol advertising versus a neutral setting. In a series of studies, Stacy and colleagues showed that alcohol-related associations to ambiguous words (homophones such as pitcher or mug) and pictures were more frequently produced by heavier than by lighter drinkers (e.g., Stacy, Leigh, & Weingardt, 1994). On the basis of these studies, Stacy et al. suggested a mechanism reflecting memory associations that influences drinking and is separate from expectancies. Such associations may also be construed as expectancies, however, in that they function as templates for the interpretation (and response directing) of open-ended stimulus configurations. The utility of separating, versus combining, such cognitive processes remains to be seen. Nevertheless, these investigations indicate that results using cognitive methods are similar to the correlational findings.

In six studies, expectancies in experimental designs have been manipulated and effects on self-reported and observed drinking have been found (Darkes & Goldman, 1993, 1998; Henderson & Goldman, 1987; Massey & Goldman, 1988; Roehrich & Goldman, 1995; Stein, Goldman, & Del Boca, 1997). As further support for a causal inference, these manipulations have decreased as well as increased drinking. Four studies have been conducted in which various placebo procedures were used to challenge expectancies (Darkes & Goldman, 1993, 1998; Henderson & Goldman, 1987; Massey & Goldman, 1988). In the most recent studies (Darkes & Goldman, 1993, 1998), light-to-heavy drinking male college students were administered beverages that they were told might or might not contain alcohol and were subsequently asked to indicate who among them had consumed alcohol. Their failure to select the actual drinkers at better-than-chance levels, coupled with information about alcohol placebo (expectancy) effects, resulted in drinking decreases 6 weeks after the challenge procedure. These data suggest that challenges might serve as prevention and intervention tools.

Increases in drinking after implicit priming of expectancy concepts were first shown by Roehrich and Goldman (1995). Although Roehrich and Goldman did not measure cognitive changes associated with expectancy priming, Stein et al. (1997) did measure the activation of expectancy concepts and compared the effect on observed drinking of expectancy activation with that of a positive mood induction. Although both the measures of expectancy activation and mood showed changes appropriate to the experimental conditions, alcohol consumption was highest after expectancy priming. Hence, a cognitive, rather than an affective, process appeared to be the primary mediational pathway for the observed drinking. These findings are consistent with those of Stacy et al. (1994), who showed that experimental manipulations of cognitive processing could influence associative memory responses. When participants were asked to generate an image of friends together on a Friday night, they were more likely to provide alcohol as an associate to expectancy cues (e.g., "feeling more relaxed") than when the image was friends together on a Thursday morning.

Summary of the Construct Validation Network

Research findings provide strong support for the inference that an alcohol expectancy memory system is part of the causal pathway through which alcohol use and alcoholism are influenced. Although inherent criterion contamination increases the potential for overestimation of this influence, at this point there is an absence of findings that would contradict the inference of causality. Instead, controversy has been limited to the structure of alcohol expectancies and associated measurement issues. We now address these concerns and later discuss theoretical processes.

EXPECTANCY STRUCTURE

The "true" or best way to characterize the structure of alcohol expectancies has been approached from two prevailing viewpoints. The first, primarily psychometric, approach views the fit to statistical and predictive criteria as preeminent. The second, process-oriented, approach focuses primarily on the mechanism of expectancy operation.

Structure From a Psychometric Viewpoint

The structure of alcohol expectancies is only just coming into focus because issues of measurement and structure have been intrinsically confounded. Considering the variations in the measurement of expectancies and other closely associated concepts (e.g., motivations, reasons for drinking, memory associations), it may be legitimate to ask whether the measured constructs overlap. Careful scrutiny, we believe, reveals more similarities than differences, and the similar relationship to alcohol consumption suggests that whatever constructs are being measured should be considered together.

Generation of Expectancy Items

Researchers have generated items from an implicit or explicit theory of the relevant domain (e.g., Earleywine & Martin, 1993; Grube, Chen, Madden, & Morgan, 1995), elicited open-ended lists of alcohol's effects from samples of the populations of interest (e.g., Brown, Goldman, Inn, & Anderson, 1980), and obtained items (and scales) from existing instruments and have perhaps added their own (e.g., Fromme, Stroot, & Kaplan, 1993). A few investigators have used free associations directly (e.g., Stacy, 1997). The number of items included has varied from a few (e.g., Leigh, 1987) to more than 100 (e.g., Christiansen, Goldman, & Inn, 1982). Response formats have included binary agree–disagree judgments (e.g., Brown et al., 1980), forced-choice adjective checklists (e.g., Southwick, Steele, Marlatt, & Lindell, 1981), Likert scales (e.g., Leigh & Stacy, 1993), and similarity ratings (Rather & Goldman, 1994). Respondents have used these formats to indicate the subjective likelihood of occurrence (Stacy, 1997); the frequency of occurrence (Rather & Goldman, 1994); the strength of specific effects (R. L. Collins, Lapp, Emmons, & Issac, 1990); or in the case of motives or reasons for drinking, how frequently they drink to obtain an effect (Cooper, Russell, Skinner, & Windle, 1992). To decipher underlying structure, item sets have been subjected to exploratory factor analysis and, more recently, to confirmatory factor analysis (CFA). Given the diversity of methods, conceptual underpinnings, and sources of items, it is perhaps no surprise that a variety of factors have been identified. Before attempting to integrate these findings, we review several issues that researchers have highlighted.

Discriminant Validity of Expectancy Factors

The first issue pertains to the discreteness of factors or, in psychometric terms, their discriminant validity. Leigh (1989b) and Leigh and Stacy (1991) criticized the Alcohol Expectancy Questionnaire (AEQ; Brown et al., 1980) for failing a confirmatory test of factor independence that was based on a criterion of perfect simple structure. This issue has since been addressed in a number of articles, beginning with Goldman, Brown, Christiansen, and Smith (1991; also see Goldman, 1994; Goldman et al., 1997; Leigh & Stacy, 1993). Such a scale construction strategy, driven by classical test theory, mandates simple structure to avoid ambiguity and redundancy in linear prediction. In fact, some expectancy scales have a simple structure (e.g., Earleywine, 1994a; Leigh & Stacy, 1993), but the number of confirmable factors is small (e.g., positive–negative or arousal–sedation).

In contrast, when investigating the organization of information in the natural world (e.g., human memory), a simple structure is often not found because actual concepts show a good deal of "fuzziness" at their boundaries (e.g., some items may load on more than one factor; e.g., is a minivan a truck or a car?). When expectancy responses to open-ended inquiries are subjected to factor analysis without eliminating natural item overlap, a simple structure will not be found. In fact, work using alternative grouping procedures such as multidimensional scaling (MDS) and cluster analysis (Rather & Goldman, 1994) shows natural expectancy structure to be similar to dimensions of affect and personality (see Larsen & Diener, 1993), with a circumplex (circular) pattern if arranged in two-dimensional space (see Figure 10.2). This circumplex likely represents an intrinsic hierarchical arrangement of natural categories. For example, expectancies such as "funny" and "social" have unique meaning, but they are also grouped together under the higher order concept of positive outcomes. Recently developed CFA models that recognize this more complex arrangement have supported the hierarchical nature of expectancies and the discriminant validity of the AEQ scales (Goldman et al., 1997). Hierarchical structure was also suggested by models offered by Leigh and Stacy (1993). Ultimately, "the best assessment strategy may be that designed for a particular purpose, rather than a single 'all-purpose' strategy" (Goldman et al., 1997, p. 154; see also Larsen & Diener, 1993). Confirmable simple structure factors, constructed for specific purposes, are not a valid "window" on the full domain of expectancies.

Basic Expectancy Factors

A related issue is whether certain factors are "basic" or closely match natural categories. Three alternative sets of constructs have emerged as candidates. First, *positive versus negative outcomes* refer to the valence of the drinking effect (e.g., sociability vs. belligerence). Second, *positive–negative reinforcement* (often called "reasons" or "motives" for drinking) refers to positive outcomes that are most sought after (e.g., having fun) and to relief from aversive states that exist before drinking (e.g., anxiety). Both overlap with the positive outcome factor above. Third, *arousing versus sedating outcomes* refers to the pharmacological effects of alcohol (e.g., stimulation and sedation). As we discuss, these constructs correspond to different locations of dimensions on an affect and personality circumplex.

The positive outcome dimension was always considered central and was included in early instruments such as the AEQ (Brown et al., 1980). Because the AEQ did not include negative expectancies and became the instrument of choice (Leigh, 1989b), the importance of negative expec-

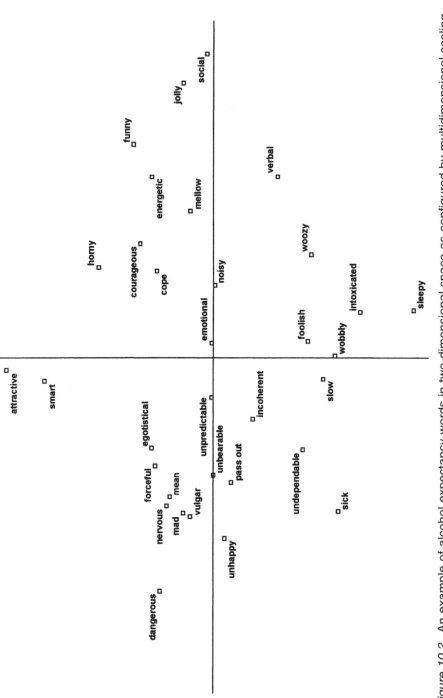

Figure 10.2. An example of alcohol expectancy words in two-dimensional space as configured by multidimensional scaling. The horizontal dimension (axis) ranges from "bad" at the left of the figure to "good" at the right of the figure, and the vertical dimension (axis) ranges from "sedated" at the bottom of the figure to "aroused" at the top of the figure. Note that a rough circle could be drawn by connecting the words at the periphery of the configuration; this arrangement is one way of characterizing a circumplex organization. The axes drawn through the circumplex could be viewed as higher order representations of the more basic elements (words).

tancies began to be debated (e.g., Leigh, 1989b). Research has shown that if an effort is made to collect negative expectancies as items, positive and negative higher order factors can be confirmed as independent, under which may be subsumed a number of lower order expectancies (Leigh & Stacy, 1993; Rather & Goldman, 1994). Although negative expectancies predict drinking in adolescents and young adults (e.g., Grube et al., 1995), they typically account for less variance than do positive expectancies (e.g., Leigh & Stacy, 1993).

One exception can be found in McMahon, Jones, and O'Donnell's (1994) study, in which negative expectancies were positively correlated with drinking in social drinkers. This finding is difficult to interpret, in that it is inconsistent with the rationale for the importance of negative expectancies as "a component of motivation to restrain alcohol use" (McMahon et al., 1994, p. 362). A likely explanation is that the Negative Alcohol Expectancy Questionnaire (McMahon & Jones, 1993) includes severe negative consequences (e.g., "If I went for a drink now I would have memory lapses") that might be endorsed only by individuals who drink heavily and experience alcohol-related problems (i.e., is criterion contaminated).

Grube et al. (1995) also reported a slight advantage (1% of variance) for negative expectancies in predicting adolescent drinking, but they did not report the actual drinking levels in their sample. Adjustments made in their data analyses suggest these rates were low and that negative expectancies were associated primarily with the absence of drinking. Negative expectancies, not surprisingly, predict short-term (3 months) treatment outcome in alcoholic individuals (Jones & McMahon, 1994), but long-term (2 years) outcome has also been related to decreases in positive expectancies (Connors et al., 1993).

A number of issues remain: Expectancies characterized as negative by researchers may not be so to all drinkers (Leigh, 1989b). Negative effects may be less predictive because they refer largely to the delayed consequences of drinking (e.g., trouble with the police) rather than to the immediate effects of alcohol use itself (e.g., have fun; Leigh, 1989b). Many negative effects may not be experienced by all drinkers (e.g., the severe effects measured by the Negative Alcohol Expectancy Questionnaire). Most important is an underlying theoretical issue; from the early days of animal research on learning, punishment (e.g., negative effects) has been known to suppress, but not eliminate, behavior. Instead, extinction requires the removal of positive reinforcement.

Positive and negative reinforcement were perhaps the earliest candidates for the basic factors (Farber, Khavari, & Douglas, 1980). Tension reduction as negative reinforcement played a prominent role in early theories of alcoholism (Conger, 1956). Although the tension-reduction view had received only mixed support (e.g., Sher, 1985), renewed interest has been generated by recent accounts of the effect of alcohol on affect (Stritzke, Patrick, & Lang, 1995). As noted shortly, hierarchical CFA based on MDS solutions have also suggested this factor as a legitimate higher order "basic" dimension of expectancy.

Positive and negative reinforcement have also reappeared recently as enhancement and coping "motives" or "reasons for drinking" (along with a third, social, motive; Cooper et al., 1992). Reasons for drinking and motives are included here with expectancies because examination of their operational definitions reveals little difference among them. The distinction seems to be that reasons for drinking and motive items ask whether or how much respondents drink for various reasons; expectancy items ask what happens when they drink. Because the association of this information with future drinking would appear to be the critical issue, it remains to be seen whether this difference taps into a different information set, or whether different levels of prediction can be achieved based on the supposedly different constructs involved (i.e., independent of differential scale characteristics).

To measure the subjective biphasic effects of alcohol (low-dose stimulation followed by higher dose sedation), Earleywine and colleagues developed and confirmed two scales that measure arousing and sedating effects (Earleywine & Erblich, 1996; Martin, Earleywine, Musty, & Perrine, 1993). Earleywine (1994b) also related these dimensions to alcoholism risk, in keeping with the differentiator model (Newlin & Thompson, 1990). These dimensions also appear in MDS solutions of expectancy words (Rather & Goldman, 1994), which, as we discuss shortly, offer an organization that allows for all the above dimensions to be acceptable choices for basic structure.

Expectancy Value, Utility, and Strength

A third issue associated with the psychometric approach to expectancy measurement is the separate evaluation of value, utility, and strength. Some investigators have argued that measuring expectancies is insufficient because individuals may differ in how much they want these effects (subjective value or utility; e.g., Fromme et al., 1993; Grube et al., 1995). Although this issue cannot yet be settled, the available research indicates that separate evaluations of value or utility do not add much to prediction beyond the assessment of expectancy alone (see Copeland, Brandon, & Quinn, 1995, for smoking prediction; see Fromme et al., 1993, and Grube et al., 1995, for alcohol).

A similar argument has been made for the subjective strength with which one holds an expectancy (e.g., R. L. Collins et al., 1990). Again, research is sparse. Although R. L. Collins et al. (1990) supported separate measurement, support came from a small subset of analyses. Furthermore, separate comparisons were made for different alcohol-containing beverages (e.g., beer vs. wine); if, as one might anticipate, participants preferred one beverage over another, high scores on one index would tend to lower scores on another.

Arguments for the separate assessment of value, utility, and strength arise from older attitude theories and psychometric considerations. If expectancy measurement taps an information-processing or memory system, however, separate assessment may not be necessary. The accessibility of particular outcomes from memory could be related inherently to their value and utility. Also, because *strength* refers to the likelihood of the activation of a concept, accessibility would reflect strength. Hence, the expectancy response itself may implicitly reflect these characteristics. Furthermore, separate assessment may call on respondents to provide information about processes to which they have no access (Nisbett & Wilson, 1977).

A counterargument is that the preponderance of evidence that supports expectancies as an important construct is based on psychometrically based questionnaires. Whether responses to questionnaire items reflect memory processes has been debated. Many psychological processes may influence responses to any scaled instrument, including those that produce error variance. Some processes may mask memory, and it is possible to respond to such instruments without accessing long-term memory (see Hastie & Park, 1986; Rather & Goldman, 1994). In connection with a construct based on stored information in memory, however, such influences would reduce the relationship between the predictor and the criterion. The reliability of the relationship observed between expectancies and drinking suggests otherwise.

Dose-Related Expectancies

Finally, it has been suggested that people hold different expectancies for different doses of alcohol (e.g., R. L. Collins et al., 1990; Southwick et al., 1981). High-dose expectancies include intoxication and drunkenness and have been found to predict drinking in individuals who customarily binge drink. Because these were cross-sectional findings, however, it is unclear whether these effects are an incentive for binge drinking or whether they reflect previous drinking experiences. Also, it remains open whether expectancies held by sober individuals influence the total amount of alcohol they will consume at a sitting or whether altered expectancies emerge once drinking has commenced.

Structure From a Process Perspective

To develop a model of expectancy process, researchers in our laboratory applied MDS and hierarchical clustering methods to decipher expectancy structure (e.g., Rather & Goldman, 1994). Unlike factor analysis, these methods do not assume that item responses are indicators of unobserved variables opaque about process (see Goldman, 1994; Goldman et al., 1997). For psychometric reasons, factor analytic methods assume that indicators that vary together are best regarded as manifestations of the same latent construct (plus error). From the perspective of memory structure, however, it may be useful to recognize that items that humans perceive as different *are* different (contain unique information) despite covarying in some circumstances. Although MDS and clustering do not as effectively parse error from structural mapping, they do allow for a direct visual examination of relationships among items (information "nodes").

Items came from young adults and hospitalized alcoholic patients who completed the phrase, "Alcohol makes one _____." This process yielded 805 items (probably exhausting the category) that were reduced in successive steps to 33 groups of 4 words with overlapping meaning. A variety of MDS procedures and participant samples consistently produced a two-dimensional solution: positive–negative and arousal–sedation. Individual items fell in a circular (circumplex) pattern (see Figure 10.2). Because the orientation of dimensions in standard MDS is arbitrary, axes could be rotated to match all the basic expectancy dimensions noted earlier. Hence, no group of expectancy dimensions may be more basic than any other. Axes can be drawn in expectancy multidimensional space to reflect any dimension a research group wishes to emphasize. With careful selection, word groups reflecting preferred higher order expectancy constructs can be confirmed by factor analysis (Darkes, Greenbaum, & Goldman, 1996a, 1997) to allow for the minimally redundant linear prediction of drinking. In this way, theories reflecting different conceptions of basic alcohol effects can be operationalized and tested by choosing the appropriate words from the circumplex. Furthermore, because the overall expectancy configuration so closely matches those found in the domains of affect and personality (see Larsen & Diener, 1993), it must be considered that alcohol expectancies are, at least in part, anticipated changes in affect and personality attributable to alcohol use.

EXPECTANCY PROCESS

To translate the structure described earlier into a working model of expectancy process merely requires viewing this structure as a still photograph of what is actually a dynamic, unfolding process. In such a model, unique expectancy concepts (nodes) relating to the reinforcing effects of alcohol and other outcomes of drinking (including images, sensorimotor and affective experiences, specific behavior patterns, and verbal representations of these concepts) are seen as constituting a network structure and as having some overall relationship to each other. Consistent with this network structure, the activation of particular nodes occurs in a predictable fashion when the individual encounters stimuli that match previously encoded material relevant to drinking. Previously encoded material may consist of external (situational) or internal (activation of other encoded information) stimuli.

Although a variety of activation algorithms could be hypothesized, one starting point is to assume simple "spreading activation" (A. M. Collins & Loftus, 1975), in which a wave of activation begins with a certain node, or group of nodes, and spreads outward in a symmetrical fashion to other nodes as a function of their proximity to the starting point (as do ripples in a pond when a pebble is dropped). Using the MDS plots as a visualization of the model (see Figure 10.3), empirically derived starting points may be estimated using procedures that locate preferred locations in the network for particular drinking groups. Therefore, as reported by Rather and Goldman (1994), heavy drinkers seem likely to first associate concepts related to positive arousal (upper right quadrant in Figure 10.3; e.g., happy, talkative) to a drinking stimulus, whereas light drinkers first activate concepts related to positive sedation (e.g., relaxed, sleepy). Because these concepts are assumed to influence the activation of affective and motor systems consistent with the activated information template, the result is more drinking accompanied by the associated behavioral patterns for heavy drinkers and a dampening of drinking as a consequence of general slowing for the light drinkers. Although these behavior patterns may reflect the actual pharmacological effects of alcohol, prior research has shown that they are not an inevitable consequence of the drug effects of alcohol.

These information patterns may induce behaviors that mimic drug effects in anticipation of what might be the later onset of actual drug effects. Results of animal research suggest that these anticipatory effects may motivate drug use and influence later drug-induced behavior (Schultz et al., 1997). The full range of behaviors observed under the influence of alcohol is unlikely to be entirely a drug effect; it also represents a set of learned patterns associated with alcohol use. As shown earlier, these patterns, although subject to change over time, are likely learned in childhood, before actual use. Hence, alcohol use is reinforced by the activation of behaviors that are not necessarily pharmacological effects of use but that occur after use, in part because the drinker has acquired information templates (i.e., response expectancies) that make it so.

An MDS plot is not the only way of visualizing these hypothetical networks. Activation can also be modeled using plots from cluster analyses. These plots may be even closer to the neurocomputational system we are trying to model, in that no assumptions need to be made about dimensional organization. In these plots, activation may be presumed to begin at all the individual nodes and to influence behavior most when activation from one

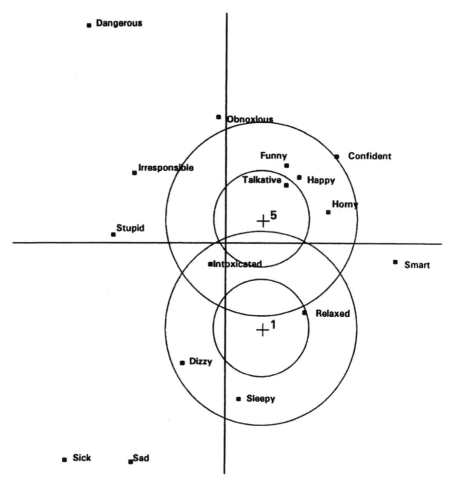

Figure 10.3. Another example of expectancy words located in two-dimensional space after being subjected to similarity scaling and multidimensional scaling (MDS). In this example, hypothetical starting points for activation of the expectancy network have been empirically located using auxiliary MDS methods. The plus adjacent to the "1" is the hypothetical starting point for light drinkers in this data set; the plus adjacent to the "5" is the hypothetical starting point for heavy drinkers. Once activation begins, it may be presumed to spread as do ripples on a smooth lake (as characterized by the concentric circles). From "Drinking-Related Differences in the Memory Organization of Alcohol Expectancies," by B. C. Rather and M. S. Goldman, 1994, *Experimental and Clinical Psychopharmacology, 2,* 176. Copyright 1994 by the American Psychological Association. Reprinted with permission.

node joins the activation from another. This type of mapping procedure also suggests that the most sought-after effects of drinking are located more closely together in heavier drinkers, thereby facilitating activation for these individuals (see Figure 10.4).

The use of multiple ways to visualize these processes underscores that these plots are not meant as literal depictions of the hypothetical networks

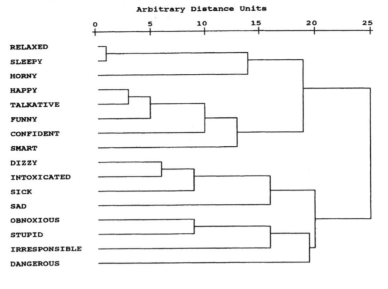

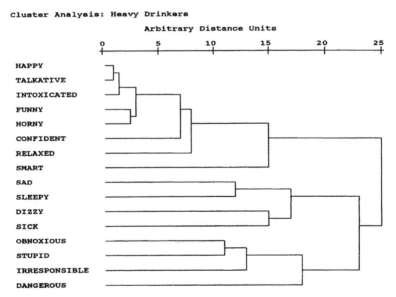

Figure 10.4. Cluster analyses of the same data shown in Figure 10.3 performed separately for light (top cluster) and heavy (bottom cluster) drinkers in this data set. Note that the words *happy, talkative, intoxicated, funny,* and *horny* are grouped much closer together for the heavy drinkers than the light drinkers. The light drinkers also most closely link *relaxed* and *sleepy* with *drinking,* unlike the heavy drinkers, who most closely link *happy* and *talkative* with drinking. From "Drinking-Related Differences in the Memory Organization of Alcohol Expectancies," by B. C. Rather and M. S. Goldman, 1994, *Experimental and Clinical Psychopharmacology, 2,* 177. Copyright 1994 by the American Psychological Association. Reprinted with permission.

but as empirically derived representations of theoretical models (see Lehmann, 1992). The use of such models also links expectancy research to recent developments in related areas, including memory research (Bower, 1992) and research on the memory underpinnings of emotional and motor behavior (e.g., Bower, 1992; see also chap. 2 in this book). Animal researchers have also recently indicated that drug reinforcement is associated with activation of brain neurochemical systems that normally mediate approach behavior (e.g., Gray, 1990; Panksepp, 1990). These same systems are thought to be the substrate for human affective response. Alcohol expectancy structure has been found to closely overlap the dimensions found for human affective response (see Russell, 1980; Watson & Tellegen, 1985; see also chap. 2 in this book). These systems presumably are activated by expectancy information templates, perhaps stored in these same areas or in cortical association areas. It is worth noting that, although network models have been criticized for being too powerful (i.e., irrefutable; see Johnson-Laird, Hermann, & Chaffin, 1984), they have been defended as useful working models from which more specific models can be developed (Chang, 1986).

Such models have the flexibility to carry out the tasks of storing information about alcohol's effects on the affective and motor systems and of activating this information to influence drinking at times and in settings that are also "programmed" into the system. The organization of such a system can reflect the different subjective experiences with alcohol that may be related to inherited biological differences in alcohol metabolism or processing. It can also reflect differences attendant to different personality patterns and temperaments. In the same way, it can store information about alcohol use acquired from observations of family members or from the general behavior of individuals in one's cultural environment (e.g., peer, ethnic and religious groups, media and advertising portrayals). This information-processing/memory system acts as a storehouse for the potential to consume alcohol, which is then translated into manifest drinking in certain circumstances.

Theorizing by Stacy and his colleagues (e.g., Stacy et al., 1994) overlaps considerably with this model. Stacy (1997), however, distinguished between expectancy processes and memory association, and between implicit and explicit memory processes, as they are manifest in the different ways of measuring expectancies. We have included all these processes within the general operation of an expectancy system. As these lines of research proceed, it appears that the operations overlap considerably, so that distinctions become less clear. For example, Stacy used the term *expectancy* only when referring to outcomes of alcohol use measured using surveys (explicit memory), whereas we have used it with reference to all the memory storage and activation processes connected with drinking. We have chosen this usage to reflect recent expectancy theories that address the ongoing control of behavior in a real-life environment, not just systems for storing and retrieving information in constrained settings, such as laboratory experiments. Recall that Tolman (1932) referred to animal behavior using expectancy formulations and certainly did not restrict himself to explicit verbal behavior.

Whether the delineation of qualitative differences between those memory processes that underpin implicit and explicit memory remains useful is yet to be resolved (see Neal & Hesketh, 1997). Such distinctions cannot be separated from the measurement operations associated with each supposed system; processing differences may be task related or a function of different systems. At present, we agree with a comment by Reber (1997) made as part of a recent symposium on implicit learning:

> Psychologists just can't seem to resist dichotomies. . . . We like to be able to decide that one theory is right and another wrong. . . . We seem ineluctably drawn to setting up poles rather than recognizing continua. Alas, this tendency often functions as a hindrance to doing good science. (p. 52)

We believe commonalities in the available findings serve as a basis for continuing advances that offer a new window on the problem of addiction.

REFERENCES

American Psychiatric Association. (1994). *Diagnostic and statistical manual of mental disorders* (4th ed.). Washington, DC: Author.

Baer, J. S., Stacy, A. W., & Lorimer, M. (1991). Biases in the perception of drinking norms among college students. *Journal of Studies on Alcohol, 52,* 580–586.

Baron, R. M., & Kenny, D. A. (1986). The moderator–mediator variable distinction in social psychological research: Conceptual, strategic, and statistical considerations. *Journal of Personality and Social Psychology, 51,* 1173–1182.

Bauer, L. O., & Hesselbrock, V. M. (1993). EEG, autonomic and subjective correlates of the risk for alcoholism. *Journal of Studies on Alcohol, 54,* 577–589.

Blum, K., Noble, E. P., Sheridan, P. J., Montgomery, A., Ritchie, T., Jagadeeswaran, P., Nogami, H., Briggs, A. H., & Cohen, J. B. (1990). Allelic association of human dopamine D_2 receptor gene and alcoholism. *Journal of the American Medical Association, 263,* 2055–2060.

Bolles, R. C. (1972). Reinforcement, expectancy, and learning. *Psychological Review, 79,* 394–409.

Bower, G. H. (1992). How might emotions affect learning? In S. Christianson (Ed.), *The handbook of emotion and memory: Research and theory* (pp. 3–31). Hillsdale, NJ: Erlbaum.

Brown, S. A., Goldman, M. S., Inn, A., & Anderson, L. R. (1980). Expectations of reinforcement from alcohol: Their domain and relation to drinking problems. *Journal of Consulting and Clinical Psychology; 48,* 419–426.

Chang, T. M. (1986). Semantic memory: Facts and models. *Psychological Bulletin, 99,* 199–220.

Chenier, G., & Goldman, M. S. (1992, August). *Implicit priming of an alcohol expectancy network.* Paper presented at the 100th Annual Convention of the American Psychological Association, Washington, DC.

Christiansen, B. A., Goldman, M. S., & Inn, A. (1982). Development of alcohol-related expectancies in adolescents: Separating pharmacological from social learning influences. *Journal of Consulting and Clinical Psychology, 50,* 336–344.

Christiansen, B. A., Smith, G. T., Roehling, P. V., & Goldman, M. S. (1989). Using alcohol expectancies to predict adolescent drinking behavior at one year. *Journal of Consulting and Clinical Psychology, 57,* 93–99.

Clark, W. B., & Hilton, M. E. (1991). *Alcohol in America: Drinking practices and problems.* Albany: State University of New York Press.

Cloninger, C. R. (1987). Neurogenetic adaptive mechanisms in alcoholism. *Science, 236,* 410–416.

Collins, A. M., & Loftus, E. F. (1975). A spreading-activation theory of semantic processing. *Psychological Review, 82,* 407–428.

Collins, R. L., Lapp, W. M., Emmons, K. M., & Issac, L. M. (1990). Endorsement and strength of alcohol expectancies. *Journal of Studies on Alcohol, 51,* 336–342.

Collins, R. L., & Searles, J. S. (1988). Alcohol and the balanced-placebo design: Were experimenter demands in expectancy really tested? Comment on Knight, Barbaree, Boland (1986). *Journal of Abnormal Psychology, 97,* 503–507.

Conger, J. J. (1956). Reinforcement theory and the dynamics of alcoholism. *Quarterly Journal of Studies on Alcohol, 17,* 296–305.

Connors, G. J., Tarbox, A. R., & Faillace, L. A. (1993). Changes in alcohol expectancies and drinking behavior among treated problem drinkers. *Journal of Studies on Alcohol, 53,* 676–683.

Cooper, M. L., Russell, M., Skinner, J. B., & Windle, M. (1992). Development and validation of a three-dimensional measure of drinking motives. *Psychological Assessment, 4,* 123–132.

Copeland, A. L., Brandon, T. H., & Quinn, E. P. (1995). The Smoking Consequences Questionnaire—Adult: Measurement of smoking outcome expectancies of experienced smokers. *Psychological Assessment, 7,* 484–494.

Darkes, J., & Goldman, M. S. (1993). Expectancy challenge and drinking reduction: Experimental evidence for a mediational process. *Journal of Consulting and Clinical Psychology, 61,* 344–353.

Darkes, J., & Goldman, M. S. (1998). Expectancy challenge and drinking reduction: Process and structure in the alcohol expectancy network. *Experimental and Clinical Psychopharmacology, 6,* 64–76.

Darkes, J., Greenbaum, P. E., & Goldman, M. S. (1996a, June). *Positive/arousal and social facilitation alcohol expectancies and concurrent alcohol use.* Paper presented at the meeting of the Research Society on Alcoholism, Washington, DC.

Darkes, J., Greenbaum, P. E., & Goldman, M. S. (1996b, August). *Disinhibition and alcohol use: The mediational role of alcohol expectancies.* Paper presented at the 104th Annual Convention of the American Psychological Association, Toronto, Ontario, Canada.

Darkes, J., Greenbaum, P. E., & Goldman, M. S. (1997, July). *Hierarchical structure in an alcohol expectancy memory network.* Paper presented at the meeting of the Research Society on Alcoholism, San Francisco.

Dunn, M. E., & Goldman, M. S. (1996). Empirical modeling of an alcohol expectancy network in elementary-school children as a function of grade. *Experimental and Clinical Psychopharmacology, 4,* 209–217.

Earleywine, M. (1994a). Confirming the factor structure of the Anticipated Biphasic Alcohol Effects Scale. *Alcoholism: Clinical and Experimental Research, 18,* 861–866.

Earleywine, M. (1994b). Anticipated biphasic effects of alcohol vary with risk for alcoholism: A preliminary report. *Alcoholism: Clinical and Experimental Research, 18,* 711–714.

Earleywine, M., & Erblich, J. (1996). A confirmed factor structure for the Biphasic Alcohol Effects Scale. *Experimental and Clinical Psychopharmacology, 4,* 107–113.

Earleywine, M., & Martin, C. S. (1993). Anticipated stimulant and sedative effects of alcohol vary with dosage and limb of the blood alcohol curve. *Alcoholism: Clinical and Experimental Research, 17,* 135–139.

Farber, P. D., Khavari, K. A., & Douglas, F. M. (1980). A factor analytic study of reasons for drinking: Empirical validation of positive and negative reinforcement dimensions. *Journal of Consulting and Clinical Psychology, 48,* 780–781.

Finn, P. R., & Pihl, R. O. (1988). Risk for alcoholism: A comparison between two different groups of sons of alcoholics on cardiovascular reactivity and sensitivity to alcohol. *Alcoholism: Clinical and Experimental Research, 12,* 742–747.

Fromme, K., Stroot, E., & Kaplan, D. (1993). Comprehensive effects of alcohol: Development and psychometric assessment of a new alcohol expectancy questionnaire. *Psychological Assessment, 5,* 19–26.

Goldman, D. (1993). Genetic transmission. In M. Galanter (Ed.), *Recent developments in alcoholism: Vol. 11. Ten years of progress* (pp. 231–248). New York: Plenum.

Goldman, M. S. (1994). The alcohol expectancy concept: Applications to assessment, prevention, and treatment of alcohol abuse. *Applied and Preventive Psychology, 3,* 131–144.

Goldman, M. S., Brown, S. A., Christiansen, B. A., & Smith G. T. (1991). Alcoholism and memory: Broadening the scope of alcohol expectancy research. *Psychological Bulletin, 110,* 137–146.

Goldman, M. S., Del Boca, F. K., & Darkes, J. (in press). Alcohol expectancy theory: The application of cognitive neuroscience. In H. T. Blane & K. E.

Leonard (Eds.), *Psychological theories of alcohol use and alcoholism.* New York: Guilford Press.

Goldman, M. S., Greenbaum, P. E., & Darkes, J. (1997). A confirmatory test of hierarchical expectancy structure and predictive power: Discriminant validation of the Alcohol Expectancy Questionnaire. *Psychological Assessment, 9,* 145–157.

Goldman, M. S., & Rather, B. C. (1993). Substance use disorders: Cognitive models and architectures. In P. Kendall & K. S. Dobson (Eds.), *Psychopathology and cognition* (pp. 245–292). Orlando, FL: Academic Press.

Gray, J. A. (1982). *The neuropsychology of anxiety: An inquiry into the function of the septohippocampal system.* Oxford, England: Oxford University Press.

Gray, J. A. (1990). Brain systems that mediate both emotion and cognition. *Cognition and Emotion, 4,* 269–288.

Grossberg, S. (1995). The attentive brain. *American Scientist, 83,* 438–449.

Grube, J. W., Chen, M. J., Madden, P., & Morgan, M. (1995). Predicting adolescent drinking from alcohol expectancy values: A comparison of additive, interactive, and nonlinear models. *Journal of Applied Social Psychology, 25,* 839–857.

Hastie, R., & Park, B. (1986). The relationship between memory and judgment depends on whether the judgment task is memory-based or on-line. *Psychological Review, 93,* 258–268.

Henderson, M. J., & Goldman, M. S. (1987, November). *Effects of a social manipulation on expectancies and subsequent drinking.* Paper presented at the meeting of the Association for the Advancement of Behavior Therapy, Boston.

Henderson, M. J., Goldman, M. S., Coovert, M. D., & Carnevalla, N. (1994). Covariance structure models of expectancy. *Journal of Studies on Alcohol, 55,* 315–326.

Hesselbrock, M. N., & Hesselbrock, V. M. (1992). Relationship of family history, antisocial personality disorder and personality traits in young men at risk for alcoholism. *Journal of Studies on Alcohol, 53,* 139–145.

Hilton, M. E. (1991). Regional diversity in US drinking practices. In W. B. Clark & M. E. Hilton (Eds.), *Alcohol in America: Drinking practices and problems* (pp. 256–279). Albany: State University of New York Press.

Johnson-Laird, P. N., Hermann, D. J., & Chaffin, R. (1984). Only connections: A critique of semantic networks. *Psychological Bulletin, 96,* 292–315.

Jones, B. T., & McMahon, J. (1994). Negative and positive alcohol expectancies as predictors of abstinence after discharge from a residential treatment program: A one-month and three-month follow-up study in men. *Journal of Studies on Alcohol, 55,* 543–548.

Katsanis, J., Iacono, W. G., McGue, M. K., & Carlson, S. R. (1997). P300 event-related heritability in monozygotic and dizygotic twins. *Psychophysiology, 34,* 47–58.

Kirsch, I. (1985). Response expectancy as a determinant of experience and behavior. *American Psychologist, 40,* 1189–1202.

Kirsch, I., & Lynn, S. J. (1999). Automaticity in clinical psychology. *American Psychologist, 54,* 504–515.

Knight, L. J., Barbaree, H. E., & Boland, F. J. (1986). Alcohol and the balanced-placebo design: The role of experimenter demands in expectancy. *Journal of Abnormal Psychology, 95,* 335–340.

Larsen, R. J., & Diener, E. (1993). Promises and problems with the circumplex model of emotion. In M. S. Clark (Ed.), *Emotion* (pp. 25–59). Newbury Park, CA: Sage.

Lehmann, F. (1992). Semantic networks. *Computers and Mathematical Applications, 23,* 1–50.

Leigh, B. C. (1987). Beliefs about the effects of alcohol on self and others. *Journal of Studies on Alcohol, 48,* 467–475.

Leigh, B. C. (1989a). Attitudes and expectancies as predictors of drinking habits: A comparison of three scales. *Journal of Studies on Alcohol, 50,* 432–440.

Leigh, B. C. (1989b). In search of the seven dwarves: Issues of measurement and meaning in alcohol expectancy research. *Psychological Bulletin, 105,* 361–373.

Leigh, B. C., & Stacy, A. W. (1991). On the scope of alcohol expectancy research: Remaining issues of measurement and meaning. *Psychological Bulletin, 110,* 147–154.

Leigh, B. C., & Stacy, A. W. (1993). Alcohol outcome expectancies: Scale construction and predictive utility in higher order confirmatory models. *Psychological Assessment, 5,* 216–229.

Lyvers, M. F., & Maltzman, I. (1991). The balanced placebo design: Effects of alcohol and beverage instructions cannot be independently assessed. *International Journal of the Addictions, 26,* 963–972.

Marlatt, G. A., & Rohsenow, D. J. (1973). Cognitive processes in alcohol use: Expectancy and the balanced-placebo design. In N. K. Mello (Ed.), *Advances in substance abuse* (Vol. 1, pp. 159–199). Greenwich, CT: JAI Press.

Martin, C. S., Earleywine, M., Musty, R. E., & Perrine, M. W. (1993). Development and validation of the Biphasic Alcohol Effects Scale. *Alcoholism: Clinical and Experimental Research, 17,* 140–146.

Massey, R. F., & Goldman, M. S. (1988, August). *Manipulating expectancies as a means of altering alcohol consumption.* Paper presented at the 96th Annual Convention of the American Psychological Association, Atlanta, GA.

McCarthy, D. M., & Smith, G. T. (1996, June). *Meta-analysis of alcohol expectancy.* Paper presented at the meeting of the Research Society on Alcoholism, Washington, DC.

McMahon, J., & Jones, B. T. (1993). Negative expectancy in motivation. *Addiction Research, 1,* 145–155.

McMahon, J., Jones, B. T., & O'Donnell, P. (1994). Comparing positive and negative alcohol expectancies in male and female social drinkers. *Addiction Research, 1,* 349–365.

Nakawatase, T. V., Yamamato, J., & Sasao, T. (1993). The association between fast-flushing response and alcohol use among Japanese Americans. *Journal of Studies on Alcohol, 54,* 48–53.

National Institute on Alcohol Abuse and Alcoholism. (1993). *Eighth special report to the U.S. Congress on alcohol and health* (NIAAA Pub. No. 93-3699). Washington, DC: U.S. Government Printing Office.

National Institute on Alcohol Abuse and Alcoholism. (1997). *Ninth special report to the U.S. Congress on alcohol and health* (NIAAA Pub. No. 97-4017). Washington, DC: U.S. Government Printing Office.

Neal, A., & Hesketh, B. (1997). Episodic knowledge and implicit learning. *Psychonomic Bulletin and Review, 4,* 24–37.

Newcomb, M. D., Chou, C., Bentler, P. M., & Huba, G. J. (1988). Cognitive motivations for drug use among adolescents: Longitudinal tests of gender differences and predictors of change in drug use. *Journal of Counseling Psychology, 35,* 426–438.

Newlin, D., & Thompson, J. (1990). Alcohol challenge with sons of alcoholics: A critical review and analysis. *Psychological Bulletin, 108,* 383–402.

Nisbett, R. E., & Wilson, T. D. (1977). Telling more than we know: Verbal reports on mental processes. *Psychological Review, 84,* 231–259.

Panksepp, J. (1990). Gray zones at the emotion/cognition interface: A commentary [Special issue]. *Cognition and Emotion, 4,* 289–302.

Palfai, T. P., Monti, P. M., Colby, S. M., & Rohsenow, D. J. (1997). Effects of suppressing the urge to drink on the accessibility of alcohol outcome expectancies. *Behavior Research and Therapy, 35,* 59–65.

Pihl, R. O., Peterson, J. B., & Finn, P. (1990). Inherited predisposition to alcoholism: Characteristics of sons of male alcoholics. *Journal of Abnormal Psychology, 99,* 291–301.

Polich, J., Pollock, V. E., & Bloom, F. E. (1994). Meta-analysis of P300 amplitude from males at risk for alcoholism. *Psychological Bulletin, 115,* 55–73.

Rather, B. C., & Goldman, M. S. (1994). Drinking-related differences in the memory organization of alcohol expectancies. *Experimental and Clinical Psychopharmacology, 2,* 167–183.

Reber, A. S. (1997). Implicit ruminations. *Psychonomic Bulletin and Review, 4,* 49–55.

Rescorla, R. A. (1988). Pavlovian conditioning: It's not what you think it is. *American Psychologist, 43,* 151–160.

Roehrich, L., & Goldman, M. S. (1995). Implicit priming of alcohol expectancy memory processes and subsequent drinking behavior. *Experimental and Clinical Psychopharmacology, 3,* 402–410.

Russell, J. A. (1980). A circumplex model of emotion. *Journal of Personality and Social Psychology, 39,* 1161–1178.

Schuckit, M. A. (1988). Reactions to alcohol in sons of alcoholics and controls. *Alcoholism: Clinical and Experimental Research, 12,* 465–470.

Schuckit, M. A. (1994). Low level response to alcohol as a predictor of future alcoholism. *American Journal of Psychiatry*, *151*, 184–189.

Schultz, W., Dayan, P., & Montague, P. R. (1997). A neural substrate of prediction and reward. *Science*, *275*, 1593–1599.

Sher, K. J. (1985). Subjective effects of alcohol: The influence of setting and individual differences in alcohol expectancies. *Journal of Studies on Alcohol*, *46*, 137–146.

Sher, K. J. (1991). *Children of alcoholics: A critical appraisal of theory and research*. Chicago: University of Chicago Press.

Sher, K. J., Byland, D. B., Wallitzer, K. J., Hartmann, J., & Ray-Prenger, C. (1994). Platelet monoamine oxidase (MAO) activity: Personality, substance use, and the stress-response dampening effect of alcohol. *Experimental and Clinical Psychopharmacology*, *2*, 53–81.

Sher, K. J., Wood, M. D., Wood, P. K., & Raskin, G. (1996). Alcohol outcome expectancies and alcohol use: A latent variable cross-lagged panel study. *Journal of Abnormal Psychology*, *105*, 561–574.

Smith, G. T., Goldman, M. S., Greenbaum, P. E., & Christiansen, B. A. (1995). Expectancy for social facilitation from drinking: The divergent paths of high-expectancy and low-expectancy adolescents. *Journal of Abnormal Psychology*, *104*, 32–40.

Southwick, L., Steele, C. M., Marlatt, G. A., & Lindell, M. (1981). Alcohol-related expectancies: Defined by phase of intoxication and drinking experience. *Journal of Consulting and Clinical Psychology*, *49*, 713–721.

Stacy, A. W. (1997). Memory activation and expectancy as prospective predictors of alcohol and marijuana use. *Journal of Abnormal Psychology*, *106*, 61–73.

Stacy, A. W., Leigh, B. C., & Weingardt, K. R. (1994). Memory accessibility and association of alcohol use and its positive outcomes. *Experimental and Clinical Psychopharmacology*, *2*, 269–282.

Stacy, A. W., Newcomb, M. D., & Bentler, P. M. (1991). Cognitive motivation and problem drug use: A 9-year longitudinal study. *Journal of Abnormal Psychology*, *100*, 502–515.

Stein, K. D., Goldman, M. S., & Del Boca, F. K. (1997, July). *Happy hour: The relative effects of alcohol expectancies and positive mood on drinking behavior*. Paper presented at the meeting of the Research Society on Alcoholism, San Francisco.

Stritzke, W. G. K., Patrick, C. J., & Lang, A. R. (1995). Alcohol and human emotion: A multidimensional analysis incorporating startle-probe methodology. *Journal of Abnormal Psychology*, *104*, 114–121.

Swaim, R. C., Oetting, E. R., Edwards, R. W., & Beauvais, F. (1989). Links from emotional distress to adolescent drug use: A path model. *Journal of Consulting and Clinical Psychology*, *57*, 227–231.

Tolman, E. C. (1932). *Purposive behavior in animals and man*. New York: Appleton-Century-Crofts.

Watson, D., & Tellegen, A. (1985). Toward a consensual structure of mood. *Psychological Bulletin, 98,* 219–235.

Wise, R. A., & Bozarth, M. A. (1987). A psychomotor stimulant theory of addiction. *Psychological Review, 94,* 469–492.

Zucker, R. A., & Gomberg, E. S. L. (1986). Etiology of alcoholism reconsidered: The case for a biopsychosocial process. *American Psychologist, 4,* 783–793.

Zucker, R. A., Kincaid, S. B., Fitzgerald, H. E., & Bingham, R. C. (1996). Alcohol schema acquisition in preschoolers: Differences between children of alcoholics and children of nonalcoholics. *Alcoholism: Clinical and Experimental Research, 19,* 1011–1017.

11

EXPECTANCIES FOR TOBACCO SMOKING

THOMAS H. BRANDON, LAURA M. JULIANO,
AND AMY L. COPELAND

Tobacco smoking kills close to a half million Americans per year. It has been identified as the leading cause of premature morbidity and mortality in the United States. Smoking is associated with increased risks of coronary heart disease, lung cancer, emphysema, chronic bronchitis, and oral cancers (Shopland & Burns, 1993). Massive public health campaigns have ensured that most Americans are aware that smoking is unhealthy. Indeed, nearly 50 million Americans have quit smoking. However, another 50 million continue to smoke, and each day 3,000 youngsters begin smoking (Centers for Disease Control and Prevention, 1993, 1995).

Despite nearly a half century of intense research, a number of practical questions still lack satisfactory answers. Among these questions are, Why do some adolescents begin smoking? Why do some smokers choose to quit? How can more smokers be motivated to attempt to quit? How can smoking cessation programs be improved? Among those who do quit, why

Preparation of this chapter was supported by Grant PBR-94 from the American Cancer Society and Grant DA10484 from the National Institute on Drug Abuse. We thank Steven J. Lynn for his helpful comments and suggestions on an earlier draft of this chapter.

do so many relapse? These deceptively simple questions have proved to have complex answers. It is now clear that all the behaviors listed are multidetermined. For example, among factors shown to influence the onset of smoking are parental smoking, peer smoking, tobacco advertising, heredity, personality, and psychiatric problems. Among factors that predict success at quitting smoking are gender, smoking history, nicotine dependence, smokers in the environment, social support, health status, life stress, and psychiatric problems such as depression, schizophrenia, and alcoholism. Because motivation to smoke is multidetermined, researchers must seek to understand the mechanisms by which each of the different factors operate.

One other factor that belongs on the list of known predictors of smoking onset and cessation is expectancies about the effects of smoking. In much of this chapter we review the evidence that smoking-related expectancies are associated with indexes of smoking motivation and behavior. In addition to identifying multiple risk factors for smoking, researchers need to search for constructs that may mediate or moderate the influences of many, if not all, the identified determinants. This is the area in which the construct of expectancy has exciting potential.

THEORETICAL MECHANISMS

Expectancy Theory

The notion of expectancy has great intuitive appeal. The formation of if–then hypotheses about the world can easily be seen as a vital aspect of the learning process and of people's everyday functioning. Because of this appeal, the concept of expectancy has a relatively long history in the relatively young science of psychology, and it has emerged in virtually every area of the field (Zuroff & Rotter, 1985). Conceptualizations of addiction, and alcohol abuse in particular, were heavily influenced by the social learning theories of Rotter (1954) and Bandura (1977b), both of whom included expectancies as key elements (Abrams & Niaura, 1987). Bandura's distinction between "self-efficacy expectations" and "outcome expectancies" has been especially influential. According to this theory, an outcome expectancy is an individual's estimate that a particular behavior will lead to certain positive outcomes. An efficacy expectation is the belief that one can successfully execute that behavior (Bandura, 1977a). When both self-efficacy and outcome expectancies are high, the individual should be motivated to perform the behavior. This expectancy dichotomy has generated an immense amount of research in social, personality, and clinical psychology. However, several theorists have argued that the distinction is not as clear-cut as Bandura suggested (cf. Kirsch, 1995; Maddux, 1995). Even within the area of smoking cessation, it has been argued that a given belief (e.g., "I can cope with an urge to smoke by relaxing") could be considered either a self-efficacy expectation (e.g., if the outcome is considered to be long-term abstinence) or an outcome expectancy (e.g., if the outcome is considered to be resisting an urge; Haaga & Stewart, 1992).

Despite this theoretical ambiguity, both self-efficacy and outcome expectancies were seized on by addiction researchers. Oddly enough, they were rarely considered together, in interaction, as Bandura's (1977b) model posited. Instead, they tended to be investigated separately. Self-efficacy received major attention with regard to the prediction of smoking cessation and relapse (e.g., Condiotte & Lichtenstein, 1981; DiClemente, Prochaska, & Gibertini, 1985). The belief that one can quit smoking has been found to be one of the best predictors of successful smoking cessation and the maintenance of abstinence. Outcome expectancies received greater attention from alcohol researchers, who used the balanced placebo design (described later) to partition the influences of expectancies and pharmacology on observed responses to drinking (Marlatt & Rohsenow, 1980). They also examined whether measured expectancies about the effects of drinking were related to indexes of drinking motivation, such as the onset of drinking, the quantity and frequency of drinking, and the success of alcoholism treatments (Goldman, Brown, & Christiansen, 1987). More recently, smoking researchers have also addressed this last type of research, often following the path forged by alcohol research. The bulk of this chapter is a review of this research, which is based on the assumption that the behavior of smoking is related to the strength of the outcome expectancies about smoking producing desirable consequences. It is not surprising that the role of self-efficacy has been ignored here because—as opposed to self-efficacy about quitting smoking—there should be little variance in the efficacy expectation that one is capable of smoking a cigarette.

Two variations on outcome expectancies are worth mentioning. The first encompasses expectancy–value models of motivation and decision making (e.g., Edwards, 1954; Fishbein & Ajzen, 1975). These models posit an interaction between the expected probability of an outcome following a behavior and the subjective value of that outcome. Given equal probabilities of occurrence, a highly desired outcome should be more motivational than a less desirable outcome. Our review includes research in which both expectancy–value and unweighted outcome expectancy models of smoking were used.

The second variation, *response expectancies*, is a subset of outcome expectancies. Response expectancies concern the occurrence of nonvolitional responses, such as fear, arousal, pain, and physiological reactions (Kirsch, 1985, 1990). Response expectancy theory assumes a direct causal connection between expectancies and the corresponding subjective experiences (Kirsch, 1985). Volitional behavior is then thought to be affected by the reinforcement value of the nonvolitional responses. Response expectancies regarding smoking would include expectancies about affective reactions to the cigarette (e.g., enhancement of positive affect or reduction of negative affect), an urge or craving for cigarettes, the taste of the cigarette, physiological reactions (e.g., heart rate acceleration), peripheral irritation reactions (e.g., coughing), weight control from smoking, and the health consequences of smoking. Most of the outcome expectancies assessed in smoking research can be conceptualized as response expectancies.

Expectancy-Based Models of Drug Motivation

Much of the research on expectancies and substance use conducted over the past two decades was based only on implicit theory about the function of expectancy in the motivation to use drugs, but there was little explication of how expectancies fit within a more elaborated model of drug use, taking into account other known risk factors and predictors. Left unaddressed were questions such as how expectancies relate to the drug urge. Are expectancies stable, traitlike attributes that are distally related to drug use, or are they more statelike variables that are proximally related? How are expectancies related to other factors thought to influence drug use, such as affective state, personality characteristics, and exposure to drug-related cues?

Recently, however, more elaborated models of drug use have been proposed that include expectancies in key causal roles. For example, Cox and Klinger (1988) posited that an alcoholic individual makes a decision to drink when positive affect expectancies of drinking outweigh expectancies for not drinking. Cox and Klinger believed that it is the emotional reaction to the expected effects of alcohol that ultimately leads to the decision to drink or abstain. For example, expectancies of enhanced positive affect will create an affective reaction of hope and approach. In contrast, expectancies that alcohol will intensify negative affect will produce a fear and avoidance reaction.

Another motivational model of drug use (Niaura et al., 1988) considers both urges and positive drug expectancies as resulting from an affective imbalance, exposure to contextual cues for drug use, or both. According to this model, the content of the expectancies should depend on the particular affective state and cues. For example, negative affect should trigger expectancies concerning relief from distress, whereas positive affect should induce anticipation of pleasurable experiences. Urges and positive drug expectancies are thought to inhibit both coping skill activation and self-efficacy expectations, thus leading to an increased likelihood of drug use or relapse.

Marlatt (1985) also provided a motivational theory of drug use and relapse. In his model, individuals who fail to use coping responses when confronted with a high-risk situation (e.g., interpersonal stress) will suffer from a loss of self-efficacy and an increase in positive drug-related outcome expectancies (e.g., expectancies about pleasurable effects of the drug). These in turn increase the chances that the individuals will use the drug. Marlatt viewed craving as the subjective state mediated by the incentive properties of positive outcome expectancies. Craving, in turn, leads to the behavioral intention to use the drug.

The models just mentioned concern the maintenance of drug use, drug relapse, or both. With regard to the initiation of smoking or other drug use, most models include positive outcome expectancies among the hypothesized risk factors. Expectancy is considered to be more proximal than other dispositional risk factors (e.g., genetic vulnerability, social environment, personality) that appear earlier in the causal chain (e.g., Babor, 1992; Bukstein, 1995; Ellickson & Hays, 1992; Flay, 1993). The exact mechanism by which expectancies influence drug use has not been well specified.

The distinction between the initiation and maintenance of drug use was addressed directly by Oei and Baldwin (1994). They posited that initiation reflects decision making involving controlled processing, during which expectancies about drug use are deliberately weighed. That is, individuals engage in the "mental algebra" implied by expectancy–value models of decision making. In contrast, drug use during the maintenance phase is governed by automatic processes (cf. Tiffany, 1990). By this time, expectancies have been incorporated into automatized drug use action plans that are consolidated in memory and that are no longer available to conscious awareness.

Although the more specified models of drug motivation just discussed have emerged in the past few years (e.g., Cox & Klinger, 1988; Marlatt, 1985; Niaura et al., 1988), unfortunately, little of the research reviewed next is directly relevant to these models. This is especially true in the smoking (as opposed to alcohol) literature. Instead, as noted earlier, most of the research has been based on general models of motivation. That is, researchers have tested the hypothesis that outcome expectancies about smoking are associated with, or predictive of, a variety of indexes of smoking motivation and behavior.

ROLE OF EXPECTANCIES

Assessment of Smoking-Related Expectancies

There are nearly as many instruments for assessing smoking expectancies as there have been studies. Smoking researchers typically have developed ad hoc expectancy instruments, ranging from single-item scales to modifications of questionnaires of alcohol expectancies. In addition, instruments designed to measure other related constructs, such as smoking motivation, reasons for smoking, attitudes about smoking, and smoking-related beliefs (e.g., Best & Hakstian, 1978; Costa, McCrae, & Bosse, 1980; Ikard, Green, & Horn, 1969; Loken, 1982; McKennell, 1970; Velicer, DiClemente, Prochaska, & Brandenburg, 1985), often have included items or scales that could be conceptualized as measuring outcome expectancies. In contrast to the alcohol expectancy research domain, where the Alcohol Expectancy Questionnaire (AEQ; Brown, Goldman, Inn, & Anderson, 1980) emerged nearly 20 years ago, standardized, validated, well-accepted instruments for measuring smoking-related expectancies are only now beginning to appear. It is difficult to determine whether the lack of such an instrument reflects the relatively lower research interest in smoking expectancies or whether the absence of an acceptable tool is what has hampered research in this area.

The main contenders for a standard instrument for measuring smoking expectancies are the recently developed Smoking Consequences Questionnaire (SCQ) and the Smoking Consequences Questionnaire–Adult (SCQ-A). The original SCQ (Brandon & Baker, 1991) was developed using a college student sample of smokers. Later, SCQ-A was developed using older, more experienced smokers (Copeland, Brandon, & Quinn, 1995). The SCQ was developed with Leigh's (1989) critique of alcohol expectancy research and instruments in mind. She cited theoretical and methodological shortcomings of the research that included (a) measurement of expectancies only for desirable consequences of drinking, ignoring undesirable consequences; (b) failure to measure the evaluative component, or desirability, of the consequences; (c) the use of dichotomous response alternatives that allows measurement of number of expectancies but is insensitive to strength of expectancies; and (d) poor internal consistency reliabilities of expectancy subscales. (See Goldman, Brown, Christiansen, & Smith, 1991, for counterarguments to many of Leigh's criticisms.)

In terms of the first two criticisms, most studies of drinking or smoking expectancies have assessed only participants' probability ratings of possible consequences. In contrast, expectancy–value theories, such as utility theory (Edwards, 1954) and social learning theory (Rotter, 1954), hold that behavior is predicted by both the probability and the desirability of possible outcomes. A few studies have assessed participants' evaluations of the consequences of drinking or smoking, as well as their probability ratings, and have combined the two ratings to form measures of subjective expected utility (SEU; Bauman & Bryan, 1980; Bauman & Chenoweth, 1984; Critchlow, 1987; Mausner, 1973). SEU scores are derived by weighting probability ratings by the desirability of the outcome. In this manner, expectancies for outcomes that are important for the participant get weighted more than unimportant outcomes, and expectancies for undesirable outcomes get negative weights. For example, two smokers may share the strong expectancy that smoking will reduce their appetite, but one may consider this a desirable outcome and the other may not. Thus, Leigh (1989) suggested that SEU should better reflect individual differences and situational influences on smoking motivation than would probability ratings alone, and the SCQ was constructed with this in mind.

The development of the SCQ was initiated in a study of college student smokers. An 80-item questionnaire was administered to 382 undergraduate smokers and ex-smokers. To assess SEU, the researchers had participants respond to the 80 items twice. The first time through the list, they were instructed to rate the desirability of each possible consequence of smoking. They then rated the likelihood of each consequence. SEU was calculated as the cross-product of the desirability and likelihood scores.

A principal-components analysis yielded 50 items that loaded on four reliable scales: (a) Negative Consequences (e.g., health risks, respiratory irritation, and negative social impression); (b) Positive Reinforcement/Sensory Satisfaction (e.g., taste, relaxation); (c) Negative Reinforcement/Negative Affect Reduction (e.g., reduction of anger, sadness, and anxiety); and (d) Appetite/Weight Control. The scale scores on the SCQ successfully discriminated among smokers with varying patterns of smoking (i.e., daily smokers, occasional smokers, ex-smokers, triers, and never-smokers), suggesting good construct validity. As expected, daily smokers tended to hold the most positive outcome expectancies about smoking, whereas nonsmokers held the least positive. (Further information relevant to the criterion-related and construct validities of the SCQ and SCQ-A are provided in later sections of this chapter.) Finally, when the four derived SEU scales were compared with the same scales based on probability ratings alone, the latter appeared to be somewhat better able to discriminate across smoking status groups. Because of this difference, and the fact that it is easier to administer and score the probability scales alone, most subsequent researchers have used the probability scales rather than the full SEU scales (e.g., K. K. Downey & Kilbey, 1995; Wetter et al., 1994).

Researchers in two laboratories have reexamined the factor structure of the SCQ. K. K. Downey and Kilbey (1993) performed a principal-components analysis of the 50 probability items selected by Brandon and Baker (1991) using 787 college students, most of whom were nonsmokers. This yielded the four original factors plus a Smoking as a Distractor factor. Wetter et al. (1994) conducted a confirmatory factor analysis, also on the 50 probability items, using 632 smokers enrolled in smoking cessation trials. They confirmed that the original four-factor solution was a better fit to their data than were alternate three-, two-, or one-factor solutions. However, their analysis did not address the question of whether a greater number of factors would have yielded an even better fit. Moreover, both studies were constrained by the content of the 50 items that had been selected by the original principal-components analysis.

Despite the promising initial findings using the SCQ, it was desirable to have an instrument that was developed and validated with smokers who were older and more experienced than the college student sample, given that the smoking rate of the average adult smoker is twice that of the sample used to develop the SCQ. Moreover, on the basis of findings from the alcohol expectancy research (Brown et al., 1980; Christiansen, Goldman, & Inn, 1982), it was hypothesized that years of smoking experience would lead to the development of more specific, less global, smoking-related outcome expectancies. In addition, a direct comparison of scales derived using the SEU scores to scales based on probability ratings alone was needed.

Copeland et al. (1995) therefore administered the original 80 expectancy items to a sample of 407 participants that included current smokers paid for participating, smokers entering a smoking cessation clinic, and ex-smokers. The mean smoking rate for this sample was more than a pack per day, twice that of the original college student sample. As hypothesized, Copeland et al. (1995) found a greater number of factors, of more homogeneous item content, than Brandon and Baker (1991) had found using college student smokers. The SEU items produced 8 subscales, and the probability items produced 10 subscales. The mean coefficient alpha reliability of the 10 probability scales was .88. The SEU and probability versions of the revised SCQ were compared on a variety of criterion-related and construct validity indexes, described next. In general, the probability version performed better than the SEU version on these tests, which led Copeland et al. (1995) to select that version as the SCQ-A and recommend its usage to smoking researchers.

That evaluative ratings did not enhance the validity of probability ratings alone is generally consistent with reports in the alcohol expectancy literature. It may be, as Goldman et al. (1991) argued, that expectancies influence rapid, automatized decision making, which is not conducive to the "mental algebra" that expectancy–value models imply. However, the book is not yet closed on this issue. Evans (1991) argued that researchers handicap themselves when they test hypothesized moderator effects—such as expectancy–value models—by creating multiplicative composites (such as SEU scales). Instead, these models must be treated as interactions between two variables and tested using multivariate statistics. Some support for this approach was found in a study by Fromme, Stroot, and Kaplan (1993), in which the independent and combined influences on alcohol use of subjective probability and evaluative ratings of alcohol's effects were examined via hierarchical regression. Fromme et al. found that evaluative ratings were related to alcohol use above and beyond the influence of probability ratings. However, the influences of evaluative ratings were less robust across both analyses and type of expected effects than were the probability ratings. Although the results of the Fromme et al. (1993) study

270   *BRANDON ET AL.*

did not settle the issue, it would be worthwhile to examine the roles of subjective probabilities and desirabilities of smoking-related outcomes in such a manner.

Expectancies and Concurrent Nicotine Use and Dependence

One of the most robust findings from research on alcohol expectancies is an association between outcome expectancies and measures of alcohol use, abuse, and dependence. In general, the frequency and quantity of alcohol consumption is positively correlated with expectancies for positive outcomes from drinking and negatively correlated with expectancies for negative outcomes (although the latter is found less reliably). Such an association between concurrent measures of substance use and outcome expectancies is neither necessary nor sufficient evidence for the role of expectancies in motivating substance use. It is not sufficient evidence because correlations cannot establish causality. It is not necessary evidence because temporal and psychometric parameters of the two types of variables may differ sufficiently to attenuate any concurrent association. Nevertheless, it is suggestive evidence, and given that it is commonly found with alcohol, researchers would expect to find such a relationship with tobacco use.

This is indeed the case. Brandon and Baker (1991) compared daily smokers, occasional smokers, ex-smokers, triers, and never-smokers on the four expectancy scales of the original SCQ. Both the SEU and probability scales differentiated the smoking status groups. For example, on the probability scales, differences emerged between smoking groups on three of the four scales: Negative Consequences, Positive Reinforcement, and Negative Reinforcement. The general pattern produced by this college student sample was that daily smokers held the most positive (or least negative) expectancies, followed by occasional smokers, triers, and never-smokers. On each of these scales, daily smokers reported expectancies that were significantly more positive than those reported by ex-smokers, triers, and never-smokers, although the differences between these groups did not always reach significance. The differences between daily and occasional smokers were significant for the Positive and Negative Reinforcement scales, but not for the Negative Consequences scale. On the fourth scale, the only between-groups difference was that daily smokers held higher expectancies than occasional smokers for appetite and weight control from smoking.

Copeland et al. (1995) examined the correlation between the probability scales of the SCQ-A and a standard measure of nicotine dependence: the Fagerström Tolerance Questionnaire. They found significant correlations with 6 of the 10 scales. Five of the 6 scales measured positive expectancies (e.g., Negative Affect Reduction, Social Facilitation). Not surprisingly, Craving/Addiction was also correlated with nicotine dependence. In contrast, the scales measuring negative expectancies (i.e., Health

Risks, Negative Physical Feelings, and Negative Social Impression) were unrelated to nicotine dependence.

Results of another study using young adults and the SCQ probability scales confirmed the association between smoking expectancies and nicotine dependence (K. K. Downey & Kilbey, 1995). K. K. Downey and Kilbey compared smokers classified as nicotine dependent (criteria from the *Diagnostic and Statistical Manual of Mental Disorders,* 3rd ed. rev.; American Psychiatric Association, 1987) with smokers who did not meet those criteria and with nonsmokers. The authors found differences between dependent smokers and the other groups on the Positive Reinforcement, Negative Reinforcement, and Appetite/Weight Control scales. Moreover, these differences were maintained even when smoking rate was controlled statistically, indicating that the association between expectancies and psychosocial symptoms of nicotine dependence reflect more than just rate of nicotine use. Interestingly, when the authors reclassified smokers as dependent or nondependent on the basis of symptoms of physical dependence (using an abbreviated version of the Fagerström Tolerance Questionnaire), only the Positive Reinforcement scale differentiated the two groups. This finding suggested that expectancies about negative reinforcement (i.e., negative affect reduction) and weight control may influence the psychosocial symptoms of nicotine dependence without being mediated by physical dependence.

A third study using the SCQ probability scales (Wetter et al., 1994) failed to show any meaningful association between the scales and measures of nicotine dependence, including smoking rate; scores on the Fagerström Tolerance Questionnaire; and the level of expired breath carbon monoxide, serum nicotine, or serum cotinine (a nicotine metabolite). However, all participants were heavy smokers seeking treatment, so there was likely a severe restriction of range on the measures of dependence. A more interesting finding was that all three scales measuring expectancies for the positive effects of smoking predicted the severity of withdrawal symptoms, negative affect, and stress during the week after cessation, symptoms assumed to reflect nicotine dependence. The scales generally maintained their predictive power even when demographic variables and the previously mentioned measures of nicotine dependence were partialed out. This finding led the authors to conjecture that outcome expectancies might be a more sensitive index of "dependence" than traditional self-report or biochemical assays.

The relationship between outcome expectancies and nicotine use and dependence has also been found using other expectancy measures. Loken (1982) compared heavy smoking, light smoking, and nonsmoking college women on 16 items assessing beliefs about the effects of smoking. The groups differed on all eight beliefs about positive effects (e.g., weight control, relaxation, tension relief) and on six of eight beliefs about negative effects (i.e., bad breath, cost, offensive to others, breathing problems, dependency, and bad odor). They did not differ on two health-related items (i.e., harmful to health and increases cancer risk). Additionally, Ahijevych and Wewers (1993) found that a global measure of positive expectancies about smoking (constructed by rewording the AEQ to address tobacco rather than alcohol) predicted 25% of the variance in nicotine dependence in a sample of Black female smokers.

This association between outcome expectancies and smoking level has also been found in adolescent smokers. In a sample of more than five thousand 6th- through 10th-grade students, Covington and Omelich (1988) found differences across smoking status groups in the strength of their beliefs about smoking producing an appearance of maturity, promoting a sense of autonomy, and reducing tension. Regular smokers held the strongest expectancies for these effects, followed by ex-smokers, experimental smokers, and nonsmokers. Similarly, with a sample of 2,339 seventh- and eighth-grade students, Gordon (1986) found differences between current smokers, triers, and never-smokers on beliefs that smoking aids relaxation, leads to positive social consequences, and is harmful. Consistent with the results of other studies, positive expectancies about smoking better distinguished smoking status than did negative expectancies.

In summary, there is clear evidence that heavier, more dependent smokers tend to hold more positive expectancies about the consequences of smoking than do lighter smokers or nonsmokers. Expectancies for positive outcomes (e.g., social facilitation, relaxation, mood enhancement) appear to be more related to nicotine consumption than are expectancies for negative outcomes (e.g., health effects). This is a pattern that has also been observed in the alcohol literature, and we return to it later.

Expectancies and the Initiation of Smoking

The association between expectancies and concurrent smoking is a first step in establishing a role for expectancies in the motivation of tobacco use. However, concurrent correlations provide little information about the causal role of expectancies. It is just as possible that smoking experience leads to positive outcome expectancies, which themselves may be no more than epiphenomena. Prospective associations between expectancies and later smoking also cannot establish causality because such associations could be the result of third variables, such as familial smoking. Nevertheless, because predictive associations rule out reverse causality, they bring researchers one step closer to conclusions about expectancy's causal role in smoking. Moreover, research in this area has the additional practical benefit of identifying markers in youth at high risk of becoming smokers, allowing for preventive interventions.

Given that most smokers begin during their teens, the bulk of research on the prediction of smoking has been conducted with children and adolescents. In fact, there has been a great deal of research on the degree to which attitudes and beliefs about smoking predict later smoking behavior. Unfortunately, there has been far less research examining outcome expectancies per se, and the handful of existing studies have all used different measures of expectancies. Despite these limitations, studies on expectancies and related constructs suggest that adolescents' expectancies about the consequences of smoking may be a useful predictor of later smoking behavior.

In the most relevant study in this area, Bauman and Chenoweth (1984) collected information about smoking expectancies and actual smoking behavior from almost 1,500 adolescents in eighth grade and then again in ninth grade. Their questionnaire consisted of 52 expected consequences of smoking, and participants rated each consequence in terms of both its desirability and likelihood. Product scores were calculated to produce SEU scores, and a factor analysis revealed six factors: Negative Physical/Social, Positive Peer Relations, Negative Peer Relations, Habit, Health, and Pleasure. The authors then conducted two sets of regression analyses. First, they used the expectancy scales to predict smoking onset at the second assessment among students who had not yet smoked by the first assessment. Depending on how they defined smoking status at the two assessments, each of the scales except Health (e.g., getting lung cancer) predicted onset of smoking, but two scales did so most consistently: low Negative Physical/Social scale expectancies (e.g., staining your fingers; looking bad to others) and high Pleasure scale expectancies (e.g., feeling good; being able to concentrate better). The authors then attempted to predict changes in smoking behavior among students who had already smoked by the first assessment. The Pleasure scale emerged as the best predictor, with the Negative Physical/Social and Health scales as the worst. Other researchers have measured "beliefs" and "attitudes" about smoking rather than expectancies per se. In general, the results of these studies suggest that junior and senior high school students who hold positive beliefs about the pleasure available from smoking are more likely to be smokers and to maintain or increase smoking in the future (Charlton & Blair, 1989; A. M. Downey & O'Rourke, 1976).

There is also some evidence that expectancies can distinguish individuals who begin smoking during adolescence (early onset) from those who delay smoking until early adulthood (late onset). Chassin, Presson, Sherman, and Edwards (1991) examined the relationship between the perceived personal consequences of smoking collected from adolescent participants and their smoking behavior during both later adolescence and early adulthood (after high school). Strong positive beliefs about the psychological consequences of smoking predicted smoking onset during both adolescence and adulthood. However, beliefs about the positive social consequences of smoking predicted adolescent smoking but not adult onset of smoking. Conversely, beliefs about the personal health consequences of smoking predicted adult onset of smoking but not adolescent onset.

Chassin et al. (1991) also compared the beliefs of late-onset smokers with nonsmokers and early-onset smokers. They found that both nonsmokers and late-onset smokers held relatively strong beliefs about the negative social consequences of smoking but that the late-onset smokers were more positive (or less negative) than nonsmokers about the psychological and health consequences. Chassin et al. posited that the belief that smoking leads to negative social consequences may prevent smoking in adolescence but that this belief becomes less important with age. A final finding from this study was that adolescent smokers who quit by the time they reached adulthood held more negative health beliefs about smoking than those who continued to smoke into adulthood.

These results are consistent with earlier findings by Morgan and Grube (1989), who assessed smoking and nonsmoking adolescents, aged 13–17 years. They found that among the older participants there was a greater difference between the smoking status groups on expectancies for the negative consequences of smoking and fewer differences on expectancies for positive consequences. Although the study design was cross-sectional, the authors concluded that the negative consequences of smoking become more important with age, even during the period of adolescence.

As a whole, the research on expectancies and the prediction of smoking onset suggests that expectancies develop in children long before any direct pharmacological experience with cigarettes. Positive expectancies about the effects of smoking tend to predict the onset of smoking. On the other hand, expectancies about negative health consequences have not as consistently predicted smoking during adolescence (Bauman & Chenoweth, 1984; Chassin et al., 1991). The negative expectancies that do appear to have predictive power are those related to the negative social consequences of smoking such as parental and peer disapproval (Bauman & Chenoweth, 1984; Chassin et al., 1991). There also appears to be age-related changes in the association between expectancies and smoking. Positive expectancies appear to be more predictive of adolescent onset of smoking, whereas negative expectancies become somewhat more important in distinguishing adult smoking status (Chassin et al., 1991; Morgan & Grube, 1989). A major difficulty in comparing across the aforementioned studies in order to draw general conclusions is the great variation in the operationalization of smoking expectancies. Worse yet, in some cases descriptions of the expectancy measures did not go beyond providing the names of the scales.

Expectancies and Prediction of Cessation Attempts and Outcomes

Another question that is open to both cross-sectional and prospective analyses involves whether smoking-related outcome expectancies can predict smokers' attempts to quit as well as their success at doing so. As with the prediction of smoking onset, affirmative findings from prospective studies would strengthen researchers' confidence in attributing a causal role to smoking expectancies, and they would also have implications for intervention. We first review research examining the association between expectancies about the effects of smoking and motivation to quit smoking. Then, in the following section, we consider whether expectancies predict the outcome of quitting attempts.

Expectancies and Cessation Attempts

Copeland et al. (1995) approached the question by comparing smokers who presented for smoking treatment with other smokers from the community who were not seeking treatment. Participants seeking treatment scored higher on three scales of the SCQ-A: Health Risk, Negative Physical Feelings, and Negative Social Impression. That is, smokers planning to quit had higher expectancies about the negative consequences of smoking, but not the positive consequences. Although the two groups differed in age and years of smoking, statistical correction for these differences did not alter the expectancy findings.

A couple of studies have examined whether smoking-related outcome expectancies predict subsequent attempts at smoking cessation. The first study assessed the smoking beliefs and attitudes of 392 smoking high school students (Hansen, Collins, Johnson, & Graham, 1985). The adolescent smokers who were most likely to have quit smoking between the initial assessment and a 4-month follow-up had reported greater positive beliefs about the short-term consequences of smoking, especially the beliefs that smoking "can give one a lift" and that it increases the "chance of making friends." That is, this study shows that positive expectancies about the effects of smoking predicted cessation, which is a counterintuitive finding.

In the second study, which had a much longer follow-up, 700 young-adult smokers (age 17–25 years) were assessed on a variety of variables, including expectancies about the personally relevant health and psychological consequences of smoking as well as the general (as opposed to personal) negative health consequences of smoking (Rose, Chassin, Presson, & Sherman, 1996). Six "motives for smoking" (which imply expectancies) were also assessed: addiction, habit, affect control, pleasure, stimulation, and sensorimotor. When the participants were contacted again 7 years later, they were asked whether they had made a serious attempt to quit within the previous 5 years. Participants who had indicated high personally relevant expectancies for negative health consequences were more likely to have attempted to quit. On the measure of general health expectancies, there was a difference between heavy and light smokers. Heavy smokers who viewed smoking as dangerous were more likely to quit, but light smokers who held the same expectancy were actually less likely to quit. Light smokers may have felt that the health consequences did not apply to them. On the motive scales, high scores on affect control predicted quitting attempts. Also, low sensorimotor scores predicted attempted cessation among women, but the inverse association was found among men.

A final study included both cross-sectional as well as prospective analyses (Velicer et al., 1985). In this study, 960 participants completed the Decisional Balance Sheet. This instrument includes two scales on which participants rate the importance of 10 positive (Pros) and 10 negative (Cons) aspects of smoking. Although not a true expectancy measure because participants do not rate the probability of smoking consequences, the Decisional Balance Sheet most likely shares significant variance with expectancy instruments.

In their cross-sectional analyses, Velicer et al. (1985) classified participants, based on their smoking status and intentions about quitting, as either "immotives" (i.e., those with no intention to quit), contemplators (i.e., those considering quitting), relapsers, recent quitters, and long-term quitters. For purposes of this discussion, we focus on the differences between immotives, contemplators, and recent quitters. On the Pro scale, no differences were found between immotives and contemplators, but both of these groups scored higher than recent quitters. On the Con scale, contemplators scored higher than immotives, but neither group differed from recent quitters. In the prospective analyses, both the Pro and Con scales predicted changes in participant classification 6 months later by participants initially classified as immotives or contemplators. That is, both high Con scores and low Pro scores were associated with progression toward quitting smoking.

In summary, although conclusions must be made cautiously in light of some of the unexplainable findings as well as the variety of methodologies used, the research does suggest a pattern in which smokers who intend or attempt to quit have expectancies that differ from smokers without intentions to quit. In particular, expectancies about the negative consequences of smoking seem to be most important at this stage, whereas positive expectancies seem to play less of a role. Smokers appear to seriously consider quitting when they acknowledge the unwanted health and social consequences of tobacco use.

Expectancies and Smoking Cessation Outcome

Despite the best intentions of those who attempt to quit, most individuals who quit smoking eventually relapse. This is true across other substances of abuse as well and, in fact, the maintenance of cessation, or relapse prevention, is one of the principle goals of modern addiction research. If outcome expectancies continue to play a part in smoking (or abstinence) motivation, as is suggested by models of relapse (Marlatt, 1985;

Niaura et al., 1988), researchers should find that long-term success is predicted by low expectancies for the positive effects of smoking, high expectancies for the negative effects of smoking, or both. Researchers have indeed found some support for this prediction.

In an early attempt to relate outcome expectancies to relapse, Shiffman (1984) obtained information about the expected effects of smoking from ex-smokers who called a relapse prevention hotline. Callers who had already lapsed and callers who had abstained in the face of a high-risk situation differed in their retrospective reports of expected effects from smoking at the time of the crisis. Those who lapsed were more likely to cite expectations of smoking resulting in reduced tension, whereas participants who did not smoke were more likely to cite the expectation of reduced craving. Expectations that smoking would result in an enhancement of positive experiences, stimulation, or relief from feelings of deprivation failed to discriminate between abstainers and lapsers.

In the two most straightforward tests of expectancies' ability to predict successful smoking cessation, the SCQ and SCQ-A, respectively, were used. In the first study, Wetter et al. (1994) found that the outcome of a smoking cessation program could be predicted from the probability scales of the SCQ collected at pretreatment, even when they controlled for demographic, treatment, dependence, negative affect, and stress variables. Smoking status (smoking vs. abstinent) was examined 1 week after quitting and at the end of treatment, 6–8 weeks later. Abstinence at 1 week was associated with high expectancy scores on the Negative Consequences scale and low scores on the Negative Reinforcement/Negative Affect Reduction scale. At the end of treatment, Negative Reinforcement scores continued to predict cessation success, but Negative Consequences scores did not. In addition, the expectancy that smoking helps control appetite and weight predicted greater end of treatment cessation. The authors were unable to explain this last finding, which was in the opposite direction of predictions.

Using the SCQ-A, Copeland et al. (1995) calculated the correlations between pretreatment expectancy scores and smoking rate 1, 2, 3, 4, and 6 months after treatment. They found a positive correlation between scores on the Negative Affect Reduction scale and smoking rates 1, 2, 4, and 6 months after treatment and between Boredom Reduction scale expectancies and smoking rates at 4 and 6 months. The other 8 scales failed to predict outcome, and the 2 that did each accounted for less than 5% of the outcome variance. Copeland et al. (1995) also examined whether expectancy ratings would change between pretreatment and 3 months' posttreatment and whether such change would be associated with participants' smoking status at the 3-month assessment. They found that compared with smoking participants, abstaining participants showed a greater decrease on four of the expectancy scales: Negative Affect Reduction, Taste/Sensorimotor, Social Facilitation, and Craving/Addiction. Of course, this analysis could not establish whether expectancy change was a cause or consequence of participants' response to treatment.

Other prospective studies have produced a variety of findings that are somewhat more difficult to interpret. Shadel and Mermelstein (1993) asked participants to recall a stressful event from the previous week. They then retrospectively rated their urges to smoke, their expectancies about the coping benefits of smoking under stress, and their self-efficacy about being able to cope with stress without smoking. The authors tested whether these self-efficacy and outcome expectancies collected after a smoking cessation treatment would predict smoking status 3 months later. As hypothesized, high self-efficacy was related to abstinence at 3 months' posttreatment. However, the influence of outcome expectancies was in the opposite direction than was predicted. That is, higher expectancies about the coping benefits of smoking were associated with a lower chance of later smoking. The interaction between the two predictor variables also indicated that the best outcomes occurred in participants with both high self-efficacy and high positive expectancies about smoking. The authors' attempts to explain this unexpected finding (in terms of high outcome expectancies serving as a warning to participants) were not particularly convincing. Shadel and Mermelstein also examined expectancy change during the course of smoking cessation treatment. Like Copeland et al. (1995), they found a decrease in positive expectancies from pre- to posttreatment. However, unlike Copeland et al., expectancy change was unrelated to outcome.

In the Rose et al. (1996) study described earlier, the authors also examined whether smoking-related beliefs and motives would predict cessation 7 years later among smokers who had reported at least one serious attempt to quit. None of the beliefs about psychological or health consequences of smoking was predictive of later smoking status. Of the six motives for smoking, two (i.e., sensorimotor and stimulation) were associated with later smoking status, but they interacted with participants' smoking rate and gender, respectively.

In another study mentioned earlier, Hansen et al. (1985) identified the adolescents who quit smoking in their study and followed them for an additional 12 months. Recall that short-term cessation had been predicted by strong positive beliefs about smoking. In contrast, participants who maintained their abstinence for 1 year tended to have more negative beliefs about smoking. Thus, this study stands out from the more common pattern of negative expectancies predicting cessation attempts and positive expectancies predicting longer term success. A limitation of this study, however, is its small sample. For example, by the final assessment, only 16 participants were smoking.

Finally, Velicer et al. (1985) examined whether scales on the Decisional Balance Sheet would predict change over 6 months among participants classified as recent quitters or relapsers. However, neither the Pro nor Con scale was predictive of change in these two groups of participants.

In summary, the best evidence for expectancies predicting success at quitting smoking has been provided by the two studies using the SCQ or the SCQ-A (Copeland et al., 1995; Wetter et al., 1994). The positive findings in these studies may have emerged because of psychometric advantages of the SCQ instruments compared with the various ad hoc expectancy measures used in most of the other studies. The outcome measures used in these two recent studies may also have greater reliability and validity than those from earlier studies. Findings from the Wetter et al. (1994) study were especially impressive, in that expectancies predicted treatment outcome above and beyond that predicted by a variety of other theoretically relevant variables, including measures of nicotine dependence, thus demonstrating the unique contribution of outcome expectancies.

A general pattern that emerges from the studies reviewed in the previous two sections is that strong expectancies about the negative effects of smoking are important for motivating the intention to quit smoking and short-term cessation. The maintenance of abstinence, in contrast, appears to be more influenced by low expectancies about the positive effects of smoking, especially those effects involving tension reduction or relief of negative affect. Put another way, smoking relapse may be triggered by high expectancies about the benefits of smoking. Although this overall pattern is discernable from the reviewed findings, enough unpredicted and unexplainable associations between expectancies and quitting motivation also emerged to justify additional systematic study.

Response Expectancies About Nicotine Withdrawal Symptoms

It is usually assumed that the variety of withdrawal symptoms (e.g., dysphoria, insomnia, irritability, nicotine craving, appetite increase, difficulty concentrating) that often accompany initial smoking cessation are psychopharmacological effects of nicotine depletion and that it is these symptoms that prevent or thwart many people's quitting attempts. We have already seen that response expectancies about the effects of smoking have predicted withdrawal symptoms in quitting smokers (Wetter et al., 1994). However, the results of a few experiments have provided evidence that expectancies about nicotine withdrawal itself can also influence perceived withdrawal symptoms.

The standard balanced placebo design was used in a study on the expectancy versus pharmacological effects of nicotine chewing gum (Gottlieb, Killen, Marlatt, & Taylor, 1987). The balanced placebo study is a 2 × 2 factorial design in which one factor is whether participants are told that they received active or placebo drug (in this case, nicotine gum), and the other factor is whether they actually did receive active or placebo drug.

Gottlieb et al. (1987) used several different dependent measures, including self-reported withdrawal symptoms (assessed with a standard instrument), cigarette use during the first 2 weeks of gum use, and the amount of gum consumed. On none of these measures did they find a drug effect. That is, there was no difference based on whether participants actually received nicotine or placebo gum. However, participants who were told that they received active nicotine gum reported fewer physical withdrawal symptoms, smoked fewer cigarettes (4.9 per day vs. 11.1 per day) during the 1st week of gum use, and were more likely to be abstinent from cigarettes during the 1st week (60% vs. 39%) compared with participants who were told that they received placebo gum. Thus, expectancies appeared to be more potent than nicotine depletion in determining withdrawal symptoms and smoking behavior shortly after quitting.

A similar study produced findings that were more mixed (Hughes, Gulliver, Amori, Mireault, & Fenwick, 1989). Hughes et al. reported that withdrawal symptoms were affected by actual nicotine receipt but not instructional set, although instructional set alone influenced nicotine craving and gum use. However, none of these differences reached traditional levels of statistical significance. Both factors influenced smoking rate during the 2 weeks after the quit date.

Another approach to testing the role of expectancies in nicotine withdrawal has involved manipulating expectancies about the effects of nicotine gum. Tate et al. (1994) gave 86 smokers placebo gum and randomly assigned them to four conditions that varied in instructions about expected withdrawal symptoms. They told participants that during the next 48 hr they could expect to experience somatic symptoms only (e.g., headache, constipation); psychological symptoms only (e.g., anxiety, depression, craving); or no withdrawal symptoms whatsoever. The fourth group was given no information about expected withdrawal. Clear expectancy effects were found only for the somatic symptoms. Participants told to expect somatic symptoms reported approximately twice as many symptoms, with twice the severity, than participants told not to expect such symptoms. In addition, participants given no expectancy information reported twice the number of somatic symptoms than those told to expect no symptoms at all. In summary, the results of these studies suggest that response expectancies about nicotine withdrawal effects can influence reported withdrawal symptoms and short-term quitting success.

Expectancies and Situational Nicotine Use

The research reviewed up to this point dealt with the relationship between expectancies and smoking behavior at a molar, or global, level. It shows that individuals who hold more favorable outcome expectancies about smoking tend to be more likely to begin smoking, to smoke at a higher rate, to resist attempting to quit smoking, and to have difficulty maintaining abstinence. In this research, both expectancies and smoking tend to be conceptualized as fairly stable, traitlike attributes (akin to Rotter's, 1978, "generalized expectancies"). Indeed, this conceptualization is probably fairly accurate. However, dealing with the association between expectancies and smoking at this molar level makes it easy to ignore the question of how expectancies actually influence behavior. An individual who holds high positive expectancies about smoking may be more likely to be a pack-a-day smoker than another individual whose expectancies are less positive. Left unanswered, however, is how expectancies determine or influence each particular act of smoking executed by that pack-a-day smoker, who will light more than 7,000 cigarettes in a year's time, taking nearly 80,000 puffs. Generalized, stable expectancies may influence situational smoking, but researchers also know that individuals may hold expectancies that are situation specific (Rotter, 1978).

Although several theories of drug motivation include such a molecular, or proximal, role of outcome expectancies (Cox & Klinger, 1988; Marlatt, 1985; Niaura et al., 1988), comparatively little research has been conducted in this area, and most of the existing research has been with alcohol (e.g., Cooney, Gillespie, Baker, & Kaplan, 1987; Corcoran & Parker, 1991; Fromme & Dunn, 1992). The most basic question is whether an individual's smoking expectancies can predict indexes of motivation to smoke (e.g., self-reported urges, psychophysiological responses, or actual tobacco self-administration) in a given situation on a given occasion.

Zinser, Baker, Sherman, and Cannon (1992) found significant correlations between eight items assessing positive smoking outcome expectancies and smokers' self-reported urges. In another study, Kozlowski, Pillitteri, Sweeney, Whitfield, and Graham (1996) divided a standard questionnaire of smoking urges (Tiffany & Drobes, 1991) into items reflecting urge per se (e.g., "I crave a cigarette right now"), intention (e.g., "I will smoke as soon as I get a chance"), and expectancy (e.g., "Smoking would make me less depressed"). When the questionnaire was given to smokers, a path analysis revealed a strong association between the Expectancy and Urge subscales, but only Urge scores were related to intention.

A study by Brandon, Wetter, and Baker (1996) provided mixed evidence for the association between expectancies and smoking motivation. They administered the original SCQ to college student smokers on two occasions: when they first entered the study and a week later, immediately before they were allowed to smoke in the laboratory. Half the participants had abstained from smoking for 24 hr before the second administration. Brandon et al. examined correlations between the SEU versions of the expectancy scales, self-reported urges to smoke, and an index of participants' nicotine self-administration (i.e., the mean of standardized increases in breath CO and the number of puffs taken) during the smoking trial.

Among all participants, they found a significant association ($r = .28$) between the second administration of the Positive Reinforcement scale and urges, measured concurrently. They found associations between expectancies and self-administration among only the abstaining smokers. Both the Positive Reinforcement and Negative Reinforcement scales from the first SCQ administration predicted nicotine consumption in the laboratory ($rs = .36$ and $.42$, respectively). On the SCQ administered before the smoking trial, only the Negative Reinforcement scale predicted consumption ($r = .38$). Interestingly, the expectancy scales continued to predict self-administration even after urge ratings were statistically controlled, indicating that the association between expectancy and administration was not mediated by urge.

Another study examining the relation between expectancies and urges was mentioned earlier (Shadel & Mermelstein, 1993). After recalling a stressful event, participants rated their urges to smoke, their expectancies about the coping benefits of smoking under stress, and their self-efficacy about being able to cope with stress without smoking. They also noted whether they had smoked in response to the event. Expectancies about the coping benefits of smoking were highly related to urge ratings ($r = .58$). Moreover, the interaction between self-efficacy ratings and outcome expectancies was also significant, indicating that outcome expectancies were largely unrelated to urges for those participants with low self-efficacy for coping without smoking (they all reported strong urges regardless of expectancies). However, participants who had high self-efficacy reported strong urges to smoke only if they also had high outcome expectancies about coping by smoking. Low self-efficacy, but not outcome expectancies or the interaction of the two, was related to whether participants had smoked on the recalled occasion. The limitation of this study was that all assessments were retrospective and therefore subject to attribution biases.

The implicit proximal role of outcome expectancies for smoking is that of a moderator variable. That is, expectancies should influence the impact of other variables (e.g., smoking cues, affect, stress) on the decision to have a cigarette. For example, negative affect should trigger smoking only in individuals who hold the expectation that smoking relieves negative affect. Some evidence for such a moderating role for alcohol expectancies has been found (Cooper, Russell, Skinner, Frone, & Mudar, 1992; McKirnan & Peterson, 1988). So far, the evidence for such a moderating effect of smoking expectancies is scanty. Brandon et al. (1996) examined interactions between affect and expectancies on both urges and self-administration variables. Among abstaining smokers, they found a significant interaction between self-reported positive affect and the Positive Reinforcement scale of the SCQ, with the greatest urges being associated with high scores on both. A similar interaction between negative affect and the Negative Reinforcement scale approached significance.

In summary, at this time there is suggestive evidence for a proximal association between smoking outcome expectancies and indexes of smoking motivation. Furthermore, there are initial data suggesting that expectancies may moderate the relation between affect and smoking motivation. In her critique of alcohol expectancy research, Leigh (1989) called for more controlled laboratory research on expectancies, with alcohol self-administration as the dependent measure, to clarify the relation between expectancies and behavior. Researchers have only just begun conducting studies of this type on smoking, and much more work is needed.

Malleability of Smoking Expectancies

How stable are smoking outcome expectancies? We already reviewed evidence that these expectancies can change over time. The strength of expectancies about smoking appear to change with age (Chassin et al., 1991; Morgan & Grube, 1989), as does the structure of such expectancies, with older, more experienced smokers holding more specific expectancies than younger smokers (Copeland et al., 1995). Expectancies also appear to change during the course of smoking cessation treatment (Copeland et al., 1995; Shadel & Mermelstein, 1993). These changes are gradual, taking place over significant periods of time, ranging from weeks to years. Yet the major psychosocial models of drug motivation (Cox & Klinger, 1988; Marlatt, 1985; Niaura et al., 1988) include drug outcome expectancies in a more statelike role, responsive to situational changes. Is there evidence for phasic changes in smoking expectancies? Unfortunately, little research has been conducted to examine this.

One of the most powerful manipulations that can be done to smokers is having them abstain. Because nicotine withdrawal seems to induce a strong smoking motivational state, one would expect to see abstinence-induced expectancy changes. However, the data are mixed. Zinser et al. (1992) found that smokers assigned to a condition requiring 24 hr of abstention reported stronger expectancies for the reinforcing effects of cigarettes, compared with smokers allowed to smoke at will. However, Brandon (1990) assigned smokers to similar conditions and compared them on the four SEU scales of the original SCQ. He found only one significant difference, which was counterdirectional to predictions: Abstaining smokers scored lower on the Negative Reinforcement scale. Brandon also hypothesized that a negative affect manipulation would increase positive outcome expectancies on the Negative Reinforcement/Negative Affect Reduction scale. Although this effect was found, the difference only approached statistical significance ($p < .10$). There were two differences between the Zinser et al. (1992) and Brandon (1990) studies that might account for the divergent findings. First, participants in the Zinser et al. study were experienced adult smokers recruited from the community, whereas Brandon's participants were college student smokers with only one third the smoking experience. The heavier smokers of the Zinser et al. study probably experienced more severe withdrawal symptoms than did the college students in Brandon's study. Second, Brandon assessed expectancies using the SCQ, an instrument that was designed to measure more traitlike, generalized smoking expectancies. The full SEU version of the questionnaire took up to 20 min to complete, which in itself may make it inappropriate for assessing phasic expectancy changes. By contrast, Zinser et al. assessed current expectancies with eight simple Likert-type items.

Clearly, more research is needed on situational factors that might influence expectancies. In particular, researchers know that exposure to smoking cues (e.g., cigarettes and matches) increases the desire to smoke (cf. Brandon, Piasecki, Quinn, & Baker, 1995), and responses to these cues have been hypothesized to begin the sequence that motivates drug use, mediated by outcome expectancies (e.g., Marlatt, 1985). Therefore, one should see expectancy changes in response to such cues, which has been found with alcohol (Cooney et al. 1987).

The issue of altering smoking outcome expectancies also has other theoretical and practical implications. Nearly all the research to date on smoking expectancies has been correlational. Although the prospective studies are consistent with a causal role of expectancies in smoking motivation, they cannot truly test it. The causal role can be tested only through an experimental design in which expectancies are manipulated and measures of smoking motivation are the dependent variables. The practical value of such a study would be to open the door to the possibility that interventions (prevention and treatment) might exploit expectancy change as a means to produce behavior change.

Copeland and Brandon (in press) recently concluded a study in which they attempted to manipulate smokers' expectancies about health risks and negative affect reduction. Participants in the expectancy challenge conditions watched videos of current and former smokers discussing either the health consequences of their smoking or how smoking was an ineffective way to regulate mood. The video viewing was followed by interviews with an experimenter who attempted to personalize the same information for participants. (A control condition included a video of smokers discussing nonmotivational aspects of their smoking pattern followed by a similar interview.)

Findings from this study show that the negative affect expectancy challenge was successful at immediately reducing participants' scores on the Negative Affect Reduction scale of the SCQ-A and that this reduction was maintained through a follow-up meeting 1 week later. However, changes in the health risk expectancies did not reach statistical significance. Dependent measures of smoking motivation (collected 1 week later to reduce demand effects) included a number of standard instruments designed to measure intention to quit smoking and progression through stages of change as well as self-reported smoking rate during the week after the manipulation and 2 and 3 months later. Results suggest that the health risk challenge, but not the negative affect reduction challenge, increased motivation to change as measured by the various questionnaires. This pattern had been hypothesized on the basis of evidence that health risk expectancies are more important for decisions to quit smoking (Copeland et al., 1995). Also, changes in health risk expectancies were associated with change on the motivation measures. No differences in participants' actual postmanipulation rate of smoking were found across conditions at 1 week, but, by the 2- and 3-month follow-ups, participants who received the health risk challenge reported smoking significantly less than other participants.

Results from Copeland and Brandon's (in press) study provide preliminary evidence that at least some types of smoking expectancies (those related to negative affect reduction) can be successfully challenged. Although changes in health risk expectancies did not reach significance, the health risk challenge did appear to produce changes in self-reported motivation to quit smoking. Health risk expectancies may be more intractable than negative affect expectancies because the former are challenged on a regular basis through public health campaigns. However, even small changes in these expectancies may have motivational power. There is a need for more experiments in which researchers attempt to manipulate expectancies. Researchers need to know which types of expectancies they are able to change, whether the change affects drug motivation, and how to produce expectancy change efficiently and with prolonged results. These questions are important not only for theoretical reasons but also because they should lead directly to the development of possible intervention strategies.

IMPLICATIONS

An Omnibus Model

Figure 11.1 illustrates an omnibus model of the role of smoking-related outcome expectations in smoking motivation. This model is derived from both existing theories and the research that we reviewed earlier. Note that the figure actually includes separate models for smoking initiation, ongoing smoking, smoking cessation, and smoking relapse. They are included in one figure for the sake of efficiency and comparison. This is not meant to be an all-inclusive model of smoking motivation, nor is it a finished product. There no doubt are other variables that could be included. In fact, the model does not include all the elements of the drug

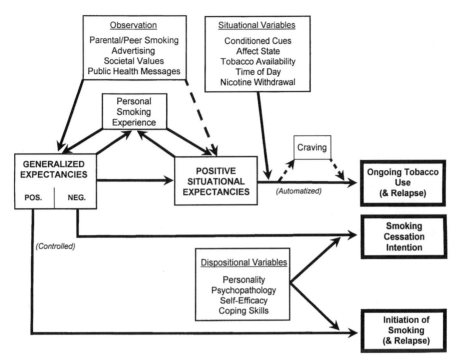

Figure 11.1. An omnibus model of the role of smoking-related outcome expectancies in smoking initiation, ongoing smoking, smoking cessation, and relapse to smoking. Outcomes are in bold.

motivational models reviewed earlier (i.e., Cox & Klinger, 1988; Marlatt, 1985; Niaura et al., 1988). Instead, it is meant to emphasize and summarize the role played by outcome expectancies. Although the model refers to tobacco smoking, reflecting the topic of this chapter, we expect that it could easily be adapted for alcohol and other drug use.

The model includes two types of smoking-related outcome expectancies: generalized expectancies and situational expectancies. Generalized expectancies are akin to what Shiffman (1989) called a "background variable." They develop as a result of both direct, personal experience with smoking as well as through observation, or vicarious learning. A few examples of sources for such learning include smoking by parents or peers, cigarette advertising, general societal values, and public health information. Note that none of the three lists of examples shown in Figure 11.1 (observations, situational variables, and dispositional variables) are assumed to be all-inclusive or to contain items that are mutually exclusive. In fact, there are probably even causal relations among items within each list.

Research suggests that smoking initiation is predicted primarily by expectancies for positive outcomes from smoking (e.g., Bauman & Chenoweth, 1984; Chassin et al., 1991), whereas the intention to quit smoking is associated with expectancies for negative outcomes (e.g., Copeland et al., 1995; Rose et al., 1996). As posited by Oei and Baldwin (1994), we believe that the intention to begin or quit smoking is based on controlled information processing, that is, an individual makes a conscious decision to change his or her behavior. We list some dispositional variables that most likely interact with expectancies in determining behavior change. These include personality characteristics, psychopathology (e.g., depression), self-efficacy about the ability to quit as well as about coping with stress in ways other than smoking, and coping skills themselves.

Situational expectancies (i.e., expectancies about the outcome of smoking in particular situations) are assumed to be influenced primarily by one's generalized expectancies and modified by personal smoking experience across situations. Because response expectancies tend to be self-confirming, the model includes arrows from both generalized and situational expectancies back to personal smoking experience. It is also possible that observational learning plays a role, such as when one observes a parent smoking after an argument. However, the observational influence is assumed to be weaker than direct experience, which accounts for the dashed line in the figure. Situational expectancies are "proximal precipitating factors" related to relapse (Shiffman, 1989). Situational expectancies must, of course, interact with the various situations (internal or external) in which smokers find themselves. These would include the presence of smoking-related cues, states of affect (e.g., boredom, sadness, elation), the assorted symptoms of nicotine withdrawal, the time of day, and even the knowledge that tobacco is available. Again influenced by Oei and Baldwin (1994) and Tiffany (1990), we assume that most tobacco use by current smokers is the result of automatized action plans. These action plans are influenced by easily accessible memories of situational expectancies (cf. Goldman et al., 1991). We must acknowledge, however, that the hypothesis that expectancies influence smoking through noncontrolled, or automatic, processes has not been tested. We have included only positive situational expectancies in the figure because these appear to be prepotent in motivating ongoing smoking, although it is possible that negative expectancies (e.g., "If I smoke in this theater, I will be thrown out") may occasionally operate to inhibit smoking.

Thus, situational expectancies are assumed to be both mediators (mediating the association between past smoking experience and tobacco use) and moderators (moderating the association between situational variables and tobacco use). We have included two routes to smoking relapse in our omnibus model. We believe that relapse can result from an intentional decision, similar to the decision to begin or quit smoking, or that it may reflect more automatized information processing. For example, consider the relapse reports of two smokers who had already abstained for several months after participating in our smoking cessation clinic. The first smoker reported that he was drinking in a bar when he suddenly realized that he had a lit cigarette in his mouth, as had always been the case when he had been in that bar before quitting. The second smoker reported that she decided to resume smoking to lose weight before she attended her son's wedding, which was 4 months away. Acknowledging the risks associated with retrospective explanations of behavior, the first smoker's relapse appears to have involved automatic action plans triggered by the situation, whereas the second smoker seems to have made a conscious decision to relapse. The possibility that smoking motivation may involve two types of processing—controlled versus automatized—is also similar to Stacy's (1997) proposal that drug use motivation may involve both implicit cognition (memory activation) and explicit cognition (outcome expectancy).

We have assigned only a tentative role (i.e., dashed arrows) for nicotine craving or urge in the model because it is not yet clear where (or if) craving belongs in the causal chain leading to smoking. Craving is linked to expectancies by models such as Marlatt's (1995), and there is evidence that they are correlated (e.g., Shadel & Mermelstein, 1993; Zinser et al., 1992). However, Tiffany (1990) argued, and presented evidence, that craving appears only when automatized smoking action plans are interrupted. Also, recall that Brandon et al. (1996) found that expectancies predicted self-administration without mediation by craving (although Kozlowski et al., 1996, found that craving mediated the relation between expectancy and intention to smoke, measured concurrently). The role of craving remains an open question that should be the subject of additional research.

Future Research

Throughout the review of research on smoking-related outcome expectancies in the previous section, we mentioned areas in which additional research is needed. Here, we summarize what we believe are the most important research directions at this time.

1. Establish causality. Interest in expectancies is predicated on the assumption that they play a causal role in smoking motivation. However, causality has not yet been demonstrated, although the prospective studies provide suggestive evidence. More studies are needed in which expectancies are manipulated. These may be laboratory analog studies like that of Copeland and Brandon (in press) or applied treatment or prevention studies.

2. Explore the nature of the causal relation. Research to date has generally been limited to examining the direct linear relation between expectancies on measures of smoking motivation. However, motivational models—including those reviewed earlier (e.g., Cox & Klinger, 1988; Marlatt, 1985; Niaura et al., 1988) as well as the omnibus model presented earlier—assume a more complex role, in which expectancies act as moderator variables, mediator variables, or both. Studies are needed that examine more than one link in these theories. That is, they need to formally test whether expectancies mediate or moderate the relation between other hypothesized variables and smoking motivation (cf. Baron & Kenny, 1986). The other variables may include self-efficacy, affect (positive and negative), nicotine dependence, and coping skills, to name a few. In the introduction, we mentioned that expectancies have exciting potential if they can be shown to serve as a higher order construct that explains the role of other variables in smoking motivation. Perhaps expectancies are even a final common pathway through which other variables exert their influence (i.e., a common mediating variable). Despite the theoretical appeal of such a model, outcome expectancies thus far have not been shown to function in this way. First, few researchers have examined expectancies in such a manner. Although some researchers have admirably tested whether expectancies predict dependent measures even after other common predictors (e.g., demographics, nicotine dependence) are controlled, few have examined the inverse: whether these predictors continue to explain variance above and beyond expectancies. Second, even when expectancies have been found to predict a statistically significant proportion of the variance in smoking motivational variables, the effect sizes have tended to be small, smaller than one would expect for a common mediating variable. However, measurement error may play a big part in attenuating these effect sizes.

3. Develop and validate a measure of phasic, or situational, expectancies. The SCQ and SCQ-A appear to be reliable and valid measures of relatively stable, traitlike expectancies for smoking. However, these instruments may not be appropriate for assessing more statelike expectancies that are subject to situational change. A standardized measure is needed to assess a smoker's expectancies about smoking a cigarette at a given moment in a given situation. Alternatively, expectancies that influence smoking in ways other than through controlled, deliberate mental algebra (i.e., expectancies that function through automatic processing) may need to be assessed in novel ways, as has begun within the alcohol field (Rather, Goldman, Roehrich, & Brannick, 1992; Stacy, 1997).

4. Examine situational change in expectancies. Once a valid measure is developed, researchers can better study the influence of situational variables on smoking expectancies. This will also allow researchers to test the validity of the various motivational models of drug use because they tend to include situational variables in their causal chain. Researchers can ask questions such as the following: Does exposure to smoking-related cues alter an individual's immediate expectancies? Also, researchers now have some evidence that positive expectancies are associated with smoking relapse. Furthermore, it is known that even a single ex-smoker who has only one postcessation cigarette is highly likely to return to regular smoking (Brandon, Tiffany, Obremski, & Baker, 1990). However, researchers do not know whether and how expectancies change after that initial cigarette and whether expectancy change is implicated in the high likelihood of full relapse. With the development of the technology for collecting real-time assessments (e.g., Stone & Shiffman, 1994), it is now possible to measure expectancy change immediately after an initial slip.

5. *Examine the memory structure of smoking expectancies.* Goldman and his colleagues (e.g., Rather & Goldman, 1994; Rather et al., 1992) have recently been approaching the study of alcohol expectancies with a different level of analysis than most of the correlational research reviewed in this chapter. They have been using semantic network models of memory to map the cognitive structure of alcohol-related expectancies. Among their findings have been differences between heavy and light drinkers in expectancy-based memory networks. When exposed to an alcohol stimulus, heavy drinkers may rapidly associate many positive and arousing outcomes of drinking, whereas light drinkers more slowly associate sedating and adverse outcomes (Rather & Goldman, 1994). It is easy to imagine similar differences in memory networks among smokers with varying experience and dependence levels. Thus, research in this vein on smoking expectancies would be informative.

6. *Use the balanced-placebo design to test response expectancies of nicotine use.* The balanced-placebo design separates the expectancy and pharmacological effects of drug use. It has been a productive design for testing the influence of alcohol expectancies on behavior (Marlatt & Rohsenow, 1980), but it has been underused with nicotine. Recent progress in the development of a convincing placebo cigarette should stimulate the use of the balanced-placebo design. Sutton (1991) suggested that the design could be used to examine the role that expectancies play in nicotine titration (i.e., the self-regulation of smoking rate in response to blood nicotine levels), nicotine's effects on performance, and the effect of a "priming dose" of nicotine on craving and relapse. Other possible dependent variables include relaxation, negative affect reduction, and stimulation, all frequently reported subjective effects of smoking. An advantage of the balanced-placebo design is that it allows a direct test of whether expectancies are causally related to the production of the expected nonvolitional responses. That is, it tests for actual response expectancies as defined by Kirsch (1985).

Implications for Intervention

Given that the association between outcome expectancies and smoking motivation is not yet well established and that causality certainly has not yet been established, firm recommendations for intervention would be premature and perhaps even irresponsible. Therefore, we keep this discussion brief and predicate it on the assumption that expectancies do indeed play a causal role in smoking. Even if expectancies do not have such a causal influence on smoking, they still may have applied use as a marker for identifying adolescents who are at risk for initiating smoking, smokers who are likely to benefit from treatment, or ex-smokers who are at risk for relapse. Cost-effective interventions could then be targeted at these individuals.

Most relevant to interventions is the observed pattern of different types of smoking expectancies being associated with different points in the natural history of smoking. The initiation of smoking appears to be most predicted by high positive expectancies and low expectancies about the negative social consequences of smoking. The maintenance of smoking is associated with high positive expectancies, especially for the reduction of negative affect by smoking. In contrast, the intention to quit and short-term success at quitting are related to high expectancies about the negative consequences of smoking, especially the negative health effects of smoking. Finally, relapse is associated with high positive expectancies again.

If these expectancies are causally related to the various stages of smoking, then interventions aimed at these stages might benefit from targeting the specific expectancies. For example, prevention programs for adolescents should focus on reducing positive expectancies and increasing expectancies for the negative social consequences of smoking. They should avoid emphasizing the delayed negative consequences of smoking, such as the deleterious health effects, which do not seem to be relevant to the early stages of smoking. In contrast, public health campaigns that emphasize those health consequences should be effective at helping smokers decide to quit. Finally, relapse prevention interventions should help clients maintain low expectancies for the positive effects of smoking, including expectancies about negative affect reduction.

Even if these expectancy targets prove to be correct, the question remains about how to affect expectancies to the degree necessary to prevent or treat smoking. It is likely that smoking-related expectancies are formed early and that they are shaped by multiple influences, including peers, parents, and the media. Actual experiences with tobacco continue to shape and reinforce these expectancies. Thus, one would expect that the alteration or weakening of these expectancies would be quite a challenge for interventions. It is remarkable that the development of techniques for changing expectancies has received so little attention by researchers of smoking, although the success of current interventions may in fact be partially mediated by expectancy change, however unintentional.

Moreover, interventions would not necessarily need to directly target smoking expectancies per se, but instead they could function by strengthening competing expectancies. For example, instead of (or in addition to) attempting to disabuse clients of their expectancies about nicotine's ability to alleviate depression or other aversive moods, a relapse prevention program could provide clients with other nonpharmacological methods for regulating their moods. That is, it could focus on increasing clients' self-efficacy and outcome expectancies about coping with stress without smoking. Indeed, there is already some evidence that cognitive therapy for depression is an effective component of smoking cessation counseling for individuals with a history of clinical depression or a proneness for negative affect (Brandon et al., 1997; Hall, Muñoz, Reus, & Sees, 1993). This is consistent with findings that smokers' beliefs about their ability to cope with stress and negative affect without smoking are related to their reported urges and nicotine self-administration under stress (Shadel & Mermelstein, 1993; Wetter, Brandon, & Baker, 1992).

CONCLUSIONS

A fair amount of research has now been generated on the topic of smoking-related outcome expectancies. An encouraging aspect of this research is that expectancies have been found to be associated with every index of smoking motivation examined. These include measures of each stage in the natural history of smoking, ranging from initiation to cessation to relapse. They include measures of nicotine dependence and nicotine withdrawal. They also include molar measures such as average smoking rate as well as molecular measures such as nicotine self-administration in response to a laboratory stressor. The range of responses that has been found to be associated with outcome expectancies is truly impressive, suggesting that expectancy is a key overarching construct relating to smoking motivation.

However, enthusiasm must be tempered by the fact that—although associations with every index of smoking motivation have been found—there have also been numerous null or counterdirectional findings. In few if any of the research areas reviewed has enough evidence accumulated to allow for highly confident conclusions about the role of expectancies. Moreover, the associations that have been observed tend to account for relatively little variance in the measures of smoking motivation. The entire area of research on smoking-related expectancies has been handicapped by a lack of both systematic research approaches and the use of accepted, standardized measurement. Instead, this body of research has an overall ad hoc quality to it. A final critical conclusion is that a causal role of outcome expectancies has not yet been satisfactorily demonstrated, although the longitudinal and laboratory studies are pointing toward such a role.

We believe that the stage is now set for more systematic investigation of smoking-related outcome expectancies and of their causal influence in tobacco smoking. The research should include examination of the mechanisms by which expectancies influence smoking. We have presented an omnibus model of expectancies in the hope that it might stimulate such research. The literature we have reviewed suggests that expectancy has unusual potential as both an explanatory construct and a target for intervention. Given the toll that smoking continues to exact on society, such potential cannot be ignored.

REFERENCES

Abrams, D. B., & Niaura, R. S. (1987). Social learning theory. In H. T. Blane & K. E. Leonard (Eds.), *Psychological theories of drinking and alcoholism* (pp. 181–226). New York: Guilford Press.

Ahijevych, K., & Wewers, M. E. (1993). Factors associated with nicotine dependence among African American women cigarette smokers. *Research in Nursing and Health, 16,* 283–292.

American Psychiatric Association. (1987). *Diagnostic and statistical manual of mental disorders* (3rd ed. rev.). Washington, DC: Author.

Babor, T. F. (1992). Nosological considerations in the diagnosis of substance use disorders. In M. Glantz & R. Pickens (Eds.), *Vulnerability to drug abuse* (pp. 53–73). Washington, DC: American Psychological Association.

Bandura, A. (1977a). Self-efficacy: Toward a unifying theory of behavioral change. *Psychological Review, 84,* 191–215.

Bandura, A. (1977b). *Social learning theory.* Englewood Cliffs, NJ: Prentice Hall.

Baron, R. M., & Kenny, D. A. (1986). The moderator–mediator variable distinction in social psychological research: Conceptual, strategic, and statistical considerations. *Journal of Personality and Social Psychology, 51,* 1173–1182.

Bauman, K. E., & Bryan, E. S. (1980). Subjective expected utility and children's drinking. *Journal of Studies on Alcohol, 41,* 952–958.

Bauman, K. E., & Chenoweth, R. L. (1984). The relationship between the consequences adolescents expect from smoking and their behavior: A factor analysis with panel data. *Journal of Applied Social Psychology, 14,* 28–41.

Best, J. A., & Hakstian, A. R. (1978). A situation-specific model for smoking behavior. *Addictive Behavior, 3,* 79–92.

Brandon, T. H. (1990). *The roles of affect and expectancies in the motivation to smoke.* Unpublished doctoral dissertation, University of Wisconsin—Madison.

Brandon, T. H., & Baker, T. B. (1991). The smoking consequences questionnaire: The subjected expected utility of smoking in college students. *Psychological Assessment, 3,* 484–491.

Brandon, T. H., Juliano, L. M., Copeland, A. L., Collins, B. N., Quinn, E. P., & Lazev, A. B. (1997, April). Matching smokers to treatment based on negative affectivity. In R. A. Brown (Chair), *Addressing depression in smoking cessation: Does it make a difference?* Symposium presented at the meeting of the Society of Behavioral Medicine, San Francisco.

Brandon, T. H., Piasecki, T., Quinn, E. P., & Baker, T. B. (1995). Cue exposure treatment in nicotine dependence. In D. C. Drummond, S. Glautier, B. Remington, & S. Tiffany (Eds.), *Addictive behaviour: Cue exposure theory and practice* (pp. 211–227). New York: Wiley.

Brandon, T. H., Tiffany, S. T., Obremski, K., & Baker, T. (1990). Postcessation cigarette use: The process of relapse. *Addictive Behaviors, 15,* 105–114.

Brandon, T. H., Wetter, D. W., & Baker, T. B. (1996). Affect, expectancies, urges and smoking: Do they conform to models of drug motivation and relapse? *Experimental and Clinical Psychopharmacology, 4,* 29–36.

Brown, S. A., Goldman, M. S., Inn, A., & Anderson, L. R. (1980). Expectations of reinforcement from alcohol: Their domain and relation to drinking patterns. *Journal of Consulting and Clinical Psychology, 50,* 336–344.

Bukstein, O. G. (1995). *Adolescent substance abuse: Assessment, prevention, and treatment.* New York: Wiley.

Centers for Disease Control and Prevention (1993). Cigarette smoking among adults—United States, 1991. *Morbidity and Mortality Weekly Report, 42,* 230–233.

Centers for Disease Control and Prevention (1995). Trends in smoking initiation among adolescents and young adults—United States, 1980–1989. *Morbidity and Mortality Weekly Report, 44,* 521–525.

Charlton, A., & Blair, V. (1989). Predicting the onset of smoking in boys and girls. *Social Science and Medicine, 29,* 813–818.

Chassin, L., Presson, C. C., Sherman, S. J., & Edwards, D. A. (1991). Four pathways to young-adult smoking status: Adolescent social-psychological antecedents in a midwestern community sample. *Health Psychology, 10,* 409–418.

Christiansen, B. A., Goldman, M. S., & Inn, A. (1982). Development of alcohol-related expectancies in adolescents: Separating pharmacological from social-learning influences. *Journal of Consulting and Clinical Psychology, 50,* 336–344.

Condiotte, M. M., & Lichtenstein, E. (1981). Self-efficacy and relapse in smoking cessation programs. *Journal of Consulting and Clinical Psychology, 49,* 648–658.

Cooney, N. L., Gillespie, R. A., Baker, L. H., & Kaplan, R. F. (1987). Cognitive changes after alcohol cue exposure. *Journal of Consulting and Clinical Psychology, 55,* 150–155.

Cooper, M. L., Russell, M., Skinner, J. B., Frone, M. R., & Mudar, P. (1992). Stress and alcohol use: Moderating effects of gender, coping, and alcohol expectancies. *Journal of Abnormal Psychology, 101,* 139–152.

Copeland, A. L., & Brandon, T. H. (in press). Testing the causal role of expectancies in motivation and behavior. *Addictive Behaviors.*

Copeland, A. L., Brandon, T. H., & Quinn, E. P. (1995). The Smoking Consequences Questionnaire–Adult: Measurement of smoking outcome expectancies of experienced smokers. *Psychological Assessment, 7,* 484–494.

Corcoran, K. J., & Parker, P. S. (1991). Alcohol Expectancy Questionnaire Tension Reduction scale as a predictor of alcohol consumption in a stressful situation. *Addictive Behaviors 16,* 129–137.

Costa, P. T., McCrae, R. R., & Bosse, R. (1980). Smoking motive factors: A review and replication. *International Journal of the Addictions, 15,* 537–549.

Covington, M., & Omelich, C. L. (1988). I can resist anything but temptation: Adolescent *expectations* for smoking cigarettes. *Journal of Applied Social Psychology, 18*, 203–227.

Cox, W. M., & Klinger, E. (1988). A motivational model of alcohol use. *Journal of Abnormal Psychology, 97*, 168–180.

Critchlow, B. (1987). A utility analysis of drinking. *Addictive Behaviors, 12*, 269–273.

DiClemente, C. C., Prochaska, J. O., & Gibertini, M. (1985). Self-efficacy and the stages of self-change of smoking. *Cognitive Therapy and Research, 9*, 181–200.

Downey, A. M., & O'Rourke, T. W. (1976). The utilization of attitudes and beliefs as indicators of future smoking behavior. *Journal of Drug Education, 6*, 283–295.

Downey, K. K., & Kilbey, M. M. (1993, August). *The relationship between alcohol and nicotine expectancies and substance dependency.* Paper presented at the 101st Annual Convention of the American Psychological Association, Toronto, Ontario, Canada.

Downey, K. K., & Kilbey, M. M. (1995). Relationship between nicotine and alcohol expectancies and substance dependence. *Experimental and Clinical Psychopharmacology, 3*, 174–182.

Edwards, W. (1954). The theory of decision making. *Psychological Bulletin, 51*, 380–417.

Ellickson, P. L., & Hays, R. D. (1992). On becoming involved with drugs: Modeling adolescent drug use over time. *Health Psychology, 11*, 377–385.

Evans, M. G. (1991). The problem of analyzing multiplicative composites: Interactions revisited. *American Psychologist, 46*, 6–15.

Fishbein, M., & Ajzen, I. (1975). *Belief, attitude, intention, and behavior: An introduction to theory and research.* Reading, MA: Addison-Wesley.

Flay, B. R. (1993). Youth tobacco use: Risks, patterns, and control. In C. T. Orleans & J. Slade (Eds.), *Nicotine addiction: Principles and management* (pp. 365–384). New York: Oxford University Press.

Fromme, K., & Dunn, M. E. (1992). Alcohol expectancies, social and environmental cues as determinants of drinking and perceived reinforcement. *Addictive Behaviors, 17*, 167–177.

Fromme, K., Stroot, E., & Kaplan, D. (1993). Comprehensive effects of alcohol: Development and psychometric assessment of a new expectancy questionnaire. *Psychological Assessment, 5*, 19–26.

Goldman, M. S., Brown, S. A., & Christiansen, B. A. (1987). Expectancy theory: Thinking about drinking. In H. T. Blane & K. E. Leonard (Eds.), *Psychological theories of drinking and alcoholism* (pp. 181–226). New York: Guilford Press.

Goldman, M. S., Brown, S. A., Christiansen, B. A., & Smith, G. T. (1991). Alcoholism etiology and memory: Broadening the scope of alcohol expectancy research. *Psychological Bulletin, 110*, 137–146.

Gordon, N. P. (1986). Never smokers, triers and current smokers: Three distinct target groups for school-based antismoking program. *Health Education Quarterly, 13,* 163–180.

Gottlieb, A. M., Killen, J. D., Marlatt, G. A., & Taylor, C. B. (1987). Psychological and pharmacological influences in cigarette smoking withdrawal: Effects of nicotine gum and expectancy on smoking withdrawal symptoms and relapse. *Journal of Consulting and Clinical Psychology, 55,* 606–608.

Haaga, D. A., & Stewart, B. L. (1992). Self-efficacy for recovery from a lapse after smoking cessation. *Journal of Consulting and Clinical Psychology, 60,* 24–28.

Hall, S. M., Muñoz, R. F., Reus, V. I., & Sees, K. L. (1993). Nicotine, negative affect, and depression. *Journal of Consulting and Clinical Psychology, 61,* 761–767.

Hansen, W. B., Collins, L. M., Johnson, C. A., & Graham, J. W. (1985). Self-initiated smoking cessation among high school students. *Addictive Behaviors, 10,* 265–271.

Hughes, J. R., Gulliver, S. B., Amori, G., Mireault, G. C., & Fenwick, J. F. (1989). Effect of instructions and nicotine on smoking cessation, withdrawal symptoms and self-administration of nicotine gum. *Psychopharmacology, 99,* 486–491.

Ikard, F. F., Green, D. E., & Horn, D. (1969). A scale to differentiate between types of smoking as related to the management of affect. *The International Journal of the Addictions, 4,* 649–659.

Kirsch, I. (1985). Response expectancy as a determinant of experience and behavior. *American Psychologist, 40,* 1189–1202.

Kirsch, I. (1990). *Changing expectancies: A key to effective psychotherapy.* Pacific Grove, CA: Brooks/Cole.

Kirsch, I. (1995). Self-efficacy and outcome expectancy: A concluding comment. In J. E. Maddux (Ed.), *Self-efficacy, adaptation, and adjustment: Theory, research, and application* (pp. 331–345). New York: Plenum.

Kozlowski, L. T., Pillitteri, J. L., Sweeney, C. T., Whitfield, K. E., & Graham, J. W. (1996). Asking questions about urges or cravings for cigarettes. *Psychology of Addictive Behaviors, 10,* 248–260.

Leigh, B. C. (1989). Attitudes and expectancies as predictors of drinking habits: A comparison of three scales. *Journal of Studies on Alcohol, 50,* 432–440.

Loken, B. (1982). Heavy smokers', light smokers' and nonsmokers' beliefs about cigarette smoking. *Journal of Applied Psychology, 67,* 616–622.

Maddux, J. E. (1995). Self-efficacy theory: An introduction. In J. E. Maddux (Ed.), *Self-efficacy, adaptation, and adjustment: Theory, research, and application* (pp. 3–33). New York: Plenum.

Marlatt, G. A. (1985). Cognitive factors in the relapse process. In G. A. Marlatt & J. R. Gordon (Eds.), *Relapse prevention* (pp. 128–200). New York: Guilford Press.

Marlatt, G. A., & Rohsenow, D. J. (1980). Cognitive processes in alcohol use: Expectancy and the balanced-placebo design. In N. K. Mello (Ed.), *Advances in substance abuse: Behavioral and biological research* (pp. 159–199). Greenwich, CT: Aijai Press.

Mausner, B. (1973). An ecological view of cigarette smoking. *Journal of Abnormal Psychology, 81*, 115–126.

Morgan, M., & Grube, J. W. (1989). Adolescent cigarette smoking: A developmental analysis of influences. *British Journal of Developmental Psychology, 7*, 179–189.

McKennell, A. C. (1970). Smoking motivation factors. *British Journal of Social and Clinical Psychology, 9*, 8–22.

McKirnan, D. J., & Peterson, P. L. (1988). Stress, expectancies, and vulnerabilities to substance abuse: A test of a model among homosexual men. *Journal of Abnormal Psychology, 97*, 461–466.

Niaura, R. S., Rohsenow, D. J., Binkoff, J. A., Monti, P. M., Pedraza, M., & Abrams, D. B. (1988). Relevance of cue reactivity to understanding alcohol and smoking relapse. *Journal of Abnormal Psychology, 97*, 133–152.

Oei, T. P., & Baldwin, A. R. (1994). Expectancy theory: A two-process model of alcohol use and abuse. *Journal of Studies on Alcohol, 55*, 525–534.

Rather, B. C., & Goldman, M. S. (1994). Drinking-related differences in the memory organization of alcohol expectancies. *Experimental and Clinical Psychopharmacology, 2*, 167–183.

Rather, B. C., & Goldman, M. S., Roehrich, L., & Brannick, M. (1992). Empirical modeling of an alcohol expectancy memory network using multidimensional scaling. *Journal of Abnormal Psychology, 101*, 174–183.

Rose, J. S., Chassin, L., Presson, C. C., & Sherman, S. J. (1996). Prospective predictors of quit attempts and smoking cessation in young adults. *Health Psychology, 15*, 261–268.

Rotter, J. B. (1954). *Social learning and clinical psychology.* Englewood Cliffs, NJ: Prentice Hall.

Rotter, J. B. (1978). Generalized expectancies for problem solving and psychotherapy. *Cognitive Therapy and Research, 2*, 1–10.

Shadel, W. G., & Mermelstein, R. J. (1993). Cigarette smoking under stress: The role of coping expectancies among smokers in a clinic-based smoking cessation program. *Health Psychology, 12*, 443–450.

Shiffman, S. (1984). Cognitive antecedents and sequelae of smoking relapse crises. *Journal of Applied Social Psychology, 14*, 296–309.

Shiffman, S. (1989). Conceptual issues in the study of relapse. In M. Gossop (Ed.), *Relapse and addictive behaviour* (pp. 149–179). London: Routledge.

Shopland, D. R., & Burns, D. M. (1993). Medical and public health implications of tobacco addiction. In C. T. Orleans & J. Slade (Eds.), *Nicotine addiction: Principles and management* (pp. 105–128). New York: Oxford University Press.

Stacy, A. W. (1997). Memory activation and expectancy as prospective predictors of alcohol and marijuana use. *Journal of Abnormal Psychology, 106*, 61–73.

Stone, A. A., & Shiffman, S. (1994). Ecological momentary assessment (EMA) in behavioral medicine. *Annals of Behavioral Medicine, 16*, 199–202.

Sutton, S. (1991). Great expectations: Some suggestions for applying the balanced placebo design to nicotine and smoking. *British Journal of Addiction, 86*, 659–662.

Tate, J. C., Stanton, A. L., Green, S. B., Schmitz, J. M., Le, T., & Marshall, B. (1994). Experimental analysis of the role of expectancy in nicotine withdrawal. *Psychology of Addictive Behaviors, 8*, 169–178.

Tiffany, S. T. (1990). A cognitive model of drug urges and drug-use behavior: Role of automatic and nonautomatic processes. *Psychological Review, 97*, 147–168.

Tiffany, S. T., & Drobes, D. J. (1991). The development and initial validation of a questionnaire on smoking urges. *British Journal of Addiction, 86*, 1467–1476.

Velicer, W. F., DiClemente, C. C., Prochaska, J. O., & Brandenburg, N. (1985). Decisional balance measure for assessing and predicting smoking status. *Journal of Personality and Social Psychology, 48*, 1279–1289.

Wetter, D. W., Brandon, T. H., & Baker, T. B. (1992). The relation of affective processing measures and smoking motivation indices among college-age smokers. *Advances in Behavior Research and Therapy, 14*, 169–193.

Wetter, D. W., Smith, S. S., Kenford, S. L., Jorenby, D. E., Fiore, M. C., Hurt, R. D., & Offord, K. (1994). Smoking outcome expectancies: Factor structure, predictive validity, and discriminant validity. *Journal of Abnormal Psychology, 103*, 801–811.

Zinser, M. C., Baker, T. B., Sherman, J. E., & Cannon, D. S. (1992). Relation between self-reported affect and drug urges and cravings in continuing and withdrawing smokers. *Journal of Abnormal Psychology, 101*, 617–629.

Zuroff, D. C., & Rotter, J. B. (1985). A history of the expectancy construct in psychology. In J. B. Dusek, V. C. Hall, & W. J. Meyer (Eds.), *Teacher expectancies* (pp. 9–36). Hillsdale, NJ: Erlbaum.

IV

SPECIFICS OF NONSPECIFIC EFFECTS

12

LISTENING TO PROZAC BUT HEARING PLACEBO: A META-ANALYSIS OF ANTIDEPRESSANT MEDICATIONS

IRVING KIRSCH AND GUY SAPIRSTEIN

Placebos are physical interventions that are administered in the guise of an active treatment but that do not have the physical properties ascribed to them. Previous reviews (Kirsch, 1990, 1997) indicate that placebos produce changes in pain, anxiety, depression, alertness, tension, sexual arousal, alcohol craving and consumption, drug withdrawal symptoms, aggression, asthma, and the full range of hypnotic responses (e.g., "trance" reports, involuntary movements, inhibition of voluntary movements, temporary amnesia, analgesia, and hallucinations). The data also indicate that placebo effects are produced by specific response expectancies and that they cannot be fully explained by other factors such as classical conditioning, ther-

We thank R. B. Lydiard and SmithKline Beecham Pharmaceuticals for supplying additional data. We also thank David Kenny for assistance with the statistical analyses and Roger P. Greenberg and Daniel E. Moerman for helpful comments on earlier versions of this chapter. From "Listening to Prozac but Hearing Placebo: A Meta-Analysis of Antidepressant Medication," by I. Kirsch and G. Sapirstein, 1998, *Prevention & Treatment* [on-line journal]. Copyright 1998 by the American Psychological Association. Adapted with permission.

apeutic relationship, or more general expectancies for improvement (Kirsch, 1997; Montgomery & Kirsch, 1996, 1997). In this chapter, we report the results of a meta-analysis in which we examined the role of expectancy in the response to antidepressant medications.

Meta-analysis provides a means of mathematically combining results from different studies, even when these studies have used different measures to assess the dependent variable. Most often, this is done using the d statistic, which is a standardized difference score. This effect size is generally calculated as the mean of the experimental group minus the mean of the control group, divided by the pooled standard deviation. Less frequently, the mean difference is divided by the standard deviation of the control group (Smith, Glass, & Miller, 1980).

Ideally, to calculate the effect size of placebos, researchers would want to subtract the effects of a no-placebo control group. However, placebos are used as controls against which the effects of physical interventions can be gauged. It is rare for an experimental condition to be included against which the effects of the placebo can be evaluated. To circumvent this problem, we decided to calculate within-cells or pre–post effect sizes, which are the posttreatment mean depression score minus the pretreatment mean depression score, divided by the pooled standard deviation (cf. Smith et al., 1980). By doing this for both placebo groups and medication groups, we could estimate the proportion of the response to antidepressant medication that is duplicated by placebo administration, a response that would be due to factors such as expectancy for improvement and the natural course of the disorder (i.e., spontaneous remission). Later in this chapter, we also separate expectancy from natural history and provide estimates of each of these effects.

Although our approach is unusual, in most cases it should provide results that are comparable to conventional methods. If there are no significant pretreatment differences between the treatment and control groups, then the subtraction of mean standardized pre–post difference scores should result in a mean effect size that is just about the same as that produced by subtracting mean standardized posttreatment scores. Suppose, for example, we have a study with the data displayed in Table 12.1. The conventionally calculated effect size would be 1.00. The pre–post effect

TABLE 12.1
Hypothetical Data for Comparing Methods of Calculating Effect Sizes

| Statistic | Treatment group | | Control group | |
	Pretreatment	Posttreatment	Pretreatment	Posttreatment
M	25.00	10.00	25.00	15.00
SD	5.50	4.50	4.50	5.50

sizes would be 3.00 for the treatment group and 2.00 for the control group. The difference between them is 1.00, which is exactly the same effect calculated from posttreatment scores alone. However, calculating the effect size in this manner also provides us with the information that the effect of the control procedure was two thirds that of the treatment procedure, information that we do not have when we consider only posttreatment scores. Of course, it is rare for two groups to have identical mean pretreatment scores, and, to the extent that those scores are different, our two methods of calculation would provide different results. However, by controlling for baseline differences, our method should provide the more accurate estimate of differential outcome.

EFFECTS OF MEDICATION AND PLACEBO

Study Characteristics

Studies assessing the efficacy of antidepressant medication were obtained through previous reviews (Davis, Janicak, & Bruninga, 1987; Free & Oei, 1989; Greenberg, Bornstein, Greenberg, & Fisher, 1992; Greenberg & Fisher, 1989; Workman & Short, 1993), supplemented by a computer search of PsycLit and MEDLINE databases from 1974 to 1995 using the search terms *drug-therapy or pharmacotherapy or psychotherapy or placebo and depression or affective disorders*. The term *psychotherapy* was included for the purpose of obtaining articles that would allow estimation of changes occurring in no-treatment and waiting-list control groups, a topic to which we return later in this chapter. Approximately 1,500 publications were produced by this literature search, and those meeting the following criteria were included in the meta-analysis.

1. The sample was restricted to patients with a primary diagnosis of depression. Studies were excluded if participants were selected because of other criteria (e.g., eating disorders, substance abuse, physical disabilities, or chronic medical conditions), as were studies in which the description of the patient population was vague (e.g., "neurotic").
2. Enough data were reported or obtainable to calculate within-conditions effect sizes. This resulted in the exclusion of studies for which neither pre–post statistical tests nor pretreatment means were available.
3. Data were reported for a placebo control group.
4. Participants were randomly assigned to experimental conditions.
5. Participants were between the ages of 18 and 75.

Of the approximately 1,500 studies examined, 20 met the inclusion criteria. Of these, all but 1 were studies of the acute phase of therapy, with treatment durations ranging from 1 to 20 weeks (M = 4.82). The 1 exception (Doogan & Caillard, 1992) was a maintenance study, with a duration of treatment of 44 weeks. Because of this difference, Doogan and Caillard's study was excluded from the meta-analysis. Thus, the analysis was conducted on 19 studies containing 2,318 participants, of whom 1,460 received medication and 858 received placebo. The medications studied were amitriptyline, amylobarbitone, fluoxetine, imipramine, paroxetine, isocarboxazid, trazodone, lithium, liothyronine, adinazolam, amoxapine, phenelzine, venlafaxine, maprotiline, tranylcypromine, and bupropion.

Calculation of Effect Sizes

In most cases, effect sizes (d) were calculated for measures of depression as the mean posttreatment score minus the mean prettreatment score, divided by the pooled standard deviation. Pretreatment standard deviations were used in place of pooled standard deviations in calculating effect sizes for four studies in which posttreatment standard deviations were not reported (Ravaris et al., 1976; Rickels & Case, 1982; Rickels et al., 1981; D. S. Robinson, Nies, & Ravaris, 1973). The methods described by Smith et al. (1980) were used to estimate effect sizes for two studies in which means and standard deviations were not reported.

In studies reporting multiple measures of depression, we calculated an effect size for each measure and then averaged them. In studies reporting the effects of two drugs, we calculated a single mean effect size for both for the primary analysis. In a subsequent analysis, we examined the effect for each drug separately. In both analyses, we calculated mean effect sizes weighted for sample size (D; Hunter & Schmidt, 1990).

Effect Sizes

Sample sizes and effect sizes for patients receiving medication or placebo are presented in Table 12.2. The mean effect sizes weighted for sample size were 1.55 SDs for the medication response and 1.16 SDs for the placebo response. Because effect sizes are obtained by dividing both treatment means by a constant (i.e., the pooled standard deviation), they can be treated mathematically like the scores from which they are derived. In particular, we have shown that, barring pretreatment between-groups differences, subtracting the mean pre–post effect size of the control groups from the mean pre–post effect size of the experimental groups is equivalent to calculating an effect size by conventional means. Subtracting mean placebo response rates from mean drug response rates reveals a mean medication effect of 0.39 SDs. This indicates that 75% of the response to the

TABLE 12.2
Studies of Placebo Control Groups

Study	Drug		Placebo	
	n	*d*	*n*	*d*
Blashki et al. (1971)	43	1.75	18	1.02
Byerley et al. (1988)	44	2.30	16	1.37
Claghorn et al. (1992)	113	1.91	95	1.49
Davidson and Turnbull (1983)	11	4.77	8	2.28
Elkin et al. (1989)	36	2.35	34	2.01
Goldberg et al. (1981)	179	0.44	93	0.44
Joffe et al. (1993)	34	1.43	16	0.61
Khan et al. (1991)	66	2.25	80	1.48
Kiev and Okerson (1979)	39	0.44	22	0.42
Lydiard (1989)	30	2.59	15	1.93
Ravaris et al. (1976)	14	1.42	19	0.91
Rickels et al. (1981)	75	1.86	23	1.45
Rickels and Case (1982)	100	1.71	54	1.17
D. S. Robinson et al. (1973)	33	1.13	27	0.76
Schweizer et al. (1994)	87	3.13	57	2.13
Stark and Hardison (1985)	370	1.40	169	1.03
van der Velde (1981)	52	0.66	27	0.10
White et al. (1984)	77	1.50	45	1.14
Zung (1983)	57	.88	40	0.95

medications examined in these studies may have been a placebo response, and, at most, 25% might be a true drug effect. This does not mean that only 25% of patients are likely to respond to the pharmacological properties of the drug. Rather, it means that for a typical patient, 75% of the benefit obtained from the active drug would also have been obtained from an inactive placebo.

Inspection of Table 12.2 reveals considerable variability in the effect sizes of drug and placebo response. As a first step toward clarifying the reason for this variability, we calculated the correlation between drug response and placebo response, which was found to be exceptionally high ($r = .90$, $p < .001$; see Figure 12.1). This indicates that the placebo response was proportionate to the drug response, with remaining variability most likely attributable to measurement error.

Our next question was the source of the common variability. One possibility is that the correlation between placebo and drug response rates were due to between-studies differences in sample characteristics (e.g., in-patients vs. outpatients, volunteers vs. referrals). Our analysis of psychotherapy studies later in this chapter provides a test of this hypothesis. If the correlation were due to between-studies differences in sample characteristics, a similar correlation should be found between the psychotherapy and no-treatment response rates. In fact, the correlation between the psychotherapy response and the no-treatment response was nonsignificant and

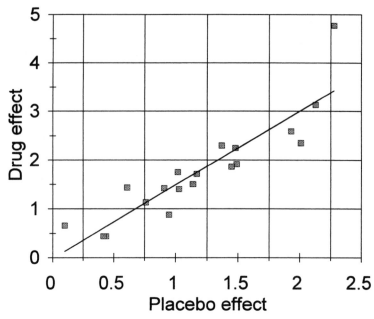

Figure 12.1. The placebo response as a predictor of the drug response. From "Listening to Prozac but Hearing Placebo: A Meta-Analysis of Antidepressant Medication," by I. Kirsch and G. Sapirstein, 1998, *Prevention & Treatment* [on-line journal], *1,* Article 0002a. Copyright 1998 by the American Psychological Association. Printed with persmission.

in the opposite direction. This indicates that common sample character-istics accounted for little if any of the relation between the treatment and control group response rates.

Another possibility is that the close correspondence between placebo and drug response was due to differences in so-called "nonspecific" variables (e.g., provision of a supportive relationship, the color of the medication, patients' expectations for change, biases in clinician's ratings, etc.), which might vary from study to study but would be common to recipients of both treatments in a given study. Alternately, the correlation might be associated with differences in the effectiveness of the various medications included in the meta-analysis. This could happen if more effective medications in-spired greater expectations of improvement among patients, prescribing physicians, or both (Frank, 1973; Kirsch, 1990). Evans (1974), for example, reported that placebo morphine was substantially more effective than pla-cebo aspirin. Finally, both factors might be operative.

We investigated this issue further by examining the magnitude of drug and placebo responses as a function of type of medication. We subdivided medication into four types: (a) tricyclics and tetracyclics, (b) selective se-rotonin reuptake inhibitors, (c) other antidepressants, and (d) other med-ications. This last category consisted of four medications (i.e., amylobarbitone, lithium, liothyronine, and adinazolam) that are not considered antidepressants.

Weighted (for sample size) mean effect sizes of the drug response as a function of type of medication are shown in Table 12.3, along with corresponding effect sizes of the placebo response and the mean effect sizes of placebo responses as a proportion of drug responses. These data revealed relatively little variability in drug response and even less variability in the ratio of the placebo response to the drug response as a function of drug type. For each type of medication, the effect sizes for the active drug response ranged from 1.43 to 1.69, and the inactive placebo response ranged from 74% to 76% of the active drug response. These data suggest that the between-drugs variability in drug and placebo response was due entirely to differences in the placebo component of the studies.

Differences between active drug responses and inactive placebo responses are typically interpreted as indications of specific pharmacological effects for the condition being treated. However, this conclusion is thrown into question by the data derived from active medications that are not considered effective for depression. It is possible that these drugs affect depression indirectly, perhaps by improving sleep or lowering anxiety. However, if this were the case and if antidepressants have a specific effect on depression, then the effect of these other medications ought to have been less than the effect of antidepressants, whereas our data indicate that the response to these nonantidepressant drugs was at least as great as that to conventional antidepressants.

A second possibility is that amylobarbitone, lithium, liothyronine, and adinazolam are in fact antidepressants. This conclusion is rendered plausible by the lack of understanding of the mechanism of clinical action of common antidepressants (e.g., tricyclics). If the classification of a drug as an antidepressant is established by its efficacy rather than by knowledge of the mechanism underlying its effects, then amylobarbitone, lithium, liothyronine, and adinazolam might be considered specifics for depression.

TABLE 12.3
Effect Sizes as a Function of Drug Type

Statistic	Antidrepressant			Other
	Tri- and tetracyclic	SSRIs	Others	
n	1,353	626	683	203
K	13	4	8	3
D drug	1.52	1.68	1.43	1.69
D placebo	1.15	1.24	1.08	1.29
D placebo–drug	0.76	0.74	0.76	0.76

Note. SSRIs = selective serotonin reuptake inhibitors; n = number of participants; K = number of studies; D = mean weighted effect size; placebo/drug = placebo response as a proportion of active drug response.

A third possibility is that these medications function as active placebos (i.e., active medications without specific activity for the condition being treated). Greenberg and Fisher (1989) summarized data indicating that the effect of antidepressant medication is smaller when it is compared with an active placebo than when it is compared with an inert placebo (also see Greenberg & Fisher, 1997). By definition, the only difference between active and inactive placebos is the presence of pharmacologically induced side effects. Therefore, differences in responses to active and inert placebos could be due to the presence of those side effects. Data from other studies indicate that most participants in studies of antidepressant medication are able to deduce whether they have been assigned to the drug condition or the placebo condition (Blashki, Mowbray, & Davies, 1971; Margraf et al., 1991; Ney, Collins, & Spensor, 1986). This is likely to be associated with their previous experience with antidepressant medication and with differences between drug and placebo in the magnitude of side effects. Experiencing more side effects, patients in active drug conditions conclude that they are in the drug group; experiencing fewer side effects, patients in placebo groups conclude that they are in the placebo condition. This can be expected to produce an enhanced placebo effect in drug conditions and a diminished placebo effect in placebo groups. Thus, the apparent drug effect of antidepressants may in fact be a placebo effect, magnified by differences in experienced side effects and the patient's subsequent recognition of the condition to which he or she has been assigned.

NATURAL HISTORY EFFECTS

Just as it is important to distinguish between a drug response and a drug effect, so, too, is it worthwhile to distinguish between a placebo response and a placebo effect (Fisher, Lipman, Uhlenhuth, Rickels, & Park, 1965). A drug response is the change that occurs after administration of the drug. The effect of the drug is that portion of the response that is due to the drug's chemical composition; it is the difference between the drug response and the response to placebo administration. A similar distinction can be made between placebo responses and placebo effects. The placebo response is the change that occurs after administration of a placebo. However, change might also occur without administration of a placebo. It may be due to spontaneous remission, regression toward the mean, life changes, the passage of time, or other factors. The placebo effect is the difference between the placebo response and changes that occur without the administration of a placebo (Kirsch, 1985, 1997).

In the preceding section, we evaluated the placebo response as a proportion of the response to antidepressant medication. The data suggest that at least 75% of the drug response is a placebo response, but it does not tell us the magnitude of the placebo effect. What proportion of the placebo response is due to expectancies generated by placebo administration, and what proportion would have occurred even without placebo administration? Those are much more difficult questions to answer. We have not been able to locate any studies in which pre- and posttreatment assessments of depression were reported for both a placebo group and a no-treatment or waiting-list control group. For that reason, we turned to psychotherapy outcome studies, in which the inclusion of untreated control groups is much more common.

We acknowledge that the use of data from psychotherapy studies as a comparison with those from drug studies is far less than ideal. Participants in psychotherapy studies might differ from those in drug studies on any number of variables. Furthermore, the assignment of participants to a no-treatment or waiting-list control group might also affect the course of their disorder. For example, Frank (1973) has argued that the promise of future treatment is sufficient to trigger a placebo response, and a waiting-list control group has been conceptualized as a placebo control group in at least one well-known outcome study (Sloane, Staples, Cristol, Yorkston, & Whipple, 1975). Conversely, one could argue that being assigned to a no-treatment control group might strengthen feelings of hopelessness and thereby increase depression. Despite these problems, the no-treatment and waiting-list control data from psychotherapy outcome studies are the best data currently available for estimating the natural course of untreated depression. Furthermore, the presence of both types of untreated control groups permits evaluation of Frank's (1973) hypothesis about the curative effects of the promise of treatment.

Study Characteristics

Studies assessing changes in depression among participants assigned to waiting-list or no-treatment control groups were obtained from the computer search described earlier, supplemented by an examination of previous reviews (Dobson, 1989; Free & Oei, 1989; L. A. Robinson, Berman, & Neimeyer, 1990). The publications produced by this literature search were examined by one of us, and those meeting the following criteria were included in the meta-analysis.

1. The sample was restricted to patients with a primary diagnosis of depression. Studies were excluded if participants were selected because of other criteria (i.e., eating disorders, substance abuse, physical disabilities, or chronic medical conditions), as were studies in which the description of the patient population was vague (e.g., "neurotic").
2. Sufficient data were reported or obtainable to calculate within-conditions effect sizes.

3. Data were reported for a waiting-list or no-treatment control group.
4. Participants were randomly assigned to experimental conditions.
5. Participants were between the ages of 18 and 75 years.

Nineteen studies were found that met these inclusion criteria, and, in all cases, sufficient data had been reported to allow direct calculation of effect sizes as the mean posttreatment score minus the mean pretreatment score, divided by the pooled standard deviation. Although they are incidental to the main purposes of this review, we examined effect sizes for psychotherapy as well as those for no-treatment and waiting-list control groups.

Effect Sizes

Sample sizes and effect sizes for patients assigned to psychotherapy, waiting list, and no treatment are presented in Table 12.4. The mean pre–post effect sizes weighted for sample size were 1.60 for the psychotherapy response and 0.37 for the waiting-list and no-treatment control groups. Participants given the promise of subsequent treatment (i.e., those in waiting-list groups) did not improve more than those not promised treatment.

TABLE 12.4
Studies of Waiting-List or No-Treatment Control Groups

Study	Psychotherapy		Control	
	n	d	n	d
Beach and O'Leary (1992)	15	2.37	15	0.97
Beck and Strong (1982)	20	2.87	10	−0.28
Catanese et al. (1979)	99	1.39	21	0.16
Comas-Diaz (1981)	16	1.87	10	−0.12
Conoley and Garber (1985)	38	1.10	19	0.21
Feldman et al. (1982)	38	2.00	10	0.42
Graff et al. (1986)	24	2.03	11	−0.03
Jarvinen and Gold (1981)	46	0.76	18	0.34
Maynard (1993)	16	1.06	14	0.36
Nezu (1986)	23	2.39	9	0.16
Rehm et al. (1981)	42	1.23	15	0.48
Rude (1986)	8	1.75	16	0.74
Schmidt and Miller (1983)	34	1.25	10	0.11
Shaw (1977)	16	2.17	8	0.41
Shipley and Fazio (1973)	11	2.12	11	1.00
Taylor and Marshall (1977)	21	1.94	7	0.27
Tyson and Range (1987)	22	0.67	11	1.45
Wierzbicki and Bartlett (1987)	18	1.17	20	0.21
Wilson et al. (1983)	16	2.17	9	−0.02

The mean effect sizes for these two conditions were 0.36 and 0.39, respectively. The correlation between effect sizes ($r = -.29$) was not significant.

Comparison of Participants in the Two Groups of Studies

Comparisons of effect sizes from different sets of studies is common in meta-analyses. Nevertheless, we examined the characteristics of the samples in the two types of studies to assess their comparability. Eighty-six percent of the participants in the psychotherapy studies were women, as were 65% of participants in the drug studies. The age range of participants was 18–75 years ($M = 30.1$) in the psychotherapy studies and 18–70 years ($M = 40.6$) in the drug studies. The duration of treatment ranged from 1 to 20 weeks ($M = 4.82$) in psychotherapy studies and 2 to 15 weeks ($M = 5.95$) in pharmacotherapy studies. The Hamilton Rating Scale for Depression (HRSD) was used in 15 drug studies involving 2,016 patients and 5 psychotherapy studies with 191 participants. An analysis of variance (ANOVA) weighted by sample size did not reveal any significant differences in pretreatment HRSD scores between patients in the drug studies ($M = 23.93$, $SD = 5.20$) and participants in the psychotherapy studies ($M = 21.34$, $SD = 5.03$). The Beck Depression Inventory (BDI) was used in 4 drug studies involving 261 patients and 17 psychotherapy studies with 677 participants. An ANOVA weighted by sample size did not reveal any significant differences in pretreatment BDI scores between participants in drug studies ($M = 21.58$, $SD = 8.23$) and those in psychotherapy studies ($M = 21.63$, $SD = 6.97$). Thus, participants in the two types of studies were comparable in initial levels of depression. These ANOVAs also failed to reveal any pretreatment differences as a function of group assignment (treatment or control) or the interaction between type of study and group assignment.

Estimating the Placebo Effect

Just as drug effects can be estimated as the drug response minus the placebo response, placebo effects can be estimated as the placebo response minus the no-treatment response. Using the effect sizes obtained from the two meta-analyses reported earlier, this would be 0.79 (1.16–0.37). Figure 12.2 displays the estimated drug, placebo, and no-treatment effect sizes as proportions of the drug response (i.e., 1.55 SDs). These data indicate that approximately one quarter of the drug response was due to the administration of an active medication, one half was a placebo effect, and the remaining quarter was due to other nonspecific factors.

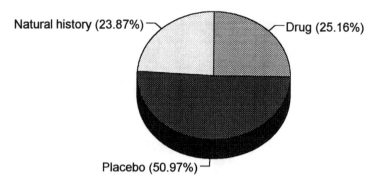

Figure 12.2. Drug effect, placebo effect, and natural history effect as proportions of the response to antidepressant medication. From "Listening to Prozac but Hearing Placebo: A Meta-Analysis of Antidepressant Medication," by I. Kirsch and G. Sapirstein, 1998, *Prevention & Treatment* [on-line journal], *1,* Article 0002a. Copyright 1998 by the American Psychological Association. Printed with permission.

DISCUSSION

No-treatment effect sizes and effect sizes for the placebo response were calculated from different sets of studies. Comparison across different samples is common in meta-analyses. For example, effect sizes derived from studies of psychodynamic therapy are often compared with those derived from studies of behavior therapy (e.g., Andrews & Harvey, 1981; Smith et al., 1980). Nevertheless, comparisons of this sort should be interpreted cautiously. Participants volunteering for different treatments might come from a different population, and when data for different conditions are drawn from different sets of studies, participants have not been assigned randomly to these conditions. Also, assignment to a no-treatment or waiting-list control group is not the same as no intervention at all. Therefore, our estimates of the placebo effect and natural history component of the response to antidepressant medication should be considered tentative. Nevertheless, when direct comparisons are not available, these comparisons provide the best available estimates of comparative effectiveness. Furthermore, in at least some cases, these estimates have been found to yield results that are comparable to those derived from direct comparisons of groups that have been randomly assigned to condition (Kirsch, 1990; Shapiro & Shapiro, 1982).

Unlike our estimate of the effect of natural history as a component of the drug response, our estimate of the placebo response as a proportion of the drug response was derived from studies in which participants from the same population were assigned randomly to drug and placebo conditions. Therefore, the estimate that only 25% of the drug response was due to the administration of an active medication can be considered reliable. Confidence in the reliability of this estimate is enhanced by the exceptionally high correlation between the drug response and the placebo response. This association is high enough to suggest that any remaining variance in drug response is error variance associated with imperfect reliability of measurement. Examining estimates of active drug and inactive placebo responses as a function of drug type further enhances confidence in the reliability of these estimates. Regardless of drug type, the inactive placebo response was approximately 75% of the active drug response.

We used highly stringent criteria in selecting studies for inclusion in this meta-analysis, and it is possible that data from a broader range of studies would have produced a different outcome. However, the effect size we have calculated for the medication effect ($D = 0.39$) is comparable to those reported in other meta-analyses of antidepressant medication (e.g., Greenberg et al., 1992; Quality Assurance Project, 1983; Smith et al., 1980; Steinbrueck, Maxwell, & Howard, 1983). Although this suggests a substantial advantage for the active medication, it does not provide enough information to calculate the proportion of the drug response that is duplicated in the placebo group. For that estimate, one must look at pre–post effects. Dividing the drug versus placebo effect size from the pre–post placebo effect size indicates that the active drug was 34% more effective than the inactive placebo, which is equivalent to the estimate that 25% of the drug response was due to the pharmacological properties of the medication. Although conventional meta-analytic effect sizes do not provide the data needed for this type of comparison, a previously published estimate reported data indicating an even larger effect for placebo than we have estimated. In their meta-analysis of the effects of monoamine oxidase inhibitors, Thase, Trivedi, and Rush (1995) calculated that medication was 15%–22% more effective than placebo for depressed inpatients. These data indicate that the pharmacological properties of monoamine oxidase inhibitors account for only 13%–18% of the drug response.

Our results are in agreement with those of other meta-analyses in revealing a substantial placebo effect in antidepressant medication and also a considerable benefit of medication over placebo. They also indicate that the placebo component of the response to medication is considerably greater than the pharmacological effect. However, there are two aspects of the data that have not been examined in other meta-analyses of antidepressant medication: (a) the exceptionally high correlation between the placebo response and the drug response and (b) the effect on depression of active drugs that are not antidepressants. Taken together, these two findings suggest the possibility that antidepressants might function as active placebos, in which the side effects amplify the placebo effect by convincing patients that they are receiving a potent drug.

In summary, the data reviewed in this meta-analysis lead to a confident estimate that the response to inert placebos is approximately 75% of the response to active antidepressant medication. Whether the remaining

25% of the drug response is a true pharmacological effect or an enhanced placebo effect cannot yet be determined because of the relatively small number of studies in which active and inactive placebos have been compared (Fisher and Greenberg, 1993). Definitive estimates of placebo component of antidepressant medication will require four-arm studies, in which the effects of active placebos, inactive placebos, active medication, and natural history (e.g., waiting-list controls) are examined. In addition, studies using the balanced placebo design would be of help, as these have been shown to diminish the ability of participants to discover the condition to which they have been assigned (Kirsch & Rosadino, 1993).

REFERENCES

Andrews, G., & Harvey, R. (1981). Does psychotherapy benefit neurotic patients? A reanalysis of the Smith, Glass, and Miller data. *Archives of General Psychiatry, 36,* 1203–1208.

Beach, S. R. H., & O'Leary, K. D. (1992). Treating depression in the context of marital discord: Outcome and predictors of response of marital therapy versus cognitive therapy. *Behavior Therapy, 23,* 507–528.

Beck, J. T., & Strong, S. R. (1982). Stimulating therapeutic change with interpretations: A comparison of positive and negative connotation. *Journal of Counseling Psychology, 29,* 551–559.

Blashki, T. G., Mowbray, R., & Davies, B. (1971). Controlled trial of amytriptyline in general practice. *British Medical Journal, 1,* 133–138.

Byerley, W. F., Reimherr, F. W., Wood, D. R., & Grosser, B. I. (1988). Fluoxetine, a selective serotonine uptake inhibitor, for the treatment of outpatients with major depression. *Journal of Clinical Psychopharmacology, 8,* 112–115.

Catanese, R. A., Rosenthal, T. L., & Kelley, J. E. (1979). Strange bedfellows: Reward, punishment, and impersonal distraction strategies in treating dysphoria. *Cognitive Therapy and Research, 3,* 299–305.

Claghorn, J. L., Kiev, A., Rickels, K., Smith, W. T., & Dunbar, G. C. (1992). Paroxetine versus placebo: A double-blind comparison in depressed patients. *Journal of Clinical Psychiatry, 53*(12), 434–438.

Comas-Diaz, L. (1981). Effects of cognitive and behavioral group treatment on the depressive symptomatology of Puerto Rican women. *Journal of Consulting and Clinical Psychology, 49,* 627–632.

Conoley, C. W., & Garber, R. A. (1985). Effects of reframing and self control directives on loneliness, depression, and controllability. *Journal of Counseling Psychology, 32,* 139–142.

Davidson, J., & Turnbull, C. (1983). Isocarboxazid: Efficacy and tolerance. *Journal of Affective Disorders, 5,* 183–189.

Davis, J. M., Janicak, P. G., & Bruninga, K. (1987). The efficacy of MAO inhibitors in depression: A meta-analysis. *Psychiatric Annals, 17,* 825–831.

Dobson, K. S. (1989). A meta-analysis of the efficacy of cognitive therapy for depression. *Journal of Consulting and Clinical Psychology, 57*, 414–419.

Doogan, D. P., & Caillard, V. (1992). Sertaline in the prevention of depression. *British Journal of Psychiatry, 160*, 217–222.

Elkin, I., Shea, M. T., Watkins, J. T., Imber, S. D., Sotsky, S. M., Collins, J. F., Glass, D. R., Pilkonis, P. A., Leber, W. R., Docherty, J. P., Fiester, S. J., & Parloff, M. B. (1989). National Institute of Mental Health Treatment of Depression Collaborative Research Program: General effectiveness of treatments. *Archives of General Psychiatry, 46*, 971–982.

Evans, F. J. (1974). The placebo response in pain reduction. In J. J. Bonica (Ed.), *Advances in neurology: 4. Pain* (pp. 289–296). New York: Raven Press.

Feldman, D. A., Strong, S. R., & Danser, D. B. (1982). A comparison of paradoxical and nonparadoxical interpretations and directives. *Journal of Counseling Psychology, 29*, 572–579.

Fisher, S., & Greenberg, R. P. (1993). How sound is the double-blind design for evaluating psychiatric drugs? *Journal of Nervous and Mental Disease, 181*, 345–350.

Fisher, S., Lipman, R. S., Uhlenhuth, E. H., Rickels, K., & Park, L. C. (1965). Drug effects and initial severity of symptomatology. *Psychopharmacologia, 7*, 57–60.

Frank, J. D. (1973). *Persuasion and healing* (Rev. ed.). Baltimore: Johns Hopkins University Press.

Free, M. L., & Oei, T. P. S. (1989). Biological and psychological processes in the treatment and maintenance of depression. *Clinical Psychology Review, 9*, 653–688.

Goldberg, H. L., Rickels, K., & Finnerty, R. (1981). Treatment of neurotic depression with a new antidepressant. *Journal of Clinical Psychopharmacology, 1*(6, Suppl.), 35S–38S.

Graff, R. W., Whitehead, G. I., & LeCompte, M. (1986). Group treatment with divorced women using cognitive–behavioral and supportive–insight methods. *Journal of Counseling Psychology, 33*, 276–281.

Greenberg, R. P., Bornstein, R. F., Greenberg, M. D., & Fisher, S. (1992). A meta-analysis of antidepressant outcome under "blinder" conditions. *Journal of Consulting and Clinical Psychology, 60*, 664–669.

Greenberg, R. P., & Fisher, S. (1989). Examining antidepressant effectiveness: Findings, ambiguities, and some vexing puzzles. In S. Fisher & R. P. Greenberg (Eds.), *The limits of biological treatments for psychological distress* (pp. 1–37). Hillsdale, NJ: Erlbaum.

Greenberg, R. P., & Fisher, S. (1997). Mood-mending medicines: Probing drug, psychotherapy, and placebo solutions. In S. Fisher & R. P. Greenberg (Eds.), *From placebo to panacea: Putting psychiatric drugs to the test* (pp. 115–172). New York: Wiley.

Hunter, J. E., & Schmidt, F. L. (1990). *Methods of meta-analysis: Correcting error and bias in research findings*. Newbury Park, CA: Sage.

Jarvinen, P. J., & Gold, S. R. (1981). Imagery as an aid in reducing depression. *Journal of Clinical Psychology, 37*, 523–529.

Joffe, R. T., Singer, W., Levitt, A. J., & MacDonald, C. (1993). A placebo controlled comparison of lithium and triiodothyronine augmentation of tricyclic antidepressants in unipolar refractory depression. *Archives of General Psychiatry, 50*, 387–393.

Khan, A., Dager, S. R., Cohen, S., Avery, D. H., Scherzo, B., & Dunner, D. L. (1991). Chronicity of depressive episode in relation to antidepressant-placebo response. *Neuropsychopharmacology, 4*, 125–130.

Kiev, A., & Okerson, L. (1979). Comparison of the therapeutic efficacy of amoxapine with that of imipramine: A controlled clinical study in patients with depressive illness. *Clinical Trials Journal, 16*(3), 68–72.

Kirsch, I. (1985). Response expectancy as a determinant of experience and behavior. *American Psychologist, 40*, 1189–1202.

Kirsch, I. (1990). *Changing expectations: A key to effective psychotherapy.* Pacific Grove, CA: Brooks/Cole.

Kirsch, I. (1997). Specifying nonspecifics: Psychological mechanisms of placebo effects. In A. Harrington (Ed.), *The placebo effect: An interdisciplinary exploration* (pp. 166–186). Cambridge, MA: Harvard University Press.

Kirsch, I., & Rosadino, M. J. (1993). Do double-blind studies with informed consent yield externally valid results? An empirical test. *Psychopharmacology, 110*, 437–442.

Kirsch, I., & Sapirstein, G. (1998). Listening to Prozac but hearing placebo: A meta-analysis of antidepressant medication. *Prevention & Treatment* [on-line journal], *1*, Article 0002a. (Available on the World Wide Web: http://journals.apa.org/prevention/volume1/pre0010002a.html)

Lydiard, R. B. (1989). Fluvoxamine, imipramine and placebo in the treatment of depressed outpatients. *Psychopharmacology Bulletin, 25*, 63–67.

Margraf, J., Ehlers, A., Roth, W. T., Clark, D. B., Sheikh, J., Agras, W. S., & Taylor, C. B. (1991). How "blind" are double-blind studies? *Journal of Consulting and Clinical Psychology, 59*, 184–187.

Maynard, C. K. (1993). Comparisons of effectiveness of group interventions for depression in women. *Archives of Psychiatric Nursing, 7*, 277–283.

Montgomery, G. H., & Kirsch, I. (1996). Mechanisms of placebo pain reduction: An empirical investigation. *Psychological Science, 7*, 174–176.

Montgomery, G. H., & Kirsch, I. (1997). Classical conditioning and the placebo effect. *Pain, 72*, 107–113.

Ney, P. G., Collins, C., & Spensor, C. (1986). Double blind: Double talk or are there ways to do better research? *Medical Hypotheses, 21*, 119–126.

Nezu, A. M. (1986). Efficacy of a social problem solving therapy approach for unipolar depression. *Journal of Consulting and Clinical Psychology, 54*, 196–202.

Quality Assurance Project. (1983). A treatment outline for depressive disorders. *Australian and New Zealand Journal of Psychiatry, 17*, 129–146.

Ravaris, C. L., Nies, A., Robinson, D. S., Ives, J. O., Lamborn, K. R., & Korson, L. (1976). A multiple-dose, controlled study of phenelzine in depression-anxiety states. *Archives of General Psychiatry, 33,* 347–350.

Rehm, L. P., Kornblith, S. J., O'Hara, M. W., Lamparski, D. J., Romano, J. M., & Volkin, J. I. (1981). An evaluation of major components in a self control therapy program for depression. *Behavior Modification, 5,* 459–489.

Rickels, K., & Case, G. W. (1982). Trazodone in depressed outpatients. *American Journal of Psychiatry, 139,* 803–806.

Rickels, K., Case, G. W., Weberlowsky, J., Csanalosi, I., Schless, A., & Weise, C. C. (1981). Amoxapine and imipramine in the treatment of depressed outpatients: A controlled study. *American Journal of Psychiatry, 138,* 20–24.

Robinson, D. S., Nies, A., & Ravaris, C. L. (1973). The MAOI, phenelzine in the treatment of depressive-anxiety states. *Archives of General Psychiatry, 29,* 407–413.

Robinson, L. A., Berman, J. S., & Neimeyer, R. A. (1990). Psychotherapy for the treatment of depression: A comprehensive review of controlled outcome research. *Psychological Bulletin, 108,* 30–49.

Rude, S. (1986). Relative benefits of assertion or cognitive self control treatment for depression as a function of proficiency in each domain. *Journal of Consulting and Clinical Psychology, 54,* 390–394.

Schmidt, M. M., & Miller, W. R. (1983). Amount of therapist contact and outcome in a multidimentional depression treatment program. *Acta Psychiatrica Scandinavica, 67,* 319–332.

Schweizer, E., Feighner, J., Mandos, L. A., & Rickels, K. (1994). Comparison of venlafaxine and imipramine in the acute treatment of major depression in outpatients. *Journal of Clinical Psychiatry, 55*(3), 104–108.

Shapiro, D. A., & Shapiro, D. (1982). Meta-analysis of comparative therapy outcome studies: A replication and refinement. *Psychological Bulletin, 92,* 581–604.

Shaw, B. F. (1977). Comparison of cognitive therapy and behavior therapy in the treatment of depression. *Journal of Consulting and Clinical Psychology, 45,* 543–551.

Shipley, C. R., & Fazio, A. F. (1973). Pilot study of a treatment for psychological depression. *Journal of Abnormal Psychology, 82,* 372–376.

Sloane, R. B., Staples, F. R., Cristol, A. H., Yorkston, N. J., & Whipple, K. (1975). *Psychotherapy versus behavior therapy.* Cambridge, MA: Harvard University Press.

Smith, M. L., Glass, G. V., & Miller, T. I. (1980). *The benefits of psychotherapy.* Baltimore: Johns Hopkins University Press.

Stark, P., & Hardison, C. D. (1985). A review of multicenter controlled studies of fluoxetine vs. imipramine and placebo in outpatients with major depressive disorder. *Journal of Clinical Psychiatry, 46*(3), 53–58.

Steinbrueck, S. M., Maxwell, S. E., & Howard, G. S. (1983). A meta-analysis of psychotherapy and drug therapy in the treatment of unipolar depression with adults. *Journal of Consulting and Clinical Psychology, 51*, 856–863.

Taylor, F. G., & Marshall, W. L. (1977). Experimental analysis of a cognitive–behavioral therapy for depression. *Cognitive Therapy and Research, 1*, 59–72.

Thase, M. E., Trivedi, M. H., & Rush, A. J. (1995). MAOIs in the contemporary treatment of depression. *Neuropsychopharmacology, 12*, 185–219.

Tyson, G. M., & Range, L. M. (1987). Gestalt dialogues as a treatment for depression: Time works just as well. *Journal of Clinical Psychology, 43*, 227–230.

van der Velde, C. D. (1981). Maprotiline versus imipramine and placebo in neurotic depression. *Journal of Clinical Psychiatry, 42*(4), 138–141.

White, K., Razani, J., Cadow, B., Gelfand, R., Palmer, R., Simpson, G., & Sloane, R. B. (1984). Tranylcypromine vs. nortriptyline vs. placebo in depressed outpatients: A controlled trial. *Psychopharmacology, 82*, 258–262.

Wierzbicki, M., & Bartlett, T. S. (1987). The efficacy of group and individual cognitive therapy for mild depression. *Cognitive Therapy and Research, 11*, 337–342.

Wilson, P. H., Goldin, J. C., & Charboneau-Powis, M. (1983). Comparative efficacy of behavioral and cognitive treatments of depression. *Cognitive Therapy and Research, 7*, 111–124.

Workman, E. A., & Short, D. D. (1993). Atypical antidepressants versus imipramine in the treatment of major depression: A meta-analysis. *Journal of Clinical Psychiatry, 54*, 5–12.

Zung, W. W. K. (1983). Review of placebo-controlled trials with bupropion. *Journal of Clinical Psychiatry, 44*, 104–114.

13

IS THE PLACEBO EFFECT DEPENDENT ON TIME? A META-ANALYSIS

HARALD WALACH AND CATARINA MAIDHOF

Despite concern that the placebo effect may be a statistical artifact (McDonald, Mazzuca, & McCabe, 1983; McDonald & McCabe, 1989), there seems to be agreement in the scientific community that it is a pervasive phenomenon in clinical trials (Turner, Deyo, Loeser, Von Korff, & Fordyce, 1994). Among the psychological mechanisms that have been hypothesized to underlie placebo effects are response expectancies (Kirsch, 1997), comfort and hope (J. D. Frank, 1989), and classical conditioning (Ader, 1983, 1985; Ader & Cohen, 1975; Wickramasekera, 1985). Because conditional responses extinguish when elicited without being reinforced by presentation of unconditional stimuli, the classical conditioning model of placebo effects predicts gradual extinction of the placebo effect over time (Wickramasekera, 1980, 1985). The meta-analysis reported in this chapter was designed to test this hypothesis.

Kupfer (1991) warned against dismissing placebo effects even in long-term studies because patients in these studies may experience considerable

Karin Seidenglanz helped with preparing the data and Stefan Schmidt with the interpretation. This work was funded by a grant from the Institut für Grenzgebiete der Psychologie, Freiburg, Germany.

alleviation of symptoms while in placebo treatment. For example, it has been reported that one third of psychiatric patients given placebo antidepressants displayed improvements that endured over a long period (Quitkin, Rabkin, Stewart, McGrath, & Harrison, 1991; Rabkin et al., 1986). Nevertheless, these authors also emphasized how little is known about the long-term effects of placebos in clinical trials (Quitkin et al., 1991). We therefore decided to systematically study the effect of time on the clinical response of patients given placebos in clinical trials. Our question was, Is the placebo effect dependent on time? On the basis of the conditioning model, we hypothesized that the placebo effect would decrease with time. We tested this hypothesis by correlating the magnitude of the placebo effect with the duration of the study. In addition, we examined the relation of various characteristics of the studies to the magnitude of the placebo response.

INCLUSION CRITERIA

Placebo-controlled studies of at least 12 weeks' duration formed the basis of this meta-analysis. We defined *placebo controlled* as the administration to a control group of substances that were considered to be pharmacologically ineffective for the disease treated but that were stated to be otherwise indistinguishable from the treatment substance. To guarantee a minimum of methodological quality, we included only randomized double-blind studies in the analysis. Only studies of human beings treated on the basis of medical indications were included. Studies on dental treatments were excluded. The population of the patients examined was limited to ill adults, as it seems possible that healthy individuals and children might react differently to placebos. The indications included psychiatric as well as organic diseases. Therapy was limited to a drug treatment, administered orally, either as tablets or capsules. This limitation was chosen because of the dependence of the placebo effect on the form of administration. It has been reported, for example, that injections can be more effective than tablets (Buckalew & Ross, 1981; Morison, Woodmansey, & Young, 1961). Studies on tolerance as well as toxicological and psychotherapeutic studies were also excluded.

Studies were obtained by searching *Medline* in 1992 and 1993 with the search terms *placebo, placebo effect, longitudinal,* and *long-term study* used separately or in combination. Additionally, a manual search was carried out in the *Journal of the American Medical Association, New England Journal of Medicine, British Medical Journal,* and *The Lancet,* and earlier publications known to us were also included to cover a somewhat longer publication period.

This search produced 464 abstracts. Eight disease categories with more than one study in each category were selected for further evaluation. The selected studies included the following diseases: psychological disorders (affective disorders, personality disorders, panic disorders, and dementia), pain, dermatological conditions, high blood pressure, diabetes mellitus, rheumatological diseases, cancer, and AIDS. This left us with 72 publications, only half of which fulfilled the inclusion criteria (n = 32). Studies on dermatological conditions, blood pressure, diabetes mellitus, and AIDS failed to meet our inclusion criteria. The main reasons for exclusion were (a) a lack of sufficient information concerning the placebo group to allow computation of success rates in that condition and (b) a treatment of duration of less than 12 weeks. Thus, the total number of publications suitable for this analysis was 26.

Some of the researchers in the long-term studies reported interim results. In analyzing the differential effects of the placebo groups as a function of duration, we entered both the interim results and the final assessment into the analyses. In addition, some of the studies had three or more treatment arms, which we segregated into separate parts. This left us with 37 units in analysis of duration effects and 29 units in other analyses. The following characteristics of the studies were recorded: duration of study, disorder treated, severity (if retrievable from publication), number of patients per group; attrition rate per group, age of the patients, intent-to-treat analysis (i.e., statistical evaluation of all randomized patients, including those who dropped out of the trial), whether it was a multisite study, publication year, and percentage of patients improved in the treatment and placebo conditions. When more than one index of improvement was reported in a study, we calculated the mean rate of improvement. Severity was coded according to information given in the original article (1 = mild, 2 = moderate, and 3 = severe). Characteristics of the studies are shown in Tables 13.1–13.4.

META-ANALYSIS RESULTS

A cursory examination of the data in Tables 13.1–13.4 indicates that the response to both placebo and verum vary widely, from 0% in dementia to an 87% improvement rate for verum in a study of panic disorder and an 80% improvement rate in a study of depression. Also, as shown in Table 13.5, improvement rates for both verum and placebo appeared to vary as a function of type of disorder. For that reason, we examined the data in two ways, first across all types of disorders and then separately by disorder.

Across studies, duration was significantly correlated with the response to treatment (r = −.33, p < .05), but not with response to placebo (r = −.19). However, an examination of the data as a function of type of disorder indicates that this underestimated both relations. Across studies of

TABLE 13.1
Study Characteristics for Affective Disorders

Study	Treatment duration (months)	Multi-center study	Intention-to-treat analysis[a]	Severity[b]	No. of drug-treated patients[c]	Drop-outs verum (n)	No. of placebo-treated patients	Drop-outs placebo (n)	Age (M)	% improved under medical treatment	% improved under placebo treatment
Prien et al. (1973)[d,e]	4	Yes	Yes	2	52	9	26	13	47.0	69	27
Prien et al. (1973)[e,f]	4	Yes	Yes	2	31	5	13	4	43.0	68	46
Seager & Bird (1962)	6	No	No	2-3	12	2	16	2	49.0	83	31
Mindham et al. (1973)[g]	6	Yes	No	1-2	34	—	27	—	47.0	76	33
Mindham et al. (1973)	6	Yes	No	1-2	16	—	15	—	47.0	81	80
Stein et al. (1980)	6	No	No	2	29	—	26	—	42.0	72	31
Klerman et al. (1974)	8	No	Yes	2	50	2	25	3	37.5	72	60
Coppen et al. (1978)	12	No	Yes	1	16	3	16	0	54.0	81	69
Montgomery et al. (1988)	12	Yes	No	2-3	88	20	94	18	—	74	43
Rouillon et al. (1989)[g]	12	Yes	Yes	2	385	53	188	22	46.0	71	59
Rouillon et al. (1989)	12	Yes	Yes	2	382	53	186	20	46.0	64	54
E. Frank et al. (1990)[e]	12	No	Yes	3	28	9	23	3	40.0	61	22
Prien et al. (1973)[a,h]	24	Yes	Yes	2	52	23	26	20	47.0	40	8
Prien et al. (1973)[f,h]	24	Yes	Yes	2	31	15	13	9	43.0	35	8
Prien et al. (1984)	24	No	Yes	2-3	114	6	34	0	39.0	47	21
E. Frank et al. (1990)[d]	24	No	Yes	3	28	9	23	3	40.0	46	13
E. Frank et al. (1990)[f]	36	No	Yes	3	28	9	23	3	40.0	46	9

[a]Statistical evaluation of all randomized patients even if they dropped out of the trial. [b]1 = mild, 2 = moderate, and 3 = severe. [c]Number of treated patients includes dropouts in studies that analyzed data according to intent to treat but excludes dropouts in studies not analyzed according to intent-to-treat criteria. [d]Unipolar. [e]Interim treatment outcome. [f]Bipolar. [g]Two treatment groups with respective control group. [h]Final treatment outcome.

TABLE 13.2
Study Characteristics for Panic Disorders

Study	Treatment duration (months)	Multi-center study	Intention-to-treat analysis	No. of drug-treated patients	Drop-outs verum (n)	No. of placebo-treated patients	Drop-outs placebo (n)	Age (M)	% improved under medical treatment	% improved under placebo treatment
Schweizer et al. (1993)[a]	2	No	Yes	71	18	35	20	33	51	29
Schweizer et al. (1993)[b]	8	No	Yes	71	5	35	1	33	45	26
Mavissakalian & Perel (1992)[a]	3	No	Yes	8	0	8	0	31	87	62
Mavissakalian & Perel (1992)[b]	6	No	Yes	8	0	8	2	31	87	13
Rickels et al. (1993)[c]	12	No	No	38	+	10	+	33	22	20
Rickels et al. (1993)[d]	12	No	No	26	+	18	+	33	10	14

[a]Interim treatment outcome. [b]Final treatment outcome. [c]Follow-up of patients from Schweizer et al. (1993). [d]Follow-up of original dropouts from Schweizer et al. (1993). +Only patients who were available for follow-up.

TABLE 13.3
Study Characteristics for Personality Disorders and Dementia

Study	Treatment duration (months)	Multi-center study	Intention-to-treat analysis	Severity	No. of drug-treated patients	Drop-outs verum (n)	No. of placebo-treated patients	Drop-outs placebo (n)	Age (M)	% improved under medical treatment	% improved under placebo treatment
Personality disorders											
Montgomery & Montgomery (1982)[a]	6	No	No	3	17	—	21	—	36	53	43
Montgomery & Montgomery (1982)	6	No	No	3	14	—	16	—	35	79	25
Dementia											
Villardita et al. (1992)	3	No	No	1–2	30	0	30	0	70	47	0
Aranda et al. (1992)	4	No	No	1–2	95	5	96	4	82	33	15
Croisile et al. (1993)	12	No	No	2	14	2	16	1	66	0	0

[a]Two treatment groups with respective control group.

TABLE 13.4
Study Characteristics for Rheumatoid Arthritis, Pain, and Cancer

Study	Treatment duration (months)	Multi-center study	Intention-to-treat analysis	Severity	No. of drug-treated patients	Drop-outs verum (n)	No. of placebo-treated patients	Drop-outs placebo (n)	Age (M)	% improved under medical treatment	% improved under placebo treatment
Rheumatoid arthritis											
Dougados et al. (1988)	4	No	Yes	3	26	4	26	2	57.5[a]	55	21.5
Tugwell et al. (1990)	6	Yes	Yes	3	72	10	72	22	55.0	37	16.5
Giannini et al. (1992)	6	Yes	No	2–3	75	11	39	2	11.0	48	36.0
Pain											
Marchand et al. (1993)[b]	2.5	No	No	2–3	30	0	12	0	36.0	20	17.5
Peters (1992)	3	No	No	—	73	4	72	11	31.5	87	22.0
Cancer											
Eri & Tveter (1993)	6	No	No	2–3	14	1	13	2	67.0	47	20.0
Jones et al. (1992)	24	Yes	Yes	2–3	168	—	168	—	61.0	37	36.0
Cummings et al. (1993)	24	No	No	2–3	85	—	83	—	71.0	54	29.0
Tangrea et al. (1992)	36	Yes	Yes	2–3	490	43	491	38	—	33	33.0

Note. Dashes indicate no entry.
[a]Median. [b]Treatment transcutaneous electric nerve stimulation (TENS).

TABLE 13.5
Improvement Rates as a Function of Disorder

Disorder	Sample size		No. improved		% improved	
	Verum	Placebo	Verum	Placebo	Verum	Placebo
Affective disorder	1,170	689	756	316	65	46
Panic disorder	79	43	39	10	49	23
Personality disorder	31	37	20	13	65	35
Dementia	139	142	45	14	32	10
Rheumatoid arthritis	173	137	77	32	45	23
Pain	103	84	70	18	68	21
Cancer	757	755	277	249	37	33
Total	2,452	1,887	1,284	652	52	34

affective disorders, there was a substantial negative correlation between duration and response to placebo ($r = -.62$, $p < .01$) and an even higher correlation between duration and response to treatment ($r = -.84$, $p < .001$). Across studies of panic disorder, these correlations were of a similar magnitude ($-.61$ for duration and placebo response and $-.77$ for duration and treatment response), but with only six units of analysis, even correlations of this magnitude were not significant. There were too few studies of other specific disorders to analyze them separately.

In a meta-analysis of antidepressant medication, Kirsch and Sapirstein (see chap. 12, this volume) reported an exceptionally high correlation ($r = .90$) between the magnitude of the placebo effect and the magnitude of treatment effect. However, their analysis was limited to studies of the acute effects of medication. To determine whether this finding could be replicated in studies of long-term maintenance effects, we calculated the correlation between treatment response and placebo in the 13 studies of affective disorder studies using only final assessment data. The correlation between placebo response and treatment response in this subsample of the studies was .77 ($p < .01$).

DISCUSSION

Our intention was to assess the duration of the placebo response in general; to that end, we included data from studies of different disorders. As expected, the magnitude of the placebo response varied considerably across categories of disorders, as did that of the verum response. This made a differential analysis necessary. The correlation between placebo improvement and duration of the study across all disorders was small and negative, indicating that the placebo response did not decrease substantially with time. However, there was a significantly negative albeit moderate correlation between duration and verum improvement, indicating that verum improvement actually decreased over time. In the subset of studies on affective disorders, the situation was different: Here, we found a strong negative correlation for placebo improvement and duration, which was even stronger for verum improvement and duration. This shows that in affective disorders, placebo improvement decreases over time, but even more so does verum improvement.

Although the placebo response may be due to conditioning, unless the active medication is in fact a placebo, the response to it is not due to conditioning. For that reason, the decrease in the verum response was not likely to have been due to extinction but may instead have been an adaptation of the patient to the pharmacological properties of the drug. However, this raises questions about whether the decrease in the placebo response was the result of extinction. Instead, it may have been due to participants' expectancies of relapse based on their previous experience with the active drug. In other words, the fading of the placebo response may be an instance of the more general phenomenon of response to placebo mimicking response to the active treatment. Conversely, it is possible that both verum and placebo effects are conditioned responses and that the decrease in both are due to extinction. However, this presents the problem of identifying an unconditional stimulus that has made these substances conditional stimuli.

Finally, our data extend the findings of Kirsch and Sapirstein (see chap. 12, this volume) to long-term maintenance studies of antidepressant medication. They reported that 75% of the verum response was duplicated by placebo and that the correlation between placebo response and verum response was .90. In our studies of affective disorders, 65% of the patients in the active drug condition improved, as did 46% of the patients in the placebo condition. Thus, 71% of the drug response was duplicated by placebo, and the correlation between placebo response and verum response was .77. Furthermore, unlike Kirsch and Sapirstein's data, which were based on standardized difference scores, ours were based on actual improvement rates. Thus, our data indicate that approximately 70% of patients who improved after administration of antidepressant medication might have improved in response to placebo.

REFERENCES

Ader, R. (1983). Behavioral conditioning and immunity. In N. Fabris, E. Garaci, J. Hadden, & N. A. Mitchison (Eds.), *Immunoregulation* (pp. 283–313). New York: Plenum.

Ader, R. (1985). Conditioned immunopharmacological effects in animals: Implications for a conditioning model of pharmacotherapy. In L. White, B. Tursky,

& G. E. Schwartz (Eds.), *Placebo: Theory, research, mechanisms* (pp. 306–323). New York: Guilford Press.

Ader, R., & Cohen, N. (1975). Behaviorally conditioned immunosuppression. *Psychosomatic Medicine, 37,* 333–340.

Aranda, B., Dumoulin, P., & Groothold, G. (1992). Kontrollierte studie zur wirkung von dihydroergocristin beim hirnorganischen psychosyndrom [Controlled study of the effect of dihydroergocristin in organic brain psychosyndrome]. *Arzneimittel-Forschung, 42,* 1406–1409.

Buckalew, L. W., & Ross, S. (1981). Relationship of perceptual characteristics to efficacy of placebo. *Psychological Reports, 49,* 955–961.

Coppen, A., Ghose, K., Montgomery, S., Rama Roa, V. A., Bailey, J., & Jorgensen, A. (1978). Continuation therapy with amitryptiline in depression. *British Journal of Psychiatry, 133,* 28–33.

Croisile, B., Trillet, M., Fondarai, J., Laurent, B., Mauguière, F., & Billardon, M. (1993). Long-term and high-dose piracetam treatment of Alzheimer's disease. *Neurology, 43,* 301–305.

Cummings, F. J., Gray, R., Tormey, D. C., Davis, T. E., Volk, H., Harris, J., Falkson, G., & Bennet, J. M. (1993). Adjuvant tamoxifen versus placebo in elderly women with node-positive breast cancer, long-term follow-up and causes of death. *Journal of Clinical Oncology, 11,* 29–35.

Dougados, M., Awada, H., & Amor, B. (1988). Cyclosporin in rheumatoid arthritis: A double-blind placebo-controlled study in 52 patients. *Annals of Rheumatic Diseases, 47,* 127–133.

Eri, L. M., & Tveter, K. J. (1993). A prospective, placebo-controlled study of the antiandrogen casodex as treatment for patients with benign prostatic hyperplasia. *Journal of Urology, 150,* 90–94.

Frank, E., Kupfer, D. J., Perel, J. M., Cornes, C., Jarret, D. B., Mallinger, A. G., Thase, M. E., McEachran, A. B., & Grochocinski, V. J. (1990). Three-year outcomes for maintenance therapies in recurrent depression. *Archives of General Psychiatry, 47,* 1093–1099.

Frank, J. D. (1989). Non-specific aspects of treatment: The view of a psychotherapist. In M. Shepherd & N. Sartorius (Eds.), *Non-specific aspects of treatment* (pp. 95–114). Bern, Switzerland: Huber.

Giannini, E. H., Brewer, E. J., Kuzmina, N., Shaikov, A., Maximov, A., Vorontsov, I., Fink, C. W., Newman, A. J., Cassidy, J. T., & Zemel, L. S. (1992). Methotrexate in resistant juvenile rheumatoid arthritis: Results of the USA–USSR double-blind, placebo controlled trial. *New England Journal of Medicine, 326,* 1043–1049.

Jones, A. L., Powles, T. J., Law, M., Tidy, A., Easton, D., Coombes, R. C., Smith, I. E., McKinna, J. A., Nash, A., Ford, H. T., & Gazet, J. C. (1992). Adjuvant aminoglutethimide for postmenopausal patients with primary breast cancer: Analysis at 8 years. *Journal of Clinical Oncology, 10,* 1547–1552.

Kirsch, I. (1997). Specifying nonspecifics: Psychological mechanisms of placebo effects. In A. Harrington (Ed.), *The placebo effect: Interdisciplinary explorations* (pp. 166–186). Cambridge, MA: Harvard University Press.

Klerman, G. L., Dimascio, A., Weissman, M., Prusoff, B., & Paykel, E. (1974). Treatment of depression by drugs and psychotherapy. *American Journal of Psychiatry, 131*, 186–191.

Kupfer, D. J. (1991). Lessons to be learned from long-term treatment of affective disorders: Potential utility in panic disorder. *Journal of Clinical Psychiatry, 52*(Suppl.), 12–16.

Marchand, S., Charest, J., Li, J., Chenard, J. R., Lavignolle, I. D., & Laurencelle, L. (1993). Is TENS purely a placebo effect? A controlled study on chronic low back pain. *Pain, 54*, 99–106.

Mavissakalian, M., & Perel, J. M. (1992). Clinical experiments in maintenance and discontinuation of imipramine therapy in panic disorder with agoraphobia. *Archives of General Psychiatry, 49*, 318–323.

McDonald, C. J., & McCabe, G. P. (1989). How much of the placebo effect is really statistical regression? [Letter to the editor]. *Statistics in Medicine, 8*, 1301–1302.

McDonald, D., Mazzuca, S., & McCabe, G. P. (1983). How much of the placebo "effect" is really statistical regression? *Statistics in Medicine, 2*, 417–427.

Mindham, R. H. S., Howland, C., & Shepherd, M. (1973). An evaluation of continuation therapy with tricyclic antidepressants in depressive illness. *Psychological Medicine, 3*, 5–17.

Montgomery, S. A., & Montgomery, D. (1982). Pharmacological prevention of suicidal behavior. *Journal of Affective Disorders, 4*, 291–298.

Montgomery, S. A., Dufour, H., Brion, S., Gailledreau, J., Laqueille, X., Ferrey, G., Moron, P., Parant-Lucena, N., Singer, L., Danion, J. M., Beuzen, J. N., & Pierredon, M. A. (1988). Prophylactic efficacy of fluexetine in unipolar depression. *British Journal of Psychiatry, 153*, 69–76.

Morison, R. A. H., Woodmansey, A., & Young, A. J. (1961). Placebo response in an arthritis trial. *Annals of Rheumatic Diseases, 20*, 179–185.

Peters, F. (1992). Multicentre study of gestrinone in cyclical breast pain. *Lancet, 339*, 205–208.

Prien, R. F., Klett, C. J., & Caffey, E. M. J. (1973). Lithium carbonate and imipramine in prevention of affective episodes. *Archives of General Psychiatry, 29*, 420–425.

Prien, R. F., Kupfer, D. J., Mansky, P. A., Small, J. G., Tuason, V. B., Voss, C. B., & Johnson, W. E. (1984). Drug therapy in the prevention of recurrences in unipolar and bipolar affective disorders. *Archives of General Psychiatry, 41*, 1096–1104.

Quitkin, F., Rabkin, J. G., Stewart, J. W., McGrath, P., & Harrison, W. (1991). Heterogeneity of clinical response during placebo treatment. *American Journal of Psychiatry, 148*, 193–196.

Rabkin, J. G., McGrath, P., Stewart, J. W., Harrison, W., Markowitz, J. S., &

Quitkin, F. (1986). Follow-up of patient who improved during placebo wash-out. *Journal of Clinical Psychopharmacology, 6,* 274–278.

Rickels, K., Schweizer, E., Weiss, S., & Zavodnick, S. (1993). Maintenance drug treatment for panic disorder: II. Short and long-term outcome after drug therapy. *Archives of General Psychiatry, 50,* 61–68.

Rouillon, F., Phillips, R., Serrurier, D., Ansart, E., & Gérard, M. J. (1989). Re-chutes de dépression unipolaire et efficacité de la maprotiline [Relapse in unipolar depression and efficacy of maprotiline]. *L'Encéphale, 15,* 527–534.

Schweizer, E., Rickels, K., Weiss, S., & Zavodnick, S. (1993). Maintenance drug treatment of panic disorder: I. Results of a prospective, placebo-controlled comparison of alprazolam and imipramine. *Archives of General Psychiatry, 50,* 51–60.

Seager, C. B., & Bird, R. L. (1962). Imipramine with electrical treatment in depression: A controlled clinical trial. *Journal of Mental Science, 108,* 704–707.

Stein, M. K., Rickels, K., & Weise, C. C. (1980). Maintenance therapy with amitryptiline: A controlled trial. *American Journal of Psychiatry, 137,* 170–171.

Tangrea, J. A., Edwards, B. K., Taylor, P. R., Hartmann, A. M., Peck, G. L., Salasche, S. J., Menon, P. A., Benson, P. M., Mellette, J. R., Guill, M. A. Robinson, J. K., Guin, J. D., Stoll, H. L., Grabski, W. J., & Winton, G. B. (1992). Long-term therapy with low-dose isotretinoin for prevention of basal cell carcinoma: A multicenter clinical trial. *Journal of the National Cancer Institute, 84,* 328–332.

Tugwell, P., Bombardier, C., Gent, M., Bennet, K. J., Bensen, W. G., Carette, S., Chalmers, A., Esdaile, J. M., Klinkhoff, A. V., Kraag, G. R., Ludwin, D., & Roberts, R. S. (1990). Low-dose cyclosporin versus placebo in patients with rheumatoid arthritis. *Lancet, 335,* 1051–1055.

Turner, J. A., Deyo, R. A., Loeser, J. D., Von Korff, M., & Fordyce, W. (1994). The importance of placebo effects in pain treatment and research. *Journal of the American Medical Association, 20,* 1609–1614.

Villardita, C., Grioli, S., Lomeo, C., Cattaneo, C., & Parini, J. (1992). Clinical studies with oxiracetam in patients with dementia of Alzheimer type and multi-infarct dementia of mild to moderate degree. *Neuropsychobiology, 25,* 24–28.

Wickramasekera, I. (1980). A conditioned response model of the placebo effect: Predictions from the model. *Biofeedback and Self-Regulation, 5,* 5–18.

Wickramasekera, I. (1985). A conditioned response model of the placebo effect: Predictions from the model. In L. White, B. Tursky, & G. E. Schwartz (Eds.), *Placebo: Theory, research, mechanisms* (pp. 255–287). New York: Guilford Press.

14

EXPECTATIONS OF SICKNESS: CONCEPT AND EVIDENCE OF THE NOCEBO PHENOMENON

ROBERT A. HAHN

In this chapter I examine the hypothesis that expectations of sickness and symptoms cause sickness and symptoms in the expectant individual. In parallel with the healing "placebo" effects of positive expectations, the effect of negative expectations on what is expected has been referred to as the "nocebo phenomenon," first named by Kennedy (1961). Included as sicknesses are "unwanted conditions of self, or substantial threats of unwanted conditions of self" (Hahn, 1995, p. 22). In broad terms, such conditions may range from relatively minor symptoms to named sicknesses, disabilities, injuries, and death. Some nocebo effects can be assessed objectively as well as subjectively. Some are transient, and others are chronic or fatal. Because expectations are primarily learned from the cultural environment, nocebo effects are likely to differ by setting. Popular belief in nocebo phenomena may be reflected in expressions such as "worried sick" and "scared to death." In this chapter I review the concepts of expectation, sickness, and causation; present evidence for nocebo etiology; suggest explanations for the phenomenon; and explore clinical and public health implications.

An *expectation* is a belief that some event is likely to occur; expectations may be accompanied by various emotional/affective states. Expectations may be specific (i.e., the individual expects a particular outcome, such as nausea or a heart attack) or generic (i.e., the individual has vague expectations that some event, such as uncertain sickness or misfortune, is impending but does not anticipate a particular outcome).

Expectations may be founded in the expectant person's conscious beliefs (e.g., "I will have a heart attack because I am under enormous stress"), or they may arise without a recognized source (e.g., "I don't know why, but I believe I will have a heart attack"). Although expressed expectations may be difficult or impossible to assess (Bayer, 1985), they must be sincere to count as possible nocebo events. Hypochondria might be a nocebo effect (i.e., if it results in the increased symptomatology expected); malingering, however, cannot be nocebo phenomenon because the professed patient deceitfully reports a condition.

Unwantedness comes in degrees, and individuals may have different thresholds regarding just how serious a condition must be to qualify as sickness (Barsky, Coeytaux, Sarnie, & Cleary, 1993). A person may not be able to determine when a substantial threat of unwanted conditions exists, as in asymptomatic hypertension; nevertheless, this person's desires and conceptions of well-being initially define what is to be threatened. Although broken legs, rabies, and heart attacks may be unwanted universally, other conditions will be unwanted because of individual circumstances. Opera singers, marathoners, and scholars may suffer different unwanted conditions. Sicknesses are not only *of* the self, they are in essence defined *by* the self.

The nocebo phenomenon considered in this chapter is distinct from placebo side effects, which occur when expectations of healing produce sickness (i.e., a positive expectation has a negative outcome). For example, a rash that occurs after the administration of a placebo remedy might be a placebo side effect. Diverse placebo side effects have been reported, although such reports usually have been based on uncontrolled studies; an incidence of 19% was found in the healthy participants in the pharmacological studies of Rosenzweig, Brohier, and Zipfel (1993). In the nocebo phenomenon, however, the individual expects sickness to be the outcome (i.e., the expectation is negative). Nocebos can also have side effects (i.e., when negative expectations produce positive outcomes or outcomes other than those expected).

Finally, placebo and nocebo effects also might occur simultaneously, such as when a patient expects both a healing outcome and another, pathological outcome. Such an occurrence has been suggested by Pogge (1963), who found that specific placebo side effects varied by treated conditions.

For example, 17% of the patients given placebo estrogen experienced nausea or vomiting, compared with 6% of the patients given placebo analgesics and 2% of the patients given placebo antiobesity drugs.

Reference to expectations as being *causal* is the same as that of commonly recognized pathogens and toxins (e.g., cigarette smoke of lung cancer; U.S. Surgeon General, 1989). Such exposures, including exposure to cigarette smoke, are not necessary causes of the given outcome; lung cancer can occur in the absence of exposure to cigarette smoke. Nor are such exposures sufficient causes of the given outcome—lung cancer does not always occur even among heavy smokers—other conditions, including the characteristics of the host, contribute to the causal process. The nocebo hypothesis is that expectations of sickness increase the likelihood that the expected sickness will occur.

RANGE OF EVIDENCE

In this section I review the range of evidence that expectations of sickness affect the sickness expected. I first examine evidence that expectations of pain and other symptoms may affect the expected outcome. I then review evidence concerning the effects of expectations of specific named sicknesses. I conclude by commenting briefly on the effects of expectations on mortality.

Expectations of Symptoms

Social psychologists have conducted diverse experiments that demonstrate the effects of negative suggestions on the experience of symptoms (Jewett, Fein, & Greenberg, 1990; Lancman, Asconape, Craven, Howard, & Penry, 1994; Luparello, Leist, Lourie, & Sweet, 1970; Schachter & Singer, 1962; Schweiger & Parducci, 1981; Sternbach, 1964); these studies have focused on specific nocebo effects. Schweiger and Parducci (1981) reported an experiment in which 34 college students were told to expect headaches when administered an electrical current. Although no current was actually administered, 24 (70.6%) of the students reported having headaches, and they confirmed their experiences of headaches even when informed that no current had been administered.

In another, double-blind experiment, Luparello, Lyons, Bleecker, and McFadden (1968) randomly assigned 20 asthmatic patients to one of four conditions: Two groups were given a bronchodilator and the other two groups a bronchoconstrictor. Half the participants in each group were told they were being given a bronchodilator, and the other half were told they were being given a bronchoconstrictor. Expectations induced by misinformation about the substance reduced its physiological effectiveness by 43%

(for the bronchoconstrictor) and 49% (for the bronchodilator). Luparello et al. also referred to a 16th-century Dominican monk who reportedly fainted either at the smell or at the distant sight of a rose and to an asthmatic patient in another study whose allergy to roses was induced by both plastic and natural roses, indicating that the effect of the rose did not result entirely from its biological or chemical properties (Mackenzie, 1896).

Another study was designed to evaluate a method for diagnosing psychogenic seizures, reported to account for as many as 20% of cases of "refractory epilepsy," in which no physical basis for seizures can be determined (Lancman et al., 1994). Lancman et al. compared the effect of suggestion on the induction of seizure behavior in patients who had psychogenic seizures and other patients who had known epilepsy. Patients were told that a medicine administered through a skin patch would induce seizures within 30 s, and that removal of the patch would end the seizures. The patch was colored and had the smell of alcohol but was not capable of inducing seizures physiologically. Of patients who had refractory epilepsy, 77% manifested seizures while wearing the patch and had symptoms such as nonresponsiveness, generalized violent thrashing, and uncoordinated movements; 19% of these patients reported seeing auras, and 44% showed postictal confusion, sleepiness, or both. None of the patients who were known to have epilepsy manifested seizures. Another study using saline injections rather than inactive patches showed similar results: Eighty-four percent of "hysterical seizure" patients had seizurelike behavior, compared with none of the epileptic patients who participated as controls (Cohen & Suter, 1982).

Another study by Jewett et al. (1990) was designed to evaluate a controversial method of testing for food allergies. Jewett et al. compared the effect of injecting the food substances—the test to be evaluated—with the effect of injecting saline diluent without the substance in question. The allergic outcomes examined included itching of the nose, watering or burning eyes, plugged-up ears, tight or scratchy throat, nausea, dizziness, sleepiness, and depression. (Patients with a history of anaphylactic reactions or documented cardiac irregularity, or other severe reactions to their allergies, were excluded from the study.) In this double-blind study, the proportion of patients who experienced symptoms was not statistically different for patients injected with the possible allergen (27%) and those injected with the *nocebo* diluent (24%). "Neutralizing" injections, administered to eliminate the reactions, were also equally effective regardless of whether they contained the possible allergen or—in this case—the diluent *placebo*. An injection became a nocebo (or placebo) not because of its contents but because of the recipient's pessimistic (or optimistic) expectations.

A study by Myers, Cairns, and Singer (1987) indicated that increases in the number of reported symptoms was associated with indications of potential side effects given in the process of informed consent. In this study, the effects of two medications and a placebo on unstable angina in three different medical settings were compared. Study participants were given informed-consent statements warning of possible minor and major gastro-intestinal side effects of treatment in two of the settings, but not in the third. Participants given the information about specific potential gastro-intestinal side effects were 2.3–2.9 times as likely to report minor gastro-intestinal side effects as patients not given the specific information. No significant differences were noted between the proportions of participants in the three comparison groups who reported major side effects that were regarded as being attributable to the pharmacological effects of treatment.

Nocebo effects also appear as a part of routine medical practice. In "anticipatory nausea," patients with cancer who have initiated a course of chemotherapy begin to experience nausea before subsequent administra-tions of chemotherapeutic agents. Anticipation may also suppress immune functioning (Bovbjerg et al., 1990). Anticipatory nausea may be provoked by the sight of the medical setting, the voices of medical personnel, or even the thought of treatment. In one study (Andrykowski et al., 1988), 57% of women with breast cancer suffered anticipatory nausea. The like-lihood of anticipatory nausea was increased if the women had experienced more severe nausea after initial chemotherapy and if they had greater levels of expectation of subsequent nausea.

Symptoms may also occur when one person observes or learns of the symptoms in others. Knowledge of symptoms in others fosters an expec-tation that one may also be subject to these symptoms. Contagion by ob-servation has been referred to as "sociogenic illness," "psychogenic illness," "mass hysteria," or, in the workplace, "assembly line hysteria" (Colligan & Stockton, 1978).

Sirois (1974) reviewed 78 documented outbreaks of "epidemic hys-teria" reported from 1872 through 1972. He restricted the analysis to a range of behaviors, required that organic causes be either not demonstrated or improbable, and rated the quality of available studies. Of the outbreaks ascertained, 44% occurred in schools, 22% in towns, and 10% in factories. Twenty-eight percent of the outbreaks involved fewer than 10 people, 32% involved 10–30 people, and 19% involved more than 30 people; 5% were of an unreported magnitude. The largest of the outbreaks noted by Sirois involved approximately 200 people.[1] Only women were involved in 74% of the outbreaks and only men in 4%. Outbreaks occurred more often among those from lower socioeconomic classes and during periods of social stress and uncertainty. The symptoms reported in these outbreaks (some-times more than one symptom per outbreak) included convulsions, which were reported in 24% of the outbreaks; abnormal movements in 18%; and

---

[1]A more recent school outbreak in 1983 involved 949 people (Modan et al., 1983).

fainting, globus-cough-laryngismus, and loss of sensation in 12% each. Symptomatology changed during the 100 years included in the analysis, from more globus-cough-laryngismus and abnormal movements to more fainting, nausea, abdominal malaise, and headaches.

Colligan and Murphy (1979) pointed out that sociogenic outbreaks are usually associated with a source believed by patients to be related to the symptoms (e.g., a strange odor or gas, a new solvent, or an insect bite). However, reported symptoms often do not fit biomedical knowledge of associations between potential toxins or pathogens and pathophysiology. People who become ill during sociogenic outbreaks often have repetitive jobs, are being exposed to unusual stress, have poor relationships with superiors, or all of these. They might be in poorer health and be absent from work more frequently than those who are not affected. Colligan and Murphy found that sociogenic outbreaks in workplace settings are substantially underreported.

Sirois (1975) estimated that sociogenic outbreaks occur in approximately 1 of every 1,000 schools per year in the province of Quebec. A review of recent school outbreaks in diverse countries indicates attack rates (i.e., the proportion of people exposed who experience the condition) of 6%–48% (Arcidiacono, Brand, Coppenger, & Calder, 1990).

The investigation conducted by Kerckhoff and Back (1968) of the 1962 "June bug" outbreak in a Montana mill is one of the few to carefully reconstruct the social patterns of the spread of a sociogenic illness. In the June bug event, those affected fainted or complained of pain, nausea, or disorientation. Of the 965 workers, 62 (6.4%) were affected; women were 8.5 times as likely to be affected as men. All the ill employees worked in dressmaking departments. People affected were 70% more likely than controls to believe that the cause of the outbreak was an insect or other physical object. People affected were 62% more likely to have worked overtime at least two or three times a week than those not affected. They were less likely to go to a supervisor with a complaint or to be members of the union. They were 2.2 times as likely to be sole breadwinners, 5.6 times as likely to be divorced, and 30% more likely to have a child under 6 years of age. The outbreak began among women who were socially isolated, subsequently spread to women who were connected by close social relationships, and finally diffused among women who were less closely connected. The phenomenon analyzed by Kerckhoff and Back might be described as "mass somatization."

Expectations of Named Sicknesses

Mood, affect, and some psychiatric conditions are often associated with negative expectations (American Psychiatric Association, 1980). For example, feelings of hopelessness are a prominent component of diverse forms of depression; insofar as the depressed patient may not specify an expected outcome, the association between depression and negative outcomes is an example of the generic nocebo effect. The results of several studies indicate an association between negative affect associated with psychiatric conditions and pathological outcomes (Black, Warrack, & Winokur, 1985a, 1985b; Bruce, Leaf, Rozal, Florio, & Hoff, 1994; Conti et al., 1989; Friedman & Booth-Kewley, 1987; Newman & Bland, 1991; Reich, 1985; Weissman, Markowitz, Ouellette, Greenwald, & Kahn, 1990; Wells et al., 1989). However, only Anda et al. (1993) used epidemological methods to control for the confounding effects of other risk factors.

Anda et al. (1993) examined the effects of depression on ischemic heart disease (IHD) incidence and mortality in a sample of U.S. adults. Individuals who did not have heart disease at the beginning of the study were examined, and those whose initial depressed affect might have been the consequence of chronic disease were excluded from the study. Depression was assessed with the General Well-Being Schedule (Dupuy, 1977). Results indicated that respondents with depressive affect were 1.6 times more likely to have nonfatal IHD and 1.5 times more likely to have fatal IHD than respondents who did not have depressive affect, independent of several other known risk factors for IHD (e.g., smoking and physical inactivity). Another investigation of hospitalized patients indicated that, independent of physical condition, patients who had suffered a myocardial infarction and who were depressed were 4.6–6.9 times as likely to die from heart disease as were patients who had suffered a myocardial infarction and who were not depressed (Frasure-Smith, Lespérance, & Talajic, 1993). Anda et al. also found a dose–response relationship between the degree of hopelessness and IHD: The greater the hopelessness, the greater the IHD incidence and mortality. Insofar as these patients were pessimistic but did not specifically expect IHD to be the outcome, this is a generic nocebo effect.

In another psychiatric condition, hypochondria, patients believe themselves to suffer from certain diseases, although medical examination reveals no physiological basis for the patients' concerns (Barsky, Wyshak, & Klerman, 1986). Cardiophobia is a form of hypochondria in which patients specifically believe that they have heart problems. A study that compared such patients with other patients without such fears showed that cardiophobic patients were less accurate in their assessment of cardiac events than were controls who do not have hypochondria (Barsky, Cleary, Barnett, Christiansen, & Ruskin, 1994). However, patients who have hypochondria are said to actually experience the events they report (Kaplan & Sadock, 1995). Thus, although the expectations of these patients are, by definition, not associated with objectively detectable physiological conditions, these patients might experience pain and other symptoms. In this sense, hypochondria is a nocebo phenomenon.

Awareness or attention to nosological categories may lead to self-scrutiny and to self-diagnosis with the considered sickness. Consideration that the condition exists promotes its "observation" in oneself. A well-recognized form of the effect of nosological self-scrutiny is "medical students' disease" (MSD), casually referred to as "sophomoritis" or "medstudentitis" (Hunter, Lohrenz, & Schwartzman, 1964; Mechanic, 1972; Ryle, 1948; Woods, Natterson, & Silverman, 1966). Woods et al. (1966) defined MSD as "the development of either symptoms or hypochondriacal anxiety about the disease being studied by the student" (p. 785). They determined that 79% of the students in their study reported having had MSD at some time during their medical education, resulting in reports of psychiatric as well as medical conditions. In most students, Woods et al. reported, symptoms or anxiety disappeared within 2 weeks or a month, most often after reassurance from other people that the student did not have the illness. In 15% of the students, MSD led to "a phobic avoidance of both study and clinical contacts related to the disease in question" (Woods et al., 1966, p. 787). Seventy percent of the students expressed a desire for psychiatric help, although only 27% actually sought help. A study in which 60 medical students were compared with 60 law students showed similar rates of hypochondriacal complaints (i.e., 8.3%); however, significantly more medical students than law students reported that they had experienced symptoms similar to those of an illness they had read about (Kellner, Wiggins, & Pathak, 1986).

There is also evidence that physical conditions such as "late whiplash" (i.e., patients report chronic neck pain, headache, and cognitive impairment after a rear-end automobile crash) also might have a strong expectational component corresponding to the cultural and socioeconomic environment in which late whiplash is reported. In previous decades, although cases of whiplash were reported primarily after severe automobile crashes, the incidence is now reported to be as common after more moderate crashes; one study showed lower whiplash rates after crashes in which the vehicles had to be towed away than after crashes in which no towing was required (Evans, 1992). Analysts of this association concluded that in most cases, the experience of pain and other symptoms was not malingering (i.e., deliberate deception) but true experience that corresponded to locally given expectations (Bayer, 1985; Mendelson, 1986). Bayer described experimental evidence of a process in which individuals initially induced to exaggerate or falsify a claim of pain then rapidly came to believe their initial reports.

In a recent study, Schrader et al. (1996) examined the prevalence of chronic crash-related symptoms in Finland, a country where the cultural awareness of late whiplash is minimal and where financial gain for chronic conditions is unlikely. The researchers found no significant differences in the prevalence of chronic neck pain or headache among people involved in rear-end automobile crashes 1–3 years after the crashes, compared with sex- and age-matched controls who had not recently been involved in automobile crashes.

Mills and Horne (1986) compared the rates of rear-end collisions, whiplash injuries, and compensation during a 12-month period (1982–1983) in New Zealand, where medical expenses and worker's compensation are awarded automatically (approximately NZ$1,038 per incident), and in Victoria, Australia, where compensation (approximately NZ$3,265 per incident) must be sought through legal means. More than 10 times as many cases of whiplash were reported in Victoria as in New Zealand, although the population of Victoria was 24% greater than that of New Zealand. In New Zealand, 0.78 whiplash injuries were reported per rear-end collision; in Victoria, 1.94 whiplash injuries were reported per rear-end collision. A subsequent report from Victoria indicated that when regulations concerning compensation for cervical whiplash were made more restrictive in 1987, the number of reported whiplash cases dropped from more than 6,000 per year in the mid-1980s to 2,500 in 1987 and to substantially lower numbers in subsequent years (McDermott, 1993).

Other physical conditions also might be affected by the cultural and socioeconomic environments. A recent meta-analysis of the association between compensation and chronic pain (i.e., primarily lower back pain) indicated that complaints of chronic pain were more common and treatment less effective when compensation was provided than when it was not (Rohling, Binder, & Langhinrichsen-Rohling, 1995). Again, it is thought that deliberate deception is not usually involved but that patients are responding to expectations of their sociocultural environment.

Expectations of Death

The studies cited earlier show both the generic and specific effects of expectations on IHD incidence and mortality (e.g., Anda et al., 1993). However, much of the evidence for the effect of expectations on mortality is anecdotal or otherwise questionable; other inferences are based on ecological studies.

An extreme form of the nocebo phenomenon was described by Mauss (1926) and then, apparently independently in Cannon's (1942) classic article, as "voodoo death." In voodoo death, which has been reported to occur in several non-Western societies, a person is said to die from intense fear after a curse. However, evidence on voodoo death is difficult to collect (Lewis, 1987) and remains controversial. For example, a physician, Eastwell, closely observed several possible instances of voodoo death in East Arnhem, Australia, and concluded that "psychological factors are secondary to the basic physical process of dehydration, but both are involved" (Eastwell, 1982, p. 17). Reid and Williams (1984), ethnographers who worked extensively in the same region, disputed most of Eastwell's claims. In contrast to Eastwell's assertion that "gross fear," including a fear of death from sorcery, is a common psychiatric condition, Reid and Williams reported that sorcery is a post hoc diagnosis of death and that patients rarely manifest such fear. Reid and Williams also reported that patients' families rarely withdrew from care and did not withhold water unless it was refused by patients. They suggested that voodoo death is a fabrication of Western observers.

The validity of voodoo death as reported in diverse cultures throughout the world is controversial; however, as Lester (1972) noted, this phenomenon is similar to the "giving up–given up complex" described by Engel (1968). The latter complex is associated with some manifestations of clinical depression; in this psychological state, the patient experiences feelings of helplessness and hopelessness, doubts his or her experience to cope or get help, and may feel abandoned and inadequate. As noted previously, such depressive states are risk factors for cardiac morbidity and mortality.

Surgical patients may also have convictions about their deaths. Weisman and Hackett (1961), in an article entitled "Predilection to Death," reported the surgeons' principle that patients who are convinced they will die during surgery should not be operated on, presumably because their convictions are usually correct. Weisman and Hackett reviewed the courses of 600 patients from one hospital (accumulated during 3 years of psychiatric consultation in a surgical ward). They carefully distinguished which patients were convinced that they were going to die during surgery and which patients were unusually apprehensive about dying during surgery. The 5 patients who were convinced that they were going to die during surgery were more likely to do so.

The results of controlled epidemiological studies also show that just having the belief that one is susceptible to heart attacks is a risk factor for coronary death; this is an example of a specific nocebo effect. Eaker, Pinsky, and Castelli (1992) examined women ages 45–64 years who were participating in the Framingham study cohort to determine the 20-year incidence of myocardial infarction and coronary death. Independent of commonly recognized risk factors for coronary death (e.g., smoking, high systolic blood pressure, and the ratio of total to high-density lipoprotein cholesterol), women who believed that they were more likely than other women to have a heart attack were 3.7 times as likely to die as a result of coronary conditions as were women who believed that they were less likely to die of such causes.

The process that triggers the expectational effects of a person's social environment on mortality need not involve direct personal contact. An association has been found between traumatic death or violence in the community environment and subsequent suicide or suicidelike behavior

(Phillips, 1974, 1977; Phillips & Carstensen, 1986). For example, the incidence of suicide may increase during the week after a suicide is reported in a newspaper or on TV, the greater the circulation of the newspaper, the greater the increase (Phillips, 1974). During the week after Marilyn Monroe's suicide in 1962, 197 suicides occurred in the United States—12% more than the number expected on the basis of past suicide patterns (Phillips, 1974). Results of another study indicated that teenagers were more susceptible to televised reports of a suicide than adults and that increases in suicides were greater for girls than boys (Phillips & Carstensen, 1986).

Increases in the number of motor-vehicle-related fatalities, which sometimes are ascribed to suicidal behavior, have also occurred after newspaper reports of a suicide. Phillips (1977) calculated that, on average, the number of motor-vehicle-related fatalities increased 9% above the expected rate during the week after front-page reporting of suicides in newspapers. When such reports appeared in newspapers that had greater-than-average circulation, the increase in motor-vehicle-related fatalities was 19%.

ELEMENTS OF AN EXPLANATION OF THE NOCEBO PHENOMENON

Although a unified and comprehensive explanation of the nocebo phenomenon has not been formulated, several interrelated elements of an explanation appear plausible and not inconsistent with one another. The nocebo phenomenon comprises three basic components to be explained: (a) the sources of expectations; (b) differential susceptibility to nocebo effects; and (c) the translation of expectations into expected experiential, behavioral, and physiological outcomes (see Figure 14.1). Explanations for the first two components are principally cultural, social, and psychological; explanations for the third are primarily psychological and psychophysical.

Sources of Expectations

A person's expectations derive largely from the society in which he or she is reared. A society's *ethnomedicine* is the part of its culture that informs members about sicknesses and their causes, symptoms, possible cures, and moral connotations (Hahn, 1995). Traditional Chinese medicine, Native American shamanism, African curing, and contemporary biomedicine are examples of ethnomedicines; each system provides adherents, both experts and laypeople, with expectations about sickness and healing.

Despite the rapid worldwide dissemination of Western biomedicine, ethnomedicines differ substantially from society to society. People in different cultural settings name conditions differently; more fundamentally,

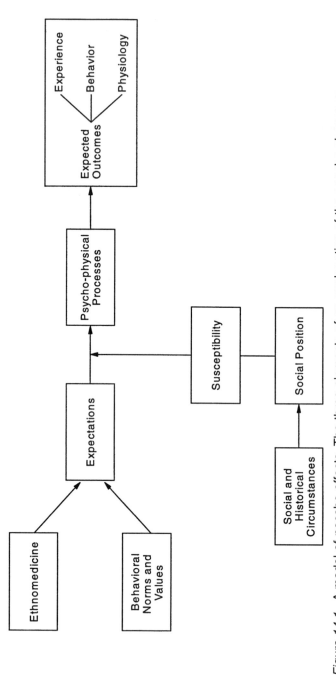

Figure 14.1. A model of nocebo effects. The three elements of an explanation of the nocebo phenomenon are sources of expectations, differential susceptibility, and the translation of expectations into expected experiential, behavioral, and physiological outcomes.

they may also conceive of conditions in radically different ways in terms of symptoms, causation, and meaning (Hahn, 1995). For example, in many non-Western settings, sickness usually has profound spiritual and moral aspects that may not be explicitly recognized in Western thought. The implication of this variation for the nocebo (and placebo) phenomenon is substantial, for its consequences will differ by setting and will parallel local expectations.

An ethnomedicine informs societal members not only about what sickness conditions to expect but also about the norms of behavior expected for patients and others. One form of behavior expected for patients in the "sick role," which, especially in relatively severe sickness conditions, may exempt patients from their usual responsibilities and also require them to seek appropriate treatment. Sick roles may differ in each society. The availability of the sick role may provide a motive—conscious or unconscious—for becoming sick because being sick gives the patient an excuse from unwanted or troubling responsibilities (Mechanic & Volkart, 1960). Identification with others who have an illness may enhance the likelihood of one's own affiliation.

The benefit of sickness to the patient is referred to as "secondary gain" and may include both the attention and care received from others and monetary benefits. For example, the patient who has hypochondria is said to use the sick role as "a ticket of admission to caretaking" (Guggenheim & Smith, 1995, p. 1262). Fishbain, Rosomoff, Cutler, and Rosomoff (1995) compared secondary gain with reinforcement in conditioned responses (i.e., a reward that induces repetitions in behavior). In addition, societies may have systems of compensation in which the patients' medical and other expenses are paid or partially paid. In some settings, payment is relatively automatic; in others, payment requires legal or other proof of injury or disability, thus encouraging the adversarial process.

The social system of compensation may motivate sickness. Evidence cited earlier concerning late whiplash and lower back pain suggests that secondary gains increase the frequency of reported injury and disability and decrease the likelihood that treatments will succeed. The environment of secondary gains may foster the expectation that the illness will persist and be difficult to cure and that the illness will be rewarded. The duration of illness and reward can be observed in other patients; therefore, both can be expected to occur. Bayer (1985) pointed out, however, that although most patients will have gains of some sort when they are patients, their losses may often outweigh their gains. Thus, "the economy of secondary gain does not seem to adequately explain why some people would be induced to misrepresent or misperceive their level of pain" (Bayer, 1985, p. 518).

One mechanism, conditioning, may be relevant to experiential, behavioral, and physiological outcomes. In 1927, Pavlov (1927/1960) demonstrated that the repeated pairing of a tone with the administration of an emetic to a dog produced vomiting behavior with subsequent presentations of only the tone; presumably, in addition to manifesting vomiting behavior, the dog experienced nausea and had physiological signs of vomiting. The phenomenon of anticipatory nausea among patients with cancer also has been attributed to conditioning. More recent studies of mice that had systemic lupus erythematosus have indicated that the repeated pairings of immunosuppressive drugs with a conditioned stimulus (e.g., saccharin drinking solution) resulted in a delay in the onset of "unremitting protein-uria" and death after the mice received only the conditioned stimulus (Ader & Cohen, 1982). In this instance, although the saccharin might be regarded as a placebo, because it induced a positive final outcome its intermediate effect of immunosuppression might be a negative outcome in other circumstances (e.g., in the presence of infectious agents; Ader & Cohen, 1991). A similar effect was found in a human adolescent who had systemic lupus erythematosus and who improved markedly with a reduced dose (and a reduced cost) of a noxious drug accompanied by conditioned stimuli (i.e., the taste of cod liver oil and the smell of a rose; Olness & Ader, 1992). Despite its apparently beneficial results in a single patient, this trial has not been repeated. Conditioning effects have also been indicated in the occurrence of asthma attacks (Dekker, Pelser, & Groen, 1957). The evidence also indicates that conditioning plays a prominent role in the placebo component of many drug and other therapies; the effectiveness of pharmacological agents longer than pharmacokinetically expected is probably explained by the accompanying placebo effects (Ader, 1989).

Kirsch (1997) reported, however, that the tenets of classical conditioning do not explain a variety of empirical outcomes (e.g., the production by a conditioned stimulus of an outcome opposite to that produced by the unconditioned stimulus). Kirsch and colleagues (Montgomery & Kirsch, 1997) have found evidence that conditioned responses in humans are mediated by the expectations of the individual (i.e., conditioning produces cognitive anticipation that in turn induces the expected outcome).

Differential Susceptibility to Nocebo Effects

Many of the studies reviewed indicate that some people are susceptible to nocebo effects in given circumstances and others are not. Many people who have "refractory epilepsy" can be induced to display seizurelike behavior by taking an inert substance that they have been told will cause seizures; however, other people who have "refractory epilepsy" and patients who have true epilepsy cannot be induced to have seizurelike behavior when exposed to the same stimuli. The attack rates of sociogenic illness in school outbreaks range from 6% to 48% and imply that 52%–94% of students exposed to similar stimuli do not become ill with the symptoms experienced by their classmates. The reason why some people are susceptible to nocebo influences under given circumstances and other people are not susceptible are unclear, although at least one plausible hypothesis corresponds to the available evidence.

A society's social structure and process may influence susceptibility to nocebo effects. A social structure is a system of institutions, each of which has designated roles, including both occupational and nonoccupational roles (e.g., parent, member of a choir, or chairperson of the Parent–Teacher Association). Social roles are sets of behavioral expectations associated with specific societal positions, each of which has differential status, power, and access to societal resources. Social roles may be critical determinants of a person's identity and susceptibility to nocebo phenomena. People who find their social positions intolerable or unavoidable are at increased risk for nocebo experiences, as indicated by reviews of sociogenic outbreaks (Colligan & Murphy, 1979; Sirois, 1974) and as exemplified by the June bug outbreak (Kerckhoff & Back, 1968). Sirois determined that sociogenic outbreaks occurred more frequently during periods of social disruption, perhaps as a result of disrupted social roles and the status associated with such roles.

Translation of Expectations Into Expected Experiential, Behavioral, and Physiological Outcomes

The mechanisms by which a negative expectation produces the expected experiential, behavioral, and physiological outcomes have not been determined. Several plausible, possibly interrelated, mechanisms are relevant to different combinations of outcomes. Prospective research on this matter is limited by ethical constraints regarding the use of procedures that might effect painful or otherwise harmful outcomes.

Experiential Outcomes

Empirical evidence for the theory of cognitive dissonance (Festinger, 1957) indicates that people who are induced to lie about or to exaggerate symptoms or sickness may subsequently begin to believe and experience what was initially a deception (Bayer, 1985). The inconsistency in beliefs about some topic—cognitive dissonance—is uncomfortable to the believer and impels resolution through the adoption of one of the inconsistent beliefs and the forgetting or denial of the other. Bayer suggested that individuals believe and incorporate the messages implied by their own behavior.

Behavioral Outcomes

A society's social structure and process also might foster specific expectations by providing behavioral models, rewards for imitation of the behavior, and an inculcation of values promoting the behavior. Observations that specific behaviors occur and are rewarded and valued lead to the expectation that this is the behavior to be performed in appropriate circumstances. Widom (1989) proposed that the "cycle of violence," in which early experiences of violence are associated with subsequent violent behavior during adolescence and adulthood, occurs through modeling, encouragement, and reinforcement (Bandura & Walters, 1963). Other researchers have shown how pain behavior is modeled on the behavior of others (Craig, 1975; Craig & Coren, 1975). Some investigators have argued that behavior associated with use of alcohol and other drugs is the result of learned behavior as much as or, in some instances, despite the physiological effects of alcohol or other drugs (Fillmore & Vogel-Sprott, 1992; Kirsch, 1997; McAndrew & Edgerton, 1969). Conditions such as hypochondria are also thought to have etiologies in the early modeling and reward of sickness behavior (Barsky et al., 1986). The cultural environment provides symptoms and sicknesses that, given motivation and valued models, are guides for adoption and performance; concepts of a sickness include ideas about how the patient is supposed to behave.

Physiological Outcomes

Although the translation of subjective cognitive and affective experiences into physiological outcomes is a relatively uncharted region of knowledge, several clues suggest how this translation might occur. There is also evidence for the physiological mechanisms involved in placebo effects. For example, the placebo effects of reduced pain after a tooth extraction are mitigated by the administration of naloxone, an opiate inhibitor (Levine, Gordon, & Fields, 1978).

Cognitive events, such as expectation, appear to have physiological aspects. In a recent study, Drevets et al. (1995) examined the flow of blood in the brain immediately after the anticipation of electrical shock to specific body parts. Participants were told to expect to be shocked in their right big toe; blood flow decreased in areas of the somatosensory area of the brain that deal with facial sensation, particularly facial expressions of emotion, while the area responsive to the big toe maintained its blood flow. Results of this experiment indicated that the expectation of pain (and other stimuli) had specific neurological consequences corresponding to the contents of the expectation. The expectation might not induce pain, but it directs attention to the perception of the pain, and it might lower the pain thresholds.

Research in the field of psychoneuroimmunology has shown diverse associations between cognitive and affective states and between neurological and immunological processes. In 1942, Cannon proposed a physiological mechanism, "persistent excessive activity of the sympathico-adrenal system" (p. 177), that was associated with the fear response and that might account for voodoo death. More recently, Ader and Cohen (1993) reviewed evidence on the immunological effects of conditioned responses (e.g., immunosuppression); there is experimental support for several mechanisms, including reduction of T cell immunity and the production of catecholamines. For example, one meta-analysis indicated that depression is associated with a diminution of immune function as measured by several markers (Herbert & Cohen, 1993).

Finally, there is evidence that certain psychological events have been associated with cardiac events (e.g., life-threatening arrhythmias). Some of the provoking stimuli were emotions such as anger, which may not be directly relevant to nocebo effects, whereas other stimuli were associated with fear and a sense of lack of control and could have been more directly related to nocebo effects (Reich, 1985). The arrhythmias are thought to be produced by neurally generated electrical stimuli to the heart rather than, as in psychoneuroimmunological effects, by means of immunological processes. Although many people who have psychologically induced arrhythmia have detectable underlying heart conditions, some do not (Reich, 1985). In a study of 117 survivors of life-threatening arrhythmias, Reich, DeSilva, Lown, and Murawski (1981) found that more than half of the patients who had no detectable cardiac pathology had experienced a negative psychological event preceding the life-threatening cardiac events. In comparison, less than 16% of the patients who had known cardiac pathology had experienced such a psychological event.

IMPLICATIONS

Results of a broad range of studies indicate that the presence in an individual of socially acquired negative expectations and the emotions with which they are associated facilitate the realization of the expectation. Beliefs can make people sick as well as healthy. The nocebo phenomenon is a little-recognized facet of culture that might be responsible for a substantial variety of pathology throughout the world. However, the evidence for this phenomenon is incomplete and ambiguous, and the extent of the phenomenon is not yet known. There is evidence that mental states such as depression affect pathological outcomes, independent of other risk factors; that symptoms may be caused by experimentally induced expectations; and that symptoms may spread in communities by being witnessed or reported. Social, psychological, and physiological mechanisms might account for the different facets of nocebo outcomes.

There are several implications of the nocebo phenomenon with regard to public health and clinical practice. First, the nocebo phenomenon is a side effect of human culture. The nocebo phenomenon suggests that the categories of a society's ethnomedicine not only describe the conditions of sickness thought to exist but that they also might foster those conditions by establishing expectations that they could occur. Furthermore, societies provide behavioral models for the manifestation of sicknesses, reward the adoption of these models, and manifest values supporting such behavior. Thus, a cultural system usually thought to serve a healing function may also have a paradoxical side effect: fostering those same pathologies that it strives to prevent or heal. Researchers should more systematically explore the ways in which, like the placebo phenomenon, the expectations of the nocebo phenomenon translate diverse cultural beliefs into physiological processes. The assessment of the extent of this noxious facet of ethnomedicines, including the Western system of biomedicine, is an important public health challenge.

Second, the methodological and medical issue that concerned Kennedy (who named the nocebo phenomenon in 1961) has not been addressed. In the assessment of the medical benefits of proposed therapies, the candidate therapy is usually (or optimally) compared with a standard treatment, a placebo treatment, or both. Reported side effects of therapies are determined in the following ways: (a) Any drug is ascribed the side effects of the broader class of drugs to which it belongs (i.e., if Drug X is the newest form of Drug A, then Drug X is assumed to have the side effects attributed to Drug A regardless of Drug X's own specific consequences); (b) before marketing a therapy, the potential side effects are determined by comparing them with standard treatment, a placebo treatment, or both; and (c) other side effects are determined by postmarketing surveillance, which uses physician reports of adverse events that patients experience after using the drug. Personnel at a major pharmaceutical company (T. Woodward, personal communication, October 1997), have estimated that in "mature drugs" (i.e., those that have been available and used for a relatively long time), more than 50% of the reported side effects are determined using postmarketing surveillance. In postmarketing surveillance, it is assumed that what occurs after the administration of the therapy in question is its consequence—an error of logic referred to as "post hoc, ergo propter hoc" (i.e., sequence, therefore consequence). Kennedy pointed out the importance of separating the effects of the therapy per se from the associated nocebo effects in the patients to whom the therapy was applied. Although Kennedy did not propose a method to separate nocebo from "true" side effects, such a procedure might be imagined in which side effects would be compared after the true therapy or procedure and a nocebo therapy or procedure.

Third, and more immediately practical, if communication about pathological conditions serves not only to describe but also to prescribe sickness by fostering expectations, then the public health community and health care practitioners must be cautious in their communications. Informed consent may be an invitation to pathology. Barsky (1988) argued that the increase in reported morbidity and disability during recent decades may have resulted from an increased awareness of and attention to health matters, the inclusion of more and more issues as "medical," and a medical and commercial environment that fosters fears about a multitude of symptoms. More needs to be known about how health messages affect audiences. Such knowledge may enhance the ability to minimize the pathological consequences of negative messages. The placebo–nocebo phenomenon suggests that it may be healthier to err on the side of optimism.

REFERENCES

Ader, R. (1989). Conditioning effects in pharmacotherapy and the incompleteness of the double-blind, crossover design. *Integrative Psychiatry, 6,* 165–170.

Ader, R., & Cohen N. (1982). Behaviorally conditioned immunosuppression and murine systemic lupus erythematosus. *Science, 215,* 1534–1536.

Ader, R., & Cohen N. (1991). The influence of conditioning on immune responses. In R. Ader & D. L. Felten (Eds.), *Psychoneuroendocrinology* (2nd ed., pp. 611–646). New York: Academic Press.

Ader, R., & Cohen, N. (1993). Psychoneuroimmunology: Conditioning and stress. *Annual Review of Psychology, 44,* 53–85.

American Psychiatric Association. (1980). *Diagnostic and statistical manual of mental disorders* (3rd ed.). Washington, DC: Author.

Anda, R., Williamson, D., Jones, C., Macera, C., Eaker, E., Glassman, A., & Marks, J. (1993). Depressed affect, hopelessness, and the risk of ischemic heart disease in a cohort of U.S. adults. *Epidemiology, 4,* 285–294.

Andrykowski, M. A., Jacobsen, P. B., Marks, E., Gorfinkle, K., Hakes, T. B., Kaufman, R. J., Currie, V. E., Holland, J. C., & Redd, W. H. (1988). Prevalence, predictors, and course of anticipatory nausea in women receiving adjuvant chemotherapy for breast cancer. *Cancer, 62,* 2607–2613.

Arcidiacono, S., Brand, J. I., Coppenger, W., & Calder, R. A. (1990). Mass sociogenic illness in a day-care center—Florida. *Morbidity and Mortality Weekly Report, 31,* 301–304.

Bandura, A., & Walters, R. H. (1963). *Social learning and personality development.* New York: Holt, Rinehart, & Winston.

Barsky, A. J. (1988). The paradox of health. *New England Journal of Medicine, 318,* 14–18.

Barsky, A. J., Cleary, P. D., Barnett, M. C., Christiansen, C. L., & Ruskin, J. N. (1994). The accuracy of symptom reporting by patients complaining of palpitations. *American Journal of Medicine, 97,* 214–221.

Barsky, A. J., Coeytaux, R. R., Sarnie, N. K., & Cleary, P. D. (1993). Hypochondriacal patients' beliefs about good health. *American Journal of Psychiatry, 150,* 1085–1089.

Barsky, A. J., Wyshak, G., & Klerman, G. L.. (1986). Hypochondriasis: An evaluation of the *DSM-III* criteria in medical outpatients. *Archives of General Psychiatry, 43,* 493–500.

Bayer, T. L. (1985). Weaving a tangled web: The psychology of deception and self-deception in psychogenic pain. *Social Science and Medicine, 5,* 517–527.

Black, D. W., Warrack, G., & Winokur, G. (1985a). Excess mortality among psychiatric patients. *Journal of the American Medical Association, 253,* 58–61.

Black, D. W., Warrack, G., & Winokur, G. (1985b). The Iowa Record-Linkage Study: II. Excess mortality among patients with 'functional' disorders. *Archives of General Psychiatry, 42,* 82–88.

Bruce, M. L., Leaf, P. J., Rozal, G. P. M., Florio, L., & Hoff, R. A. (1994). Psychiatric status and 9 year mortality data in the New Haven Epidemiologic Catchment Area Study. *American Journal of Psychiatry, 151,* 716–721.

Bovbjerg, D. H., Redd, W. H., Maier, L. A., Holland, J. C., Lesko, L. M., Niedzwiecki, D., Rubin, S. C., & Hakes, T. B. (1990). Anticipatory immune suppression and nausea in women receiving cyclic chemotherapy for ovarian cancer. *Journal of Consulting and Clinical Psychology, 58,* 153–157.

Cannon, W. B. (1942). Voodoo death. *American Anthropologist, 44,* 169–181.

Cohen, R. J., & Suter, C. (1982). Hysterical seizures: Suggestion as a provocative EEG test. *Annals of Neurology, 11,* 391–395.

Colligan, M. J., & Murphy, L. R. (1979). Mass psychogenic illness in organizations: An overview. *Journal of Occupational Psychology, 52,* 77–90.

Colligan, M. J., & Stockton, W. (1978, June). The mystery of assembly-line hysteria. *Psychology Today,* pp. 93–116.

Conti, S., Savron, G., Bartolucci, G., Grandi, S., Magelli, C., Semprini, F., Saviotti, F. M., Trombini, G., Fava, G. A., & Magnani, B. (1989). Cardiac neurosis and psychopathology. *Psychotherapy and Psychosomatics, 52,* 88–91.

Craig, K. D. (1975). Social modelling determinants of pain processes. *Pain, 1,* 375–378.

Craig, K. D., & Coren, S. (1975). Signal detection analyses of social modelling influences on pain expressions. *Journal of Psychosomatic Research, 19,* 105–112.

Dekker, E., Pelser, H. E., & Groen, J. (1957). Conditioning as a cause of asthmatic attacks: A laboratory study. *Journal of Psychosomatic Research, 2,* 97–108.

Drevets, W. C., Burton, J., Videen, T. O., Snyder, A. Z., Simpson, J. R., Jr., & Raichle, M. E. (1995). Blood flow changes in human somatosensory cortex during anticipated stimulation. *Nature, 373,* 249–252.

Dupuy, H. J. (1977). A concurrent validational study of the NCHS general well-being schedule. In *Vital and health statistics* (Series 2, No. 73, DHEW Pub. No. HRA 78–1347). Washington, DC: U.S. Government Printing Office.

Eaker, E., Pinsky, J., & Castelli, W. P. (1992). Myocardial infarction and coronary death among women: Psychosocial predictors from a 20-year follow-up of women in the Framingham Study. *American Journal of Epidemiology, 135,* 854–864.

Eastwell, H. D. (1982). Voodoo death and the mechanism for dispatch of the dying in East Arnhem, Australia. *American Anthropologist, 84,* 5–18.

Engel, G. L. (1968). A life setting conducive to illness: The giving-up–give-up complex. *Annals of Internal Medicine, 69,* 293–300.

Evans, R. W. (1992). Some observations on whiplash injuries. *Neurology Clinics, 10,* 975–977.

Festinger, L. (1957). *A theory of cognitive dissonance.* Palo Alto, CA: Stanford University Press.

Fillmore, M., & Vogel-Sprott, M. (1992). Expected effect of caffeine on motor performance predicts the type of response to placebo. *Psychopharmacology, 106,* 209–214.

Fishbain, D. A., Rosomoff, J., Cutler, R. B., & Rosomoff, R. S. (1995). Secondary gain concept: A review of the scientific evidence. *Clinical Journal of Pain, 11,* 6–21.

Frasure-Smith, N., Lespérance, F., & Talajic, M. (1993). Depression following myocardial infarction: Impact on 6-month survival. *Journal of the American Medical Association, 270,* 1819–1825.

Friedman, H. S., & Booth-Kewley, S. (1987). The "disease-prone personality": A meta-analytic view of the construct. *American Psychologist, 42,* 539–555.

Guggenheim, F. G., & Smith, G. R. (1995). Somatoform disorders. In H. I. Kaplan & B. J. Saddock (Eds.), *Comprehensive textbook of psychiatry* (pp. 1251–1270). Baltimore: Williams & Wilkins.

Hahn, R. A. (1995). *Sickness and healing: An anthropological perspective.* New Haven, CT: Yale University Press.

Herbert, T. B., & Cohen, S. (1993). Depression and immunity: A meta-analytic review. *Psychological Bulletin, 113,* 472–486.

Hunter, R. C. A., Lohrenz, J. G., & Schwartzman, A. E. (1964). Nosophobia and hypochondriasis in medical students. *Journal of Nervous and Mental Disease, 139,* 147–152.

Jewett, D. L., Fein, G., & Greenberg, M. H. (1990). A double-blind study of symptom provocation to determine food sensitivity. *New England Journal of Medicine, 323,* 429–433.

Kaplan, H. I., & Sadock, B. J. (Eds.). (1995). *Comprehensive textbook of psychiatry.* Baltimore: Williams & Wilkins.

Kellner, R., Wiggins, R. G., & Pathak, D. (1986). Hypochondriacal fears and beliefs in medical students. *Archives of General Psychiatry, 43,* 487–489.

Kennedy, W. P. (1961). The nocebo reaction. *Medical World, 91,* 203–205.

Kerckhoff, A. C., & Back, K. W. (1968). *The June bug: A study of hysterical contagion.* New York: Appleton-Century-Crofts.

Kirsch, I. (1997). Specifying nonspecifics: Psychological mechanisms of placebo effects. In A. Harrington (Ed.), *The placebo effect: Interdisciplinary explorations* (pp. 166–186). Cambridge, MA: Harvard University Press.

Lancman, M. E., Asconape, J. J., Craven, W. J., Howard, G., & Penry, J. K. (1994). Predictive value of induction of psychogenic seizures by suggestion. *Annals of Neurology, 35,* 359–361.

Lester, D. (1972). Voodoo death: Some new thoughts on an old explanation. *American Anthropologist, 74,* 386–390.

Levine, J. D., Gordon, N. C., & Fields, H. L. (1978). The mechanism of placebo analgesia. *The Lancet, 23,* 654–657.

Lewis, G. (1987). Fear of sorcery and the problem of death by suggestion. *Social Science and Medicine, 24,* 997–1010.

Luparello, T. J., Leist, N., Lourie, C. H., & Sweet, N. (1970). The interaction of psychologic stimuli and pharmacologic agents on airway reactivity in asthmatic subjects. *Psychosomatic Medicine, 32,* 509–513.

Luparello, T., Lyons, H. A., Bleecker, E. R., & McFadden, E. R., Jr. (1968). Influences of suggestion on airway reactivity in asthmatic subjects. *Psychosomatic Medicine, 30,* 819–825.

Mackenzie, J. N. (1896). The production of the so-called 'rose cold' by means of an artificial rose. *American Journal of Medical Science, 91,* 45–57.

Mauss, M. (1926). Effet physique chez l'individu de l'idée de mort sugerée par la collectivité [Physical effect in the individual of the idea of death suggested by the collectivity]. *Journal de Psychologie Normale et Pathologique, 23,* 653–669.

McAndrew, C., & Edgerton, R. B. (1969). *Drunken comportment: A social explanation.* Chicago: Aldine-Atherton.

McDermott, F. T. (1993). Reduction in cervical 'whiplash' after new motor vehicle accident legislation in Victoria. *Medical Journal of Australia, 158,* 720–721.

Mechanic, D. (1972). Social psychologic factors affecting the presentation of bodily complaints. *New England Journal of Medicine, 286,* 1132–1139.

Mechanic, D., & Volkart, E. H. (1960). Illness behavior and medical diagnoses. *Journal of Health and Human Behavior, 1,* 86–94.

Mendelson, G. (1986). Chronic pain and compensation: A review. *Journal of Pain and Symptom Management, 1,* 135–144.

Mills, H., & Horne, G. (1986). Whiplash—Manmade disease? *New Zealand Medical Journal, 99,* 73–74.

Modan, B., Swartz, T. A., Tirosh, M., Costin, C., Weissenberg, E., Donagi, A., Acker, C., Revach, M., & Vettorazzi, G. (1983). The Arjenyattah epidemic: A mass phenomenon: Spread and triggering factors. *Lancet, 24,* 1472–1474.

Montgomery, G. H., & Kirsch, I. (1997). Classical conditioning and the placebo effect. *Pain, 72,* 107–113.

Myers, M. G., Cairns, J. A., & Singer, J. (1987). The consent form as a possible cause of side effects. *Clinical Pharmacology and Therapy, 42,* 250–253.

Newman, S. C., & Bland, R. C. (1991). Mortality in a cohort of patients with schizophrenia: A record linkage study. *Canadian Journal of Psychiatry, 36,* 239–245.

Olness, K., & Ader, R. (1992). Conditioning as an adjunct in the pharmacology of lupus erythematosus. *Journal of Developmental and Behavioral Pediatrics, 13,* 124–125.

Pavlov, I. P. (1960). *Conditioned reflexes* (G. V. Anrep, Trans.). Oxford, England: Oxford University Press. (Original work published 1927)

Phillips, D. P. (1974). The influence of suggestion on suicide: Substantive and theoretical implications of the Werther effect. *American Sociological Review, 39,* 340–354.

Phillips, D. P. (1977). Motor vehicle fatalities increase just after publicized suicide stories. *Science, 196,* 1464–1465.

Phillips, D. P., & Carstensen, L. L. (1986). Clustering of teenage suicides after television news stories about suicide. *New England Journal of Medicine, 315,* 685–689.

Pogge, R. C. (1963). The toxic placebo: Part I. Side and toxic effects reported during the administration of placebo medicine. *Medical Times, 91,* 773–778.

Reich, P. (1985). Psychological predisposition to life-threatening arrhythmias. *Annual Review of Medicine, 36,* 397–405.

Reich, P., DeSilva, R. A., Lown, B., & Murawski, B. J. (1981). Acute psychological disturbances preceding life threatening arrhythmias. *Journal of the American Medical Association, 246,* 233–235.

Reid, J., & Williams, N. (1984). Voodoo death in Arnhem land: Whose reality? [Commentary]. *American Anthropological Association, 84,* 121–133.

Rohling, M. L., Binder, L. M., & Langhinrichsen-Rohling, J. (1995). Money matters: A meta-analytic review of the association between financial compensation and the experience and treatment of chronic pain. *Health Psychology, 14,* 537–547.

Rosenzweig, P., Brohier, S., & Zipfel, A. (1993). The placebo effect in healthy volunteers: Influence of experimental conditions on the adverse events profile during phase I studies. *Clinical Pharmacology and Therapeutics, 54,* 578–583.

Ryle, J. A. (1948). The twenty-first Maudsley lecture: Nosophobia. *Journal of Mental Science, 394,* 1–17.

Schachter, S., & Singer, J. E. (1962). Cognitive, social, and physiological determinants of emotional state. *Psychological Review, 69,* 379–399.

Schrader, H., Obelienniene, D., Bovim, G., Surkiene, D., Mickeviciene, D., Mickeviciene, I., & Sand, T. (1996). Natural evolution of late whiplash syndrome outside the medicolegal context. *Lancet, 347,* 1207–1211.

Schweiger, A., & Parducci, A. (1981). Nocebo: The psychologic induction of pain. *Pavlovian Journal of Biological Science, 16,* 140–143.

Sirois, F. (1974). Epidemic hysteria. *Acta Psychiatrica Scandinavia, 51,* 7–44.

Sirois, F. (1975). À propos de la fréquence des épidémies d'hystérie [Regarding the frequency of epidemics of hysteria]. *Union Medicale de Canada, 104,* 121–123.

Sternbach, R. A. (1964). The effects of instructional sets on autonomic responsivity. *Psychophysiology*, *1*, 67–72.

U.S. Surgeon General. (1989). *Reducing the health consequences of smoking: 25 years of progress* (DHHS Pub. No. CDC 89–8411). Rockville, MD: U.S. Department of Health and Human Services.

Weisman, A. D., & Hackett, T. P. (1961). Predilection to death: Death and dying as a psychiatric problem. *Psychosomatic Medicine*, *23*, 232–256.

Weissman, M. M., Markowitz, J. S., Ouellette, R., Greenwald, S., & Kahn, J. P. (1990). Panic disorder and cardiovascular/cerebrovascular problems: Results from a community survey. *American Journal of Psychiatry*, *147*, 1504–1508.

Wells, K. B., Stewart, A., Hays, R. D., Burnam, M. A., Rogers, W., Daniels, M., Berry, S., Greenfield S., & Ware, J. (1989). The functioning and well-being of depressed patients. *Journal of the American Medical Association*, *262*, 914–919.

Widom, C. S. (1989). The cycle of violence. *Science*, *244*, 160–166.

Woods, S. M., Natterson, J., & Silverman, J. (1966). Medical students' disease: Hypochondriasis in medical education. *Journal of Medical Education*, *41*, 785–790.

15

EXPECTANCIES: THE IGNORED COMMON FACTOR IN PSYCHOTHERAPY

JOEL WEINBERGER AND ANDREW EIG

Most psychotherapy outcome research comes to two conclusions. First, psychotherapy is effective. Second, different kinds of treatment are about equally effective. If there are reliable differences between different kinds of treatments, they appear to be much smaller than would be predicted by the theories underlying the treatments. Reviewers (Lambert & Bergin, 1994; Lambert, Shapiro, & Bergin, 1986; Luborsky, Singer, & Luborsky, 1975; Stiles, Shapiro, & Elliott, 1986), meta-analyses (D. A. Shapiro & Shapiro, 1982; Smith, Glass, & Miller, 1980), and the best individual studies (Elkin et al., 1989; Sloane, Staples, Cristol, Yorkston, & Whipple, 1975) all agree on these points.

The first bit of news is reassuring; it is nice to know that psychotherapists and their patients have not been engaging in an elaborate, time-consuming, and expensive waste of time, as some have alleged (e.g., Brody, 1983; Eysenck, 1966). The second finding, often termed *outcome equivalence*, is more problematic. How can diverse treatments, whose philosophies and treatment techniques seem to be at odds with one another, be equivalent? Apparently, the reasons given by theorists for why their pet therapies work may not be correct. Psychologists may know that psychotherapy works, but they do not seem to have solid answers about why or how. One explanation that has received much currency today is that there are similarities underlying these apparently diverse treatments. These "common factors" are then called on to explain outcome equivalence. The differences between treatments then become unimportant. They are relatively irrelevant to outcome; they are cachet or window dressing. Common factors are deemed to be the true sources of therapeutic change.[1]

The usual argument is that all forms of psychotherapy use these common factors to similar degrees. Weinberger (1995) has presented a different view. He favored the common factor explanation of outcome equivalence but argued that the different schools have emphasized certain of these factors to the relative neglect of others. Outcome equivalence is then as much a product of the neglect of common factors as it is of their use. Weinberger identified five common factors strongly supported by empirical research and traced their emphasis or lack thereof in the psychodynamic, humanistic–experimental, behavioral, and cognitive approaches to psychotherapeutic treatment: the therapeutic relationship, expectations, confronting or facing problems, experiences of mastery or cognitive control over problems, and attributions of therapeutic outcome.

The therapeutic relationship is emphasized by the psychodynamic and humanistic–experimental treatments. It is relatively neglected by the cognitive and behavioral approaches. Confronting issues is most central to the behavioral treatments and most neglected by the psychodynamic and humanistic–experiential approaches. Provision of mastery experiences holds a central place in cognitive therapy but is relatively neglected by the psychodynamic and humanistic–experiential approaches. Expectations and attributions are not emphasized by any major school of psychotherapy. They are therefore the most neglected of the common factors. *Expectations* usually refer to expectancies going into treatment; *attributions* usually refer to expectancies following treatment. They can therefore be lumped together under a metafactor of expectancies.

In this chapter, we focus on the almost universally ignored factor of expectancies. We review research and provide clinical material that demonstrates the power of expectancies in human functioning generally and in psychotherapy in particular. We then discuss its place in the major types of psychotherapy and why it tends to be ignored in systematic formulations of these treatments.[2] Next, we discuss the treatment implications of taking

---

[1]Although this idea of common factors has become popular only recently, it has a long history that probably began with Rosenzweig (1936). Arkowitz (1992), Kleinke (1994), and Weinberger (1993) all have reviewed this history. Goldfried (1982) has reprinted many of the original papers.

[2]This review focuses on individual psychotherapy. There is also a huge literature on group and family psychotherapy. Expectancies are also relevant to these forms of treatment. Furthermore, in family treatment, they are often explicitly addressed (e.g., Haley, 1963).

expectancies seriously. Finally, we argue that despite its critical importance to psychotherapy outcome, there is more to psychotherapeutic treatment than expectancies and relate this point to another neglected treatment issue: long-term psychotherapy.

POWER OF EXPECTANCIES

Placebo Effects

There are overwhelming data attesting to the power of expectancies in medical treatment. This usually falls under the rubric of placebo effects. In these studies, a supposedly medically active intervention is compared with a treatment alike in every way except for the hypothesized medically active ingredient. The prototypical experiment involves comparing the effects of a sugar pill with an experimental drug. Surgical procedures have also been tested in this manner. The idea behind such studies is to determine whether a procedure is efficacious or "only" a placebo. That is, the experiment compares medical procedures with expectancies set up by mimicking those procedures. Besides providing a rigorous test for experimental medical procedures, these studies attest to the power of placebos or expectancies. Cure rates are often astonishingly high in the placebo control groups. For example, Volgyesi (1954) found placebos to be far more effective than no treatment for patients suffering from bleeding ventricular and duodenal ulcers. He reported a 70% placebo cure rate. Boissel et al. (1986) reported a 77% success rate for the placebo treatment of angina pectoris. Thomsen, Bretlau, Tos, and Johnsen (1983) examined placebo surgery on patients suffering from Méniere's disease. They also found a 77% success rate for the placebo treatment. The active surgical procedure had only a 70% success rate. Many more such examples can be found in the reviews of Critelli and Neumann (1984), Horvath (1988), Kirsch (1985, 1990), Ross and Buchalew (1983), Ross and Olson (1982), A. K. Shapiro and Morris (1978), and Turner, Gallimore, and Fox-Henning (1980). Kirsch's review has shown that placebos can be effective analgesics, tranquilizers, and stimulants. They can create or reduce sensitivity to stimulation and to pain. They can produce or inhibit arousal, aggressiveness, social anxiety, and drowsiness. In other words, placebos and therefore expectancies can affect just about anything. A. K. Shapiro and Morris (1978) argued that most medical procedures before the 20th century owed their effectiveness to placebo or expectancy. Thus, expectancy is an extremely powerful variable in human health functioning.

A well-known and dramatic clinical vignette can demonstrate the power of this phenomenon much more strongly than the mere recitation of data. Klopfer (1957) reported that a patient with advanced cancer persuaded his physician to try a new experimental cancer drug on him. Within 2 weeks, there was virtually no cancerous tissue left. After a couple of months of complete health, this patient read that the drug had proved ineffective in clinical trials. He almost immediately relapsed. His physician recognized what was happening and convinced him that a double dose of the drug would be effective. The patient again recovered and remained well for another couple of months. However, once more, he had the misfortune of reading that the drug had been declared completely ineffective. His cancer returned and he died within days.

Educational and Experimenter Expectancy Effects

Expectancies are also powerful in educational settings. Students often perform up (or down) to teacher expectations (Jussim & Eccles, 1992; Rosenthal, 1973; Rosenthal & Jacobson, 1968). Such effects often last well beyond the student–teacher interactions that caused them. They can have profound effects on long-term student expectations and performance (Jussim, 1986). The implications for female and minority school achievement are obvious.

Interactions need not be meaningful for expectancies to show effects. A huge literature, spearheaded by Rosenthal (1966), shows that the expectancies of an experimenter in a psychology experiment can powerfully affect results. In a typical study, one group of experimenters is led to believe that the results will be in one direction, whereas another group is told that they will be in the opposite direction. The results of hundreds of studies demonstrate that experimenters find what they expect to find. This is not a consequence of fraud or subterfuge. The experimenters thought they were conducting the studies honestly and were often surprised when informed of the experimental manipulation and its outcome. Rosenthal and Rubin (1978) provided a comprehensive review of this work. These studies have led to the advocacy of double-blind experiments. They also show, unequivocally, the power of expectancies. In experimenter expectancy studies, interactions are brief and relatively neutral. Furthermore, the participant has no stake in the outcome and the experimenter is not trying to influence him or her (quite the reverse; the experimenter wants to exert as little influence as possible to avoid biasing the results). Imagine, then, the potential influence of expectancies in psychotherapy. This is a situation in which interactions are ongoing and emotionally charged and in which the patient and therapist both have large stakes in the outcome.

Explanatory Style

Expectancies do not have to be activated through environmental manipulations. People come equipped with chronic, highly accessible expectancies. These are readily observed in stereotypes. There are also documented individual differences in chronic expectancies that relate to physical and psychological health. Peterson and Seligman (1984) and Peterson, Maier, and Seligman (1993) have summarized data showing that people have characteristic and relatively stable expectancies concerning the consequences of negative events. They called these traitlike characteristics "explanatory style" or "attributional style." They have found that explanatory style predicts mood change, psychotherapy outcome, and even longevity.

EXPECTANCIES IN PSYCHOTHERAPY

In this section, we summarize the literature on expectancies in psychotherapy. This literature is not as large as that on medical placebos but it is still compelling. There are three ways that expectancies have been examined: expectancies of people about to enter treatment, expectancies after treatment that therapeutic gains will be maintained, and the chronic expectancies that people have about the consequences of events of their lives. Before we describe the data, we present another clinical vignette as a way of demonstrating the power of placebo and expectancies in human terms.

One of us (Weinberger) was treating a child of about 10 years of age who, among other things, had difficulty sleeping. I suggested to the parents that they fill an appropriately impressive medicine bottle with tap water and tell their son that this would help him sleep. Each night they were to carefully measure out an exact amount and administer it to him. As time passed, they were to administer less and less until he slept without it. I explained to the boy that I was prescribing a powerful sleeping agent for children and that its dosage would be gradually reduced until he did not need it anymore. The intervention was working wonderfully when one day the parents came into my office in an agitated state. I asked what was wrong. They replied that the previous night when they went to get the "medication" from the refrigerator where it was stored, they discovered that the bottle was almost empty; they did not know what to do. The placebo had worked so well that the parents had come to believe in the medication. I had to remind them that it was tap water and that all they had to do was to refill the bottle. However, filling it with ordinary tap water worried them; they were afraid it would stop working, as if the original tap water had some special properties. After some discussion, I was able to convince them to refill it and the treatment went on successfully. The boy eventually did not need the "medicine," and psychotherapy was able to deal with important issues underlying his fear of sleeping. I was even able to tell him that the medication was a placebo without him suffering a negative effect or a relapse.

Pretreatment Expectancies

In most of the studies described next, patients were administered symptom and mood measures at a pretreatment visit to a clinic. At a later date, they returned to the clinic and these measures were readministered. Only then did actual treatment proceed. These investigations revealed significant positive change in the pretreatment interval (Frank, Nash, Stone, & Imber, 1963; Friedman, 1963; Kellner & Sheffield, 1971; Piper & Wogan, 1970; A. K. Shapiro, Struening, & Shapiro, 1980). The degree of pretreatment improvement was often found to be correlated with patients' treatment expectations (Friedman, 1963; Goldstein, 1960). This effect was obtained across a wide variety of treatment modalities (Howard, Kopta, Krause, & Orlinsky, 1986). Thus, Beckham (1989) found improvement immediately after the scheduling of the first cognitive therapy session. Furthermore, Frank, Gliedman, Imber, Stone, and Nash (1959) obtained improvement before the administration of a placebo.

On the basis of these and other data, Frank (1978) concluded that psychotherapy is more effective when the patient has positive expectations. Kirsch (1985, 1990) reviewed the literature extensively and came to a similar conclusion. D. A. Shapiro (1981) took this one step further and averred that expectancies can completely account for the effects of psychotherapy. In his later writings, Frank (e.g., 1983) seemed to espouse this position as well. Whatever the strength of this effect relative to other therapeutic factors (and we address this point later in this chapter), it is beyond dispute that the mere promise of treatment can lead to positive effects. This is presumably due to the creation of positive expectancies.

Posttreatment Expectancies

Even though psychotherapy tends to be effective, there is a real danger of relapse after treatment termination (see, e.g., Elkin, 1994). This has led some researchers (e.g., Brody, 1994) to conclude that the effects of psychotherapy are evanescent. However, whether patients relapse or regress seems to be at least partly a function of posttreatment expectancies. It turns out that patients' attributions about the causes of their improvement (or lack thereof) influences its stability (cf. Weinberger, 1995). When patients attribute therapeutic change to internal factors such as personality change or new coping skills, such change tends to be long term. Alternatively, if patients attribute therapeutic change to external factors such as the therapist or his or her bag of tricks, change tends to be short-lived. In the former case, the patient sees herself or himself as an effective agent and expects to remain so. In the latter case, he or she sees improvement as being caused by external forces and expects to be unable to cope when these external aids are no longer available (cf. Liberman, 1978; Weinberger, 1994). The locus of attribution (internal or external) therefore sets up self-fulfilling expectancies (Weinberger, 1995).

Bandura (1986, 1989) built an impressive body of work that clearly demonstrates the importance of posttreatment expectancies. He found that self-efficacy (i.e., the belief or expectation that one will be effective) predicted posttreatment behavior better than did the actual end-of-treatment behavior. The greater the self-efficacy, the better the posttreatment performance. Patients were able to do what they expected to be able to do and shunned or failed endeavors that they believed were beyond their coping capabilities. That is, the more effective people thought they were, the better they performed at posttreatment and the less likely they were to relapse. This perception, belief, or expectation was a better predictor of future coping than how they were actually doing at the time. It was a better predictor than their actual outcome behavior.

Personality Differences in Expectancies

Finally, the traitlike consistencies people show in their expectancies are related to psychotherapy outcome. We have already alluded to these when we mentioned Peterson and Seligman's (1984; Peterson et al., 1993) work on explanatory style.

Explanatory style refers to the way a person explains an event. There are three dimensions on which such explanations fall: internal–external, global–specific, and stable–unstable. The person can take personal responsibility or attribute the cause of the event to external forces; this is the internal–external dimension. The person can presume that the event affects many other aspects of his or her life or is unique to the situation; this is the global–specific dimension. Finally, the person can expect the consequences of the event to be long lasting or ephemeral; this is the stable–unstable dimension. If a negative event is seen as internal, global, and stable, it can have very deleterious effects. A negative event interpreted to be external, specific, and unstable is of relatively minor consequence. There is less work on positive events, and the results are not as clear. The effects of negative explanatory style are quite striking, however.

Explanatory style has been shown to predict mood changes in psychodynamic psychotherapy (Peterson, Luborsky, & Seligman, 1983), and it can predict relapse in cognitive and drug therapy (Evans et al., cited in Hollon & Garber, 1990; Hollon, Evans, & DeRubeis, 1988; Seligman et al., 1988). Negative explanatory style can also be changed by cognitive psychotherapy (Hollon & Garber, 1990; Whisman, 1993).

EXPECTANCIES AND MAJOR SCHOOLS OF PSYCHOTHERAPY

The research literature and anecdotal evidence on expectancies are compelling. Expectancies play a significant role in psychotherapy. What do the major schools of treatment have to say about them? Where do they fit in, and what part do they play in their understanding of psychotherapy? In this section, we review what the psychodynamic, cognitive, and behavioral schools say about expectancies. (We do not review the humanistic–experiential school because we could not find any statements about this factor.) We also review data on the place of expectancies in each of these schools.

Psychodynamic Psychotherapy

Freud (1905/1956) identified expectation, tiggered by hope and faith, as an important factor in psychotherapy. However, outside of assertions of this sort, there is virtually no systematic research or theory on the operation of this factor in psychodynamic psychotherapy. Instead, there are scattered reports that expectancies affect the course and outcome of psychodynamic treatment (Gomes-Schwartz, Hadley, & Strupp, 1978; Luborsky, 1984). The findings of Howard, Lueger, Maling, and Martinovich (1993) that anxious and depressed patients begin to feel hopeful in the first few weeks of psychodynamic treatment, and that this precedes symptomatic change, also speak to the power of expectancies.

There are theoretical assertions about the power of expectancies in psychodynamic psychotherapy. They are not usually thought of in these terms, however. For example, the analysis of transference (Freud, 1912/1958) involves identifying and then altering expectancies. Transference essentially involves expecting others to behave as significant others did in the past and then misconstruing their actual behavior so that it is seen to conform to these expectancies. Patients are thought to improve to the extent that their perceptions become more colored by reality and less by their transference-based expectancies (Brenner, 1982; Fenichel, 1945; Fromm-Reichman, 1950; Langs, 1982; Silverman, 1974). This point of view was most clearly articulated by Alexander and French (1946), who argued that therapist behavior that disconfirms patient transference expectancies leads to a corrective emotional experience. Horwitz (1974) reported that such corrective experiences had salutary effects in long-term psychodynamic psychotherapy. Strupp and Binder (1984) applied this principle to create a form of short-term dynamic psychotherapy. Their book is a training manual for this type of treatment and provides some data supportive of it.

One type of psychodynamically oriented psychotherapy makes explicit use of expectancies in its model of cure. Klerman and Weissman's (1982) interpersonal psychotherapy expressly aims to instill hope in depressed patients. That is, patient response expectancies, their sense of hope-lessness about their depression, are directly addressed.

For the most part, however, there is little research support for the place of expectancies in psychodynamic psychotherapy. Even in the arena of theory and of clinical case material, where psychodynamic writers focus most of their efforts, little attention is devoted to expectancies and their effects. What we have described covers much of it. Expectancies are a truly neglected aspect of this form of treatment.

Behavioral Psychotherapy

Most of the attention given to expectancies in writings on behavior therapy has fallen on one of its central therapeutic techniques: exposure. In their early writings, behaviorists attributed the ameliorative effects of exposure to learning principles such as extinction (Stampfl & Levis, 1967), reciprocal inhibition (Wolpe, 1973), and counterconditioning (Davison, 1968). Modern behavior therapists are not so sure anymore (Emmelkamp, 1982, 1994). One of the current candidates for explaining exposure effects is expectancies.

Kirsch and Henry (1977); Leitenberg, Agras, Barlow, and Oliveau (1969); and Marcia, Rubin, and Efran (1969) reported that manipulating expectancies affected responses to exposure in systematic desensitization. Lick and Bootzin (1975) concluded that disguising the therapeutic intent of systematic desensitization, to inhibit its expectancy generating potential, significantly lowered its effectiveness. In some cases, its ability to reduce anxiety was eliminated altogether. Kazdin and Wilcoxin (1976) also con-cluded that at least part of the effects of this intervention were due to the generation of positive expectancies. Southworth and Kirsch (1988) re-ported data leading to a similar conclusion for in vivo exposure. Kirsch (1990) reported that there were at least 15 studies comparing systematic desensitization with well-designed expectancy control treatments. Thirteen of these studies showed no differences in effectiveness. One reported greater effectiveness for the expectancy condition. Only one study reported better outcome for systematic desensitization. It seems that expectancy interven-tions are the equal of exposure and that at least part of the effects of exposure are due to expectancy modification.

Cognitive Therapy

Cognitive therapists allude to the role of expectancies in psycho-therapy but usually assign it secondary importance. They have conducted virtually no research on it. Only recently have they begun paying serious attention to expectancies, usually in the form of what they call "nonspecific effects" (see, e.g., Ilardi & Craighead, 1994).

Beck (1976) said that one of the goals of cognitive therapy is to enable patients to see themselves as winners. Similarly, Teasdale (1985) viewed changes in perceived controllability as being responsible for some of the success engendered by cognitive therapy. Both writers seemed to be referring to something like Bandura's (1989) concept of self-efficacy, although neither made this connection. More directly related to the effects of expectancies is Hollon and Garber's (1990) assertion that the type of depression typically treated in cognitive therapy is partly a result of patients' negative expectancies.

Despite these theoretical bows in the direction of expectancy, this factor is not central to theorizing about the effectiveness of cognitive therapy. The fundamental tenet of cognitive therapy is that change is due to alterations in the patient's characteristic ways of thinking (Beck, 1976; Beck, Rush, Shaw, & Emery, 1979). This has come to be called the "cognitive mediation hypothesis" (DeRubeis et al., 1990). Changes in expectancies are said to flow from and are secondary to these cognitive alterations.

But a great deal of data show that expectancies have their effects before any changes in thinking. It therefore cannot be a consequence of those changes. Thus, Fennell and Teasdale (1987) found that depressed patients' feelings of hopelessness about their eventual recovery, a kind of "metadepression" (the authors referred to it as depression about depression), predicted cognitive therapy outcome. Gaston, Marmar, Gallagher, and Thompson (1989) found that cognitive therapy patients who expected treatment to be efficacious had superior outcomes. In addition, Beckham (1989) reported that a substantial amount of improvement in cognitive therapy occurred after the first session has been scheduled but before it had taken place. Hollon and Beck (1994) and Whisman (1993) concluded that the cognitive mediation hypothesis has by no means been proved. They suggested that nonspecific effects may account for more of the outcome variance.

Perhaps the most thorough demonstration that cognitive mediation cannot be the sole or even major agent of change in cognitive therapy can be found in a recent review by Ilardi and Craighead (1994). They examined cognitive therapy studies that reported on the temporal course of change in depression. Seven such studies showed that, on the average, 64% of overall improvement had occurred by the 4th week of treatment; five studies showed that more than 55% of improvement had occurred by the 3rd week. The lowest level of improvement by Week 4 was slightly more than 40% (Elkin et al., 1989); the highest was 80% (Murphy, Simons, Wetzel, & Lustman, 1984). For Week 3, the lowest was slightly less than 50% (Hollon et al., cited in Mandell, 1987); the highest was slightly under 70% (Beckham, 1989). Because the specific techniques designed to facilitate changes in depressive thought are not even introduced into treatment for several sessions, and because it presumably takes a while for them to yield their effects, cognitive mediation cannot account for these changes. Ilardi and Craighead concluded that this documented early change must have been mediated by nonspecific processes, which would include expectancies. Thus, it is likely that expectancies are a factor that help to account for at least 40% of outcome variance in cognitive therapy.

EXPLAINING EFFECTS OF EXPECTANCIES IN PSYCHOTHERAPY

It seems clear that expectancies are a force in human functioning generally and in psychotherapy in particular. How do they generate their effects? The major schools of treatment have no answer because they do not consider expectancies in their models of change. From early in the history of experimental psychology, expectancies were viewed as artifacts needing to be controlled (see Kirsch, 1985, 1990; Weinberger, 1995). Much current work has maintained this focus. Thus, a great deal of discussion has been devoted to controlling for or eliminating experimenter expectancy effects, usually through the use of double-blind designs (Rosenthal & Rosnow, 1991). Relatively little attention has been devoted to understanding them and less to increasing their effects, however (see Rosenthal & Rubin, 1978).

The placebo studies that led to awareness of expectancy effects in medical and psychotherapeutic interventions have a similar history. The original investigations sought to determine whether medical interventions were effective. Because of this goal, any effects not directly attributable to the intervention of interest had to be controlled for and were of no inherent interest. Placebo control groups were designed for this purpose. Differences between placebo and experimental groups could be confidently attributed to medical effects. If there were no differences, the procedure or medication was deemed worthless. When this design was transposed to psychological interventions, many felt that such interventions were effective only insofar as they surpassed the effectiveness of the placebo group (e.g., Prioleau, Murdock, & Brody, 1983). When they did not, some reviewers argued that psychotherapy was ineffective (e.g., Brody, 1983). The effects of the placebos and the expectancies that underlay them were not considered worthy of consideration (cf. Weinberger, 1995).

PANDORA MODEL OF EXPECTANCY: HOPE

The major model of the effects of expectancies is the classic work of Frank (1973, 1978, 1982; Frank & Frank, 1991). According to Frank, patients entering psychotherapy are usually demoralized because of unsuccessful efforts to negotiate their problems. They hope and expect that psychotherapy will help them to surmount what they heretofore could not. This hope and positive expectation serve to remoralize them. The restoration of hope is the curative factor in psychotherapy. We like to think of Frank's model as the "Pandora theory of psychotherapeutic improvement."

> There were ... all the griefs and hardships to which man from that day has been subject.... At last the stream slackened, and Pandora, who had been paralyzed with fear and horror, found strength to shut her box. The only thing left in it now, however, was the one good gift the gods had put in among so many evil ones. This was hope, and since that time the hope that is in man's heart is the only thing which has made him able to bear the sorrows that Pandora brought upon him. (Codidge, 1964, p. 72)

According to Frank (1973, 1978, 1982) four factors help to mobilize hope and restore morale: (a) an emotionally charged confiding relationship; (b) a healing setting; (c) a rationale or myth that plausibly explains the patient's difficulties and offers a sensible solution; and (d) a believable treatment or ritual for restoring health. Frank collected a great deal of data supporting his model. The data cited earlier showing that improvement takes place before treatment begins were mostly generated by Frank's thinking (see Frank, 1973, for an overview of much of this work). Ilardi and Craighead (1994) made use of Frank's model to explain the positive early effects of cognitive therapy not attributable to cognitive mediation. They posited that these early effects may be due to reductions in the hopelessness that accompany entering treatment.

Frank's (1973, 1978, 1982) model is not a complete explanation of expectancy effects. The activation of hope cannot explain the fact that placebos have effects on people who are not demoralized. It also cannot explain the negative effects of placebo treatments and expectancies that are sometimes reported. How can hope lead to negative outcomes? Frank's model also cannot explain the unpleasant side effects often associated with overall positive placebo effects or the specificity often obtained in expectancy studies. Hope should lead to a general improvement in mood functioning, not to specific predictable changes (Kirsch, 1990).

Thus, although Frank's (1973, 1978, 1982) Pandora hypothesis of hope may explain some of the effects of expectancies, it does not constitute a complete account. Researchers are left having to acknowledge that although expectancies play a large role in psychotherapy outcome, they really do not know how or why.

TREATMENT IMPLICATIONS

Psychologists' understanding of the principles underlying expectancy effects in psychotherapy (or anywhere else) is extremely limited. They do, however, know a bit about how to augment such effects. In this section, we discuss some of this and how it might be applied to enhance psychotherapy.

Harris and Rosenthal (1985) identified variables that communicate expectancies in psychology experiments. These include distance, the frequency and duration of interaction, eye contact, smiling, and verbal rewards and punishments. The underlying variable seems to be interpersonal closeness, although the authors did not say so. It may be that therapists ought to try to communicate more caring to their patients. Therapists already know that a positive relationship is an important factor in successful psychotherapy (Weinberger, 1995). Perhaps this is partly because of the greater chance of communicating expectancies when people feel close. This is a researchable question and should be examined.

Frank (1982), Nau, Caputo, and Borkovec (1974), and D. A. Shapiro (1981) have found that the presentation of a credible treatment rationale (or "myth," as Frank, 1982, called it) helps to generate positive expectancies. Kazdin and Krouse (1983) found that such rationales were especially effective when they were said to be novel and scientifically based. A. K. Shapiro and Morris (1978) concluded that physician enthusiasm can enhance medical outcomes. Ilardi and Craighead (1994) reviewed evidence indicating that homework assigned early in cognitive therapy increased hope and was related to rapid early improvement. This suggests that it would be a good idea for therapists to enthusiastically explain to their patients how they believe their treatment works and how it is "cutting edge." They should probably back up this explanation with any available research findings. They should then assign some doable task that follows logically from the rationale.

These suggestions have found support in research carried out by Zwick and Attkisson (1985). Those investigators prepared patients for psychotherapy by showing them a videotape describing treatment. A control group did not view a videotape. The experimental group showed more accurate expectancies and fewer symptoms than did the control group. These results were maintained through treatment and at 1-month follow-up. Deane, Spicer, and Leathem (1992) replicated the initial effects, but the differences had evaporated by a 2-month follow-up. Therefore, the value of these findings may be considered equivocal pending future replication attempts. A more impressive finding was reported by Fennell and Teasdale (1987). They had patients, about to begin cognitive–behavior therapy, read a booklet describing the treatment and its rationale. Before the second session, the patients were asked about what they had read. Endorsement of the booklet rationale was not related to current or pretreatment depression. However, it was highly correlated with posttreatment depression. Furthermore, it predicted rapid, early (by Session 4) improvement.

The aforementioned results only scratch the surface. Researchers must also investigate individual differences; group effects are not enough. This is particularly important in a field in which treatment decisions are made idiographically, not on the basis of average (nomothetic) effects. Craig and Hennessy (1989) reviewed what is known about sex differences in expectations about psychotherapy. The data are meager. Women seem to expect therapists to be confrontational, genuine, nurturant, tolerant, and trustworthy. They expect that as patients they will be called on to be responsible and self-motivated. Men seem to expect therapists to demonstrate self-disclosure, directiveness, criticalness, and an analytic orientation. Sipps and Janeczek (1986) argued that such differences are more attributable to sex role orientation than actual gender. Perhaps therapists ought to think about these variables when they offer their rationales or assign homework.

In summary, positive expectancies can be enhanced through therapist friendly and caring behavior; enthusiasm; provision of a credible, scientifically-based rationale; and assignment of doable homework. These factors ought to be adjusted on an individual basis and may vary according to gender role endorsement. Unfortunately, little more is known. Much further research is necessary (cf. Kirsch, 1990).

ARE EXPECTANCIES EVERYTHING?

We have been focusing on the importance of expectancies to psychotherapeutic outcome, and the evidence is clear: Expectancies are critical to outcome. But is that all there is to treatment, as A. K. Shapiro and Morris (1978) and Frank and Frank (1991) suggested? We believe that the answer is no. In this section, we try to demonstrate this and to identify some other common factors that are causally relevant to psychotherapeutic outcome.

Meta-analyses have generally indicated that psychotherapy is superior to placebo control groups. Smith et al. (1980) found that psychotherapy was about twice as effective as placebo control groups. They used a relatively liberal definition of "placebo control" (i.e., anything a researcher has identified as a placebo). Barker, Funk, and Houston (1988) defined placebo controls more strictly in their meta-analysis of psychotherapy outcome studies. They found 17 studies in which the control conditions (the placebos) were as credible as the (mostly behavioral) treatments to which they were being compared. The regular treatments were about twice as effective as the controls. At follow-up, however, the gap had narrowed. Genuine treatments were still more effective but now only slightly so. These meta-analyses indicate two things. First, psychotherapy is superior to placebo. Second, placebo treatments are effective in their own right. There are also suggestions that the differences between the two diminish over time. Shea et al. (1992) reported a similar diminishing of differences between treatments and a placebo control group in their well-conducted Depression Collaborative Study. This finding needs more documentation. If it holds up, it has powerful implications. We touch on these implications in the final section of this chapter, which concerns long-term psychotherapy.

Earlier in this chapter, we cited Weinberger's (1995) arguments for the causal relevance of several common factors relevant to psychotherapeutic outcome. In addition to expectancies, he named the therapeutic relationship, exposure or confronting problems, and mastery or cognitive control. We review these factors now to determine whether they explain something of psychotherapy outcome above and beyond that explained by expectancies.

Therapeutic Relationship

Patients often attribute therapeutic improvement to a positive therapeutic relationship (Mathews et al., 1976; Rabavilas, Boulougouris, & Perissaki, 1979; Sloane et al., 1975). There are objective data that support these feelings. Klee, Abeles, and Muller (1990) reported that the therapeutic bond increased in successful, but not in unsuccessful, psychotherapy. Miller, Taylor, and West (1980) found a strong relationship between therapist empathy and outcome. Gaston, Marmar, Gallagher, and Thompson (1989) found that the therapeutic alliance accounted for more than 35% of outcome variance, even after controlling for initial symptomatology. Beutler (1989), Lambert (1992), and Waterhouse and Strupp (1984) reported that the therapeutic relationship accounted for more outcome variance than did other measured variables. Finally, Hovarth and Symonds (1991) conducted a meta-analysis that revealed that the working alliance reliably affected outcome. (See Weinberger, 1995, for more on this.)

It is clear that the therapeutic relationship is causally relevant to treatment outcome. What is not clear is why (cf. Henry, Strupp, Schacht, & Gaston, 1994; Weinberger, 1995). It may simply be a potent activator of positive expectancies, as we suggested earlier when we discussed interpersonal closeness in the context of experimenter expectancy effects. Or it may be effective in its own right. These possibilities are not mutually exclusive. Both may be correct, or the two factors may interact in a synergistic fashion.

One set of studies that points toward an independent contribution of the therapeutic relationship was conducted by Silverman and his colleagues (see Silverman & Weinberger, 1985, for a review). In those studies, a relationship-enhancing subliminal message, presented before psychotherapy sessions, led to improved outcome compared with a subliminal control message. It is difficult to see how expectancies could have played a role because patients could not consciously recognize the message. Clearly, much more research is needed to clarify this matter.

Exposure

We have reviewed evidence showing that many of the effects of exposure can be attributed to expectancies or, at least, do not surpass expectancy effects. There is a body of evidence, however, that speaks to the efficacy of exposure that cannot be attributed to expectancies. Pennebaker (1989, 1990) had participants (college students, not patients) write or talk about negative or traumatic experiences. Compared with those who wrote of other types of experiences, these individuals showed fewer stressful physiological reactions, healthier immune functioning, and fewer health problems. These effects continued for months after the intervention. It is not likely that these participants could have formed positive expectancies relating to these results. They were not recruited on the basis of any suffering. They did not know what the experimenter was after. They were participating in a psychological experiment of unknown purpose, usually for class credit or money. Interactions with experimenters were formal and brief. For these reasons, a therapeutic relationship could not have played a role in these findings either. By way of independent confirmation and extension to psychotherapy, Liberman (1978) obtained similar results for psychotherapy outcome. In one of his psychotherapy control conditions, he had patients speak into a tape recorder for 30 min. The outcome for these patients was superior to that of a control group that did not experience this intervention and similar to the treatment group. Furthermore, these results held at a 1-year follow-up. Liberman did not predict (expect) such results, and they preceded Pennebaker's work. They, too, cannot be easily explained by expectancies. Clearly, there is something causally relevant about exposure.

Mastery

Interestingly, mastery or cognitive control, so central to cognitive conceptions, has the least amount of data supporting its status as an important independent common factor. Jarrett and Nelson (1987) and Teasdale and Fennell (1982) found that the cognitive therapy techniques of hypothesis testing and logical analysis (sometimes called "Socratic dialogue") are associated with reductions in depression in the middle-to-late stages of cognitive–behavioral therapy. The efficacy of cognitive restructuring techniques in the late stages of cognitive treatment has been supported many times (DeRubeis et al., 1990; Hayes, Castonduay, & Goldfried, 1992; Persons & Burns, 1985; Teasdale & Fennell, 1982). Whisman (1993) reviewed the available evidence.

The aforementioned studies suggest a statistically significant role for cognitive mediation in cognitive therapy. The effects seem to manifest themselves late in treatment. The effects also seem to be relatively small. Recall that more than half of the gain in cognitive treatment occurs by the third or fourth session. Findings such as these have led reviewers (Hollon & Beck, 1994; Whisman, 1993) to question the value of the cognitive mediation hypothesis and to wonder whether cognitive therapy owes much of its effectiveness to nonspecific factors (expectancies and the therapeutic alliance).

LONG-TERM PSYCHOTHERAPY

The ubiquity of expectancy effects and the research that shows so much of outcome accounted for by the first few weeks of treatment leads to questions about the value of long-term psychotherapy. One can reasonably argue that long-term psychotherapy is a waste of time and money. After all, if the majority of outcome variance seems to be accounted for by the first few weeks of treatment (Ilardi & Craighead, 1994), what is going on for the remaining years of treatment? Furthermore, Smith et al. (1980) found no differences between long- and short-term psychotherapy.

The picture is not that simple, however. Patients seem to be more satisfied with long- than short-term psychotherapy (Seligman, 1995). They may be deluded, or it may be like a cognitive dissonance effect. That is, they have spent so much time and money in treatment that they need justify it by saying how worthwhile it was. Alternatively, they may know something that most psychotherapy researchers do not. We lean toward the latter conclusion.

The Smith et al. (1980) finding of no difference between short- and long-term psychotherapy is misleading. The mean length of treatment in the studies they examined was 16 weeks. This is hardly what is usually meant by "long-term treatment." All the studies cited thus far in this chapter and the vast majority of the studies cited in the psychotherapy outcome literature are really investigations of short-term psychotherapy. They have nothing to say about long-term treatment, especially treatment lasting years.

There are many studies that have examined the efficacy of long-term psychotherapy. Most of them have examined psychoanalysis and are published in psychoanalytic journals. As a result, they are generally unknown in the other fields of psychology. The best known is the Menninger Foundation Psychotherapy Research Project (see Wallerstein, 1986, for an overview), which followed patients for more than 30 years. There are many other studies (reviewed by Bachrach, Galatzer-Levy, Skolnikoff, & Waldron, 1991, and Doidge, 1993), involving hundreds of patients, with follow-ups ranging from about 2–10 years. In toto, these studies have demonstrated positive treatment outcomes, with treatment length being positively related to the overall results. These findings are in stark contrast to the findings of Smith et al. (1980). But they are based on treatment lasting years, whereas the Smith et al. results are based on treatments lasting weeks or months.

Expectancy effects are prominent early in treatment and may be the source of many of the ameliorative effects of short-term psychotherapy (cf. Ilardi & Craighead, 1994). However, other factors may play a larger role in the effects of long-term treatment. Short-term treatments may simply not allow enough time for these other factors to take effect. The satisfaction expressed by patients in long-term psychotherapy (Seligman, 1995) may then be justified. There is some research support for this view. Jones, Ghannam, Nigg, and Dyer (1993) and Jones (1998) presented data that show that the effects of psychotherapy increase steadily for a few months and then plateau. After a period of no improvement, outcome improves again, this time for years, and is maintained at follow-up.

These data suggest that the first spurt may be attributable to expectancy and (possibly) to relationship variables. The cause of the second improvement in functioning is not yet known. Admittedly, this hypothesis is currently speculative. A great deal more research would be needed to support this view. There is also a need for serious comparisons between long- and short-term psychotherapy, which are now conspicuous by their absence.

REFERENCES

Alexander, F., & French, T. M. (1946). *Psychoanalytic psychotherapy: Principles and applications*. New York: Ronald Press.

Arkowitz, H. (1992). Integrative theories of therapy. In D. K. Freedheim (Ed.), *History of psychotherapy: A century of change* (pp. 261–303). Washington, DC: American Psychological Association.

Bachrach, H. M., Galatzer-Levy, R., Skolnikoff, A., & Waldron, S. (1991). On the efficacy of psychoanalysis. *Journal of the American Psychoanalytic Association, 39*, 871–916.

Bandura, A. (1986). *Social foundations of thought and action*. Englewood Cliffs, NJ: Prentice Hall.

Bandura, A. (1989). Human agency in social cognitive theory. *American Psychologist, 44*, 1175–1181.

Barker, S. L., Funk, S. C., & Houston, B. K. (1988). Psychological treatment versus nonspecific factors: A meta-analysis of conditions that engender comparable expectations of improvement. *Clinical Psychology Review, 8*, 579–594.

Beck, A. T. (1976). *Cognitive therapy and the emotional disorders*. Madison, CT: International Universities Press.

Beck, A. T., Rush, A. J., Shaw, F. B., & Emery, G. (1979). *The cognitive therapy of depression*. New York: Guilford Press.

Beckham, E. E. (1989). Improvement after evaluation in psychotherapy of depression: Evidence of a placebo effect? *Journal of Clinical Psychology, 43*, 945–950.

Beutler, L. E. (1989). Differential treatment selection: The role of diagnosis in psychotherapy. *Psychotherapy, 26*, 271–281.

Boissel, J. P., Philippon, A. M., Gauthier, E., Schbath, J., Destors, J. M., & the B.I.S. Research Group. (1986). Time course of long-term placebo therapy effects in angina pectoris. *European Heart Journal, 7*, 1030–1036.

Brenner, C. (1982). *The mind in conflict*. Madison, CT: International Universities Press.

Brody, N. (1983). Where are the emperor's clothes? *Behavioral and Brain Sciences, 6*, 303–308.

Brody, N. (1994). .5+ or −.5: Continuity and change in personality dispositions. In T. F. Heatherton & J. Weinberger (Eds.), *Can personality change?* (pp. 59–82). Washington, DC: American Psychological Association.

Codidge, O. (Ed.). (1964). *Greek myths*. Boston: Houghton Mifflin.

Craig, S. S., & Hennessy, J. J. (1989). Personality differences and expectations about counseling. *Journal of Counseling Psychology, 36*, 401–407.

Critelli, J. W., & Neumann, K. F. (1984). The placebo: Conceptual analysis of construct in transition. *American Psychologist, 39*, 32–39.

Davison, G. C. (1968). Systematic desensitization as a counter-conditioning process. *Journal of Abnormal Psychology, 73*, 91.

Deane, F. P., Spicer, J., & Leathem, J. (1992). Effects of videotaped preparatory information on expectations, anxiety, and psychotherapy outcome. *Journal of Consulting and Clinical Psychology, 60*, 980–984.

DeRubeis, R. J., Evans, M. D., Hollon, S. D., Garvey, M. J., Grove, W. M., & Tuason, V. B. (1990). How does cognitive therapy work? Cognitive change and symptom change in cognitive therapy and pharmacotherapy for depression. *Journal of Clinical and Consulting Psychology, 58*, 862–869.

Doidge, N. (1993). *An overview of empirical studies on the efficacy of psychoanalysis and psychoanalytic psychology*. Unpublished manuscript.

Elkin, I. (1994). The NIMH Treatment of Depression Collaborative Research Program: Where we began and where we are. In A. E. Bergin & S. L. Garfield (Eds.), *Handbook of psychotherapy and behavior change* (4th ed., pp. 114–142). New York: Wiley.

Elkin, I., Shea, M. T., Watkins, J. T., Imber, S. D., Sotsky, S. M., Collins, J. F., Glass, D. R., Pilkonis, P. A., Leber, W. R., Docherty, J. P., Fiester, S. J., & Parloff, M. B. (1989). National Institute of Mental Health Treatment of Depression Collaborative Research Program: General effectiveness of treatments. *Archives of General Psychiatry, 46*, 971–988.

Emmelkamp, P. M. G. (1982). *Phobic and obsessive-compulsive disorders: Theory, research and practice.* New York: Plenum.

Emmelkamp, P. M. G. (1994). Behavior therapy with adults. In A. E. Bergin & S. L. Garfield (Eds.), *Handbook of psychotherapy and behavior change* (4th ed., pp. 379–427). New York: Wiley.

Eysenck, H. S. (1966). *The effects of psychotherapy.* New York: International Science Press.

Fenichel, O. (1945). *The psychoanalytic theory of neurosis.* New York: Norton.

Fennell, M. J., & Teasdale, J. D. (1987). Cognitive therapy for depression: Individual differences and the process of change. *Cognitive Therapy and Research, 11,* 253–271.

Frank, J. D. (1973). *Persuasion and healing.* Baltimore: Johns Hopkins University Press.

Frank, J. D. (1978). Expectation and therapeutic outcome: The placebo effect and the role induction interview. In J. D. Frank, R. Hoen-Saric, S. D. Imber, B. L. Liberman, & A. R. Stone (Eds.), *Effective ingredients in psychotherapy* (pp. 1–34). New York: Brunner/Mazel.

Frank, J. D. (1982). Therapeutic components shared by all psychotherapy. In J. H. Harvey & M. M. Parks (Eds.), *The master lecture series: Vol. 1. Psychotherapy research and behavior change* (pp. 5–38). Washington, DC: American Psychological Association.

Frank, J. D. (1983). The placebo is psychotherapy. *Behavioral and Brain Sciences, 6,* 291–292.

Frank, J. D., & Frank, J. B. (1991). *Persuasion and healing.* Baltimore: Johns Hopkins University Press.

Frank, J. D., Gliedman, L. H., Imber, S. D., Stone, A. R., & Nash, E. H. (1959). Patient's expectancies and relearning as factors determining improvement in psychotherapy. *American Journal of Psychiatry, 115,* 961–968.

Frank, J. D., Nash, E. H., Stone, A. R., & Imber, S. D. (1963). Immediate and long-term symptomatic course of psychiatric outpatients. *American Journal of Psychiatry, 120,* 429–439.

Freud, S. (1956). Psychical treatment. In J. Strachey (Ed. & Trans.), *The standard edition of the complete psychological works of Sigmund Freud* (Vol. 7, p. 289). London: Hogarth Press. (Original work published 1905)

Freud, S. (1958). Papers on technique. In J. Strachey (Ed. and Trans.), *The standard edition of the complete psychological works of Sigmund Freud* (Vol. 12, pp. 85–174). London: Hogarth Press. (Original work published 1912)

Friedman, H. J. (1963). Patient expectancy and symptom reduction. *Archives of General Psychiatry, 8,* 61–67.

Fromm-Reichman, F. (1950). *Principles of intensive psychotherapy.* Chicago: University of Chicago Press.

Gaston, L., Marmar, C. R., Gallagher, D., & Thompson, L. W. (1989). Impact of confirming patients expectations of change processes in behavioral, cognitive, and brief dynamic psychotherapy. *Psychotherapy, 3,* 296–302.

Goldfried, M. R. (Ed.). (1982). *Converging themes in psychotherapy*. New York: Springer.

Goldstein, A. P. (1960). Patient's expectancies and non-specific therapy as a basis for spontaneous remission. *Journal of Clinical Psychology, 16,* 399–403.

Gomes-Schwartz, B., Hadley, S. W., & Strupp, H. H. (1978). Individual psychotherapy and behavior therapy. *Annual Review of Psychology, 29,* 435–471.

Haley, J. (1963). *Strategies of psychotherapy*. New York: Grune & Stratton.

Harris, M. J., & Rosenthal, R. (1985). Mediation of interpersonal expectancy effects: 31 meta-analyses. *Psychological Bulletin, 97,* 363–386.

Hayes, A. M., Castonduay, L., & Goldfried, M. R. (1992). *The relationship between the focus of therapist interventions and treatment response in cognitive therapy for depression*. Manuscript submitted for publication.

Henry, W. P., Strupp, H. H., Schacht, T. E., & Gaston, L. (1994). Psychodynamic approaches. In A. E. Bergin & S. L. Garfield (Eds.), *Handbook of psychotherapy and behavior change* (4th ed., pp. 467–508). New York: Wiley.

Hollon, S. D., & Beck, A. T. (1994). Cognitive and cognitive behavioral therapies. In A. E. Bergin & S. L. Garfield (Eds.), *Handbook of psychotherapy and behavior change* (4th ed., pp. 428–466). New York: Wiley.

Hollon, S. D., Evans, M. D., & DeRubeis, R. J. (1988). Preventing relapse following treatment for depression: The cognitive pharmacotherapy project. In T. M. Field, P. M. McCabe, & N. Schneiderman (Eds.), *Stress and coping across development* (pp. 227–243). Hillsdale, NJ: Erlbaum.

Hollon, S. D., & Garber, J. (1990). Cognitive therapy for depression: A social cognitive perspective. *Personality and Social Psychology Bulletin, 16,* 58–73.

Horvath, P. (1988). Placebos as common factors in decades of psychotherapy research. *Psychological Bulletin, 104,* 214–225.

Horwitz, L. (1974). *Clinical prediction in psychotherapy*. Northvale, NJ: Jason Aronson.

Hovarth, A. O., & Symonds, B. D. (1991). Relation between working alliance and outcome in psychotherapy: A meta-analysis. *Journal of Counseling Psychology, 38,* 139–149.

Howard, K. I., Kopta, S. M., Krause, M. S., & Orlinsky, D. E. (1986). The dose–effect relationship in psychotherapy. *American Psychologist, 41,* 159–164.

Howard, K. I., Lueger, R. J., Maling, M. S., & Martinovich, Z. (1993). A phase model of psychotherapy outcome: Causal mediation of change. *Journal of Consulting and Clinical Psychology, 61,* 678–685.

Ilardi, S. S., & Craighead, W. E. (1994). The role of nonspecific factors in cognitive–behavioral therapy for depression. *Clinical Psychology: Science and Practice, 1,* 138–156.

Jarrett, R. B., & Nelson, R. O. (1987). Mechanisms of change in cognitive therapy of depression. *Behavior Therapy, 18,* 227–241.

Jones, E. E. (1998). Depression: Intervention as assessment. In J. W. Barron (Ed.), *Making diagnosis meaningful: Enhancing evaluation and treatment of psychological disorders* (pp. 267–297). Washington, DC: American Psychological Association.

Jones, E. E., Ghannam, J., Nigg, J. T., & Dyer, J. F. P. (1993). A paradigm for single-case research: The time series study of a long-term psychotherapy for depression. *Journal of Consulting and Clinical Psychology, 61,* 381–394.

Jussim, L. (1986). Self-fulfilling prophecies: A theoretical and integrative review. *Psychological Review, 93,* 429–445.

Jussim, L., & Eccles, J. (1992). Teacher expectations: II. Construction and reflection of student achievement. *Journal of Personality and Social Psychology, 63,* 947–961.

Kazdin, A. E., & Krouse, R. (1983). The impact of variations in treatment rationales on expectancies for therapeutic change. *Behavior Therapy, 14,* 657–671.

Kazdin, A. E., & Wilcoxin, L. A. (1976). Systematic desensitization and nonspecific factor treatment effects: A methodological evaluation. *Psychological Bulletin, 83,* 729–758.

Kellner, R., & Sheffield, B. F. (1971). The relief of distress following attendance at a clinic. *British Journal of Psychiatry, 118,* 195–198.

Kirsch, I. (1985). Response expectancy as a determinant of experience and behavior. *American Psychologist, 40,* 1189–1202.

Kirsch, I. (1990). *Changing expectations: A key to effective psychotherapy.* Pacific Grove, CA: Brooks/Cole.

Kirsch, I., & Henry, D. (1977). Extinction vs. credibility in the desensitization of speech anxiety. *Journal of Consulting and Clinical Psychology, 45,* 1052–1059.

Klee, M. R., Abeles, N., & Muller, R. T. (1990). Therapeutic alliance: Early indicators, course and outcome. *Psychotherapy, 27,* 166–174.

Kleinke, C. L. (1994). *Common factors in psychotherapy.* Pacific Grove, CA: Brooks/Cole.

Klerman, G. L., & Weissman, M. M. (1982). Interpersonal psychotherapy: Theory and research. In A. J. Rush (Ed.), *Short-term psychotherapies for depression: Behavioral, interpersonal, cognitive, and psychodynamic approaches* (pp. 88–106). New York: Guilford Press.

Klopfer, B. (1957). Psychological variables in human cancer. *Journal of Projective Techniques, 21,* 331–340.

Lambert, M. J. (1992). Psychotherapy outcome research: Implications for integrative and eclectical psychotherapists. In J. C. Norcross & M. R. Goldfried (Eds.), *Handbook of psychotherapy integration* (pp. 94–129). New York: Basic Books.

Lambert, M. J., & Bergin, A. E. (1994). The effectiveness of psychotherapy. In A. E. Bergin & S. L. Garfield (Eds.), *Handbook of psychotherapy and behavior change* (4th ed., pp. 143–189). New York: Wiley.

Lambert, M. J., Shapiro, D. A., & Bergin, A. E. (1986). Evaluations of therapeutic outcomes. In S. L. Garfield & A. E. Bergin (Eds.), *Handbook of psychotherapy and behavior change* (3rd ed., pp. 157–212). New York: Wiley.

Langs, R. (1982). *Psychotherapy: A basic text.* Northvale, NJ: Aronson.

Leitenberg, H., Agras, W. S., Barlow, D. H., & Oliveau, D. C. (1969). Contributions of selective positive reinforcement and therapeutic instructions to systematic desensitization. *Journal of Abnormal Psychology, 74,* 382–387.

Liberman, B. L. (1978). The role of mastery in psychotherapy: Maintenance of improvement and prescriptive change. In J. D. Frank, R. Hoehn-Saric, S. D. Imber, B. L. Liberman, & A. R. Stone (Eds.), *Effective ingredients of successful psychotherapy* (pp. 35–72). New York: Brunner/Mazel.

Lick, J., & Bootzin, R. (1975). Expectancy factors in the treatment of fear: Methodological and theoretical issues. *Psychological Bulletin, 82,* 917–931.

Luborsky, L. (1984). *Principles of psychoanalytic psychotherapy: A manual for supportive-expressive (SE) methods.* New York: Basic Books.

Luborsky, L., Singer, B., & Luborsky, S. (1975). Comparative studies of psychotherapies: Is it true that "Everyone has won and all must have prizes"? *Archives of General Psychiatry, 32,* 995–1008.

Mandell, M. (1987). *Changes in components of syndrome depression associated with cognitive therapy, pharmacotherapy, and combined cognitive therapy and pharmacotherapy.* Unpublished doctoral dissertation, University of Minnesota, Minneapolis.

Marcia, J. E., Rubin, B. M., & Efran, J. S. (1969). Systematic desensitization: Expectancy change or counterconditioning? *Journal of Abnormal Psychology, 74,* 382–387.

Mathews, A. M., Johnston, D. W., Lancashire, M., Munby, M., Shaw, P. M., & Gelder, M. G. (1976). Imaginal flooding and exposure to real phobic situations: Treatment outcome with agoraphobic patients. *British Journal of Psychiatry, 129,* 362–371.

Miller, W. R., Taylor, C. A., & West, J. C. (1980). Focused versus broad-spectrum behavior for problem drinkers. *Journal of Consulting and Clinical Psychology, 48,* 590–601.

Murphy, G. E., Simons, A. D., Wetzel, R. D. S., & Lustman, P. J. (1984). Cognitive therapy and pharmacotherapy, singly and together in the treatment of depression. *Archives of General Psychiatry, 41,* 33–41.

Nau, D. S., Caputo, L. A., & Borkovec, T. D. (1974). The relationship between credibility of therapy and simulated therapy effects. *Journal of Behavior Therapy and Experimental Psychiatry, 5,* 129–134.

Pennebaker, J. W. (1989). Confession, inhibition, and disease. *Advances in Experimental Social Psychology, 22,* 211–214.

Pennebaker, J. W. (1990). *Opening up: The healing power of confiding in others.* New York: Morrow.

Persons, J. B., & Burns, D. D. (1985). Mechanisms of action of cognitive therapy: Relative contribution of technical and interpersonal intervention. *Cognitive Therapy and Research, 9,* 539–551.

Peterson, C., Luborsky, L., & Seligman, M. E. P. (1983). Attributions and depressive mood shifts: A case study using symptom-context method. *Journal of Abnormal Psychology, 91*, 96–103.

Peterson, C., Maier, S. F., & Seligman, M. E. P. (1993). *Learned helplessness: A theory for the age of personal control.* New York: Oxford University Press.

Peterson, C., & Seligman, M. E. P. (1984). Causal explanations as a risk factor for depression: Theory and evidence. *Psychological Review, 91*, 347–374.

Piper, W. E., & Wogan, M. (1970). Placebo effect in psychotherapy: An extension of earlier findings. *Journal of Consulting and Clinical Psychology, 34*, 447.

Prioleau, L., Murdock, M., & Brody, N. (1983). An analysis of psychotherapy versus placebo studies. *Behavioral and Brain Sciences, 6*, 275–310.

Rabavilas, A. D., Boulougouris, J. D., & Perissaki, C. (1979). Therapist qualities related to outcome with exposure in vivo in neurotic patients. *Journal of Behavior Therapy and Experimental Psychiatry, 10*, 293–294.

Rosenthal, R. (1966). *Experimenter effects in behavioral research.* New York: Appleton-Century-Crofts.

Rosenthal, R. (1973, July). The Pygmalion effect. *Psychology Today*, pp. 56–63.

Rosenthal, R., & Jacobson, L. (1968). *Pygmalion in the classroom: Teacher expectation and pupils' intellectual development.* New York: Holt, Rinehart, & Winston.

Rosenthal, R., & Rosnow, R. L. (1991). *Essentials of behavioral research.* New York: McGraw-Hill.

Rosenthal, R., & Rubin, R. L. (1978). Interpersonal expectancy effects: The first 345 studies. *Behavioral and Brain Sciences, 3*, 377–386.

Rosenzweig, S. (1936). Some implicit common factors in diverse methods of psychotherapy. *American Journal of Orthopsychiatry, 6*, 412–415.

Ross, M., & Buchalew, L. W. (1983). The placebo as an agent in behavior manipulation: A review of problems, issues, and affected measures. *Clinical Psychology Review, 3*, 457–471.

Ross, M., & Olson, J. M. (1982). Placebo effects in medical research and practice. In J. R. Eiser (Ed.), *Social psychology and behavior medicine* (pp. 441–458). New York: Wiley.

Seligman, M. E. P. (1995). The effectiveness of psychotherapy: The *Consumer Reports* Study. *American Psychologist, 50*, 965–974.

Seligman, M. E. P., Castellon, C., Cacciola, J., Shulman, P., Luborsky, L., Ollove, M., & Downing, R. (1988). Explanatory style change during cognitive therapy for unipolar depression. *Journal of Abnormal Psychology, 97*, 13–18.

Shapiro, A. K., & Morris, L. A. (1978). The placebo effect in medical and psychological therapies. In S. L. Garfield & A. E. Bergin (Eds.), *Handbook of psychotherapy and behavior change* (2nd ed., pp. 369–410). New York: Wiley.

Shapiro, A. K., Struening, E., & Shapiro, E. (1980). The reliability and validity of a placebo test. *Journal of Psychiatric Research, 15*, 253–290.

Shapiro, D. A. (1981). Comparative credibility of treatment rationales: Three tests of expectancy theory. *British Journal of Clinical Psychology, 21*, 111–122.

Shapiro, D. A., & Shapiro, D. (1982). Meta-analysis of comparative psychotherapy outcome studies: A replication and refinement. *Psychological Bulletin, 92,* 581–604.

Shea, M. T., Elkin, I., Imber, S. D., Sotsky, S. M., Watkins, J. T., Collins, J. F., Pilkonis, P. A., Beckham, E., Glass, D. R., Dolan, R. T., & Parloff, M. B. (1992). Course of depressive symptoms over follow-up: Findings from the National Institute of Mental Health Treatment of Depression Collaborative Research Program. *Archives of General Psychiatry, 49,* 782–787.

Silverman, L. H. (1974). Some psychoanalytic considerations of non-psychoanalytic therapies: On the possibility of integrating treatment approaches and related issues. *Psychotherapy: Research and Practice, 2,* 298–305.

Silverman, L. H., & Weinberger, J. (1985). Mommy and I are one: Implications for psychotherapy. *American Psychologist, 40,* 1296–1308.

Sipps, G. J., & Janeczek, R. G. (1986). Expectancies for counselors in relation to subject gender traits. *Journal of Counseling Psychology, 33,* 214–216.

Sloane, R. B., Staples, F. R., Cristol, A. H., Yorkston, N. J., & Whipple, K. (1975). *Psychotherapy vs. behavior therapy.* Cambridge, MA: Harvard University Press.

Smith, M. L., Glass, G. V., & Miller, F. I. (1980). *The benefits of psychotherapy.* Baltimore: Johns Hopkins University Press.

Southworth, S., & Kirsch, I. (1988). The role of expectancy in exposure-generated fear reduction in agoraphobia. *Behavior Research and Therapy, 26,* 113–120.

Stampfl, T. G., & Levis, D. J. (1967). Essentials of implosive therapy: A learning-theory-based psychodynamic behavioral therapy. *Journal of Abnormal Psychology, 72,* 496–503.

Stiles, W. B., Shapiro, D. A., & Elliott, R. (1986). Are all psychotherapies equivalent? *American Psychologist, 41,* 165–180.

Strupp, H. H., & Binder, J. L. (1984). *Psychotherapy in a new key: A guide to time-limited psychotherapy.* New York: Basic Books.

Teasdale, J. D. (1985). Psychological treatments for depression: How do they work? *Behavior Research and Therapy, 23,* 157–165.

Teasdale, J. D., & Fennell, M. J. (1982). Immediate effects on depression of cognitive therapy interventions. *Cognitive Therapy and Research, 6,* 343–352.

Thomsen, J., Bretlau, P., Tos, M., & Johnsen, N. J. (1983). Placebo effect in surgery for Meniere's disease: Three-year follow-up. *Otolaryngology-Head and Neck Surgery, 91,* 183–186.

Turner, J. L., Gallimore, R., & Fox-Henning, C. (1980). An annotated bibliography of placebo research. *JSAS Catalog of Selected Documents in Psychology, 10*(33, Ms. No. 2063).

Volgyesi, F. A. (1954). "School for patients," hypnosis therapy, and psychoprophylaxis. *British Journal of Medical Hypnotism, 5,* 8–17.

Wallerstein, R. (1986). *Forty-two lives in treatment: A study of psychoanalysis and psychotherapy.* New York: Guilford Press.

Waterhouse, G. J., & Strupp, H. H. (1984). The patient–therapist relationship:

Research from the psychodynamic perspective. *Clinical Psychology Review, 4,* 77–92.

Weinberger, J. (1993). Common factors in psychotherapy. In J. Gold & G. Stricker (Eds.), *Handbook of psychotherapy integration* (pp. 43–56). New York: Plenum.

Weinberger, J. (1994). Conclusion: Can personality change? In T. F. Heatherton & J. Weinberger (Eds.), *Can personality change?* (pp. 333–350). Washington, DC: American Psychological Association.

Weinberger, J. (1995). Common factors aren't so common: The common factors dilemma. *Clinical psychology: Science and practice, 2,* 45–69.

Whisman, M. A. (1993). Mediators and moderators of change in cognitive therapy of depression. *Psychological Bulletin, 114,* 248–264.

Wolpe, J. (1973). *The practice of behavioral therapy* (2nd ed.). New York: Pergamon.

Zwick, R., & Attkisson, C. C. (1985). Effectiveness of a client pretherapy orientation videotape. *Journal of Counseling Psychology, 32,* 514–524.

16

HYPNOSIS AND RESPONSE EXPECTANCIES

JAMES R. COUNCIL

Hypnosis has a special relationship to response expectancy theory. Not only does response expectancy provide a straightforward explanation of many hypnotic phenomena, but hypnosis also provides an excellent vehicle for investigating expectancy effects. Indeed, much of the early validity evidence for Kirsch's (e.g., 1985, 1991) response expectancy theory came from hypnosis research.

Until recently, expectancy effects have been viewed as artifacts that obscure the essence of hypnosis (Orne, 1959). Unfortunately, this perspective has often led investigators to abandon a topic as being due to "nothing but" expectancy. Kirsch's (1985, 1991) response expectancy theory has provided a theoretical framework to organize the findings on hypnosis and expectancy, and the evidence has grown steadily to show that hypnotic response expectancies are well worth studying in their own right.

Expectancy constructs have been applied to hypnosis since the days of mesmerism. This chapter provides a comprehensive review of the research and theory leading up to current research on response expectancies and hypnosis.

383

WHAT IS HYPNOSIS?

Despite its long history, there has been a chronic failure among experts to agree on a definition of hypnosis. In response to this problem, Division 30 (Psychological Hypnosis) of the American Psychological Association generated a definition of hypnosis based on the consensus of a group of eminent hypnosis scholars (Kirsch, 1994). The main points of this definition are as follows:

1. *Hypnosis is a procedure during which a health professional or researcher suggests that a client, patient, or participant experience changes in sensations, perceptions, thoughts, or behavior.* Hypnosis involves an interpersonal interaction between the hypnotist and client. With regard to the topic of this chapter, the hypnotist could be seen as issuing communications designed to induce expectancies for the occurrence of hypnotic responses.

2. *The hypnotic context is generally established by an induction procedure.* Hypnotic inductions may help clients relax and attend to the hypnotic experience, but their primary function is to establish the hypnotic context. In fact, labeling the situation as one in which hypnotic responses are expected and appropriate may be the only common feature across the myriad methods that have been used to induce hypnosis.

3. *People respond to hypnosis in different ways. Some people are highly responsive to hypnotic suggestions and others are less responsive.* People who are highly responsive to hypnosis tend to describe their experiences as vivid, absorbing, and even profound. At the other extreme are those who merely think about the suggestions and respond only to comply with experimental demands (Radtke & Spanos, 1981; Wagstaff, 1981). Most people fall in between these extremes. Individual differences in hypnotic suggestibility can be reliably and validly measured with standardized hypnotic suggestibility scales. The major scales used in current research include the Stanford Hypnotic Susceptibility Scale, Form C (Weitzenhoffer & Hilgard, 1962) and the Harvard Group Scale of Hypnotic Susceptibility (HGSHS; Shor & Orne, 1962). Standardized hypnotizability scales typically begin with a scripted eye-fixation/relaxation induction procedure, followed by a set of standard suggestions of varying difficulty. Responses are scored pass–fail according to objective criteria (e.g., swatting at a hallucinated mosquito). Subjective scoring criteria have also been developed in which respondents rate the vividness or "reality" of their responses (Kirsch, Council, & Wickless, 1990).

4. *People who have been hypnotized do not lose control over their behavior.* As White (1941) put it, the hypnotized individual strives to "behave like a hypnotized person as this is continuously defined by the operator and understood by the subject" (p. 483). Good hypnotic clients actively process information in the hypnotic situation, thinking and imagining

along with suggestions (Barber, Spanos, & Chaves, 1974). This kind of conscious involvement in the hypnotic experience is essential for the generation of positive hypnotic response expectancies (Kirsch, 1991).

5. *Hypnosis has been used in the treatment of pain, depression, anxiety, stress, habit disorders, and many other psychological and medical problems.* Clinical applications of hypnosis usually involve behaviors and experiences that clients perceive as being beyond their conscious control. Such problems belong to the class of nonvolitional responses with which response expectancy theory is primarily concerned (see Kirsch, 1991).

6. *In addition to its use in clinical settings, hypnosis is used in research, with the goal of learning more about the nature of hypnosis itself as well as its impact on sensation, perception, learning, memory, and physiology.* This part of the definition acknowledges the importance of hypnosis to psychology. Hypnosis moved steadily into the mainstream of psychology after attracting the attention of Freud (Breuer & Freud, 1895/1964), James (1890), and Hull (1933), and research on hypnotic response expectancies should ensure its continued integration into general psychological theory.

PLACE OF EXPECTANCY IN HYPNOSIS THEORY

The idea that expectancy can influence responses to hypnosis can be traced to experiments conducted in 1784 to investigate Mesmer's claims about animal magnetism (Franklin et al., 1784; Pattie, 1967). The studies demonstrated that mesmeric phenomena was caused by the belief that one was being "magnetized." For example, falsely informing participants that mesmeric forces were being directed at them would elicit the typical phenomena.

Expectancy-related constructs continued to be developed in 19th-century theories of hypnosis, especially those of Braid and Bernheim. William James (1890) emphasized expectancy throughout his chapter on hypnosis in the *Principles of Psychology*. James's discussion of expectancy effects conforms to Kirsch's (1991) theory of response expectancies. For example, James (1890) noted that "the prime condition of success is that the participant should confidently *expect* to be entranced" (p. 594). Later in the chapter, James supported Bernheim's proposal that the "symptoms" elicited by Charcot, and even the sleepy, inert appearance of hypnotic participants was due to expectancies.

In this synopsis of hypnosis research and theory, James (1890) praised the German physician, Albert Moll, for producing the best compendium on that subject to date (Moll, 1890). Moll emphasized the role of expectancy in creating hypnotic responses, which may explain James's similar emphasis. Moll (1890) maintained that two fundamental principles determine hypnotic behavior:

> (1) men have a certain proneness to allow themselves to be influenced by others through their ideas, and in particular to believe much without making conscious logical deductions; (2) a psychological effect tends to appear in a man if he is expecting it. (p. 221)

Moll (1890) recounted a number of anecdotes and experiments demonstrating the role of belief and expectancy in producing perceptual, motoric, and physiological alterations in hypnotic and nonhypnotic contexts. In his opinion, these phenomena stemmed from the participant focusing attention on the desired effect and firmly believing the effect would occur. For example, Moll elicited hallucinations by leading blindfolded participants to believe that they were being mesmerized, replicating the findings of the Franklin Commission of 1784.

Moll (1890) anticipated a number of contemporary findings. For example, he noted that watching a responsive participant model hypnotic behavior tends to enhance the observer's expectancies of responding to hypnotic suggestions. Consistently with Kirsch's (1985) response expectancy theory, Moll viewed expectancy as a general process influencing both hypnotic and other nonvolitional responses. Regarding responses to placebo sleeping medication, Moll (1890) said, "They slept because they expected to do so. When they learn that the medicine is not a sleeping draught they no longer expect sleep, and do not sleep" (p. 224).

Contemporary Theories

Several approaches to expectancy are taken in current theories of hypnosis. At one extreme are theorists who minimize its importance. For example, Weitzenhoffer (1953) ascribed to expectancy a negligible effect on hypnotic behavior, one that is "easily masked by more potent factors" (p. 283). The omission of any discussion of expectancy in E. R. Hilgard's (1977) influential book, *Divided Consciousness*, also illustrates the minor role that expectancy constructs play in some theories of hypnosis.

Orne (1959) saw that expectancies help determine behavior in hypnotic situations but viewed their role as artifactual (i.e., expectancies contribute to a "role-played artifact" that must be distinguished from the "essence" of hypnosis). In contrast to Orne's model, cognitive–behavioral (Barber, 1969) and social psychological (Sarbin & Coe, 1972; Spanos, 1996) theorists view expectancy as an essential part of the process by which hypnotic behavior is generated. Barber (1969) and Sarbin and Coe (1972) agreed that hypnosis involves strategically enacted, goal-directed behavior but focused on different aspects of expectancy in hypnosis.

Sarbin's (Sarbin & Anderson, 1963; Sarbin & Coe, 1972) role-theoretical analysis of hypnotic behavior emphasizes a person's perceptions of the responses appropriate to the role of the hypnotized individual. Hypnotic role expectations stem from general cultural knowledge of hypnosis and from expectancy statements made by the hypnotist in the hypnotic situation.

In addition to role perceptions, Barber (1969, 1970, 1972) stressed perceptions of how appropriate the situation is for hypnotic behavior, the perceived difficulty of particular suggestions, and beliefs about one's ability to experience hypnotic phenomena. Barber attached considerable importance to these expectancy-related cognitions as determinants of motivation and involvement in the hypnotic situation. According to Barber et al. (1974), positive expectancies lead participants to involve themselves in goal-directed fantasies, which in turn produce hypnotic experiences and responses.

Kirsch's Response Expectancy Theory

This extension of social learning theory has been a relatively recent contribution to theories of hypnosis (Kirsch, 1985, 1991; Kirsch & Council, 1989). Kirsch proposed that the occurrence of a particular hypnotic response is a function of the participant's expectancy (subjective probability) that it will occur. Various expectancy-related cognitions (e.g., role perceptions, situational perceptions, perceived task difficulty, and expected hypnotic suggestibility) affect hypnotic responses via their influence on response expectancies. People expect to experience particular suggested effects to the extent that they perceive the response as being consistent with the role of a hypnotic participant, perceive the situation as hypnotic, judge the response to be "easy," and judge themselves to be good participants (Kirsch, 1991).

RESEARCH ON HYPNOSIS AND RESPONSE EXPECTANCY

The most obvious and straightforward way to examine the effects of response expectancies on hypnotic behavior is to ask participants to predict how they will respond to hypnosis, so research using this method is reviewed first. Other studies, discussed later, have used various methods to manipulate expectancies for responding to suggestions.

Self-Predictions

Global Ratings

Barber (1972) reviewed studies in which participants made global predictions of their response to hypnosis (Barber & Calverley, 1966, 1969;

Derman & London, 1965; Melei & Hilgard, 1964). Overall, the results of these studies show that global predictions were moderately but significantly correlated with hypnotic suggestibility. However, because most of these studies included participants who had previously been hypnotized, the correlations could have been due to factors other than response expectancies.

Barber and Calverley (1969) asked naive participants to rate how deeply hypnotized they expected to be before a standard hypnotic induction and suggestions. Some participants were given a formal hypnotic induction before the suggestions, and others were simply asked to place themselves in hypnosis. For both instructional sets, the expectancy measure was significantly correlated with suggestibility scores. Subsequent research has also shown moderate correlations between global predictions and suggestibility in naive participants (Ashford & Hammer, 1978; Diamond, Gregory, Lenny, Steadman, & Tallone, 1974; Saavedra & Miller, 1983).

Overall, research using global predictions of hypnotic suggestibility has supported the importance of response expectancy, but it has not indicated a particularly robust relationship. However, most of these studies used small samples, which may lead to unreliable findings. Furthermore, social learning theory (Bandura, 1986; Rotter, Chance, & Phares, 1972) suggests that providing more information about the hypnotic situation and experiences should improve prediction by allowing participants to generalize more accurately from their own experiences.

Specific Ratings

Shor (1971) had participants read a brief description of the hypnotic induction and a description of each test suggestion and objective scoring criterion before reporting expected responses. His finding that specific predictions showed little or no relationship to the corresponding responses led Shor to conclude that his measures were probably not sufficiently sensitive or flexible to capture expectancy effects.

Following Shor's (1971) methodology, Council, Kirsch, Vickery, and Carlson (1983) assessed specific hypnotic response expectancies after a detailed rationale for several different induction procedures. This method resulted in substantially higher correlations between expectancy and various measures of hypnotic suggestibility than had previously been reported, with correlations ranging from .47 to .65. In addition, they found that participants could significantly predict their responses to specific suggestions. Council et al. (1983) proposed two reasons for the discrepancy with Shor's (1971) earlier results. First, the self-predictions were based on more detailed descriptions of the induction and test suggestions. Second, whereas Shor (1971) had used pass–fail scoring for predictions and responses, Council et al. used continuously scored ratings for each suggestion. Because variables such as expectancies and hypnotic responsivity are continuous, it seems likely that Shor's methodology resulted in lost information and an underestimation of existing relationships.

Subsequent studies using refined expectancy measures have confirmed this strong association between expectancy and responses to suggestion (Council, Kirsch, & Hafner, 1986; Gearan, Schoenberger, & Kirsch, 1995; Johnston, Chajkowaski, DuBreuil, & Spanos, 1989; Kirsch, Silva, Comey, & Reed, 1995; Vickery & Kirsch, 1991). Kirsch et al. (1995) presented three data sets in which hypnotic suggestibility was correlated with absorption, fantasy proneness, dissociation, attitudes toward hypnosis, and response expectancies. Overall, hypnotic response expectancy was the most powerful predictor, substantially overriding the effects of trait and ability variables.

As a whole, the results of these studies suggest that people can significantly predict how they will respond to hypnotic inductions and test suggestions. That expectancy would become an important predictor of hypnotic suggestibility was hardly apparent from earlier studies. However, recent studies with refined methodology indicate that expectancy is the most powerful single predictor of hypnotic suggestibility (Kirsch & Council, 1992). It is now clear that more accurate predictions are associated with better knowledge of the hypnotic situation and hypnotic responses, the experience of a hypnotic induction, higher confidence in ratings, and higher suggestibility. The data also indicate that predictions are better for cognitive–behavioral skill training procedures than traditional hypnotic inductions (Kirsch, Council, & Vickery, 1984). However, once participants experience a trance induction, predictions of responsivity to suggestions become more accurate (Council et al., 1986).

Experimental Studies

There are two basic approaches to manipulating hypnotic response expectancies. The first is to change people's beliefs about hypnotic procedures, such as by telling them that particular inductions are more or less effective or that responding to suggestions is easier or harder. The second is to change people's self-perceptions of whether they would be good hypnotic participants.

Global Experimenter Predictions

One of the simplest ways to manipulate expectancies is by an authoritative statement that responding to a suggestion will be easy or difficult. Barber and Calverley (1966) reported that telling participants that responding to suggestions would be easy rather than difficult resulted in significantly higher scores on a suggestibility scale. In another study, participants who were told that a tape-recorded hypnotic induction would be highly effective earned significantly higher hypnotic suggestibility scores than participants told the tape would be highly ineffective in producing hypnosis (Barber & Calverley, 1964). It seems likely that the differences were due to the suppression of responding by negative expectations because positive expectancy instructions did not lead to higher-than-normal scores (Barber & Wilson, 1979). In a more recent study, Vickery and Kirsch (1991) told participants that their responsivity to hypnosis would either increase, decrease, or stay the same over repeated testing. These instructions influenced expectancies as well as performance, and the positive expectancy instructions were as effective as a more extensive skill training procedure in increasing hypnotic suggestibility.

Specific Experimenter Predictions

In contrast to researchers using experimenter statements to manipulate global expectancies, other researchers have presented information designed to influence expectancies for specific experiences. Gandolfo (1971) told participants that they either would or would not be able to resist a posthypnotic suggestion to experience difficulty in writing and concentrating. The participants who had been told that they would successfully resist the suggestion performed significantly better on a digit-symbol task than did other participants. Similarly, Silva and Kirsch (1987) reported that telling hypnotized participants that they were going "deeper" into hypnosis either strengthened or breached the suggested amnesia depending on whether participants had been told previously that deep hypnosis enables recall of forgotten material.

Expectancy-inducing information of this sort has been shown to affect responses to suggestions in a number of conceptually similar studies (Bartis & Zamansky, 1986; Kirsch, Council, & Mobayed, 1987; Lynn, Nash, Rhue, Frauman, & Sweeny, 1984; Lynn, Snodgrass, Rhue, & Hardaway, 1987; Spanos, Cobb, & Gorassini, 1985; Spanos, Weekes, & de Groh, 1984; Zamansky, reviewed in Council, Kirsch, & Grant, 1996). In some of these studies, some participants were told that they would not be able to resist suggestions, whereas others were told that they would be able to do so. In the other studies, participants were asked to imagine one thing (e.g., a powerful stream of water pushing their arms upward) while hearing a contrary suggestion (e.g., their arms becoming heavier and being pushed down). Before hypnosis, some of these participants were told to expect the image to have a greater effect, whereas others were told that the suggestion would be more effective. In all of these studies, the participant's behavior paralleled the prehypnotic expectancy information.

In a replication of E. R. Hilgard's (1977) study on the "hidden observer" phenomenon, Spanos and Hewitt (1980) manipulated information about the "observer." In the original demonstration, E. R. Hilgard told participants that they had a "hidden part" that was more aware of experiences than their "hypnotized part." Later, the participants were painfully stimulated and given suggestions for analgesia. Although participants reported low levels of pain during hypnotic analgesia, when their "hidden observers" were contacted, they reported high pain levels of pain. This was interpreted as evidence of dissociation during hypnosis (E. R. Hilgard, 1977). In Spanos and Hewitt's replication, half the participants were instructed as in E. R. Hilgard's original study. The other half were told that their hidden part knew less than their hypnotized part. Participants' overt and hidden reports of cold pressor pain during hypnotic analgesia were consistent with their previously induced expectancies. In effect, Spanos and Hewitt had created a "stupid observer" that did not conform to predictions from neodissociation theory.

Spanos also demonstrated how investigators can imply that treatments are more or less effective by the order in which they are presented in within-subjects designs. Stam and Spanos (1980) tested hypnotic analgesia and waking analgesia under different instructional sets. Waking and hypnotic analgesia were produced by similar suggestions, with the difference that waking analgesia suggestions were not preceded by a hypnotic induction. Waking analgesia was more effective than hypnotic analgesia when tested after hypnotic analgesia and when the experimenter instructed the participant that waking analgesia would be more effective than the hypnotic analgesia. When Stam and Spanos presented waking analgesia first, followed by hypnotic analgesia, they replicated the usual findings that hypnotic analgesia was superior. Baker and Kirsch (1993) replicated this result comparing hypnosis with placebo analgesia: Hypnotic analgesia was more effective when it was tested last. However, when the placebo was described as a drug that increases suggestibility, there was no difference in effectiveness. Baker and Kirsch also reported that both hypnotic suggestibility and pain reduction were correlated with expectancy and that with expectancy controlled, the relation between hypnotic suggestibility and pain reduction was nonsignificant.

Modeling

Self-predictions about responding to suggestions may also be influenced through exposure to a hypnotized model (Barber, 1972; Brown & Krasner, 1969; Klinger, 1970). As with other observational learning (Bandura, 1986), participants tend to base their self-predictions on their observations of the model. The results of several studies have demonstrated that prior exposure to a hypnotized model can influence hypnotic performance. Klinger (1970) and Botto, Fisher, and Soucy (1977) compared the effects on hypnotic suggestibility of viewing responsive versus nonresponsive models. Both studies showed that participants who were exposed to an unresponsive model had significantly lower suggestibility scores on the HGSHS than did participants exposed to a responsive model. Brown and Krasner (1969) obtained similar results with a different modeling procedure. The results of these studies indicate that viewing a model fail suggestions has a pronounced negative effect on the participant's responsivity but that viewing responsive models does not enhance hypnotic responsivity over standard procedures. The weak effect of responsive models is supported by reports that the addition of peer modeling (Diamond, 1972) and experimenter modeling (Council et al., 1983) does not appreciably enhance the effectiveness of cognitive–behavioral procedures containing verbal instructions for response enhancement.

Whereas in the studies described earlier a globally responsive or unresponsive model was presented, other research has manipulated the model's success on a specific subset of items. Coe and Steen (1981) presented one of two videotapes to participants, with each tape showing a confederate failing a different half of the items on the HGSHS. There was modest support for the prediction that participants would pass positively modeled items and fail negatively modeled items. Botto and Fisher (1978) also used a model who passed or failed a subset of HGSHS items. When participants were tested on the complete HGSHS, there was a significant increase in scores for positively modeled items and a significant decrease in scores for negatively modeled items.

Verbally Induced Expectancies

Juhasz and Sarbin (1966) told research participants that a series of bottles labeled *1* through *10* went in order from the lowest to the highest concentration of salt. In reality, all the bottles contained unsalted distilled water. Starting with the bottle marked *1*, participants tasted the water through the series of bottles. Almost all reported tasting salt, and many maintained that they would testify at a murder trial about the reality of their perceptions. Council and Loge (1988) replicated and extended Juhasz and Sarbin's design to investigate whether hypnotic suggestibility would be related to responsiveness to expectancy inductions. In that study, participants pretested for hypnotic suggestibility were seated in front of a row of bottles said to contain an increasingly strong odor of lemon and a row of weights said to become progressively heavier. As in Sarbin and Juhasz's study, all the stimuli were exactly the same. Whether the tasks were presented in a hypnotic context, greater hypnotic suggestibility was associated with more perceived changes in the stimuli and greater confidence in the reality of those perceptions. These findings suggest that suggestible people may be especially receptive to expectancy inducing information.

Experiential Manipulations

In contrast to the preceding studies, which set up apparatuses to induce expectancies for sensory experiences, the results of other research has reinforced suggested experiences with actual sensations. Wilson (1967) covertly reinforced nonhypnotic suggestions with real experiences (e.g., he lit a tiny bulb to impart a faint red tinge to the room while the participant heard a suggestion that the room was turning red). This procedure significantly increased participants' responsivity to suggestions. Covertly reinforcing suggestions with actual experiences can be seen as generating an expectancy that the participant will also have the experiences described in later suggestions.

Wickless and Kirsch (1989) replicated and extended Wilson's (1967) study using both a verbal expectancy manipulation and Wilson's experiential treatment to enhance hypnotic response expectancies. The verbal manipulation consisted of bogus feedback from a battery of personality tests, which informed participants that they had "excellent hypnotic talent." Combining the experiential and verbal expectancy manipulations was particularly effective in increasing hypnotic responsivity: more than 70% of the participants in this sample scored as highly suggestible. Note that the test suggestions were not ones that had been experientially reinforced. Furthermore, even after being told about the manipulations, participants maintained their high levels of responsiveness. Thus, enhancing response expectancies can lead to lasting changes in suggestibility.

Bogus Feedback

Wickless and Kirsch's (1989) use of bogus feedback from personality tests is a good example of studies that try to change expectancies by changing participants' beliefs about themselves. In effect, a participant receives a "diagnosis" indicating that he or she will be a very good or very poor hypnotic subject. Wickless and Kirsch's (1989) bogus feedback treatment appeared to heighten responsivity to suggestions relative to a no-treatment control condition, but it was most effective in conjunction with the experiential treatment. Several other researchers have used bogus personality feedback as an expectancy manipulation (Goebel & Stewart, 1971; Gregory & Diamond, 1973; Saavedra & Miller, 1983). Although the results were mixed, they generally indicated that both positive and negative feedback influenced hypnotic suggestibility.

Hypnotic Placebos

Other researchers have attempted to convince participants that a procedure has changed them so they will become more responsive to hypnotic suggestions. This type of procedure could be called a hypnotic placebo; much as a sugar pill in a drug study, a hypnotic placebo should change a person's belief about his or her inner state. Also like a drug placebo, a hypnotic placebo should produce effects through no other mechanism than expectancy. Finally, as physicians know, the trappings or rituals that accompany the administration of placebo medication greatly contribute to its effectiveness.

The "sugar pill" comparison is apt for Glass and Barber's (1961) study because these investigators used placebo medication to induce hypnosis. Glass and Barber established a medical context by using various props and procedures (e.g., medical attire and examination of reflexes by a physician). In this context, participants were given in inert pill described as a "powerful hypnotic drug." This treatment was as effective as a formal 20-min trance induction in increasing responsivity to suggestion. Baker and Kirsch (1987) also used a "hypnotic drug" placebo in research on hypnotic analgesia. They reported that its effects on pain reports were equivalent to those of a standard hypnotic induction.

In a conceptually similar treatment, Council et al. (1983) used the setting of a psychophysiological laboratory to lend credibility to a placebo manipulation involving "biofeedback." Participants were presented with the rationale that a hypnotic state could be generated through the use of biofeedback and were then exposed to a treatment incorporating physiological apparatuses, oscilloscopes, and a false feedback tone. Participants judged this procedure to be as credible as a traditional trance induction and a cognitive–behavioral "skill" induction. Although the placebo induction produced slightly lower scores on a measure of overt responses to suggestions, it was equivalent to the trance and skill inductions on subjective measures of responsivity.

Kroger and Schneider (1959) unintentionally used a similar placebo induction with their "brain wave synchronizer," a variable stroboscopic light that they claimed induced hypnosis by altering alpha rhythms through photic driving. In a replication of that study, Hammer and Arkins (1964) demonstrated that the synchronizer alone had no effect on hypnotic suggestibility and that it worked as claimed only when participants were told that it would induce hypnosis.

EXPECTANCY: A FINAL PATHWAY TO HYPNOTIC SUGGESTIBILITY

In *Personality and Hypnosis: A Study of Imaginative Involvement*, Josephine Hilgard (1970) proposed that imaginative involvement was the final pathway to hypnosis. She viewed imaginative involvement as a trait that could develop through various childhood experiences. Whatever its origin, according to J. Hilgard, imaginative involvement was a personality trait necessary for hypnotic suggestibility. This work encouraged other theorists to emphasize imagination as the basis for hypnosis. For example, Tellegen and Atkinson (1974) expanded the conception of imaginative involvement as a trait underlying hypnosis with their construct *absorption*. Concurrently, cognitive–behavioral theorists were presenting *goal-directed fantasy* (Barber et al., 1974; Spanos, 1971) as a cognitive skill underlying hypnotic responsiveness. By the mid-1970s, the emphasis on imagination became so pervasive in hypnosis theory that Spanos and Barber (1974) described it as a unifying force in a field that had been fraught with contention.

However, increased research led to questions of how directly hypnotic suggestibility relates to imagination. (For a more detailed discussion, see Council et al., 1996, and Kirsch & Council, 1989, 1992.) Some of the negative findings came from studies that contrasted imagery and expectancy as determinants of hypnotic suggestibility (reviewed by Council et al., 1996). In general, the findings showed that the information or rationales presented about imaginal procedures determined whether imagery inhibited or facilitated responses to suggestions.

Another line of evidence concerned the relation of self-report imagination scales to scores on hypnotic suggestibility scales. The first report was by Council et al. (1986), who found that absorption and hypnotic suggestibility were significantly correlated only when the scales were administered in the same research setting. Because of its theoretical implications, that study was replicated and extended by a number of researchers (reviewed by Council, 1993; Council et al., 1996). As a whole, the evidence indicated that correlations were spuriously inflated when measures of imagination and hypnotic suggestibility were completed in the same research context. With controls for context effects, imagination scales were only weakly related to hypnotic suggestibility.

Other personality and cognitive influences on hypnotic suggestibility can also be ruled out as basic factors underlying hypnotic suggestibility. In their review of personality and situational correlates of response to hypnotic suggestion, Kirsch and Council (1992) concluded that decades of research had failed to reveal that personality questionnaires and other self-report measures had more than a minuscule relationship to hypnotic suggestibility. Although imagination scales appeared to reliably predict suggestibility, the relation was largely mediated by expectancy. Likewise, most situational variables bore minor relationships to hypnotic suggestibility.

The exceptions to these discouraging findings have involved expectancy. Self-report expectancy measures of response have shown consistent positive correlations with hypnotic suggestibility, and methodological improvements have strengthened the correlations. In fact, the Council et al. (1986) report indicated that expectancy may be the final common pathway to hypnotic suggestibility. Council et al. presented a causal model that included predictions of hypnotic responsivity and depth made before a hypnotic induction, hypnotic response expectancy and depth reports made after inductions, and outcome measures of hypnotic depth as well as objective and subjective responses to the test suggestions. Path analysis showed that postinduction expectancies were by far the strongest predictor of scores on both test suggestions and a measure of hypnotic depth. Furthermore, the analysis indicated that a person's subjective experiences during a trance induction (i.e., hypnotic depth) had a strong effect on expectancies for subsequent responses to suggestions but no direct effect on suggestibility scores.

In addition to the literature on self-report measures of expectancy, a number of experiments manipulating hypnotic response expectancies have demonstrated significant effects on responses to hypnotic suggestions. Most importantly, Wickless and Kirsch's (1989) experiential expectancy manipulation greatly enhanced hypnotic suggestibility scores over baseline levels. This kind of result should not occur if hypnotic suggestibility is based on some underlying trait.

In summary, the research evidence indicates that response expectancies strongly determine hypnotic behavior. Furthermore, decades of research on a wide range of personality, ability, and situational variables have failed to reveal any variables with comparable predictive power. However, it would be premature at this point to pronounce expectancy as *the* final pathway to hypnosis. A conservative appraisal of the research evidence would be that expectancy is the strongest single predictor of hypnotic suggestibility, and much of the effect of other variables (e.g., absorption and fantasy proneness) is mediated by expectancy. However, some other variables may also make a small independent contribution to responsiveness to suggestion.

The proposal that expectancy is an immediate cause of hypnotic suggestibility is a null hypothesis that cannot be proved true (Kirsch, 1991). However, it could be disconfirmed if other variables can be shown to intervene between response expectancies and hypnotic behavior. To date, there has been no evidence that such intervening variables exist. Until there is, response expectancy should stand as the most parsimonious explanation for hypnotic suggestibility.

REFERENCES

Ashford, B., & Hammer, A. G. (1978). The role of expectancies in the occurrence of posthypnotic amnesia. *International Journal of Clinical and Experimental Hypnosis, 26*, 281–291.

Baker, S., & Kirsch, I. (1987, August). Hypnotic and placebo analgesia in subjects not selected for hypnotizability. In J. Chaves (Chair), *Hypnotic analgesia, placebo effects, and expectancy*. Symposium conducted at the 95th Annual Convention of the American Psychological Association, New York.

Baker, S., & Kirsch, I. (1993). Hypnotic and placebo analgesia: Order effects and the placebo label. *Contemporary Hypnosis, 10,* 117–126.

Bandura, A. (1986). *Social foundations of thought and action: A social cognitive theory.* Englewood Cliffs, NJ: Prentice Hall.

Barber, T. X. (1969). *Hypnosis: A scientific approach.* New York: Psychological Dimensions.

Barber, T. X. (1970). *LSD, marijuana, yoga and hypnosis.* Chicago: Aldine.

Barber, T. X. (1972). Suggested (hypnotic) behavior: The trance paradigm versus an alternative paradigm. In E. Fromm & R. E. Shor (Eds.), *Hypnosis: Research developments and perspectives* (pp. 115–182). New York: Aldine-Atherton.

Barber, T. X., & Calverley, D. S. (1966). Toward a theory of hypnotic behavior: Experimental evaluation of Hull's postulate that hypnotic susceptibility is a habit phenomenon. *Journal of Personality, 34,* 416–433.

Barber, T. X., & Calverley, D. S. (1969). Multidimensional analysis of "hypnotic" behavior. *Journal of Abnormal Psychology, 74,* 209–220.

Barber, T. X., Spanos, N. P., & Chaves, J. F. (1974). *Hypnotism, imagination and human potentialities.* Elmsford, NY: Pergamon Press.

Barber, T. X., & Wilson, S. C. (1979). The Barber Suggestibility Scale and the Creative Imagination Scale: Experimental and clinical applications. *American Journal of Clinical Hypnosis, 21,* 84–108.

Bartis, S., & Zamansky, H. (1986). Dissociation in hypnotic amnesia. *American Journal of Clinical Hypnosis, 29,* 103–108.

Botto, R. W., & Fisher, S. (1978). Preliminary report on social learning behavior in the hypnotic situation: Modeling or mimicry. In F. H. Frankel & H. S. Zamansky (Eds.), *Hypnosis at its bicentennial* (pp. 175–183). New York: Plenum.

Botto, R. W., Fisher, S., & Soucy, G. P. (1977). The effect of a good and a poor model on hypnotic susceptibility in a low demand situation. *International Journal of Clinical and Experimental Hypnosis, 25,* 175–183.

Breuer, J., & Freud, S. (1964). *Studies on hysteria.* (A. A. Brill, Trans.). Boston: Beacon Press. (Original work published 1895)

Brown, H. A., & Krasner, L. (1969). The role of subject expectancies in hypnosis. *International Journal of Clinical and Experimental Hypnosis, 12,* 180–188.

Coe, W. C., & Steen, P. (1981). Examining the relationship between believing one will respond to hypnotic suggestions and hypnotic responsiveness. *American Journal of Clinical Hypnosis, 24,* 22–32.

Council, J. R. (1993). Context effects in personality research. *Current Directions in Psychological Science, 2,* 31–34.

Council, J. R., Kirsch, I., & Grant, D. L. (1996). Expectancy, imagination, and hypnotic susceptibility. In R. Kunzendorf, B. Wallace, & N. P. Spanos (Eds.), *Imagination and hypnosis* (pp. 41–65). Amityville, NY: Baywood.

Council, J. R., Kirsch, I., & Hafner, L. P. (1986). Expectancy versus absorption in the prediction of hypnotic responding. *Journal of Personality and Social Psychology, 50,* 182–189.

Council, J. R., Kirsch, I., Vickery, A. R., & Carlson, D. (1983). "Trance" versus "skill" hypnotic inductions: The effects of credibility, expectancy, and experimenter modeling. *Journal of Consulting and Clinical Psychology, 51*, 432–440.

Council, J. R., & Loge, D. (1988). Suggestibility and confidence in false perceptions: A pilot study. *British Journal of Experimental and Clinical Hypnosis, 5*, 95–98.

Derman, D., & London, P. (1965). Correlates of hypnotic susceptibility. *Journal of Consulting Psychology, 29*, 537–545.

Diamond, M. J. (1972). The use of observationally presented information to modify hypnotic susceptibility. *Journal of Abnormal Psychology, 79*, 174–180.

Diamond, M. J., Gregory, J., Lenny, E., Steadman, C., & Tallone, J. M. (1974). An alternative approach to personality correlates of hypnotizability: Hypnosis-specific mediational attitudes. *International Journal of Clinical and Experimental Hypnosis, 22*, 346–353.

Franklin, B., de Bory, G., Lavoisier, A. L., Bailly, J. S., Majault Sallin, D'Arcet, J., Guillotin, J. I., & Leroy, J. B. (1784). *Rapport des Commissaires charges par le roy de l'examen du magnetisme animal* [Report of the commissioners charged by the king with the examination of animal magnetism]. Paris: Bibliotheque Royale.

Gearan, P., Schoenberger, N. E., & Kirsch, I. (1995). Modifying hypnotizability: A new component analysis. *International Journal of Clinical and Experimental Hypnosis, 43*, 70–89.

Gandolfo, R. L. (1971). Role of expectancy, amnesia, and hypnotic induction in the performance of posthypnotic behavior. *Journal of Abnormal Psychology, 77*, 324–328.

Glass, L. B., & Barber, T. X. (1961). A note on hypnotic behavior, the definition of the situation and the placebo effect. *Journal of Nervous and Mental Disease, 132*, 539–541.

Goebel, R. A., & Stewart, C. G. (1971). Effects of experimenter bias and induced subject expectancy on hypnotic susceptibility. *Journal of Personality and Social Psychology, 16*, 263–272.

Gregory, J., & Diamond, M. J. (1973). Increasing hypnotic susceptibility by means of positive expectancies and written instructions. *Journal of Abnormal Psychology, 62*, 363–367.

Hammer, A. G., & Arkins, W. J. (1964). The role of photic stimulation in the induction of hypnotic trance. *International Journal of Clinical and Experimental Hypnosis, 12*, 81–87.

Hilgard, E. R. (1977). *Divided consciousness: Multiple controls in human thought and action.* New York: Wiley.

Hilgard, J. R. (1970). *Personality and hypnosis: A study of imaginative involvement.* Chicago: University of Chicago Press.

Hull, C. L. (1933). *Hypnosis and suggestibility: An experimental approach.* New York: Appleton-Century-Crofts.

James, W. (1890). *The principles of psychology* (Vol. 2). New York: Holt.

Johnston, J. C., Chajkowaski, J., DuBreuil, S. C., & Spanos, N. P. (1989). The effects of manipulated expectancies on behavioural and subjective indices of hypnotisability. *Australian Journal of Clinical and Experimental Hypnosis, 17,* 121–130.

Juhasz, J. B., & Sarbin, T. R. (1966). On the false alarm metaphor in psychophysics. *Psychological Record, 16,* 323–327.

Kirsch, I. (1985). Response expectancy as a determinant of experience and behavior. *American Psychologist, 40,* 1189–1202.

Kirsch, I. (1991). *Changing expectations: A key to effective psychotherapy.* Pacific Grove, CA: Brooks/Cole.

Kirsch, I. (1994). APA definition and description of hypnosis: Defining hypnosis for the public. *Contemporary Hypnosis, 11,* 142–143.

Kirsch, I., & Council, J. R. (1989). Response expectancy as a determinant of hypnotic behavior. In N. P. Spanos & J. F. Chaves (Eds.), *Hypnosis: The cognitive–behavioral perspective* (pp. 360–379). Buffalo, NY: Prometheus Books.

Kirsch, I., & Council, J. R. (1992). Situational and personality correlates of suggestibility. In E. Fromm & M. Nash (Eds.), *Contemporary hypnosis research* (pp. 267–291). New York: Guilford Press.

Kirsch, I., Council, J. R., & Mobayed, C. (1987). Imagery versus response expectancy as determinants of hypnotic behavior. *British Journal of Experimental and Clinical Hypnosis, 4,* 25–31.

Kirsch, I., Council, J. R., & Vickery, A. R. (1984). The role of expectancy in eliciting hypnotic responses as a function of type of induction. *Journal of Consulting and Clinical Psychology, 52,* 708–709.

Kirsch, I., Council, J. R., & Wickless, C. (1990). Subjective scoring for the Harvard Group Scale of Hypnotic Susceptibility, Form A. *International Journal of Clinical and Experimental Hypnosis, 38,* 112–124.

Kirsch, I., Silva, C. E., Comey, G., & Reed, S. (1995). A spectral analysis of cognitive and personality variables in hypnosis: Empirical disconfirmation of the two-factor model of hypnotic responding. *Journal of Personality and Social Psychology, 69,* 167–175.

Klinger, B. I. (1970). Effect of peer model responsiveness and length of induction procedure on hypnotic responsiveness. *Journal of Abnormal Psychology, 75,* 15–18.

Kroger, W. S., & Schneider, S. A. (1959). An electronic aid for hypnotic induction: A preliminary report. *International Journal of Clinical and Experimental Hypnosis, 71,* 93–98.

Lynn, S. J., Nash, M. R., Rhue, J. W., Frauman, D. C., & Sweeny, C. (1984). Nonvolition, expectancies, and hypnotic rapport. *Journal of Abnormal Psychology, 93,* 295–303.

Lynn, S. J., Snodgrass, M., Rhue, J. W., & Hardaway, R. (1987). Goal-directed fantasy, hypnotic susceptibility, and expectancies. *Journal of Personality and Social Psychology, 53,* 933–938.

Melei, J. P., & Hilgard, E. R. (1964). Attitudes toward hypnosis, self predictions, and hypnotic susceptibility. *International Journal of Clinical and Experimental Hypnosis, 12,* 99–108.

Moll, A. (1890). *Hypnotism.* London: Scott.

Orne, M. T. (1959). The nature of hypnosis: Artifact and essence. *Journal of Abnormal and Social Psychology, 58,* 277–299.

Pattie, F. (1967). A brief history of hypnotism. In J. E. Gordon (Ed.), *Handbook of clinical and experimental hypnosis* (pp. 10–43). New York: Macmillan.

Radtke, H. L., & Spanos, N. P. (1981). Was I hypnotized? A social psychological analysis of hypnotic depth reports. *Psychiatry, 44,* 359–376.

Rotter, J. B., Chance, J. E., & Phares, E. J. (Eds.). (1972). *Applications of a social learning theory of personality.* New York: Holt, Rinehart & Winston.

Saavedra, R. L., & Miller, R. J. (1983). The influence of experimentally induced expectations on responses to the Harvard Group Scale of Hypnotic Susceptibility, Form A. *International Journal of Clinical and Experimental Hypnosis, 31,* 37–46.

Sarbin, T. R., & Anderson, M. I. (1963). Base-rate expectancies and perceptual alterations in hypnosis. *British Journal of Clinical Psychology, 2,* 112–121.

Sarbin, T. R., & Coe, W. C. (1972). *Hypnosis: A social psychological analysis of influence communication.* New York: Holt, Rinehart & Winston.

Shor, R. E. (1971). Expectations of being influenced and hypnotic performance. *International Journal of Clinical and Experimental Hypnosis, 19,* 154–166.

Shor, R. E., & Orne, E. C. (1962). *Harvard Group Scale of Hypnotic Susceptibility, Form A.* Palo Alto, CA: Consulting Psychologists Press.

Silva, C. E., & Kirsch, I. (1987). Breaching amnesia by manipulating expectancy. *Journal of Abnormal Psychology, 96,* 325–329.

Spanos, N. P. (1971). Goal-directed fantasy and the performance of hypnotic test suggestions. *Psychiatry, 34,* 86–96.

Spanos, N. P. (1996). *Multiple identities and false memories: A sociocognitive perspective.* Washington, DC: American Psychological Association.

Spanos, N. P., & Barber, T. X. (1974). Toward a convergence in hypnosis research. *American Psychologist, 29,* 500–511.

Spanos, N. P., Cobb, P. C., & Gorassini, D. R. (1985). Failing to resist hypnotic test suggestions: A strategy for self-presenting as deeply hypnotized. *Psychiatry, 48,* 282–292.

Spanos, N. P., & Hewitt, E. C. (1980). The hidden observer in hypnotic analgesia: Discovery or experimental creation? *Journal of Personality and Social Psychology, 39,* 1201–1214.

Spanos, N. P., Weekes, J. R., & de Groh, M. (1984). The "involuntary" countering of suggested requests: A test of the ideomotor hypothesis of hypnotic responsiveness. *British Journal of Experimental and Clinical Hypnosis, 1,* 3–11.

Stam, H. J., & Spanos, N. P. (1980). Experimental designs, expectancy effects, and hypnotic analgesia. *Journal of Abnormal Psychology, 89,* 751–762.

Tellegen, A., & Atkinson, G. (1974). Openness to absorbing and self-altering experiences ("absorption"), a trait related to hypnotic susceptibility. *Journal of Abnormal Psychology, 83,* 268–277.

Vickery, A. R., & Kirsch, I. (1991). The effects of brief expectancy manipulations on hypnotic responsiveness. *Contemporary Hypnosis, 8,* 167–171.

Wagstaff, G. F. (1981). *Hypnosis, compliance and belief.* New York: St. Martin's Press.

Weitzenhoffer, A. M. (1953). *Hypnotism: An objective study in suggestibility.* New York: Wiley.

Weitzenhoffer, A. M., & Hilgard, E. (1962). *Stanford Hypnotic Susceptibility Scale: Form C.* Palo Alto, CA: Consulting Psychologists Press.

White, R. W. (1941). A preface to a theory of hypnotism. *Journal of Abnormal and Social Psychology, 36,* 477–505.

Wickless, C., & Kirsch, I. (1989). The effects of verbal and experiential expectancy manipulations on hypnotic susceptibility. *Journal of Personality and Social Psychology, 57,* 762–768.

Wilson, D. L. (1967). The role of confirmation of expectancies in hypnotic induction. *Dissertation Abstracts International, 28,* 4787B. (University Microfilms No. 66-6781)

AUTHOR INDEX

Numbers in italics refer to listings in the reference sections.

Barsky, A. J., 334, 339, 348, 351, *351,*
352
Bartis, S., 390, *397*
Bartlett, F. C., 94, 96, 97, *117*
Bartlett, T. S., 312, *320*
Bartolucci, G., *352*
Basbaum, A. I., 164, *168*
Baucom, D. H., *12*
Bauer, L. O., 235, *255*
Baum, W. M., 34, *36*
Bauman, K. E., 268, 274, 275, 287, *294*
Bautista, S. M., 74, 77, *89*
Bayer, T. L., 334, 340, 345, 347, *352*
Beach, S. R. H., 312, *316*
Beauvais, F., 236, *261*
Beck, A. T., 18, *36,* 58, 60, 80, 82, 86,
86, 126, 128, 129, 135, *141,*
366, 373, 375, *377*
Beck, J. G., 176, 178, *194, 195*
Beck, J. T., 312, *316*
Becker, M. H., 29, *36*
Beckham, E., *381*
Beckham, E. E., 362, 366, *375*
Beecher, H. K., 156, 159, *167, 168*
Beidel, D. C., 132, *144*
Beirness, D. J., 223, *229*
Bekerian, D. A., 96, *117*
Bellezza, F. S., 97, *118*
Belli, R. F., 113, *118*
Bennet, J. M., *330*
Bennet, K. J., *332*
Bensen, W. G., *332*
Benson, P. M., *332*
Bentler, P. M., 240, *260, 261*
Bergin, A. E., 357, *378*
Berman, J. S., 311, *319*
Berns, G. S., 50, *60*
Berridge, K. C., 45, *62,* 228, *231*
Berry, S., *356*
Best, J. A., 268, *294*
Beutler, L. E., *12,* 371, *375*
Beuzen, J. N., *331*
Beyer, J., 133, *141*
Bichard, S., 137, 138, *143*
Biggs, V. E., *196*
Billardon, M., *330*
Billings, A. G., 80, *90*
Billings, F. J., 111, *120*
Binder, J. L., 364, *381*
Binder, L. M., 341, *355*
Bingham, R. C., 239, *262*
Binkoff, J. A., *298*

Bird, R. L., 324, *332*
Birnbaum, D., 83, *90*
BIS Research Group, *375*
Black, D. W., 339, *352*
Blackwell, D. M., 108, 115, *122*
Blair, V., 274, *295*
Blalock, S. J., 27, *36*
Bland, R. C., 339, *354*
Blankstein, K. R., 74, *88*
Blashki, T. G., 307, 310, *316*
Bleecker, E., 198, *212,* 335, *354*
Bless, H., 104–107, *123*
Blois, W. O., 111, *123*
Bloom, F. E., 235, *260*
Blum, K., 234, *255*
Boissel, J. P., 359, *375*
Boland, F. J., 242, *259*
Bolles, R. C., 22, 23, *36,* 42, 44, 60,
216, *229, 237, 255*
Bombardier, C., *332*
Booth-Kewley, S., 339, *353*
Bootzin, R., 162, *168,* 365, *379*
Borkovec, T. D., 26, *36,* 369, *379*
Bornstein, J. C., 162, *169*
Bornstein, R. F., 305, *317*
Bosse, R., 268, *295*
Bothwell, R. K., 113, *123*
Botto, R. W., 391, 392, *397*
Boulougouris, J. D., 371, *380*
Bovbjerg, D. H., *91,* 337, *352*
Bovim, G., *355*
Bower, G. H., 43, 52, 54, 55, 60, 71, 83,
84, *86, 91,* 97, *118,* 254, *255*
Bowers, J. M., 96, *117*
Boyd, S., *212*
Boykin, A., 33, *38*
Bozarth, M. A., 228, 232, 234, *262*
Brand, J. I., 338, *351*
Brandenburg, N., 268, *299*
Brandon, T. H., 215, *229,* 248, *256,*
268–271, 282–285, 289, 290,
293, 294, 295, 299
Brannick, M., 290, *298*
Brashares, H. J., 72, 73, 77, *86*
Brawley, L., 33, *38*
Brenner, C., 364, *375*
Bretlau, P., 359, *381*
Breuer, J., 385, *397*
Brewer, E. J., *330*
Briggs, A. H., *255*
Brion, S., *331*
Brody, N., 357, 362, 367, *375, 380*

Evans, M. D., 363, *375, 377*
Evans, M. G., 270, *296*
Evans, R. W., 340, *353*
Eysenck, H. S., 357, *376*

Faillace, L. A., 240, *256*
Falbo, J., 133, *144*
Falkson, G., *330*
Farber, P. D., 247, *257*
Fava, G. A., *352*
Fazio, A. F., 312, *319*
Fazio, R. H., 137, *141*
Feather, N. T., 17, *36*
Fedele, L., 154, *168*
Feighner, J., *319*
Fein, G., 335, *353*
Feine, J. S., 147, *170*
Feldman, D. A., 312, *317*
Feldman, J. A., 45, *60*
Feldman, S., 33, *38*
Fenichel, O., 364, *376*
Fennell, M. J., 366, 369, 372, *376, 381*
Fenwich, J. F., 281, *297*
Fernandez, E., 150, 151, *168*
Ferrey, G., *331*
Festinger, L., 347, *353*
Fields, H. L., 153, 162, 164, 165, 167, *168–170*, 348, *354*
Fiester, S. J., *317, 375*
Fillmore, M., 219–222, 226, 230, 348, *353*
Finger, K., 112, *122*
Fink, C. W., *330*
Finn, P., 235, *257, 260*
Finnerty, R., *317*
Finney, J. W., 80, *90*
Fiore, M. C., *299*
Firestone, P., 69, *88*
Fishbain, D. A., 345, *353*
Fishbein, M., 4, *11*, 18, 23, 30, *36*, 136, *141*, 163, 167, 265, *296*
Fisher, S., 305, 310, 316, *317*, 391, 392, *397*
Fiske, S. T., 35, *36*, 100, *119*
Fitzgerald, H. E., 239, *262*
Flay, B. R., 267, *296*
Fletcher, G. J. O., 97, *122*
Flett, G. L., 74, *88*
Florio, L., 339, *352*
Foley, M. A., 102, 104, *120*
Folkman, S., 81, 83, *89*

Fondarai, J., *330*
Fong, G. T., 100, *122*
Ford, H. T., *330*
Fordyce, W., 321, *332*
Forgas, J. P., 83, *88*
Forster, J., 104, 106, 107, *119, 123*
Fowles, D. C., 53, *60*
Fox-Henning, C., 359, *381*
Fradkin, B., 69, *88*
Frank, E., 324, *330*
Frank, J. B., 367, 370, *376*
Frank, J. D., 308, 311, *317*, 321, *330*, 362, 367–370, *376*
Franklin, B., 385, *398*
Franko, D., 71, 72, *88*
Frasure-Smith, N., 339, *353*
Frauman, D. C., 390, *399*
Free, M. L., 305, 311, *317*
French, T. M., 364, *374*
Freud, S., 364, *376*, 385, *397*
Fried, L., 127, *142*
Friedman, H. J., 362, *376*
Friedman, H. S., 339, *353*
Friend, R., 132, *144*
Frijda, N. H., 32, *36*
Froldi, M., *212*
Fromme, K., 244, 248, *257*, 270, 282, *296*
Fromm-Reichman, F., 364, *376*
Frone, M. R., 74, *88*, 283, *295*
Fulero, S., 94, *122*
Funk, S. C., 370, *374*

Gabora, N. J., 115, *123*
Gailledreau, J., *331*
Galanter, E., 44, *62*
Galatzer-Levy, R., 373, *374*
Gallagher, D., 366, 371, *376*
Gallimore, R., 359, *381*
Gandolfo, R. L., 390, *398*
Ganguli, R., 85, *90*
Garagiola, U., 154, *168*
Garber, J., 363, 366, *377*
Garber, R. A., 312, *316*
Gardiner, J. M., 116, *119*
Garrick, T., 80, *88*
Garry, M., 111, 113, *118, 119*
Garvey, M. J., *375*
Gaston, L., 366, 371, *376, 377*
Gauld, A., 97, *119*
Gauthier, E., *375*

414   AUTHOR INDEX

Weixel, L. J., 4, *12*, 220, *231*
Wells, G. L., 103, *123*
Wells, K. B., 339, *356*
West, J. C., 371, *379*
Wetter, D. W., 269, 272, 278, 280, 282, 293, 295, 299
Wetzel, C. G., 68, *91*
Wetzel, R. D. S., 366, *379*
Wewers, M. E., 273, *294*
Wheeler, L., 83, *91*
Whipple, K., 311, *319*, 357, *381*
Whisman, M. A., 363, 366, 372, 373, *382*
White, K., 307, *320*
White, R. W., 384, *401*
Whitehead, G. I., *317*
Whitfield, K. E., 282, *297*
Wickless, C., 11, *13*, 126, 137, *142*, *144*, 384, 393, 396, 399, *401*
Wickramasekera, I., 153, *171*, 321, *332*
Widom, C. S., 348, *356*
Wiedenfeld, S. A., 85, *91*
Wierzbicki, M., 312, *320*
Wigal, J. K., 207, *211*
Wiggins, R. G., 340, *353*
Wilcoxin, L. A., 365, *378*
Wilde, G. J. S., 201, *212*
Williams, D. A., *12*
Williams, N., 341, *355*
Williams, S. L., 25, *39*, 127–130, 133, 134, 138, *144*
Williamson, D., *351*
Wilson, D. L., 393, *401*
Wilson, P. H., 312, *320*
Wilson, S. C., 390, *397*
Wilson, T. D., 67, 68, 89, *91*, 249, *260*
Wincze, J. P., 176, 178, 183, *194–196*
Windle, M., 244, *256*
Winokur, G., 339, *352*
Winton, G. B., *332*
Wise, R. A., 228, *232*, 234, *262*
Wogan, M., 362, *380*

Wolchik, S. A., 178, *196*
Wolf, S., 7, *13*
Woll, S. B., 97, *118*
Wolpe, J., 177, *196*, 365, *382*
Wood, D. R., *316*
Wood, M. D., 240, *261*
Wood, P. K., 240, *261*
Woodmansey, A., 322, *331*
Woods, S. M., 340, *356*
Woodward, T., 350
Woodward, W. R., 18, *39*
Woody, S. R., *12*
Workman, E. A., 305, *320*
Wright, J., 83, *91*
Wright, W. F., 83, *91*
Wyer, R. S., 94, *123*
Wyshak, G., 339, *352*

Yamamato, J., 234, *259*
Yorkston, N. J., 311, *319*, 357, *381*
Young, A. J., 322, *331*

Zack, M., 225, *232*
Zadny, J., 94, *123*
Zamansky, H., 390, *397*
Zangwill, O. L., 97, *124*
Zanna, M. P., 17, *38*, 137, *141*
Zanussi, C., *212*
Zara, C., *212*
Zaragoza, M., 96, *121*
Zaragoza, M. S., 104, 113, *124*
Zavodnick, S., *332*
Zemel, L. S., 330
Zimring, F. M., 156, 166, *169*
Zinser, M. C., 282, 284, 289, *299*
Zipfel, A., 334, *355*
Zucker, R. A., 236, 239, *262*
Zung, W. W. K., 307, *320*
Zuroff, D. C., 71, 88, 264, *299*
Zwick, R., 369, *382*

SUBJECT INDEX

ABOUT THE EDITOR

Irving Kirsch, PhD, is a professor of psychology at the University of Connecticut. The concept of response expectancy was first introduced in his 1985 *American Psychologist* article, titled "Response Expectancy as a Determinant of Experience and Behavior." A former president of Division 30 of the American Psychological Association, Dr. Kirsch is the author or editor of 5 books, including *Changing Expectations: A Key to Effective Psychotherapy* (Brooks/Cole, 1990), which was the first full explication of response expectancy theory. In addition, he has authored 29 book chapters and more than 130 journal articles on placebo effects, hypnosis, psychotherapy, history of psychology, and philosophy of science. His work has been published in *American Psychologist, Psychological Bulletin, Behavioral and Brain Sciences, Psychological Science,* and other leading journals. In addition, his work has received extensive coverage in *Science, Lancet, The New York Times, Smithsonian,* and *New Scientist* and on national and international radio and television programs. Dr. Kirsch is the North American Editor of *Contemporary Hypnosis* and a member of the editorial boards of the *International Journal of Clinical and Experimental Hypnosis, American Journal of Clinical Hypnosis,* and *Hypnosis International Monographs.*